T0354269

THE
MINDFULNESS
IN PLAIN ENGLISH
Collection

THE
MINDFULNESS
IN PLAIN ENGLISH
Collection

Bhante Henepola Gunaratana

Wisdom

Wisdom Publications
199 Elm Street
Somerville MA 02144 USA
wisdompubs.org

*Library of Congress Cataloging-in-Publication Data is available for the original
editions collected in this volume:*
Mindfulness in Plain English: LCCN 2011025555
The Four Foundations of Mindfulness in Plain English: LCCN 2012005119
Beyond Mindfulness in Plain English: LCCN 2009009950

ISBN 978-1-61429-479-5   ebook ISBN 978-1-61429-504-4

21 20 19 18 17
5 4 3 2 1

Cover design by Gopa&Ted2, Inc. Set in Fairfield LH Light 11 pt. /16 pt.

Wisdom Publications' books are printed on acid-free paper and meet the
guidelines for permanence and durability of the Committee on Production
Guidelines for Book Longevity of the Council on Library Resources.

♻This book was produced with environmental mindfulness.
For more information, please visit wisdompubs.org/wisdom-environment.

Printed in the United States of America.

Contents

Preface   ix

Acknowledgments   xi

Introduction   xiii

MINDFULNESS IN PLAIN ENGLISH | 1

1 Meditation: Why Bother?   3

2 What Meditation Isn't   13

3 What Meditation Is   25

4 Attitude   35

5 The Practice   41

6 What to Do with Your Body   59

7 What to Do with Your Mind   65

8 Structuring Your Meditation   75

9 Setup Exercises   83

10 Dealing with Problems   93

11 Dealing with Distractions 1   111

12 Dealing with Distractions 2   117

13 Mindfulness (*Sati*)   133

14 Mindfulness versus Concentration   145

15 Meditation in Everyday Life   153

16 What's in It for You   165

Afterword: The Power of Loving-Friendliness   173

Appendix: The Context of the Tradition   195

The Four Foundations of Mindfulness in Plain English | 199

The Four Foundations of Mindfulness Sutta   201

Part 1: *Mindfulness of the Body*   205

  1 Breath   207

  2 Four Postures   219

  3 Clear Comprehension   233

  4 Parts and Elements   247

  5 Death and Impermanence   261

Part 2: *Mindfulness of Feelings*   273

  6 Sensations and Emotions   275

  7 Harmful and Beneficial Feelings   287

Part 3: *Mindfulness of Mind*   299

  8 Mind and Consciousness   301

  9 Mental States   311

Part 4: *Mindfulness of Dhamma*   323

  10 Hindrances   325

  11 Clinging and the Fetters   337

  12 Factors of Enlightenment   351

  13 Four Truths and Eight Steps   365

Beyond Mindfulness in Plain English | 375

  1 The Concentration Path   377

  2 Concentration and the Jhanas   387

  3 Getting Ready for Jhana Meditation   399

  4 Wishing the Best for Yourself and Others   417

  5 Breath Meditation   435

  6 Why Can't We Concentrate Strongly Right Now? 445

  7 The Purpose of Practice   463

  8 The Jhana States   481

 9 Access Concentration   489
10 The First Jhana   499
11 The Second and Third Jhanas   519
12 The Fourth Jhana   531
13 The Immaterial Jhanas   547
14 The Supramundane Jhanas   557

Glossary   567
Index   583
About the Author   609

Preface to the Collection

I am so pleased that, on the occasion of my ninetieth birthday, Wisdom Publications is bringing out, for the first time in a single volume, this comprehensive collection of my core, in-plain-English teachings on mindfulness.

This collection includes the full texts of three books: *Mindfulness in Plain English, The Four Foundations of Mindfulness in Plain English,* and *Beyond Mindfulness in Plain English.* This volume also includes an integrated glossary and index, covering all three works together.

The *Mindfulness in Plain English* text is the expanded edition that Wisdom brought out on the occasion of its twentieth anniversary. I first published this book in Taiwan in 1991, and the first Wisdom edition came out in 1993. I am truly humbled to learn how many people—all over the world—have been touched by this book. Indeed it has been translated into more than twenty languages. I wrote *Mindfulness in Plain English* to be a gentle but thorough introduction to the practice of *vipassana.* Though it has come to be known as beloved introduction for newcomers to the Buddha's teaching, I hope this collection may be a cause for everyone to read this book again, mindfully and with fresh eyes. You may be surprised by what may touch your heart for the first time. You may think of

Mindfulness in Plain English as a book for beginners—yet, when it comes to this rich practice, aren't we all beginners?

Appearing next in this collection is *The Four Foundations of Mindfulness in Plain English*. This book is built around the *Satipatthana Sutta*, a Pali text in which the Buddha thoroughly lays out the groundwork of meditation practice. Studying the four foundations of mindfulness, the four bases on which mindfulness practice is built, is a powerful way to simultaneously deepen and broaden your practice of mindfulness. Studying these foundations—mindfulness of feelings, of the body, of the mind, and of the Dhamma—will make clear to you the principles that underlie mindfulness practice. Deep familiarity with these bedrock elements will help you bring the practice of mindfulness more fully into every aspect of your life.

Then, having gone deep down into the substrates of mindfulness with *The Four Foundations*, with *Beyond Mindfulness in Plain English* I invite you to explore *samatha*, practices of concentration that, together with *vipassana*, complete the single integrated set of tools that the Buddha taught for becoming free of suffering. Through samatha practice, you can gain access to the *jhanas*, the deeper states of meditation that reveal to us, in increasingly subtle and far-reaching ways, the true nature of the mind—and of freedom.

Taken together as a whole, *The Mindfulness in Plain English Collection* can serve as a comprehensive handbook for meditators along the entirety of the Buddha's path. And I am honored to be able to offer it to you.

May it serve you well.

With metta,
Bhante Henepola Gunaratana
Bhavana Society
High View, West Virginia

Acknowledgments

MINDFULNESS IN PLAIN ENGLISH

I am deeply grateful to the many friends who have helped me prepare this book for publication. I would especially like to express my deepest appreciation and sincere gratitude to John M. Peddicord, Daniel J. Olmsted, Matthew Flickstein, Carol Flickstein, Patrick Hamilton, Genny Hamilton, Bill Mayne, Bhikkhu Dang Pham Jotika, Elizabeth Reid, Bhikkhu Sona, Reverend Sister Sama, and Chris O'Keefe for their most valuable suggestions, comments, criticisms, and support. I would also like to acknowledge the entire team at Wisdom Publications for their help in bringing this book and this new edition out into the world.

THE FOUR FOUNDATIONS OF MINDFULNESS IN PLAIN ENGLISH

I sincerely thank Ajahn Sona, one of our students at the Bhavana Society, for his valuable help in getting this book started. I am grateful to Josh Bartok and Laura Cunningham at Wisdom Publications for making many valuable suggestions to complete this book and for shepherding it to completion, and to Brenda Rosen who contributed enormous time and effort to develop the manuscript.

Beyond Mindfulness in Plain English

Throughout this book I have given a number of quotations from the canon of Pali suttas, our best record of what the Buddha himself taught. Since this is not an academic work, we have not used notes. Nonetheless I'd like to acknowledge the many fine translators whose work I've drawn on: Bhikkhu Bodhi, Nyanaponika Maha Thera, Bhikkhu Nanamoli, John D. Ireland, and Gil Fronsdal. A few translations are my own, and several come from the *Visuddhimagga* by Buddhaghosa, translated by Bhikkhu Nanamoli.

I am profoundly grateful to John Peddicord for the generous gifts of his time and patience. This book, like *Mindfulness in Plain English*, could not have come into being without his extensive hard work in its development.

I am also thankful to Josh Bartok of Wisdom Publications for making many valuable suggestions to complete the work. Others who contributed their time and effort include Barry Boyce, Brenda Rosen, Fran Oropeza, Bhante Rahula, Bhante Buddharakita, and Bhikkhuni Sobhana. I am grateful to all of you.

Bhante Henepola Gunaratana

Introduction

*I*n my experience the most effective way to express something new is to use the simplest language possible. I have also learned from teaching that the more rigid the language—that is to say, the less it reflects the inevitable variety of people's experience—the less effective that teaching is. Who wants to meet with stern and rigid language? Especially when learning new things or encountering things we do not normally engage with in daily life. That approach can make meditation, the practice of mindfulness, seem like an activity reserved for the select. This collection of three books presents the antidote to that view! The books are straightforward, written in ordinary, everyday language. Yet within these pages you'll find rich instructions that allow you to discover for yourself the true power of mindfulness. I wrote *Mindfulness in Plain English* in response to the many requests I'd received for just such an introduction. You may find it especially useful if you are taking up mindfulness meditation on your own, without access to a teacher.

In the decades since Wisdom Publications first released *Mind-fulness in Plain English*, we've seen mindfulness become more and more embedded in modern society and culture—in education, psychotherapy, art, yoga, medicine, and the burgeoning science of the brain. And more and more people are seeking out mindfulness to reduce stress, to improve physical and psychological well-being, and to be more effective, skillful, and kind in relationships, at work, and throughout their lives.

WHAT IS MINDFULNESS?

The basic premise of mindfulness is simple. We can train ourselves to become aware of the things we do with the body, such as walking, standing, talking, eating, drinking, writing, reading, playing, and other physical activities. And we can also develop moment-to-moment awareness of our emotions, sensations, thoughts, and other mental activities. Mindfulness, in other words, trains us to bring full awareness to whatever we are doing right now.

You may be wondering, "Why is full awareness important?" As anyone who tries mindfulness practice quickly discovers, the more aware we are of our actions and of the feelings, thoughts, and perceptions that give rise to them, the more insight we have into why we are doing what we are doing. Awareness allows us to see whether our actions spring from beneficial or harmful impulses. Beneficial motivations include generosity, friendliness, compassion, and wisdom; harmful actions are caused primarily by greed, hatred, and delusion. When we are mindful of the deep roots from which our thoughts, words, and deeds grow, we have the opportunity to cultivate those that are beneficial and weed out those that are harmful.

The Buddha is very clear that the primary aim of all his teachings is "the end of suffering." Mindfulness helps us to recognize that beneficial actions bring peace of mind and happiness to our everyday lives. They also help us progress on the Buddha's path toward *nibbana*—liberation, complete freedom from suffering. Similarly, mindfulness teaches us that actions motivated by greed, hatred, and delusion make us miserable and anxious. They imprison us in *samsara*, the life-after-life cycle of repeated suffering.

When we practice mindfulness, before we speak we ask ourselves: "Are these words truthful and beneficial to me and to others? Will they bring peace or will they create problems?" When we think mindfully, we ask: "Does this thought make me calm and happy, or distressed and fearful?" Before we act, we ask: "Will this action cause suffering for me and for others?" Being mindful gives us the opportunity to choose: "Do I want joy and contentment or misery and worry?"

Mindfulness also trains us to remember to pay attention to the changes that are continually taking place inside our body and mind and in the world around us. Normally we forget to pay attention because the countless things that are happening simultaneously distract our minds. We get carried away by the superficial and lose sight of the flow. The mind wants to see what is next, what is next, and what is next. We get excited by the show and forget that it is, indeed, simply a show.

The Buddha taught: "That which is impermanent is suffering." The truth of these words becomes clear when we simply pay attention. Eventually the mind gets tired of moving from one impermanent thing to the next. Losing interest in the futile pursuit, the mind rests and finds joy. In Pali the word for "to remember" is *sati*, which is also the word that is translated as "mindfulness." Remembering is simply paying direct, nonverbal attention to what is happening from one moment to the next.

Resting comfortably in awareness, we relax into things as they are right now in this very moment, not slipping away into what happened in the past or will happen in the future. Normally we tend to blame the world for our pain and suffering. But with *sati*, mindful remembering, we understand that the only place to find peace and freedom from suffering is this very place, right here in our own body and mind.

Present-moment recollection of our body and mind can be trained until it becomes almost automatic. The heart pumps blood without our reminding it to do so. The mind can also be taught to act the same way. With training, the faculty of mindfulness can become as continuous as breathing. As mental events arise, mindfulness empowers us to choose: Will we merely suffer from pain or will we examine the pain to understand why it arises and then create different causes? If we ignore the causes, we continue to suffer. Living with awareness requires effort, especially in the beginning, but following the Buddha's example, with practice anyone can master it.

The Four Foundations

More than 2,600 years ago the Buddha exhorted his senior monks who were responsible for passing his teachings on to others to train their students in the four foundations of mindfulness. The practice of contemplating, or as we might say, meditating on, the four foundations—mindfulness of the body, feelings, mind, and *dhammas* (or phenomena)—is recommended for people at every stage of the spiritual path. As the Buddha explains in the *Foundations of Mindfulness Sutta (Satipatthana Sutta)*, everyone—trainees who have become interested in the Buddhist path, monks and nuns, and even *arahants*, advanced meditators who have reached the goal of liberation from suffering—"should be exhorted, settled, and established in the development of these four foundations of mindfulness."

In this sutta the Buddha is primarily addressing the community of *bhikkhus*, his monastic students who have dedicated their lives to spiritual practice. Given this, you might wonder whether people with families and jobs and busy Western lives can benefit from mindfulness practice. If the Buddha's words were meant only for monastics, he would have given this talk in a monastery. But he spoke in a village filled with shopkeepers, farmers, and other ordinary folk. Since mindfulness can help men and women from all walks of life relieve suffering, we can assume that the word "bhikkhu" here is used to mean anyone seriously interested in meditation. In that sense, we are all bhikkhus.

Let's look briefly at each of the four foundations. By asking us to practice *mindfulness of the body*, the Buddha is reminding us to recognize that the body is not a solid unified thing but rather a collection of parts (nails, teeth, skin, bones, heart, lungs, and so on). Remembering that the body is composed of many parts helps us to see "the body as body"—not as my body or as myself, but simply as a physical form like all other physical forms. Like all forms, the body comes into being, remains present for a time, and then passes away. Since it experiences injury, illness, and death, the body is unsatisfactory as a source of lasting happiness. Since it is not myself, the body can also be called "selfless." When mindfulness helps us to recognize that the body is impermanent, unsatisfactory, and selfless, in the Buddha's words, we "know the body as it really is."

Similarly, by asking us to practice *mindfulness of feelings*, the Buddha is telling us to contemplate "the feeling in the feelings." These words remind us that, like the body, feelings can be subdivided. Traditionally, there are only three types—pleasant feelings, unpleasant feelings, and neutral feelings. Each type is one "feeling" in the mental awareness that we call "feelings." At any given moment we are able to notice only one type. We regard feelings in this way to help us develop a simple nonjudgmental awareness of what we are experiencing—seeing a particular feeling as one of many feelings rather than as *my* feeling or as part of *me*. As we watch each emotion or sensation as it arises, remains present, and passes away, we observe that any feeling is impermanent. Since a pleasant feeling does not last and an unpleasant feeling is often painful, we understand that feelings are unsatisfactory. Seeing a feeling as an emotion or sensation rather than as *my* feeling, we come to know that feelings are selfless. Recognizing these truths, we "know feelings as they really are."

The same process applies to *mindfulness of mind*. Although we talk about "the mind" as if it were a single thing, mind or consciousness is actually a succession of particular instances of "mind in mind." As mindfulness practice teaches us, consciousness arises from moment to moment on the basis of information coming to us from the senses—what we see, hear, smell, taste, and touch—and from internal mental states such as memories, imaginings, and daydreams. When we look at the mind, we are not looking at mere consciousness. The mind alone cannot exist, only particular states of mind that appear depending on external or internal conditions. Paying attention to the way each thought arises, remains present, and passes away, we learn to stop the runaway train of one unsatisfactory thought leading to another and another and another. We gain a bit of detachment and understand that we are not our thoughts. In the end we come to know "mind as it really is."

By telling us to practice *mindfulness of dhammas*, or phenomena, the Buddha is not simply saying that we should be mindful of his teachings, though that is one meaning of the term *dhamma*. He is also reminding us that the dhamma that we contemplate is within us. The history of the world is full of truth seekers. The Buddha was one of them. Almost all sought the truth outside themselves. Before he attained enlightenment, the Buddha also searched outside of himself. He was looking for his maker, the cause of his existence, whom he called the "builder of this house." But he never found what he was looking for. Instead he discovered that he himself was subject to birth, growth, decay, death, sickness, sorrow, lamentation, and defilement. When he looked outside himself, he saw that everyone else was suffering from these same problems. This recognition helped him to see that no one outside himself could free him from his own suffering. So he began to search within. This inner seeking is known as "come and see." Only when he began to search inside did he find the answer. Then he said:

Many a birth I wandered in samsara,
seeking but not finding the builder of this house.
Sorrowful is it to be born again and again.
O housebuilder, thou art seen!
Thou shall not build a house again.
All thy rafters are broken.
Thy ridgepole is shattered.
The mind has attained the unconditioned.

The great discovery of the Buddha is that the truth is within us. The entire Dhamma that he taught is based on this realization. When we look inside we come to understand the significance of the four noble truths—the Buddha's essential first teaching. Where do we find suffering? We experience it within ourselves. And where is the cause of our suffering, our craving? It too is within us. And how can we reach the end of it, the cessation of suffering? We find the way within ourselves. And where do we develop skillful understanding, thinking, speech, action, livelihood, effort, mindfulness, and concentration, the Buddha's noble eightfold path—the method for ending suffering? We develop all of these qualities within our own body and mind. The roots of suffering are within us. And the method for eliminating suffering is within us as well.

When we practice mindfulness we follow the Buddha's example and look inside. We become aware that our own greed, hatred, and delusion are the causes of our unhappiness. When we replace these poisons with generosity, loving-friendliness, compassion, appreciative joy, patience, cordiality, gentleness, and wisdom, we find the happiness and peace of mind we have been seeking. As I always remind my students, "The meditation you do on the cushion is your homework. The rest of your life is your fieldwork. To practice mindfulness you need both."

The other meaning of dhammas is simply "phenomena." When we follow the Buddha's advice and "dwell contemplating dhamma in dhammas," we come to understand that each individual phenomenon within reality as we experience it, including physical objects, feelings, perceptions, mental activities, and consciousness, comes into being, remains, and then passes away. In the same way, the deep-rooted negative habits of the unenlightened mind, the fetters that bind us to one unsatisfactory life after another, are impermanent. With effort each fetter—including greed, hatred, and belief in the existence of a permanent self or soul—can be recognized and removed. In essence the Dhamma path is quite straightforward. We eliminate our harmful habits one by one and cultivate beneficial qualities based on our understanding of each of the Buddha's teachings. In the end the last fetter falls away and we achieve liberation from suffering.

The Goals of Practice

While many people are drawn to meditation because of its wonderful benefits for relaxation, relief from stress and pain, and the general health of the body and mind, it's important to keep another set of goals in mind. With dedicated effort and regular practice, we can look forward to five significant spiritual accomplishments:

First, meditation helps us become fully aware of what is going on in the mind and body here and now. All too often we sleepwalk through our days musing about the past or daydreaming about the future. Mindfulness teaches us to cut through the fog and bring our focus to the present moment.

Second, because of this new awareness, we are able to evaluate more clearly the purpose and suitability of everything we say and do. As a result, we make wiser and more beneficial choices.

Third, meditation trains us to see our own body, feelings, perceptions, thoughts, and consciousness exactly as they are, from moment to moment. Seeing ourselves clearly is the essential first step to making positive life changes.

Fourth, as our practice deepens we see the world around us in a special way, without distortion. We come to understand that everything that exists—including us—is interdependent with everything else, and that everything is always changing. For this reason, we realize, no person, place, thing, or situation can ever be permanently satisfying.

And finally, we learn to dedicate ourselves fully to reflection or meditation, recognizing that only by following the Buddha's example can we hope to find lasting happiness and peace.

In a nutshell, insight meditation trains the mind to be aware twenty-four hours a day. With this new clarity we begin to perceive material objects as less solid than our ordinary senses tell us they are. We discover they are only as real as a mirage shimmering in the desert. In the same way, we recognize that our thoughts and feelings are always in flux. In truth they are only as permanent as soap bubbles. Awareness frees us from the desire to grasp on to things and other people with the thought "this is mine." Awareness liberates us from viewing our own body and mind as fixed and unchanging with the thought "I am this" or "this is my self."

Beyond Mindfulness

Having gone deep down into the substrates of mindfulness with the four foundations, I invite you to explore *samatha*, deeper levels of concentration that, together with *vipassana*, complete the single integrated set of tools that the Buddha taught for becoming free of suffering.

While the words *mindfulness* and even *vipassana* are now common in the West and meditation practice itself has received lots of attention, deep-concentration meditation is only recently beginning to receive widespread attention from Westerners interested in contemplative practice. The progressive stages of deep concentration, called *jhanas* in Pali, were widely considered a kind of meditators' Olympics, a pursuit suited only to extraordinary beings who lived in caves or monasteries, far beyond the ken of "normal people," folks with busy daily lives. But in the first decades of this century, interest is turning toward samatha and the path of the jhanas. And that is a good thing, because concentration meditation is truly a parallel yet complementary path to mindfulness and insight meditation. The two are intertwined and support each other. Over the last two millennia, these two paths were codified and refined as parallel paths for a very good reason: they both work and they work best together. The two are really one. In truth the Buddha did not teach vipassana and samatha as separate systems. The Buddha gave us one meditation path, one set of tools for becoming free from suffering. Vipassana is like the knife that helps us cut out the hindrances to liberation at the root, and samatha makes our insight extraordinarily powerful and extraordinarily deft. They are truly effective only when they work together.

Beyond Mindfulness in Plain English, the final book in this collection, was intended to serve as a clear, comprehensible meditators' handbook, laying out the path of concentration meditation in a fashion as close to step-by-step as possible. Once you have begun to cultivate a mindfulness practice, you are ready to take the next step—beyond mindfulness.

The four foundations and the jhanas are powerful teachings. In fact, the Buddha promises that anyone who practices his mindfulness instructions, exactly as they are given, without leaving anything out, can attain enlightenment—permanent liberation from suffering—in this very life, even in as short a time as seven days!

Amazing as that guarantee sounds, it makes perfect sense. Imagine how clear your mind would be if you were mindful during every waking moment for just one day from morning to evening. Then imagine how clear it would be if you spent two days with mindfulness, three days, four days. When we remain mindful all the time, it's easy to make good choices. The mind is purified and becomes luminous. Every day that we practice mindfulness moves us closer to liberation.

I hope that, whatever reasons have brought you to this collection or have brought this collection to you, you will find within it clear pointers to an incomparably beneficial path.

Mindfulness
in Plain English

1. Meditation: Why Bother?

*M*editation is not easy. It takes time and it takes energy. It also takes grit, determination, and discipline. It requires a host of personal qualities that we normally regard as unpleasant and like to avoid whenever possible. We can sum up all of these qualities in the American word *gumption*. Meditation takes gumption. It is certainly a great deal easier just to sit back and watch television. So why bother? Why waste all that time and energy when you could be out enjoying yourself? Why? Simple. Because you are human. Just because of the simple fact that you are human, you find yourself heir to an inherent unsatisfactoriness in life that simply will not go away. You can suppress it from your awareness for a time, you can distract yourself for hours on end, but it always comes back, and usually when you least expect it. All of a sudden, seemingly out of the blue, you sit up, take stock, and realize your actual situation in life.

There you are, and you suddenly realize that you are spending your whole life just barely getting by. You keep up a good front. You manage to make ends meet somehow and look OK from the outside. But those periods of desperation, those times when you feel everything caving in on you—you keep those to yourself. You are a mess, and you know it. But you hide it beautifully. Meanwhile, way down under all of that, you just know that there has to be some other way to live, a better way to look at the world, a way to touch life more fully. You click into it by chance now and then: You get a good job. You fall in love. You win the game. For a while, things are different. Life takes on a richness and clarity that makes all the bad times and humdrum fade away. The whole texture of your experience changes and you say to yourself, "OK, now I've made it; now I will be happy." But then that fades too, like smoke in the wind. You are left with just a memory—that, and the vague awareness that something is wrong.

You feel that there really is a whole other realm of depth and sensitivity available in life; somehow, you are just not seeing it. You wind up feeling cut off. You feel insulated from the sweetness of experience by some sort of sensory cotton. You are not really touching life. You are not "making it" again. Then even that vague awareness fades away, and you are back to the same old reality. The world looks like the usual foul place. It is an emotional roller coaster, and you spend a lot of your time down at the bottom of the ramp, yearning for the heights.

So what is wrong with you? Are you a freak? No. You are just human. And you suffer from the same malady that infects every human being. It is a monster inside all of us, and it has many arms: chronic tension, lack of genuine compassion for others, including the people closest to you, blocked up feelings and emotional deadness—many, many arms. None of us is entirely free from it. We may deny it. We try to suppress it. We build a whole culture around hiding from it, pretending it is not there, and distracting ourselves with goals, projects, and concerns about status. But it never goes away. It is a constant undercurrent in every thought and every perception, a little voice in the back of the mind that keeps saying, "Not good enough yet. Need to have more. Have to make it better. Have to be better." It is a monster, a monster that manifests everywhere in subtle forms.

Go to a party. Listen to the laughter, those brittle-tongued voices that express fun on the surface, and fear underneath. Feel the tension, the pressure. Nobody really relaxes. They are faking it. Go to a ball game. Watch the fans in the stand. Watch the irrational fits of anger. Watch the uncontrolled frustration bubbling forth from people that masquerades under the guise of enthusiasm or team spirit. Booing, catcalls, and unbridled egotism in the name of team loyalty, drunkenness, fights in the stands—these are people trying desperately to release tension from within; these are not people who are at peace with themselves. Watch the news on TV. Listen to the lyrics of popular songs. You find the same theme repeated over and over in variations: jealousy, suffering, discontent, and stress.

Life seems to be a perpetual struggle, an enormous effort against staggering odds. And what is our solution to all this dissatisfaction? We get stuck in the "if only" syndrome. If only I had more money, then I would be happy. If only I could find somebody who really loved me; if only I could lose twenty pounds; if only I had a color TV, a hot tub, and curly hair; and on and on forever. Where does all this junk come from, and more important, what can we do about it? It comes from the conditions of our own minds. It is a deep, subtle, and pervasive set of mental habits, a Gordian knot that we have tied bit by bit and that we can only unravel in just that same way, one piece at a time. We can tune up our awareness, dredge up each separate piece, and bring it out into the light. We can make the unconscious conscious, slowly, one piece at a time.

The essence of our experience is change. Change is incessant. Moment by moment life flows by, and it is never the same. Perpetual fluctuation is the essence of the perceptual universe. A thought springs up in your head and half a second later, it is gone. In comes another one, and then that is gone too. A sound strikes your ears, and then silence. Open your eyes and the world pours in, blink and it is gone. People come into your life and go. Friends leave, relatives die. Your fortunes go up, and they go down. Sometimes you win, and just as often, you lose. It is incessant: change, change, change; no two moments ever the same.

There is not a thing wrong with this. It is the nature of the universe. But human culture has taught us some odd responses to this endless flowing. We categorize experiences. We try to stick each perception, every mental change in this endless flow, into one of three mental pigeonholes: it is good, bad, or neutral. Then, according to which box we stick it in, we perceive with a set of fixed habitual mental responses. If a particular perception has been labeled "good," then we try to freeze time right there. We grab onto that particular thought, fondle it, hold it, and we try to keep it from escaping. When that does not work, we go all-out in an effort to repeat the experience that caused the thought. Let us call this mental habit "grasping."

Over on the other side of the mind lies the box labeled "bad." When we perceive something "bad," we try to push it away. We try to deny it, reject it, and get rid of it any way we can. We fight against our own experience. We run from pieces of ourselves. Let us call this mental habit "rejecting." Between these two reactions lies the "neutral" box. Here we place the experiences that are neither good nor bad. They are tepid, neutral, uninteresting. We pack experience away in the neutral box so that we can ignore it and thus return our attention to where the action is, namely, our endless round of desire and aversion. So this "neutral" category of experience gets robbed of its fair share of our attention. Let us call this mental habit "ignoring." The direct result of all this lunacy is a perpetual treadmill race to nowhere, endlessly pounding after pleasure, endlessly fleeing from pain, and endlessly ignoring 90 percent of our experience. Then we wonder why life tastes so flat. In the final analysis this system does not work.

No matter how hard you pursue pleasure and success, there are times when you fail. No matter how fast you flee, there are times when pain catches up with you. And in between those times, life is so boring you could scream. Our minds are full of opinions and criticisms. We have built walls all around ourselves and are trapped in the prison of our own likes and dislikes. We suffer.

"Suffering" is a big word in Buddhist thought. It is a key term and should be thoroughly understood. The Pali word is *dukkha,* and it does not just mean the agony of the body. It means that deep, subtle sense of dissatisfaction that is a part of every mind-moment and that results directly from the mental treadmill. The essence of life is suffering, said the Buddha. At first glance this statement seems exceedingly morbid and pessimistic. It even seems untrue. After all, there are plenty of times when we are happy. Aren't there? No, there are not. It just seems that way. Take any moment when you feel really fulfilled and examine it closely. Down under the joy, you will find that subtle, all-pervasive undercurrent of tension that no matter how great this moment is, it is going to end. No matter how much you just gained, you are inevitably either going to lose some of it or spend the rest of your days guarding what you have and scheming how to get more. And in the end, you are going to die; in the end, you lose everything. It is all transitory.

Sounds pretty bleak, doesn't it? Luckily, it's not—not at all. It only sounds bleak when you view it from the ordinary mental perspective, the very perspective at which the treadmill mechanism operates. Underneath lies another perspective, a completely different way to look at the universe. It is a level of functioning in which the mind does not try to freeze time, does not grasp on to our experience as it flows by, and does not try to block things out and ignore them. It is a level of experience beyond good and bad, beyond pleasure and pain.

It is a lovely way to perceive the world, and it is a learnable skill. It is not easy, but it can be learned.

Happiness and peace are really the prime issues in human existence. That is what all of us are seeking. This is often a bit hard to see because we cover up those basic goals with layers of surface objectives. We want food, wealth, sex, entertainment, and respect. We even say to ourselves that the idea of "happiness" is too abstract: "Look, I am practical. Just give me enough money and I will buy all the happiness I need." Unfortunately, this is an attitude that does not work. Examine each of these goals and you will find that they are superficial. You want food. Why? Because I am hungry. So you are hungry—so what? Well, if I eat, I won't be hungry, and then I'll feel good. Ah ha! "Feel good": now there is the real item. What we really seek are not the surface goals; those are just means to an end. What we are really after is the feeling of relief that comes when the drive is satisfied. Relief, relaxation, and an end to the tension. Peace, happiness—no more yearning.

So what is this happiness? For most of us, the idea of perfect happiness would be to have everything we wanted and be in control of everything, playing Caesar, making the whole world dance a jig according to our every whim. Once again, it does not work that way. Take a look at the people in history who have actually held this type of power. They were not happy people. Certainly, they were not at peace with themselves. Why not? Because they were driven to control the world totally and absolutely, and they could not. They wanted to control all people, yet there remained people who refused to be controlled. These powerful people could not control the stars. They still got sick. They still had to die.

You can't ever get everything you want. It is impossible. Luckily, there is another option. You can learn to control your mind, to step outside of the endless cycle of desire and aversion. You can learn not to want what you want, to recognize desires but not be controlled by them. This does not mean that you lie down on the road and invite everybody to walk all over you. It means that you continue to live a very normal-looking life, but live from a whole new viewpoint. You do the things that a person must do, but you are free from that obsessive, compulsive drivenness of your own desires. You want something, but you don't need to chase after it. You fear something, but you don't need to stand there quaking in your boots. This sort of mental cultivation is very difficult. It takes years. But trying to control everything is impossible; the difficult is preferable to the impossible.

Wait a minute, though. Peace and happiness! Isn't that what civilization is all about? We build skyscrapers and freeways. We have paid vacations, TV sets; we provide free hospitals and sick leaves, Social Security and welfare benefits. All of that is aimed at providing some measure of peace and happiness. Yet the rate of mental illness climbs steadily, and the crime rates rise faster. The streets are crawling with aggressive and unstable individuals. Stick your arms outside the safety of your own door, and somebody is very likely to steal your watch! Something is not working. A happy person does not steal. One who is at peace with him- or herself does not feel driven to kill. We like to think that our society is employing every area of human knowledge in order to achieve peace and happiness, but this is not true.

We are just beginning to realize that we have overdeveloped the material aspects of existence at the expense of the deeper emotional and spiritual aspects, and we are paying the price for that error. It is one thing to talk about degeneration of moral and spiritual fiber in America today, and another thing to actually do something about it. The place to start is within ourselves. Look carefully inside, truthfully and objectively, and each of us will see moments when "I am the delinquent" and "I am the crazy person." We will learn to see those moments, see them clearly, cleanly, and without condemnation, and we will be on our way up and out of being so.

You can't make radical changes in the pattern of your life until you begin to see yourself exactly as you are now. As soon as you do that, changes will flow naturally. You don't have to force anything, struggle, or obey rules dictated to you by some authority. It is automatic; you just change. But arriving at that initial insight is quite a task. You have to see who you are and how you are without illusion, judgment, or resistance of any kind. You have to see your place in society and your function as a social being. You have to see your duties and obligations to your fellow human beings, and above all, your responsibility to yourself as an individual living with other individuals. And finally, you have to see all of that clearly as a single unit, an irreducible whole of interrelationship. It sounds complex, but it can occur in a single instant. Mental cultivation through meditation is without rival in helping you achieve this sort of understanding and serene happiness.

The *Dhammapada*, an ancient Buddhist text (which anticipated Freud by thousands of years), says: "What you are now is the result of what you were. What you will be tomorrow will be the result of what you are now. The consequences of an evil mind will follow you like the cart follows the ox that pulls it. The consequences of a purified mind will follow you like your own shadow. No one can do more for you than your own purified mind—no parent, no relative, no friend, no one. A well-disciplined mind brings happiness."

Meditation is intended to purify the mind. It cleanses the thought process of what can be called psychic irritants, things like greed, hatred, and jealousy, which keep you snarled up in emotional bondage. Meditation brings the mind to a state of tranquility and awareness, a state of concentration and insight.

In our society, we are great believers in education. We believe that knowledge makes a person civilized. Civilization, however, polishes a person only superficially. Subject our noble and sophisticated gentle-person to the stresses of war or economic collapse, and see what happens. It is one thing to obey the law because you know the penalties and fear the consequences; it is something else entirely to obey the law because you have cleansed yourself from the greed that would make you steal and the hatred that would make you kill. Throw a stóne into a stream. The running water would smooth the stone's surface, but the inside remains unchanged. Take that same stone and place it in the intense fires of a forge, and it all melts; the whole stone changes inside and out. Civilization changes a person on the outside. Meditation softens a person from within, through and through.

Meditation is called the Great Teacher. It is the cleansing crucible fire that works slowly but surely, through understanding. The greater your understanding, the more flexible and tolerant, the more compassionate you can be. You become like a perfect parent or an ideal teacher. You are ready to forgive and forget. You feel love toward others because you understand them, and you understand others because you have understood yourself. You have looked deeply inside and seen self-illusion and your own human failings, seen your own humanity and learned to forgive and to love. When you have learned compassion for yourself, compassion for others is automatic. An accomplished meditator has achieved a profound understanding of life, and he or she inevitably relates to the world with a deep and uncritical love.

Meditation is a lot like cultivating a new land. To make a field out of a forest, first you have to clear the trees and pull out the stumps. Then you till the soil and fertilize it, sow your seed, and harvest your crops. To cultivate your mind, first you have to clear out the various irritants that are in the way—pull them right out by the root so that they won't grow back. Then you fertilize: you pump energy and discipline into the mental soil. Then you sow the seed, and harvest your crops of faith, morality, mindfulness, and wisdom.

Faith and morality, by the way, have a special meaning in this context. Buddhism does not advocate faith in the sense of believing something because it is written in a book, attributed to a prophet, or taught to you by some authority figure. The meaning of faith here is closer to confidence. It is knowing that something is true because you have seen it work, because you have observed that very thing within yourself. In the same way, morality is not a ritualistic obedience to a code of behavior imposed by an external authority. It is rather a healthy habit pattern that you have consciously and voluntarily chosen to impose upon yourself because you recognize its superiority to your present behavior.

The purpose of meditation is personal transformation. The "you" that goes in one side of the meditation experience is not the same "you" that comes out the other side. Meditation changes your character by a process of sensitization, by making you deeply aware of your own thoughts, words, and deeds. Your arrogance evaporates, and your antagonism dries up. Your mind becomes still and calm. And your life smoothes out. Thus meditation, properly performed, prepares you to meet the ups and downs of existence. It reduces your tension, fear, and worry. Restlessness recedes and passion moderates. Things begin to fall into place, and your life becomes a glide instead of a struggle. All of this happens through understanding.

Meditation sharpens your concentration and your thinking power. Then, piece by piece, your own subconscious motives and mechanics become clear to you. Your intuition sharpens. The precision of your thought increases, and gradually you come to a direct knowledge of things as they really are, without prejudice and without illusion.

So are these reasons enough to bother? Scarcely. These are just promises on paper. There is only one way you will ever know if meditation is worth the effort: learn to do it right, and do it. See for yourself.

2. What Meditation Isn't

*M*editation is a word. You have heard this word before, or you would never have picked up this book. The thinking process operates by association, and all sorts of ideas are associated with the word "meditation." Some of them are probably accurate, and others are hogwash. Some of them pertain more properly to other systems of meditation and have nothing to do with vipassana practice. Before we proceed, it behooves us to blast some of that residue out of our neuron circuits so that new information can pass unimpeded. Let us start with some of the most obvious stuff.

We are not going to teach you to contemplate your navel or to chant secret syllables. You are not conquering demons or harnessing invisible energies. There are no colored belts given for your performance, and you don't have to shave your head or wear a turban. You don't even have to give away all your belongings and move to a monastery. In fact, unless your life is immoral and chaotic, you can probably get started right away and make some progress. Sounds fairly encouraging, wouldn't you say?

There are many books on the subject of meditation. Most of them are written from a point of view that lies squarely within one particular religious or philosophical tradition, and many of the authors have not bothered to point this out. They make statements about meditation that sound like general laws but are actually highly specific procedures exclusive to that particular system of practice. Worse yet is the panoply of complex theories and interpretations available, often at odds with one another. The result is a real mess: an enormous jumble of conflicting opinions accompanied by a mass of extraneous data. This book is specific. We are dealing exclusively with the vipassana system of meditation. We are going to teach you to watch the functioning of your own mind in a calm and detached manner so you can gain insight into your own behavior. The goal is awareness, an awareness so intense, concentrated, and finely tuned that you will be able to pierce the inner workings of reality itself.

There are a number of common misconceptions about meditation. We see the same questions crop up again and again from new students. It is best to deal with these things at once, because they are the sort of preconceptions that can block your progress right from the outset. We are going to take these misconceptions one at a time and dissolve them.

Misconception 1: Meditation is just a relaxation technique.

The bugaboo here is the word *just*. Relaxation is a key component of meditation, but vipassana-style meditation aims at a much loftier goal. The statement is essentially true for many other systems of meditation. All meditation procedures stress concentration of the mind, bringing the mind to rest on one item or one area of thought. Do it strongly and thoroughly enough, and you achieve a deep and blissful relaxation, called *jhana*. It is a state of such supreme tranquility that it amounts to rapture, a form of pleasure that lies above and beyond anything that can be experienced in the normal state of consciousness. Most systems stop right there. *Jhana* is the goal, and when you attain that, you simply repeat the experience for the rest of your life. Not so with vipassana meditation. Vipassana seeks another goal: awareness. Concentration and relaxation are considered necessary concomitants to awareness. They are required precursors, handy tools, and beneficial byproducts. But they are not the goal. The goal is insight. Vipassana meditation is a profound religious practice aimed at nothing less than the purification and transformation of your everyday life. We will deal more thoroughly with the differences between concentration and insight in chapter 14.

MISCONCEPTION 2: MEDITATION MEANS GOING INTO A TRANCE.

Here again the statement could be applied accurately to certain systems of meditation, but not to vipassana. Insight meditation is not a form of hypnosis. You are not trying to black out your mind so as to become unconscious, or trying to turn yourself into an emotionless vegetable. If anything, the reverse is true: you will become more and more attuned to your own emotional changes. You will learn to know yourself with ever greater clarity and precision. In learning this technique, certain states do occur that may appear trancelike to the observer. But they are really quite the opposite. In hypnotic trance, the subject is susceptible to control by another party, whereas in deep concentration, the meditator remains very much under his or her own control. The similarity is superficial, and in any case, the occurrence of these phenomena is not the point of vipassana. As we have said, the deep concentration of *jhana* is simply a tool or steppingstone on the route to heightened awareness. Vipassana, by definition, is the cultivation of mindfulness or awareness. If you find that you are becoming unconscious in meditation, then you aren't meditating, according to the definition of that word as used in the vipassana system.

Misconception 3: Meditation is a mysterious practice that cannot be understood.

Here again, this is almost true, but not quite. Meditation deals with levels of consciousness that lie deeper than conceptual thought. Therefore, some of the experiences of meditation just won't fit into words. That does not mean, however, that meditation cannot be understood. There are deeper ways to understand things than by the use of words. You understand how to walk. You probably can't describe the exact order in which your nerve fibers and your muscles contract during that process. But you know how to do it. Meditation needs to be understood that same way—by doing it. It is not something that you can learn in abstract terms, or something to be talked about. It is something to be experienced. Meditation is not a mindless formula that gives automatic and predictable results; you can never really predict exactly what will come up during any particular session. It is an investigation and an experiment, an adventure every time. In fact, this is so true that when you do reach a feeling of predictability and sameness in your practice, you can read that as an indication that you have gotten off track and are headed for stagnation. Learning to look at each second as if it were the first and only second in the universe is essential in vipassana meditation.

Misconception 4: The purpose of meditation is to become psychic.

No. The purpose of meditation is to develop awareness. Learning to read minds is not the point. Levitation is not the goal. The goal is liberation. There is a link between psychic phenomena and meditation, but the relationship is complex. During early stages of the meditator's career, such phenomena may or may not arise. Some people may experience some intuitive understanding or memories from past lives; others do not. In any case, these phenomena are not regarded as well-developed and reliable psychic abilities, and they should not be given undue importance. Such phenomena are in fact fairly dangerous to new meditators in that they are quite seductive. They can be an ego trap, luring you right off the track. Your best approach is not to place any emphasis on these phenomena. If they come up, that's fine. If they don't, that's fine, too. There is a point in the meditator's career where he or she may practice special exercises to develop psychic powers. But this occurs far down the line. Only after the meditator has reached a very deep stage of *jhana* will he or she be advanced enough to work with such powers without the danger of their running out of control or taking over his or her life. The meditator will then develop them strictly for the purpose of service to others. In most cases, this state of affairs occurs only after decades of practice. Don't worry about it. Just concentrate on developing more and more awareness. If voices and visions pop up, just notice them and let them go. Don't get involved.

MISCONCEPTION 5: MEDITATION IS DANGEROUS, AND A PRUDENT PERSON SHOULD AVOID IT.

Everything is dangerous. Walk across the street and you may get hit by a bus. Take a shower and you could break your neck. Meditate, and you will probably dredge up various nasty matters from your past. The suppressed material that has been buried for quite some time can be scary. But exploring it is also highly profitable. No activity is entirely without risk, but that does not mean that we should wrap ourselves in a protective cocoon. That is not living, but is premature death. The way to deal with danger is to know approximately how much of it there is, where it is likely to be found, and how to deal with it when it arises. That is the purpose of this manual. Vipassana is development of awareness. That in itself is not dangerous; on the contrary, increased awareness is a safeguard against danger. Properly done, meditation is a very gentle and gradual process. Take it slow and easy, and the development of your practice will occur very naturally. Nothing should be forced. Later, when you are under the close scrutiny and protective wisdom of a competent teacher, you can accelerate your rate of growth by taking a period of intensive meditation. In the beginning, though, easy does it. Work gently and everything will be fine.

MISCONCEPTION 6: MEDITATION IS FOR SAINTS AND SADHUS, NOT FOR REGULAR PEOPLE.

This attitude is very prevalent in Asia, where monks and holy men are accorded an enormous amount of ritualized reverence, somewhat akin to the American attitude of idolizing movie stars and baseball heroes. Such people are stereotyped, made larger than life, and saddled with all sorts of characteristics that few human beings can ever live up to. Even in the West, we share some of this attitude about meditation. We expect the meditator to be an extraordinarily pious figure in whose mouth butter would never dare to melt. A little personal contact with such people will quickly dispel this illusion. They usually prove to be people of enormous energy and gusto, who live their lives with amazing vigor.

It is true, of course, that most holy men meditate, but they don't meditate because they are holy men. That is backward. They are holy men *because* they meditate; meditation is how they got there. And they started meditating before they became holy, otherwise they would not be holy. This is an important point. A sizable number of students seems to feel that a person should be completely moral before beginning to meditate. It is an unworkable strategy. Morality requires a certain degree of mental control as a prerequisite. You can't follow any set of moral precepts without at least a little self-control, and if your mind is perpetually spinning like a fruit cylinder in a slot machine, self-control is highly unlikely. So mental culture has to come first.

There are three integral factors in Buddhist meditation—morality, concentration, and wisdom. These three factors grow together as your practice deepens. Each one influences the other, so you cultivate the three of them at once, not separately. When you have the wisdom to truly understand a situation, compassion toward all parties involved is automatic, and compassion means that you automatically restrain yourself from any thought, word, or deed that might harm yourself or others; thus, your behavior is automatically moral. It is only when you don't understand things deeply that you create problems. If you fail to see the consequences of your actions, you will blunder. The person who waits to become totally moral before he begins to meditate is waiting for a situation that will never arise. The ancient sages say this person is like a man waiting for the ocean to become calm so that he can take a bath.

To understand this relationship more fully, let us propose that there are levels of morality. The lowest level is adherence to a set of rules and regulations laid down by somebody else. It could be your favorite prophet. It could be the state, the head of your tribe, or a parent. No matter who generates the rules, all you have to do at this level is know the rules and follow them. A robot can do that. Even a trained chimpanzee could do it, if the rules were simple enough and he were smacked with a stick every time he broke one. This level requires no meditation at all. All you need are the rules and somebody to swing the stick.

The next level of morality consists of obeying the same rules even in the absence of somebody who will smack you. You obey because you have internalized the rules. You smack yourself every time you break one. This level requires a bit of mind control. But if your thought pattern is chaotic, your behavior will be chaotic, too. Mental cultivation reduces mental chaos.

There is a third level of morality, which might better be termed as "ethics." This level is a quantum leap up the scale from the first two levels, a complete shift in orientation. At the level of ethics, a person does not follow hard and fast rules dictated by authority. A person chooses to follow a path dictated by mindfulness, wisdom, and compassion. This level requires real intelligence, and an ability to juggle all the factors in every situation to arrive at a unique, creative, and appropriate response each time. Furthermore, the individual making these decisions needs to have dug him- or herself out of a limited personal viewpoint. The person has to see the entire situation from an objective point of view, giving equal weight to his or her own needs and those of others. In other words, he or she has to be free from greed, hatred, envy, and all the other selfish junk that ordinarily keeps us from seeing the other person's side of the issue. Only then can he or she choose the precise set of actions that will be truly optimal for that situation. This level of morality absolutely demands meditation, unless you were born a saint. There is no other way to acquire the skill. Furthermore, the sorting process required at this level is exhausting. If you tried to juggle all those factors in every situation with your conscious mind, you'd overload yourself. The intellect just can't keep that many balls in the air at once. Luckily, a deeper level of consciousness can do this sort of processing with ease. Meditation can accomplish the sorting process for you. It is an eerie feeling.

One day you've got a problem—let's say, to handle Uncle Herman's latest divorce. It looks absolutely unsolvable, an enormous muddle of "maybes" that would give King Solomon himself a headache. The next day you are washing the dishes, thinking about something else entirely, and suddenly the solution is there. It just pops out of the deep mind, and you say, "Ah ha!" and the whole thing is solved. This sort of intuition can only occur when you disengage the logic circuits from the problem and give the deep mind the opportunity to cook up the solution. The conscious mind just gets in the way. Meditation teaches you how to disentangle yourself from the thought process. It is the mental art of stepping out of your own way, and that's a pretty useful skill in everyday life. Meditation is certainly not an irrelevant practice strictly for ascetics and hermits. It is a practical skill that focuses on everyday events and has immediate applications in everybody's life. Meditation is not "other-worldly."

Unfortunately, this very fact constitutes the drawback for certain students. They enter the practice expecting instantaneous cosmic revelation, complete with angelic choirs. What they usually get is a more efficient way to take out the trash and better ways to deal with Uncle Herman. They are needlessly disappointed. The trash solution comes first. The voices of archangels take a bit longer.

MISCONCEPTION 7: MEDITATION IS RUNNING AWAY FROM REALITY.

Incorrect. Meditation is running straight into reality. It does not insulate you from the pain of life but rather allows you to delve so deeply into life and all its aspects that you pierce the pain barrier and go beyond suffering. Vipassana is a practice done with the specific intention of facing reality, to fully experience life just as it is and to cope with exactly what you find. It allows you to blow aside the illusions and free yourself from all the polite little lies you tell yourself all the time. What is there is there. You are who you are, and lying to yourself about your own weaknesses and motivations only binds you tighter to them. Vipassana meditation is not an attempt to forget yourself or to cover up your troubles. It is learning to look at yourself exactly as you are to see what is there and accept it fully. Only then can you change it.

MISCONCEPTION 8: MEDITATION IS A GREAT WAY TO GET HIGH.

Well, yes and no. Meditation does produce lovely blissful feelings sometimes. But they are not the purpose, and they don't always occur. Furthermore, if you do meditation with that purpose in mind, they are less likely to occur than if you just meditate for the actual purpose of meditation, which is increased awareness. Bliss results from relaxation, and relaxation results from release of tension. Seeking bliss from meditation introduces tension into the process, which blows the whole chain of events. It is a catch-22: you can only experience bliss if you don't chase after it. Euphoria is not the purpose of meditation. It will often arise, but should be regarded as a byproduct. Still, it is a very pleasant side effect, and it becomes more and more frequent the longer you meditate. You won't hear any disagreement about this from advanced practitioners.

MISCONCEPTION 9: MEDITATION IS SELFISH.

It certainly looks that way. There sits the meditator parked on a little cushion. Is she out donating blood? No. Is she busy working with disaster victims? No. But let us examine her motivation. Why is she doing this? The meditator's intention is to purge her own mind of anger, prejudice, and ill will, and she is actively engaged in the process of getting rid of greed, tension, and insensitivity. Those are the very items that obstruct her compassion for others. Until they are gone, any good works that she does are likely to be just an extension of her own ego, and of no real help in the long run. Harm in the name of help is one of the oldest games. The grand inquisitor of the Spanish Inquisition spouted the loftiest of motives. The Salem witchcraft trials were conducted for the "public good." Examine the personal lives of advanced meditators, and you will often find them engaged in humanitarian service. You will seldom find them as crusading missionaries who are willing to sacrifice certain individuals for the sake of a supposedly pious idea. The fact is that we are more selfish than we know. The ego has a way of turning the loftiest activities into trash if it is allowed free range. Through meditation, we become aware of ourselves exactly as we are, by waking up to the numerous subtle ways that we act out our own selfishness. Then we truly begin to be genuinely selfless. Cleansing yourself of selfishness is not a selfish activity.

MISCONCEPTION 10: WHEN YOU MEDITATE, YOU SIT AROUND THINKING LOFTY THOUGHTS.

Wrong again. There are certain systems of contemplation in which this sort of thing is done. But that is not vipassana. Vipassana is the practice of awareness, awareness of whatever is there, be it supreme truth or trivial trash. What is there, is there. Of course, lofty thoughts may arise during your practice. They are certainly not to be avoided. Neither are they to be sought. They are just pleasant side effects. Vipassana is a simple practice. It consists of experiencing your own life events directly, without preferences and without mental images pasted onto them. Vipassana is seeing your life unfold from moment to moment without biases. What comes up, comes up. It is very simple.

MISCONCEPTION 11: A COUPLE OF WEEKS OF MEDITATION AND ALL MY PROBLEMS WILL GO AWAY.

Sorry, meditation is not a quick cure-all. You will start seeing changes right away, but really profound effects are years down the line. That is just the way the universe is constructed. Nothing worthwhile is achieved overnight. Meditation is tough in some respects, requiring a long discipline and a sometimes painful process of practice. At each sitting you gain some results, but they are often very subtle. They occur deep within the mind, and only manifest much later. And if you are sitting there constantly looking for huge, instantaneous changes, you will miss the subtle shifts altogether. You will get discouraged, give up, and swear that no such changes could ever occur. Patience is the key. Patience. If you learn nothing else from meditation, you will learn patience. Patience is essential for any profound change.

3. What Meditation Is

*M*editation is a word, and words are used in different ways by different speakers. This may seem like a trivial point, but it is not. It is quite important to distinguish exactly what a particular speaker means by the words he or she uses. Probably every culture on earth has produced some sort of mental practice that could be termed meditation. It all depends on how loose a definition you give to that word. The techniques worldwide are enormously varied, but we will make no attempt to survey them. There are other books for that. For the purpose of this volume, we will restrict our discussion to those practices best known to Western audiences and most often associated with the term meditation.

Within the Judeo-Christian tradition we find two overlapping practices called prayer and contemplation. Prayer is a direct address to a spiritual entity. Contemplation is a prolonged period of conscious thought about a specific topic, usually a religious ideal or scriptural passage. From the standpoint of mental cultivation, both of these activities are exercises in concentration. The normal deluge of conscious thought is restricted, and the mind is brought to one conscious area of operation. The results are those you find in any concentrative practice: deep calm, a physiological slowing of the metabolism, and a sense of peace and well-being.

Out of the Hindu tradition comes yogic meditation, which is also purely concentrative. The traditional basic exercises consist of focusing the mind on a single object—a stone, a candle flame, a syllable, or whatever—and not allowing it to wander. Having acquired the basic skill, the yogi proceeds to expand his practice by taking on more complex objects of meditation—chants, colorful religious images, energy channels in the body, and so forth. Still, no matter how complex the object of meditation, the meditation itself remains purely an exercise in concentration.

Within the Buddhist tradition, concentration is also highly valued. But a new element is added and more highly stressed: the element of awareness. All Buddhist meditation aims at the development of awareness, using concentration as a tool toward that end. The Buddhist tradition is very wide, however, and there are several diverse routes to this goal. Zen meditation uses two separate tacks. The first is the direct plunge into awareness by sheer force of will. You sit down and you just sit, meaning that you toss out of your mind everything except pure awareness of sitting. This sounds very simple. It is not. (A brief trial will demonstrate just how difficult it really is.) The second Zen approach, used in the Rinzai school, is that of tricking the mind out of conscious thought and into pure awareness. This is done by giving a student an unsolvable riddle, which he must solve nonetheless, and by placing him in a horrendous training situation. Since he cannot escape from the pain of the situation, he must flee into a pure experience of the moment: there is nowhere else to go. Zen is tough. It is effective for many people, but it is really tough.

Another stratagem, tantric Buddhism, is nearly the reverse. Conscious thought, at least the way we usually do it, is the manifestation of ego, the "you" that you usually think that you are. Conscious thought is tightly connected with self-concept. The self-concept or ego is nothing more than a set of reactions and mental images that are artificially pasted to the flowing process of pure awareness. Tantra seeks to obtain pure awareness by destroying this ego image. This is accomplished by a process of visualization. The student is given a particular religious image to meditate upon, for example, one of the deities from the tantric pantheon. She does this in so thorough a fashion that she becomes that entity. She takes off her own identity and puts on another. This takes a while, as you might imagine, but it works. During the process, she is able to watch the way in which the ego is constructed and put in place. She comes to recognize the arbitrary nature of all egos, including her own, and she escapes from bondage to the ego. She is left in a state where she may have an ego if she so chooses—either her own or whichever other she might wish—or she can do without one. Result: pure awareness. Tantra is not exactly a piece of cake either.

Vipassana is the oldest of Buddhist meditation practices. The method comes directly from the *Satipatthana Sutta,* a discourse attributed to the Buddha himself. Vipassana is a direct and gradual cultivation of mindfulness or awareness. It proceeds piece by piece over a period of years. One's attention is carefully directed to an intense examination of certain aspects of one's own existence. The meditator is trained to notice more and more of the flow of life experience. Vipassana is a gentle technique, but it also is very, very thorough. It is an ancient and codified system of training your mind, a set of exercises dedicated to the purpose of becoming more and more aware of your own life experience. It is attentive listening, mindful seeing, and careful testing. We learn to smell acutely, to touch fully, and really pay attention to the changes taking place in all these experiences. We learn to listen to our own thoughts without being caught up in them.

The object of vipassana practice is to learn to see the truths of impermanence, unsatisfactoriness, and selflessness of phenomena.

We think we are doing this already, but that is an illusion. It comes from the fact that we are paying so little attention to the ongoing surge of our own life experiences that we might just as well be asleep. We are simply not paying enough attention to notice that we are not paying attention. It is another catch-22.

Through the process of mindfulness, we slowly become aware of what we really are, down below the ego image. We wake up to what life really is. It is not just a parade of ups and downs, lollipops and smacks on the wrist. That is an illusion. Life has a much deeper texture than that if we bother to look, and if we look in the right way.

Vipassana is a form of mental training that will teach you to experience the world in an entirely new way. You will learn for the first time what is truly happening to you, around you, and within you. It is a process of self-discovery, a participatory investigation in which you observe your own experiences while participating in them. The practice must be approached with this attitude: "Never mind what I have been taught. Forget about theories and prejudices and stereotypes. I want to understand the true nature of life. I want to know what this experience of being alive really is. I want to apprehend the true and deepest qualities of life, and I don't want to just accept somebody else's explanation. I want to see it for myself."

If you pursue your meditation practice with this attitude, you will succeed. You'll find yourself observing things objectively, exactly as they are—flowing and changing from moment to moment. Life then takes on an unbelievable richness that cannot be described. It has to be experienced.

The Pali term for insight meditation is *vipassana bhavana*. *Bhavana* comes from the root *bhu*, which means to grow or to become. Therefore *bhavana* means to cultivate, and the word is always used in reference to the mind; *bhavana* means mental cultivation. *Vipassana* is derived from two roots. *Passana* means seeing or perceiving.

Vi is a prefix with a complex set of connotations that can be roughly translated as "in a special way," and also *into* and *through* "a special way." The whole meaning of the word *vipassana* is looking into something with clarity and precision, seeing each component as distinct, and piercing all the way through to perceive the most fundamental reality of that thing. This process leads to insight into the basic reality of whatever is being examined. Put these words together and *vipassana bhavana* means the cultivation of the mind toward the aim of seeing in the special way that leads to insight and full understanding.

In vipassana meditation we cultivate this special way of seeing life. We train ourselves to see reality exactly as it is, and we call this special mode of perception *mindfulness*. This process of mindfulness is really quite different from what we usually do. We usually do not look into what is actually there in front of us. We see life through a screen of thoughts and concepts, and we mistake those mental objects for reality. We get so caught up in this endless thought-stream that reality flows by unnoticed. We spend our time engrossed in activity, caught up in an eternal pursuit of pleasure and gratification and eternal flight from pain and unpleasantness. We spend all of our energies trying to make ourselves feel better, trying to bury our fears, endlessly seeking security. Meanwhile, the world of real experience flows by untouched and untasted. In vipassana meditation we train ourselves to ignore the constant impulses to be more comfortable, and we dive into reality instead. The irony of it is that real peace comes only when you stop chasing it—another catch-22.

When you relax your driving desire for comfort, real fulfillment arises. When you drop your hectic pursuit of gratification, the real beauty of life comes out. When you seek to know reality without illusion, complete with all its pain and danger, real freedom and security will be yours. This is not a doctrine we are trying to drill into you; it is an observable reality, something you can and should see for yourself.

Buddhism is 2,500 years old, and any thought system of such vintage has time to develop layers and layers of doctrine and ritual. Nevertheless, the fundamental attitude of Buddhism is intensely empirical and antiauthoritarian. Gotama the Buddha was a highly unorthodox individual and a real antitraditionalist. He did not offer his teaching as a set of dogmas, but rather as a set of propositions for each individual to investigate for him- or herself. His invitation to one and all was, "Come and see." One of the things he said to his followers was, "Place no head above your own." By this he meant, don't just accept somebody else's word. See for yourself.

We want you to apply this attitude to every word you read in this manual. We are not making statements that you should accept merely because we are authorities in the field. Blind faith has nothing to do with this. These are experiential realities. Learn to adjust your mode of perception according to instructions given in the book, and you will see for yourself. That, and only that, will provide grounds for your faith. Essentially, insight meditation is a practice of investigative personal discovery.

Having said this, we will present here a very short synopsis of some of the key points of Buddhist philosophy. We make no attempt to be thorough, since that has been quite nicely done in many other books. But since this material is essential to understanding vipassana, some mention must be made.

From the Buddhist point of view, we human beings live in a very peculiar fashion. We view impermanent things as permanent, though everything is changing all around us. The process of change is constant and eternal. Even as you read these words, your body is aging. But you pay no attention to that. The book in your hand is decaying. The print is fading, and the pages are becoming brittle.

The walls around you are aging. The molecules within those walls are vibrating at an enormous rate, and everything is shifting, going to pieces, and slowly dissolving. You pay no attention to that either. Then one day you look around you. Your skin is wrinkled and your joints ache. The book is a yellowed, faded thing; and the building is falling apart. So you pine for lost youth, cry when your possessions are gone. Where does this pain come from? It comes from your own inattention. You failed to look closely at life. You failed to observe the constantly shifting flow of the world as it passed by. You set up a collection of mental constructions—"me," "the book," "the building"—and you assumed that those were solid, real entities. You assumed that they would endure forever. They never do. But now you can tune in to the constant change. You can learn to perceive your life as an ever-flowing movement. You can learn to see the continuous flow of all conditioned things. You can. It is just a matter of time and training.

Our human perceptual habits are remarkably stupid in some ways. We tune out 99 percent of all the sensory stimuli we actually receive, and we solidify the remainder into discrete mental objects. Then we react to those mental objects in programmed, habitual ways.

An example: There you are, sitting alone in the stillness of a peaceful night. A dog barks in the distance, which, in itself, is neither good nor bad. Up out of that sea of silence come surging waves of sonic vibration. You start to hear the lovely complex patterns, and they are turned into scintillating electronic stimulations within the nervous system. The process should be used as an experience of impermanence, unsatisfactoriness, and selflessness. We humans tend to ignore it totally. Instead, we solidify that perception into a mental object. We paste a mental picture on it and launch into a series of emotional and conceptual reactions to it. "There is that dog again. He is always barking at night. What a nuisance. Every night he is a real bother. Somebody should do something. Maybe I should call a cop. No, a dog catcher—I'll call the pound. No, maybe I'll just write a nasty letter to the guy who owns that dog. No, too much trouble. I'll just get earplugs." These are just perceptual mental habits. You learn to respond this way as a child by copying the perceptual habits of those around you. These perceptual responses are not inherent in the structure of the nervous system. The circuits are there, but this is not the only way that our mental machinery can be used. That which has been learned can be unlearned. The first step is to realize what you are doing as you are doing it, to stand back and quietly watch.

From the Buddhist perspective, we humans have a backward view of life. We look at what is actually the cause of suffering and see it as happiness. The cause of suffering is that desire-aversion syndrome that we spoke of earlier. Up pops a perception. It could be anything—an attractive woman, a handsome guy, a speedboat, the aroma of baking bread, a truck tailgating you, anything. Whatever it is, the very next thing we do is to react to the stimulus with a feeling about it.

For example, take worry. We worry a lot. Worry itself is the problem. Worry is a process; it has steps. Anxiety is not just a state of existence but a procedure. What you've got to do is to look at the very beginning of that procedure, those initial stages before the process has built up a head of steam. The very first link of the worry chain is the grasping-rejecting reaction. As soon as a phenomenon pops into the mind, we try mentally to grab onto it or push it away. That sets the worry response in motion. Luckily, there is a handy little tool called vipassana meditation that you can use to short-circuit the whole mechanism.

Vipassana meditation teaches us how to scrutinize our own perceptual process with great precision. We learn to watch the arising of thought and perception with a feeling of serene detachment. We learn to view our own reactions to stimuli with calmness and clarity.

We begin to see ourselves reacting without getting caught up in the reactions themselves. The obsessive nature of thought slowly dies. We can still get married. We can still get out of the path of the truck. But we don't need to go through hell over either one.

This escape from the obsessive nature of thought produces a whole new view of reality. It is a complete paradigm shift, a total change in the perceptual mechanism. It brings with it the bliss of emancipation from obsessions. Because of these advantages, Buddhism views this way of looking at things as a correct view of life; Buddhist texts call it seeing things as they really are.

Vipassana meditation is a set of training procedures that gradually open us to this new view of reality as it truly is. Along with this new reality goes a new view of that most central aspect of reality: "me." A close inspection reveals that we have done the same thing to "me" that we have done to all other perceptions. We have taken a flowing vortex of thought, feeling, and sensation and solidified that into a mental construct. Then we have stuck a label onto it: "me." Forever after, we treat it as if it were a static and enduring entity. We view it as a thing separate from all other things. We pinch ourselves off from the rest of that process of eternal change that is the universe, and then we grieve over how lonely we feel. We ignore our inherent connectedness to all other beings and decide that "I" have to get more for "me"; then we marvel at how greedy and insensitive human beings are. And on it goes. Every evil deed, every example of heartlessness in the world, stems directly from this false sense of "me" as distinct from everything else.

If you explode the illusion of that one concept, your whole universe changes. Don't expect to be able to do this overnight, though. You spent your whole life building up that concept, reinforcing it with every thought, word, and deed over all those years. It is not going to evaporate instantly. But it will pass if you give it enough time and attention. Vipassana meditation is a process by which that concept is dissolved. Little by little, you chip away at it, just by observing it.

The "I" concept is a process. It is something we are constantly doing. With vipassana we learn to see that we are doing it, when we are doing it, and how we are doing it. Then that mindset moves and fades away, like a cloud passing through a clear sky. We are left in a state where we can decide to do it or not, whichever seems appropriate to the situation. The compulsiveness is gone: now we have a choice.

These are all major insights. Each one is a deep-reaching under-standing of one of the fundamental issues of human existence. They do not occur quickly, nor without considerable effort. But the payoff is big. They lead to a total transformation of your life. Every second of your existence thereafter is changed. The meditator who pushes all the way down this track achieves perfect mental health, a pure love for all that lives, and complete cessation of suffering. That is no small goal. But you don't have to go the whole way to reap benefits. The benefits start right away, and they pile up over the years. It is a cumulative function: the more you sit, the more you learn about the real nature of your own existence. The more hours you spend in meditation, the greater your ability to calmly observe every impulse and intention, thought and emotion, just as it arises in the mind. Your progress to liberation is measured in hours on the cushion. And you can stop during the process any time you feel you've had enough. There is no mandating rule but your own desire to see the true quality of life, to enhance your own existence and that of others.

Vipassana meditation is inherently experiential, not theoretical. In the practice of meditation you become sensitive to the actual expe-rience of living, to how things actually feel. You do not sit around developing sublime thoughts about living. You live. Vipassana medi-tation, more than anything else, is learning to live.

4. Attitude

*W*ithin the last century, Western science has made a startling discovery: We are part of the world we view. The very process of our observation changes the things we observe. For example, an electron is an extremely tiny item. It cannot be viewed without instrumentation, and that apparatus dictates what the observer will see. If you look at an electron in one particular way, it appears to be a particle, a hard little ball that bounces around in nice straight paths. When you view it another way, an electron appears to be a wave form, glowing and wiggling all over the place, with nothing solid about it at all. An electron is an event more than a thing, and the observer participates in that event by the very act of his or her observation. There is no way to avoid this interaction.

Eastern science has recognized this basic principle for a very long time. The mind itself is a set of events, and you participate in those events every time you look inward. Meditation is participatory observation: What you are looking at responds to the process of looking. In this case, what you are looking at is you, and what you see depends on how you look. Thus the process of meditation is extremely delicate, and the result depends absolutely on the state of mind of the meditator. The following attitudes are essential to success in practice; most of them have already been presented, but we bring them together again here as a series of rules for application:

(1) *Don't expect anything.* Just sit back and see what happens. Treat the whole thing as an experiment. Take an active interest in the test itself, but don't get distracted by your expectations about the results. For that matter, don't be anxious for any result whatsoever. Let the meditation move along at its own speed and in its own direction. Let the meditation teach you. Meditative awareness seeks to see reality exactly as it is. Whether that corresponds to our expectations or not, it does require a temporary suspension of all of our preconceptions and ideas. We must store our images, opinions, and interpretations out of the way for the duration of the session. Otherwise we will stumble over them.

(2) *Don't strain.* Don't force anything or make grand, exaggerated efforts. Meditation is not aggressive. There is no place or need for violent striving. Just let your effort be relaxed and steady.

(3) *Don't rush.* There is no hurry, so take your time. Settle yourself on a cushion and sit as though you have the whole day. Anything really valuable takes time to develop. Patience, patience, patience.

(4) *Don't cling to anything, and don't reject anything.* Let come what comes, and accommodate yourself to that, whatever it is. If good mental images arise, that is fine. If bad mental images arise, that is fine, too. Look on all of it as equal, and make yourself comfortable with whatever happens. Don't fight with what you experience, just observe it all mindfully.

(5) *Let go.* Learn to flow with all the changes that come up. Loosen up and relax.

(6) *Accept everything that arises.* Accept your feelings, even the ones you wish you did not have. Accept your experiences, even the ones

you hate. Don't condemn yourself for having human flaws and failings. Learn to see all the phenomena in the mind as being perfectly natural and understandable. Try to exercise a disinterested acceptance at all times with respect to everything you experience.

(7) *Be gentle with yourself.* Be kind to yourself. You may not be perfect, but you are all you've got to work with. The process of becoming who you will be begins first with the total acceptance of who you are.

(8) *Investigate yourself.* Question everything. Take nothing for granted. Don't believe anything because it sounds wise and pious and some holy man said it. See for yourself. That does not mean that you should be cynical, impudent, or irreverent. It means you should be empirical. Subject all statements to the actual test of your own experience, and let the results be your guide to truth. Insight meditation evolves out of an inner longing to wake up to what is real and to gain liberating insight into the true structure of existence. The entire practice hinges upon this desire to be awake to the truth. Without it, the practice is superficial.

(9) *View all problems as challenges.* Look upon negativities that arise as opportunities to learn and to grow. Don't run from them, condemn yourself, or bury your burden in saintly silence. You have a problem? Great. More grist for the mill. Rejoice, dive in, and investigate.

(10) *Don't ponder.* You don't need to figure everything out. Discursive thinking won't free you from the trap. In meditation, the mind is purified naturally by mindfulness, by wordless bare attention. Habitual deliberation is not necessary to eliminate those things that are keeping you in bondage. All that is necessary is a clear,

nonconceptual perception of what they are and how they work. That alone is sufficient to dissolve them. Concepts and reasoning just get in the way. Don't think. See.

(11) *Don't dwell upon contrasts.* Differences do exist between people, but dwelling upon them is a dangerous process. Unless carefully handled, this leads directly to egotism. Ordinary human thinking is full of greed, jealousy, and pride. A man seeing another man on the street may immediately think, "He is better looking than I am." The instant result is envy or shame. A girl seeing another girl may think, "I am prettier than she is." The instant result is pride. This sort of comparison is a mental habit, and it leads directly to ill feeling of one sort or another: greed, envy, pride, jealousy, or hatred. It is an unskillful mental state, but we do it all the time. We compare our looks with others, our success, accomplishments, wealth, possessions, or IQ, and all of this leads to the same state—estrangement, barriers between people, and ill feeling.

The meditator's job is to cancel this unskillful habit by examining it thoroughly, and then replacing it with another. Rather than noticing the differences between oneself and others, the meditator trains him- or herself to notice the similarities. She centers her attention on those factors that are universal to all life, things that will move her closer to others. Then her comparisons, if any, lead to feelings of kinship rather than of estrangement.

Breathing is a universal process. All vertebrates breathe in essentially the same manner. All living things exchange gases with their environment in some way or other. This is one of the reasons that breathing has been chosen as a focus of meditation. The meditator is advised to explore the process of his or her own breathing as a vehicle for realizing our inherent connectedness with the rest of life. This does not mean that we shut our eyes to all the differences around us.

Differences do exist. It means simply that we de-emphasize contrasts and emphasize the universal factors that we have in common.

The recommended procedure is as follows: When we as meditators perceive any sensory object, we are not to dwell upon it in the ordinary egoistic way. We should rather examine the very process of perception itself. We should watch what that object does to our senses and our perception. We should watch the feelings that arise and the mental activities that follow. We should note the changes that occur in our own consciousness as a result. In watching all these phenomena, we must be aware of the universality of what we are seeing. The initial perception will spark pleasant, unpleasant, or neutral feelings. That is a universal phenomenon, occurring in the minds of others just as it does in our own, and we should see that clearly. By following these feelings various reactions may arise. We may feel greed, lust, or jealousy. We may feel fear, worry, restlessness, or boredom. These reactions are also universal. We should simply note them and then generalize. We should realize that these reactions are normal human responses, and can arise in anybody.

The practice of this style of comparison may feel forced and artificial at first, but it is no less natural than what we ordinarily do. It is merely unfamiliar. With practice, this habit pattern replaces our normal habit of egoistic comparison and feels far more natural in the long run. We become very understanding people as a result. We no longer get upset by the "failings" of others. We progress toward harmony with all life.

5. The Practice

Although there are many subjects of meditation, we strongly recommend that you start with focusing your undivided attention on your breathing to gain some degree of basic concentration. Remember that in doing this, you are not practicing a deep absorption or pure concentration technique. You are practicing mindfulness, for which you need only a certain amount of basic concentration. You want to cultivate mindfulness culminating in the insight and wisdom to realize the truth as it is. You want to know the workings of your body-mind complex exactly as they are. You want to get rid of all psychological annoyances to make your life truly peaceful and happy.

The mind cannot be purified without seeing things as they really are. "Seeing things as they really are" is such a heavily loaded and ambiguous phrase. Many beginning meditators wonder what we mean, since it seems like anyone who has clear eyesight should be able to see objects as they are.

When we use this phrase in reference to insight gained from meditation, however, we do not mean seeing things superficially, with our regular eyes, but seeing things as they are in themselves, with wisdom. Seeing with wisdom means seeing things within the framework of our body-mind complex without prejudices or biases that spring from greed, hatred, and delusion. Ordinarily, when we watch the working of our body-mind complex, we tend to ignore things that are not pleasant to us and hold on to the things that are. This is because our minds are generally influenced by desire, resentment, and delusion. Our ego, self, or opinions get in our way and color our judgment.

When we mindfully watch our bodily sensations, we should not confuse them with mental formations, for bodily sensations can arise completely independent of the mind. For instance, we sit comfortably. After a while, there can arise some uncomfortable feeling in our back or our legs. Our mind immediately experiences that discomfort and forms numerous thoughts around the feeling. At that point, without confusing the feeling with the mental formations, we should isolate the feeling as feeling and watch it mindfully. Feeling is one of the seven universal mental factors. The other six are contact, perception, attention, concentration, life force, and volition.

Other times, a certain emotion, such as resentment, fear, or lust, may arise. During these times we should watch the emotion exactly as it is, without confusing it with anything else. When we bundle our aggregates of form, feeling, perceptions, mental formations, and consciousness into one and regard all of them as a feeling, we get confused because the source of the feeling becomes obscured. If we simply dwell upon the feeling without separating it from other mental factors, our realization of truth becomes very difficult.

We want to gain insight into the experience of impermanence to overcome our unhappiness and ignorance: our deeper knowledge of unhappiness overcomes the greed that causes our unhappiness, and our realization of selflessness overcomes the ignorance that arises from the notion of self. Toward these insights, we begin by seeing the mind and body as separate; and having comprehended them separately, we should also see their essential interconnectedness. As our insight becomes sharpened, we become more and more aware of the fact that all aggregates, mental and physical, are cooperating, and that none can exist without the others. We can truly understand the meaning of the famous metaphor of the blind man who has a healthy body and the disabled person who has good eyes. Both of them, alone, are limited. But when the disabled person climbs on the shoulders of the blind man, together they can travel and achieve their goals easily. The mind and body are like this. The body alone can do nothing for itself; it is like a log unable to move or do anything by itself except to become subject to impermanence, decay, and death. The mind can do nothing without the support of the body. When we mindfully watch both body and mind, we can see how many wonderful things they do together.

By sitting in one place, we may gain some degree of mindfulness. Going to a retreat and spending several days or several months watching our feelings, perceptions, countless thoughts, and various states of consciousness may make us eventually calm and peaceful. But normally we do not have that much time to spend in one place, meditating all the time. Therefore, we should find a way to apply our mindfulness to our daily life in order for us to be able to handle daily unforeseeable eventualities.

What we face every day is unpredictable. Things happen due to multiple causes and conditions, since we live in a conditional and impermanent world. Mindfulness is our emergency kit, readily available at any time. When we face a situation in which we feel indignation, if we mindfully investigate our own mind, we will discover bitter truths about ourselves: for example, that we are selfish; we are egocentric; we are attached to our ego; we hold on to our opinions; we think we are right and everybody else is wrong; we are prejudiced; we are biased; and at the bottom of all of this, we do not really love ourselves. This discovery, though bitter, is a most rewarding experience. And in the long run, this discovery delivers us from deeply rooted psychological and spiritual suffering.

Mindfulness practice is the practice of being 100 percent honest with ourselves. When we watch our own mind and body, we notice certain things that are unpleasant to realize. Since we do not like them, we try to reject them. What are the things we do not like? We do not like to detach ourselves from loved ones or to live with unloved ones. We include not only people, places, and material things into our likes and dislikes, but opinions, ideas, beliefs, and decisions as well. We do not like what naturally happens to us. We do not like, for instance, growing old, becoming sick, becoming weak, or showing our age, for we have a great desire to preserve our appearance. We do not like it when someone points out our faults, for we take great pride in ourselves. We do not like someone to be wiser than we are, for we are deluded about ourselves. These are but a few examples of our personal experience of greed, hatred, and ignorance.

When greed, hatred, and ignorance reveal themselves in our daily lives, we use our mindfulness to track them down and comprehend their roots. The root of each of these mental states is within ourselves. If we do not, for instance, have the root of hatred, nobody can make us angry, for it is the root of our anger that reacts to somebody's actions or words or behavior. If we are mindful, we will diligently use our wisdom to look into our own mind. If we do not have hatred in us, we will not be concerned when someone points out our shortcomings. Rather, we will be thankful to the person who draws our attention to our faults. We have to be extremely wise and mindful to thank the person who exposes our faults for helping us to tread the upward path of self-improvement. We all have blind spots. The other person is our mirror in which we see our faults with wisdom. We should consider the person who shows us our shortcomings as one who excavates a hidden treasure of which we were unaware, since it is by knowing the existence of our deficiencies that we can improve ourselves. Improving ourselves is the unswerving path to the perfection that is our goal in life. Before we try to surmount our defects, we should know what they are. Then, and only then, by overcoming these weaknesses, can we cultivate noble qualities hidden deep down in our subconscious mind.

Think of it this way: if we are sick, we must find out the cause of our sickness. Only then can we get treatment. If we pretend that we are not sick, even though we are suffering, we will never get treatment. Similarly, if we think that we don't have these faults, we will never clear our spiritual path. If we are blind to our own flaws, we need someone to point them out to us. When they point out our faults, we should be grateful to them like the Venerable Sariputta, who said: "Even if a seven-year-old novice monk points out my mistakes, I will accept them with utmost respect for him." Venerable Sariputta was a monk who was 100 percent mindful and had no faults. Since he did not have any pride, he was able to maintain this position. Although we are not arahants, we should determine to emulate his example, for our goal in life also is to attain what he attained.

Of course, the person pointing out our mistakes may not be totally free from defects himself, but he can see our faults just as we can see his, which he does not notice until we point them out to him. Both pointing out shortcomings and responding to someone pointing out our own shortcomings should be done mindfully. If someone becomes unmindful in indicating faults and uses unkind and harsh language, he might do more harm than good to himself as well as to the person whose shortcomings he points out. One who speaks with resentment cannot be mindful and is unable to express himself clearly. One who feels hurt while listening to harsh language may lose his mindfulness and not hear what the other person is really saying. We should speak mindfully and listen mindfully to be benefited by talking and listening. When we listen and talk mindfully, our minds are free from greed, selfishness, hatred, and delusion.

Our Goal

As meditators, we all must have a goal, for if we do not, and blindly follow somebody's instructions on meditation, we will simply be groping in the dark. There must certainly be a goal for whatever we do consciously and willingly. It is not the vipassana meditator's goal to become enlightened before other people or to have more power or make more profit than others. Meditators are not in competition with each other for mindfulness.

Our goal is to reach the perfection of all the noble and wholesome qualities latent in our subconscious mind. This goal has five elements to it: purification of mind, overcoming sorrow and lamentation, overcoming pain and grief, treading the right path leading to attainment of eternal peace, and attaining happiness by following that path. Keeping this fivefold goal in mind, we can advance with hope and confidence.

Practice

Once you sit, do not change the position again until the end of the time you determined at the beginning. Suppose you change your original position because it is uncomfortable, and assume another position. What happens after a while is that the new position becomes uncomfortable. Then you want another and after a while it, too, becomes uncomfortable. So you may go on shifting, moving, changing one position to another the whole time you are on your meditation cushion, and you may not gain a deep and meaningful level of concentration. Therefore, you must make every effort not to change your original position. We will discuss how to deal with pain in chapter 10.

To avoid changing your position, determine at the beginning of meditation how long you are going to meditate. If you have never meditated before, sit motionlessly for not longer than twenty minutes. As you repeat your practice, you can increase your sitting time. The length of sitting depends on how much time you have for sitting meditation practice and how long you can sit without excruciating pain.

We should not have a time schedule to attain the goal, for our attainment depends on how we progress in our practice based on our understanding and development of our spiritual faculties. We must work diligently and mindfully toward the goal without setting any particular time schedule to reach it. When we are ready, we get there. All we have to do is to prepare ourselves for that attainment.

After sitting motionlessly, close your eyes. Our mind is analogous to a cup of muddy water. The longer you keep a cup of muddy water still, the more the mud settles down and the water will be seen clearly. Similarly, if you keep quiet without moving your body, focusing your entire undivided attention on the subject of your meditation, your mind settles down and begins to experience the bliss of meditation.

To prepare for this attainment, we should keep our mind in the present moment. The present moment is changing so fast that a casual observer does not seem to notice its existence at all. Every moment is a moment of events and no moment passes by without an event. We cannot notice a moment without noticing events taking place in that moment. Therefore, the moment we try to pay bare attention to is the present moment. Our mind goes through a series of events like a series of pictures passing through a projector. Some of these pictures are coming from our past experiences and others are our imaginations of things that we plan to do in the future.

The mind can never be focused without a mental object. Therefore we must give our mind an object that is readily available every present moment. One such object is our breath. The mind does not have to make a great effort to find the breath. Every moment the breath is flowing in and out through our nostrils. As our practice of insight meditation is taking place every waking moment, our mind finds it very easy to focus itself on the breath, for it is more conspicuous and constant than any other object.

After sitting in the manner described and having shared your loving-friendliness with everybody, take three deep breaths. After taking three deep breaths, breathe normally, letting your breath flow in and out freely, effortlessly, and begin focusing your attention on the rims of your nostrils. Simply notice the feeling of breath going in and out. When one inhalation is complete and before exhaling begins, there is a brief pause. Notice it and notice the beginning of exhaling. When the exhalation is complete, there is another brief pause before inhaling begins. Notice this brief pause, too. This means that there are two brief pauses of breath—one at the end of inhaling and the other at the end of exhaling. These two pauses occur in such a brief moment you may not be aware of their occurrence. But when you are mindful, you can notice them.

Do not verbalize or conceptualize anything. Simply notice the incoming and outgoing breath without saying, "I breathe in," or "I breathe out." When you focus your attention on the breath, ignore any thought, memory, sound, smell, taste, etc., and focus your attention exclusively on the breath, nothing else.

At the beginning, both the inhalations and exhalations are short because the body and mind are not calm and relaxed. Notice the feeling of that short inhaling and short exhaling as they occur without saying, "short inhaling," or "short exhaling." As you continue to notice the feeling of short inhaling and short exhaling, your body and mind become relatively calm. Then your breath becomes long. Notice the feeling of that long breath as it is without saying, "Long breath." Then notice the entire breathing process from the beginning to the end. Subsequently the breath becomes subtle, and the mind and body become calmer than before. Notice this calm and peaceful feeling of your breathing.

WHAT TO DO WHEN THE MIND WANDERS AWAY

In spite of your concerted effort to keep the mind on your breathing, the mind will likely wander away. It may go to past experiences, and suddenly you may find yourself remembering places you've visited, people you met, friends not seen for a long time, a book you read long ago, the taste of food you ate yesterday, and so on. As soon as you notice that your mind is no longer on your breath, mindfully bring it back and anchor it there. However, in a few moments you may be caught up again thinking how to pay your bills, to make a telephone call to your friend, write a letter to someone, do your laundry, buy your groceries, go to a party, plan your next vacation, and so forth. As soon as you notice that your mind is not on your object, bring it back mindfully. Following are some suggestions to help you gain the concentration necessary for the practice of mindfulness.

1. Counting

In a situation like this, counting may help. The purpose of counting is simply to focus the mind on the breath. Once your mind is focused on the breath, give up counting. This is a device for gaining concentration. There are numerous ways of counting. Any counting should be done mentally. Do not make any sound when you count. Following are some of the ways of counting.

a) While breathing in, count "one, one, one, one . . ." until the lungs are full of fresh air. While breathing out count "two, two, two, two . . ." until the lungs are empty of fresh air. Then while breathing in again count "three, three, three, three, three . . ." until the lungs are full again and while breathing out count again "four, four, four, four . . ." until the lungs are empty of fresh air. Count up to ten and repeat as many times as necessary to keep the mind focused on the breath.

b) The second method of counting is counting rapidly up to ten. While counting "one, two, three, four, five, six, seven, eight, nine, and ten," breathe in, and again while counting "one, two, three, four, five, six, seven, eight, nine, and ten," breathe out. This means that with one inhalation you should count up to ten and with one exhalation you should count up to ten. Repeat this way of counting as many times as necessary to focus the mind on the breath.

c) The third method of counting is to count in succession up to ten. At this time, count "one, two, three, four, five" (only up to five) while inhaling and then count "one, two, three, four, five, six" (up to six) while exhaling. Again, count "one, two, three, four, five, six, seven" (only up to seven) while inhaling. Then count "one, two, three, four, five, six, seven, eight" while exhaling. Count up to nine while inhaling and count up to ten while exhaling. Repeat this way of counting as many times as necessary to focus the mind on the breath.

d) The fourth method is to take a long breath. When the lungs are full, mentally count "one" and breathe out completely until the lungs are empty of fresh air. Then count mentally "two." Take a long breath again and count "three" and breathe out completely as before. When the lungs are empty of fresh air, count mentally "four." Count your breath in this manner up to ten. Then count backward from ten to one. Count again from one to ten and then ten to one.

e) The fifth method is to join inhaling and exhaling. When the lungs are empty of fresh air, count mentally "one." This time you should count both inhalation and exhalation as one. Again inhale, exhale, and mentally count "two." This way of counting should be done only up to five and repeated from five to one. Repeat this method until your breathing becomes refined and quiet.

Remember that you are not supposed to continue your counting all the time. As soon as your mind is locked at the nostril tip where the inhalation and exhalation touch and you begin to feel that your breathing is so refined and quiet that you cannot notice inhalation and exhalation separately, you should give up counting. Counting is used only to train the mind to concentrate on one object.

2. Connecting

After inhaling do not wait to notice the brief pause before exhaling but connect the inhaling with exhaling, so you can notice both inhaling and exhaling as one continuous breath.

3. Fixing

After joining inhaling with exhaling, fix your mind on the point where you feel your inhaling and exhaling breath touching. Inhale and exhale as one single breath moving in and out touching or rubbing the rims of your nostrils.

4. Focus your mind like a carpenter

A carpenter draws a straight line on a board that he wants to cut. Then he cuts the board with his saw along the straight line he drew. He does not look at the teeth of his saw as they move in and out of the board. Rather he focuses his entire attention on the line he drew so he can cut the board straight. Similarly, keep your mind straight on the point where you feel the breath at the rims of your nostrils.

5. Make your mind like a gatekeeper

A gatekeeper does not take into account any detail of the people entering a house. All he does is notice people entering the house and leaving the house through the gate. Similarly, when you concentrate you should not take into account any detail of your experiences. Simply notice the feeling of your inhaling and exhaling breath as it goes in and out right at the rims of your nostrils.

As you continue your practice, your mind and body become so light that you may feel as if you are floating in the air or on water. You may even feel that your body is springing up into the sky. When the grossness of your in-and-out breathing has ceased, subtle in-and-out breathing arises. This very subtle breath is your mind's object of focus. This is the sign of concentration. This first appearance of a sign-object will be replaced by a more and more subtle sign-object. This subtlety of the sign can be compared to the sound of a bell. When a bell is struck with a big iron rod, you hear a gross sound at first. As the sound fades away, the sound becomes very subtle. Similarly, the in-and-out breath appears at first as a gross sign. As you keep paying bare attention to it, this sign becomes very subtle. But the consciousness remains totally focused on the rims of the nostrils. Other meditation objects become clearer and clearer, as the sign develops. But the breath becomes subtler and subtler as the sign develops. Because of this subtlety, you may not notice the presence of your breath. Don't get disappointed thinking that you lost your breath or that nothing is happening to your meditation practice. Don't worry. Be mindful and determined to bring your feeling of breath back to the rims of your nostrils. This is the time you should practice more vigorously, balancing your energy, faith, mindfulness, concentration, and wisdom.

FARMER SIMILE

Suppose there is a farmer who uses buffaloes for plowing his rice field. As he is tired in the middle of the day, he unfastens his buffaloes and takes a rest under the cool shade of a tree. When he wakes up, he does not find his animals. He does not worry, but simply walks to the water place where all the animals gather for drinking in the hot midday and he finds his buffaloes there. Without any problem he brings them back and ties them to the yoke again and starts plowing his field.

Similarly, as you continue this exercise, your breath becomes so subtle and refined that you might not be able to notice the feeling of breath at all. When this happens do not worry. It has not disappeared. It is still where it was before—right at the nostril tips. Take a few quick breaths and you will notice the feeling of breathing again. Continue to pay bare attention to the feeling of the touch of breath at the rims of your nostrils.

As you keep your mind focused on the rims of your nostrils, you will be able to notice the sign of the development of meditation. You will feel the pleasant sensation of a sign. Different meditators experience this differently. It will be like a star, or a round gem, or a round pearl, or a cotton seed, or a peg made of heartwood, or a long string, or a wreath of flowers, or a puff of smoke, or a cobweb, or a film of cloud, or a lotus flower, or the disc of the moon, or the disc of the sun.

Earlier in your practice you had inhaling and exhaling as objects of meditation. Now you have the sign as the third object of meditation. When you focus your mind on this third object, your mind reaches a stage of concentration sufficient for your practice of insight meditation. This sign is strongly present at the rims of the nostrils. Master it and gain full control of it so that whenever you want, it should be available. Unite the mind with this sign that is available in the present moment and let the mind flow with every succeeding moment. As you pay bare attention to it, you will see that the sign itself is changing every moment. Keep your mind with the changing moments. Also, notice that your mind can be concentrated only on the present moment. This unity of the mind with the present moment is called momentary concentration. As moments are incessantly passing away one after another, the mind keeps pace with them, changing with them, appearing and disappearing with them without clinging to any of them. If we try to stop the mind at one moment, we end up in frustration because the mind cannot be held fast. It must keep up with what is happening in the new moment. As the present moment can be found any moment, every waking moment can be made a concentrated moment.

To unite the mind with the present moment, we must find something happening in that moment. However, you cannot focus your mind on every changing moment without a certain degree of concentration to keep pace with the moment. Once you gain this degree of concentration, you can use it for focusing your attention on anything you experience—the rising and falling of your abdomen, the rising and falling of the chest area, the rising and falling of any feeling, or the rising and falling of your breath or thoughts and so on.

To make any progress in insight meditation you need this kind of momentary concentration. That is all you need for the insight meditation practice because everything in your experience lives only for one moment. When you focus this concentrated state of mind on the changes taking place in your mind and body, you will notice that your breath is the physical part and the feeling of breath, consciousness of the feeling, and the consciousness of the sign are the mental parts. As you notice them you can notice that they are changing all the time. You may have various types of sensations, other than the feeling of breathing, taking place in your body. Watch them all over your body. Don't try to create any feeling that is not naturally present in any part of your body. But notice whatever sensation arises in the body. When thought arises notice it, too. All you should notice in all these occurrences is the impermanent, unsatisfactory, and selfless nature of all your experiences whether mental or physical.

As your mindfulness develops, your resentment for the change, your dislike for the unpleasant experiences, your greed for the pleasant experiences, and the notion of selfhood will be replaced by the deeper awareness of impermanence, unsatisfactoriness, and selflessness. This knowledge of reality in your experience helps you to foster a more calm, peaceful, and mature attitude toward your life. You will see what you thought in the past to be permanent is changing with such inconceivable rapidity that even your mind cannot keep up with these changes. Somehow you will be able to notice many of the changes. You will see the subtlety of impermanence and the subtlety of selflessness. This insight will show you the way to peace and happiness, and will give you the wisdom to handle your daily problems in life.

When the mind is united with the breath flowing all the time, we will naturally be able to focus the mind on the present moment. We can notice the feeling arising from contact of breath with the rim of our nostrils. As the earth element of the air that we breathe in and out touches the earth element of our nostrils, the mind feels the flow of air in and out. The warm feeling arises at the nostrils or any other part of the body from the contact of the heat element generated by the breathing process. The feeling of impermanence of breath arises when the earth element of flowing breath touches the nostrils. Although the water element is present in the breath, the mind cannot feel it.

Also, we feel the expansion and contraction of our lungs, abdomen, and lower abdomen, as the fresh air is pumped in and out of the lungs. The expansion and contraction of the abdomen, lower abdomen, and chest are parts of the universal rhythm. Everything in the universe has the same rhythm of expansion and contraction just like our breath and body. All of them are rising and falling. However, our primary concern is the rising and falling phenomena of the breath and minute parts of our minds and bodies.

Along with the inhaling breath, we experience a small degree of calmness. This little degree of calmness turns into tension if we don't breathe out in a few moments. As we breathe out this tension is released. After breathing out, we experience discomfort if we wait too long before having fresh air brought in again. This means that every time our lungs are full we must breathe out and every time our lungs are empty we must breathe in. As we breathe in, we experience a small degree of calmness, and as we breathe out, we experience a small degree of calmness. We desire calmness and relief of tension and do not like the tension and feeling resulting from the lack of breath. We wish that the calmness would stay longer and the tension disappear more quickly than it normally does. But the tension will not go away as fast as we wish nor will the calmness stay as long as we wish. And again we get agitated or irritated, for we desire the calmness to return and stay longer and the tension to go away quickly and not to return again. Here we see how even a small degree of desire for permanence in an impermanent situation causes pain or unhappiness. Since there is no self-entity to control this situation, we will become more disappointed.

However, if we watch our breathing without desiring calmness and without resenting the tension arising from breathing in and out, and experience only the impermanence, the unsatisfactoriness, and selflessness of our breath, our mind becomes peaceful and calm.

The mind does not stay all the time with the feeling of breath. It goes to sounds, memories, emotions, perceptions, consciousness, and mental formations as well. When we experience these states, we should forget about the feeling of breath and immediately focus our attention on these states—one at a time, not all of them at one time. As they fade away, we let our mind return to the breath, which is the home base the mind can return to from quick or long journeys to various states of mind and body. We must remember that all these mental journeys are made within the mind itself.

Every time the mind returns to the breath, it comes back with a deeper insight into impermanence, unsatisfactoriness, and selflessness. The mind becomes more insightful from the impartial and unbiased watching of these occurrences. The mind gains insight into the fact that this body, these feelings, the various states of consciousness and numerous mental formations are to be used only for the purpose of gaining deeper insight into the reality of this body-mind complex.

6. What to Do with Your Body

*T*he practice of meditation has been going on for several thousand years. That is quite a bit of time for experimentation, and the procedure has been very, very thoroughly refined. Buddhist practice has always recognized that the mind and body are tightly linked and that each influences the other. Thus, there are certain recommended physical practices that will greatly help you to master this skill. And these practices should be followed. Keep in mind, however, that these postures are practice aids. Don't confuse the two. Meditation does not mean sitting in the lotus position. It is a mental skill. It can be practiced anywhere you wish. But these postures will help you to learn this skill, and they speed your progress and development. So use them.

General Rules

The purpose of the various postures is threefold. First, they provide a stable feeling in the body. This allows you to remove your attention from such issues as balance and muscular fatigue, so that you can center your concentration on the formal object of meditation. Second, they promote physical immobility, which is then reflected by an immobility of mind. This creates a deeply settled and tranquil concentration. Third, they give you the ability to sit for a long period of time without yielding to the meditator's three main enemies—pain, muscular tension, and falling asleep.

The most essential thing is to sit with your back straight. The spine should be erect with the spinal vertebrae held like a stack of coins, one on top of the other. Your head should be held in line with the rest of the spine. All of this is done in a relaxed manner. No stiffness. You are not a wooden soldier, and there is no drill sergeant. There should be no muscular tension involved in keeping the back straight. Sit light and easy. The spine should be like a firm young tree growing out of soft ground. The rest of the body just hangs from it in a loose, relaxed manner. This is going to require a bit of experimentation on your part. We generally sit in tight, guarded postures when we are walking or talking and in sprawling postures when we are relaxing. Neither of those will do. But they are cultural habits and they can be relearned.

Your objective is to achieve a posture in which you can sit for the entire session without moving at all. In the beginning, you will probably feel a bit odd to sit with a straight back. But you will get used to it. It takes practice, and an erect posture is very important. This is what is known in physiology as a position of arousal, and with it goes mental alertness. If you slouch, you are inviting drowsiness. What you sit on is equally important. You are going to need a chair or a cushion, depending on the posture you choose, and the firmness of the seat must be chosen with some care. Too soft a seat can put you right to sleep. Too hard can induce pain.

Clothing

The clothes you wear for meditation should be loose and soft. If they restrict blood flow or put pressure on nerves, the result will be pain and/or that tingling numbness that we normally refer to as our "legs going to sleep." If you are wearing a belt, loosen it. Don't wear tight pants or pants made of thick material. Long skirts are a good choice for women. Loose pants made of thin or elastic material are fine for anybody. Soft, flowing robes are the traditional garb in Asia, and they come in an enormous variety of styles such as sarongs and kimonos. Take your shoes off, and if your stockings are tight and binding, take them off, too.

TRADITIONAL POSTURES

When you are sitting on the floor in the traditional Asian manner, you need a cushion to elevate your spine. Choose one that is relatively firm and at least three inches thick when compressed. Sit close to the front edge of the cushion and let your crossed legs rest on the floor in front of you. If the floor is carpeted, that may be enough to protect your shins and ankles from pressure. If it is not, you will probably need some sort of padding for your legs. A folded blanket will do nicely. Don't sit all the way back on the cushion. This position causes its front edge to press into the underside of your thigh, causing nerves to pinch. The result will be leg pain.

There are a number of ways you can fold your legs. We will list four in ascending order of preference.

a) *Native American style.* Your right foot is tucked under the left knee and left foot is tucked under your right knee.

b) *Burmese style.* Both of your legs lie flat on the floor from knee to foot. They are parallel with one in front of the other.

c) *Half lotus.* Both of your knees touch the floor. One leg and foot lie flat along the calf of the other leg.

d) Full lotus. Both knees touch the floor, and your legs are crossed at the calf. Your left foot rests on the right thigh, and your right foot rests on the left thigh. Both soles turn upward.

In all these postures, your hands are cupped one on the other, and they rest on your lap with the palms turned upward. The hands lie just below the navel with the bend of each wrist pressed against the thigh. This arm position provides firm bracing for the upper body. Don't tighten your neck or shoulder muscles. Relax your arms. Your diaphragm is held relaxed, expanded to maximum fullness. Don't let tension build up in the stomach area. Your chin is up. Your eyes can be open or closed. If you keep them open, fix them on the tip of your nose or in a middle distance straight in front. You are not looking at anything. You are just putting your eyes where there is nothing in particular to see, so that you can forget about vision. Don't strain, don't stiffen, and don't be rigid. Relax; let the body be natural and supple. Let it hang from the erect spine like a rag doll.

Half and full lotus positions are the traditional meditation postures in Asia. And the full lotus is considered the best. It is the most solid by far. Once you are locked into this position, you can be completely immovable for a very long period. Since it requires a considerable flexibility in the legs, not everybody can do it. Besides, the main criterion by which you choose a posture for yourself is not what others say about it. It is your own comfort. Choose a position that allows you to sit the longest without pain, without moving. Experiment with different postures. The tendons will loosen with practice. And then you can work gradually toward the full lotus.

Using a Chair

Sitting on the floor may not be feasible for you because of pain or some other reason. No problem. You can always use a chair instead. Pick one that has a level seat, a straight back, and no arms. It is best to sit in such a way that your back does not lean against the back of the chair. The furniture of the seat should not dig into the underside of your thighs. Place your legs side by side, feet flat on the floor. As with the traditional postures, place both hands on your lap, cupped one upon the other. Don't tighten your neck or shoulder muscles, and relax your arms. Your eyes can be open or closed.

In all the above postures, remember your objectives. You want to achieve a state of complete physical stillness, yet you don't want to fall asleep. Recall the analogy of the muddy water. You want to promote a totally settled state of the body, which will engender a corresponding mental settling. There must also be a state of physical alertness, which can induce the kind of mental clarity you seek. So experiment. Your body is a tool for creating desired mental states. Use it judiciously.

7. What to Do with Your Mind

The meditation we teach is called insight meditation. As we have already said, the variety of possible objects of meditation is nearly unlimited, and human beings have used an enormous number down through the ages. Even within the vipassana tradition there are variations. There are meditation teachers who teach their students to follow the breath by watching the rise and fall of the abdomen. Others recommend focusing attention on the touch of the body against the cushion, or hand against hand, or the feeling of one leg against the other. The method we are explaining here, however, is considered the most traditional and is probably what Gotama Buddha taught his students. The *Satipatthana Sutta*, the Buddha's original discourse on mindfulness, specifically says that one must begin by focusing the attention on the breathing and then go on to note all other physical and mental phenomena that arise.

We sit, watching the air going in and out of our noses. At first glance, this seems an exceedingly odd and useless procedure. Before going on to specific instructions, let us examine the reason behind it. The first question we might have is why use any focus of attention at all? We are, after all, trying to develop awareness. Why not just sit down and be aware of whatever happens to be present in the mind? In fact, there are meditations of that nature. They are sometimes referred to as unstructured meditation, and they are quite difficult.

The mind is tricky. Thought is an inherently complicated procedure. By that we mean that we become trapped, wrapped up, and stuck in the thought chain. One thought leads to another, which leads to another, and another, and another, and so on. Fifteen minutes later we suddenly wake up and realize we spent that whole time stuck in a daydream or sexual fantasy or a set of worries about our bills or whatever.

There is a difference between being aware of a thought and thinking a thought. That difference is very subtle. It is primarily a matter of feeling or texture. A thought you are simply aware of with bare attention feels light in texture; there is a sense of distance between that thought and the awareness viewing it. It arises lightly like a bubble, and it passes away without necessarily giving rise to the next thought in that chain. Normal conscious thought is much heavier in texture. It is ponderous, commanding, and compulsive. It sucks you in and grabs control of consciousness. By its very nature it is obsessional, and it leads straight to the next thought in the chain, with apparently no gap between them.

Conscious thought sets up a corresponding tension in the body, such as muscular contraction or a quickening of the heartbeat. But you won't feel tension until it grows to actual pain, because normal conscious thought is also greedy. It grabs all your attention and leaves none to notice its own effect. The difference between being aware of the thought and thinking the thought is very real. But it is extremely subtle and difficult to see. Concentration is one of the tools needed to be able to see this difference.

Deep concentration has the effect of slowing down the thought process and speeding up the awareness viewing it. The result is the enhanced ability to examine the thought process. Concentration is our microscope for viewing subtle internal states. We use the focus of attention to achieve one-pointedness of mind with calm and constantly applied attention. Without a fixed reference point you get lost, overcome by the ceaseless waves of change flowing round and round within the mind.

We use breath as our focus. It serves as that vital reference point from which the mind wanders and is drawn back. Distraction cannot be seen as distraction unless there is some central focus to be distracted from. That is the frame of reference against which we can view the incessant changes and interruptions that go on all the time as a part of normal thinking.

Ancient Pali texts liken meditation to the process of taming a wild elephant. The procedure in those days was to tie a newly captured animal to a post with a good strong rope. When you do this, the elephant is not happy. He screams and tramples and pulls against the rope for days. Finally it sinks through his skull that he can't get away, and he settles down. At this point you can begin to feed him and to handle him with some measure of safety. Eventually you can dispense with the rope and post altogether and train your elephant for various tasks. Now you've got a tamed elephant that can be put to useful work. In this analogy the wild elephant is your wildly active mind, the rope is mindfulness, and the post is your object of meditation, your breathing. The tamed elephant who emerges from this process is a well-trained, concentrated mind that can then be used for the exceedingly tough job of piercing the layers of illusion that obscure reality. Meditation tames the mind.

The next question we need to address is: Why choose breathing as the primary object of meditation? Why not something a bit more interesting? Answers to this are numerous. A useful object of meditation should be one that promotes mindfulness. It should be portable, easily available, and cheap. It should also be something that will not embroil us in those states of mind from which we are trying to free ourselves, such as greed, anger, and delusion. Breathing satisfies all these criteria and more. Breathing is something common to every human being. We all carry it with us wherever we go. It is always there, constantly available, never ceasing from birth till death, and it costs nothing.

Breathing is a nonconceptual process, a thing that can be experienced directly without a need for thought. Furthermore, it is a very living process, an aspect of life that is in constant change. The breath moves in cycles—inhalation, exhalation, breathing in, and breathing out. Thus, it is a miniature model of life itself.

The sensation of breath is subtle, yet it is quite distinct when you learn to tune in to it. It takes a bit of an effort to find it. Yet anybody can do it. You've got to work at it, but not too hard. For all these reasons, breathing makes an ideal object of meditation. Breathing is normally an involuntary process, proceeding at its own pace without a conscious will. Yet a single act of will can slow it down or speed it up. Make it long and smooth or short and choppy. The balance between involuntary breathing and forced manipulation of breath is quite delicate. And there are lessons to be learned here on the nature of will and desire. Then, too, that point at the tip of the nostril can be viewed as a sort of a window between the inner and outer worlds. It is a nexus point and energy transfer spot where stuff from the outside world moves in and becomes a part of what we call "me," and where a part of "me" flows forth to merge with the outside world. There are lessons to be learned here about self-identity and how we form it.

Breath is a phenomenon common to all living things. A true experiential understanding of the process moves you closer to other living beings. It shows you your inherent connectedness with all of life. Finally, breathing is a present-moment process. By that we mean it is always occurring in the here and now. We don't normally live in the present, of course. We spend most of our time caught up in memories of the past or looking ahead to the future, full of worries and plans. The breath has none of that "other-timeness." When we truly observe the breath, we are automatically placed in the present. We are pulled out of the morass of mental images and into a bare experience of the here and now. In this sense, breath is a living slice of reality. A mindful observation of such a miniature model of life itself leads to insights that are broadly applicable to the rest of our experience.

The first step in using the breath as an object of meditation is to find it. What you are looking for is the physical, tactile sensation of the air that passes in and out of the nostrils. This is usually just inside the tip of the nose. But the exact spot varies from one person to another, depending on the shape of the nose. To find your own point, take a quick deep breath and notice the point just inside the nose or on the upper lip where you have the most distinct sensation of passing air. Now exhale and notice the sensation at the same point. It is from this point that you will follow the whole passage of breath. Once you have located your own breath point with clarity, don't deviate from that spot. Use this single point in order to keep your attention fixed. Without having selected such a point, you will find yourself moving in and out of the nose, going up and down the windpipe, eternally chasing after the breath, which you can never catch because it keeps changing, moving, and flowing.

If you ever sawed wood you already know the trick. As a carpenter, you don't stand there watching the saw blade going up and down. You would get dizzy. You fix your attention on the spot where the teeth of the blade dig into the wood. It is the only way you can saw a straight line. As a meditator, you focus your attention on that single spot of sensation inside the nose. From this vantage point, you watch the entire movement of breath with clear and collected attention. Make no attempt to control the breath. This is not a breathing exercise of the sort done in yoga. Focus on the natural and spontaneous movement of the breath. Don't try to regulate it or emphasize it in any way. Most beginners have some trouble in this area. In order to help themselves focus on the sensation, they unconsciously accentuate their breathing. The result is a forced and unnatural effort that actually inhibits concentration rather than helping it. Don't increase the depth of your breath or its sound. This latter point is especially important in group meditation. Loud breathing can be a real annoyance to those around you. Just let the breath move naturally, as if you were asleep. Let go and allow the process to go along at its own rhythm.

This sounds easy, but it is trickier than you think. Do not be discouraged if you find your own will getting in the way. Just use that as an opportunity to observe the nature of conscious intention. Watch the delicate interrelation between the breath, the impulse to control the breath, and the impulse to cease controlling the breath. You may find it frustrating for a while, but it is highly profitable as a learning experience, and it is a passing phase. Eventually, the breathing process will move along under its own steam, and you will feel no impulse to manipulate it. At this point you will have learned a major lesson about your own compulsive need to control the universe.

Breathing, which seems so mundane and uninteresting at first glance, is actually an enormously complex and fascinating procedure. It is full of delicate variations, if you look. There is inhalation and exhalation, long breath and short breath, deep breath, shallow breath, smooth breath, and ragged breath. These categories combine with one another in subtle and intricate ways. Observe the breath closely. Really study it. You find enormous variations and a constant cycle of repeated patterns. It is like a symphony. Don't observe just the bare outline of the breath. There is more to see here than just an in-breath and an out-breath. Every breath has a beginning, middle, and end. Every inhalation goes through a process of birth, growth, and death, and every exhalation does the same. The depth and speed of your breathing changes according to your emotional state, the thought that flows through your mind, and the sounds you hear. Study these phenomena. You will find them fascinating.

This does not mean, however, that you should be sitting there having little conversations with yourself inside your head: "There is a short ragged breath and there is a deep long one. I wonder what's next?" No, that is not vipassana. That is thinking. You will find this sort of thing happening, especially in the beginning. This too is a passing phase. Simply note the phenomenon and return your attention toward the observation of the sensation of breath. Mental distractions will happen again. But return your attention to your breath again, and again, and again, and again, for as long as it takes until distraction no longer occurs.

When you first begin this procedure, expect to face some difficulties. Your mind will wander off constantly, darting around like a bumblebee and zooming off on wild tangents. Try not to worry. The monkey-mind phenomenon is well known. It is something that every seasoned meditator has had to deal with. They have pushed through it one way or another, and so can you. When it happens, just note the fact that you have been thinking, daydreaming, worrying, or whatever. Gently, but firmly, without getting upset or judging yourself for straying, simply return to the simple physical sensation of the breath. Then do it again the next time, and again, and again, and again.

Somewhere in this process, you will come face to face with the sudden and shocking realization that you are completely crazy. Your mind is a shrieking, gibbering madhouse on wheels barreling pell-mell down the hill, utterly out of control and helpless. No problem. You are not crazier than you were yesterday. It has always been this way, and you just never noticed. You are also no crazier than everybody else around you. The only real difference is that you have confronted the situation; they have not. So they still feel relatively comfortable. That does not mean that they are better off. Ignorance may be bliss, but it does not lead to liberation. So don't let this realization unsettle you. It is a milestone actually, a sign of real progress. The very fact that you have looked at the problem straight in the eye means that you are on your way up and out of it.

In the wordless observation of the breath, there are two states to be avoided: thinking and sinking. The thinking mind manifests most clearly as the monkey-mind phenomenon we have just been discussing. The sinking mind is almost the reverse. As a general term, *sinking* denotes any dimming of awareness. At its best, it is sort of a mental vacuum in which there is no thought, no observation of the breath, no awareness of anything. It is a gap, a formless mental gray area rather like a dreamless sleep. Sinking mind is a void. Avoid it.

Vipassana meditation is an active function. Concentration is a strong, energetic attention to one single item. Awareness is a bright clean alertness. *Samadhi* and *sati*—these are the two faculties we wish to cultivate. And sinking mind contains neither. At its worst, it will put you to sleep. Even at its best it will simply waste your time.

When you find you have fallen into the state of sinking mind, just note the fact and return your attention to the sensation of breathing. Observe the tactile sensation of the in-breath. Feel the touch sensation of the out-breath. Breathe in, breathe out, and watch what happens. When you have been doing that for some time—perhaps weeks or months—you will begin to sense the touch as a physical object. Simply continue the process; breathe in and breathe out. Watch what happens. As your concentration deepens you will have less and less trouble with monkey mind. Your breathing will slow down, and you will track it more and more clearly, with fewer and fewer interruptions. You begin to experience a state of great calm in which you enjoy complete freedom from those things we called psychic irritants. No greed, lust, envy, jealousy, or hatred. Agitation goes away. Fear flees. These are beautiful, clear, blissful states of mind. They are temporary, and they will end when the meditation ends. Yet even these brief experiences will change your life. This is not liberation, but these are steppingstones on the path that leads in that direction. Do not, however, expect instant bliss. Even these steppingstones take time, effort, and patience.

The meditation experience is not a competition. There is a definite goal. But there is no timetable. What you are doing is digging your way deeper and deeper through layers of illusion toward realization of the supreme truth of existence. The process itself is fascinating and fulfilling. It can be enjoyed for its own sake. There is no need to rush.

At the end of a well-done meditation session, you will feel a delightful freshness of mind. It is a peaceful, buoyant, and joyous energy that you can then apply to the problems of daily living. This in itself is reward enough. The purpose of meditation is not to deal with problems, however, and problem-solving ability is a fringe benefit and should be regarded as such. If you place too much emphasis on the problem-solving aspect, you will find your attention turning to those problems during the session, sidetracking concentration.

Don't think about your problems during your practice. Push them aside very gently. Take a break from all that worrying and planning. Let your meditation be a complete vacation. Trust yourself, trust your own ability to deal with these issues later, using the energy and freshness of mind that you built up during your meditation. Trust yourself this way and it will actually occur.

Don't set goals for yourself that are too high to reach. Be gentle with yourself. You are trying to follow your own breathing continuously and without a break. That sounds easy enough, so you will have a tendency at the outset to push yourself to be scrupulous and exacting. This is unrealistic. Take time in small units instead. At the beginning of an inhalation, make the resolve to follow the breath just for the period of that one inhalation. Even this is not so easy, but at least it can be done. Then, at the start of the exhalation, resolve to follow the breath just for that one exhalation, all the way through. You will still fail repeatedly, but keep at it.

Every time you stumble, start over. Take it one breath at a time. This is the level of the game where you can actually win. Stick with it—fresh resolve with every breath cycle, tiny units of time. Observe each breath with care and precision, taking it one split second on top of another, with fresh resolve piled one on top of the other. In this way, continuous and unbroken awareness will eventually result.

Mindfulness of breathing is a present-moment awareness. When you are doing it properly, you are aware only of what is occurring in the present. You don't look back, and you don't look forward. You forget about the last breath, and you don't anticipate the next one. When the inhalation is just beginning, you don't look ahead to the end of that inhalation. You don't skip forward to the exhalation that is to follow. You stay right there with what is actually taking place. The inhalation is beginning, and that's what you pay attention to; that and nothing else.

This meditation is a process of retraining the mind. The state you are aiming for is one in which you are totally aware of everything that is happening in your own perceptual universe, exactly the way it happens, exactly when it is happening; total, unbroken awareness in present time. This is an incredibly high goal, and not to be reached all at once. It takes practice, so we start small. We start by becoming totally aware of one small unit of time, just one single inhalation. And, when you succeed, you are on your way to a whole new experience of life.

8. Structuring Your Meditation

*E*verything up to this point has been theory. Now let's dive into the actual practice. Just how do we go about this thing called meditation?

First of all, you need to establish a formal practice schedule, a specific period when you will do vipassana meditation and nothing else. When you were a baby, you did not know how to walk. Somebody went to a lot of trouble to teach you that skill. They dragged you by the arms. They gave you lots of encouragement, made you put one foot in front of the other until you could do it by yourself. Those periods of instruction constituted a formal practice in the art of walking.

In meditation, we follow the same basic procedure. We set aside a certain time, specifically devoted to developing this mental skill called mindfulness. We devote these times exclusively to that activity, and we structure our environment so there will be a minimum of distraction. This is not the easiest skill in the world to learn. We have spent our entire life developing mental habits that are really quite contrary to the ideal of uninterrupted mindfulness. Extricating ourselves from those habits requires a bit of strategy. As we said earlier, our minds are like cups of muddy water. The object of meditation is to clarify this sludge so that we can see what is going on in there. The best way to do that is just let it sit. Give it enough time and it will settle down. You wind up with clear water. In meditation, we set aside a specific time for this clarifying process. When viewed from the outside, it looks utterly useless. We sit there apparently as productive as a stone gargoyle. Inside, however, quite a bit is happening. The mental soup settles down, and we are left with a clarity of mind that prepares us to cope with the upcoming events of our lives.

That does not mean that we have to do anything to force this settling. It is a natural process that happens by itself. The very act of sitting still and being mindful causes this settling. In fact, any effort on our part to force this settling is counterproductive. That is repression, and it does not work. Try to force things out of the mind and you merely add energy to them. You may succeed temporarily, but in the long run you will only have made them stronger. They will hide in the unconscious until you are not watching, then they will leap out and leave you helpless to fight them off.

The best way to clarify the mental fluid is to just let it settle all by itself. Don't add any energy to the situation. Just mindfully watch the mud swirl, without any involvement in the process. Then, when it settles at last, it will stay settled. We exert energy in meditation, but not force. Our only effort is gentle, patient mindfulness.

The meditation period is like a cross section of your whole day. Everything that happens to you is stored away in the mind in some form, mental or emotional. During normal activity, you get so caught up in the press of events that the basic issues with which you are dealing are seldom thoroughly handled. They become buried in the unconscious, where they seethe and foam and fester. Then you wonder where all that tension came from.

All of this material comes forth in one form or another during your meditation. You get a chance to look at it, see it for what it is, and let it go. We set up a formal meditation period in order to create a conducive environment for this release. We reestablish our mindfulness at regular intervals. We withdraw from those events that constantly stimulate the mind. We back out of all that activity that prods the emotions. We go off to a quiet place and we sit still, and it all comes bubbling out. Then it goes away. The net effect is like recharging a battery. Meditation recharges your mindfulness.

WHERE TO SIT?

Find yourself a quiet place, a secluded place, a place where you will be alone. It doesn't have to be some ideal spot in the middle of a forest. That's nearly impossible for most of us, but it should be a place where you feel comfortable, and where you won't be disturbed. It should also be a place where you won't feel on display. You want all of your attention free for meditation, not wasted on worries about how you look to others. Try to pick a spot that is as quiet as possible. It doesn't have to be a soundproof room, but there are certain noises that are highly distracting, and they should be avoided. Music and talking are about the worst. The mind tends to be sucked in by these sounds in an uncontrollable manner, and there goes your concentration.

There are certain traditional aids that you can employ to set the proper mood. A darkened room with a candle is nice. Incense is nice. A little bell to start and end your sessions is nice. These are paraphernalia, though. They provide encouragement to some people, but they are by no means essential to the practice.

You will probably find it helpful to sit in the same place each time. A special spot reserved for meditation and nothing else is an aid for most people. You soon come to associate that spot with the tranquility of deep concentration, and that association helps you to reach deep states more quickly. The main thing is to sit in a place that you feel is conducive to your own practice. That requires a bit of experimentation. Try several spots until you find one where you feel comfortable.

You only need to find a place where you don't feel self-conscious, and where you can meditate without undue distraction.

Many people find it helpful and supportive to sit with a group of other meditators. The discipline of regular practice is essential, and most people find it easier to sit regularly if they are bolstered by a commitment to a group sitting schedule. You've given your word, and you know you are expected to keep it. Thus, the "I'm too busy" syndrome is cleverly skirted. You may be able to locate a group of practicing meditators in your own area. It doesn't matter if they practice a different form of meditation, so long as it's one of the silent forms. On the other hand, you also should try to be self-sufficient in your practice. Don't rely on the presence of a group as your sole motivation to sit. Properly done, sitting is a pleasure. Use the group as an aid, not as a crutch.

WHEN TO SIT?

The most important rule here is this: When it comes to sitting, the description of Buddhism as the Middle Way applies. Don't overdo it. Don't underdo it. This doesn't mean you just sit whenever the whim strikes you. It means you set up a practice schedule and keep to it with a gentle, patient tenacity. Setting up a schedule acts as an encouragement. If, however, you find that your schedule has ceased to be an encouragement and become a burden, then something is wrong. Meditation is not a duty or an obligation.

Meditation is a psychological activity. You will be dealing with the raw stuff of feelings and emotions. Consequently, it is an activity that is very sensitive to the attitude with which you approach each session. What you expect is what you are most likely to get. Your practice will therefore go best when you are looking forward to sitting. If you sit down expecting grinding drudgery, that is probably what will occur.

So set up a daily pattern that you can live with. Make it reasonable. Make it fit with the rest of your life. And if it starts to feel like you're on an uphill treadmill toward liberation, then change something.

First thing in the morning is a great time to meditate. Your mind is fresh then, before you've gotten yourself buried in responsibilities. Morning meditation is a fine way to start your day. It tunes you up and gets you ready to deal with things efficiently. You cruise through the rest of the day just a bit more lightly. Be sure you are thoroughly awake, though. You won't make much progress if you are sitting there nodding off, so get enough sleep. Wash your face, or shower before you begin. You may want to do a bit of exercise beforehand to get the circulation flowing. Do whatever you need to do in order to wake up fully, then sit down to meditate. Do not, however, let yourself get hung up in the day's activities. It's just too easy to forget to sit. Make meditation the first major thing you do in the morning.

The evening is another good time for practice. Your mind is full of all the mental rubbish that you have accumulated during the day, and it is great to get rid of that burden before you sleep. Your meditation will cleanse and rejuvenate your mind. Reestablish your mindfulness, and your sleep will be real sleep.

When you first start meditation, once a day is enough. If you feel like meditating more, that's fine, but don't overdo it. There's a burnout phenomenon we often see in new meditators. They dive right into the practice fifteen hours a day for a couple of weeks, and then the real world catches up with them. They decide that this meditation business just takes too much time. Too many sacrifices are required. They haven't got time for all of this. Don't fall into that trap. Don't burn yourself out the first week. Make haste slowly. Make your effort consistent and steady. Give yourself time to incorporate the meditation practice into your life, and let your practice grow gradually and gently.

As your interest in meditation grows, you'll find yourself making more room in your schedule for practice. It's a spontaneous phenomenon, and it happens pretty much by itself—no force necessary.

Seasoned meditators manage three or four hours of practice a day. They live ordinary lives in the day-to-day world, and they still squeeze it all in. And they enjoy it. It comes naturally.

How Long to Sit?

A similar rule applies here: sit as long as you can, but don't overdo it. Most beginners start with twenty or thirty minutes. Initially, it's difficult to sit longer than that with profit. The posture is unfamiliar to Westerners, and it takes a bit of time for the body to adjust. The mental skills are equally unfamiliar, and that adjustment takes time, too.

As you grow accustomed to the procedure, you can extend your meditation little by little. We recommend that after a year or so of steady practice you should be sitting comfortably for an hour at a time.

Here is an important point, though: vipassana meditation is not a form of asceticism. Self-mortification is not the goal. We are trying to cultivate mindfulness, not pain. Some pain is inevitable, especially in the legs. We will thoroughly cover pain, and how to handle it, in chapter 10. There are special techniques and attitudes that you will learn for dealing with discomfort. The point to be made here is this: This is not a grim endurance contest. You don't need to prove anything to anybody. So don't force yourself to sit with excruciating pain just to be able to say that you sat for an hour. That is a useless exercise in ego. And don't overdo it in the beginning. Know your limitations, and don't condemn yourself for not being able to sit forever, like a rock.

As meditation becomes more and more a part of your life, you can extend your sessions beyond an hour. As a general rule, just determine what is a comfortable length of time for you at this point in your life. Then sit five minutes longer than that.

There is no hard and fast rule about length of time for sitting. Even if you have established a firm minimum, there may be days when it is physically impossible for you to sit that long. That doesn't mean that you should just cancel the whole idea for that day. It's crucial to sit regularly. Even ten minutes of meditation can be very beneficial.

Incidentally, you decide on the length of your session before you meditate. Don't do it while you are meditating. It's too easy to give in to restlessness that way, and restlessness is one of the main items that we want to learn to mindfully observe. So choose a realistic length of time, and then stick to it.

You can use a watch to time your session, but don't peek at it every two minutes to see how you are doing. Your concentration will be completely lost, and agitation will set in. You'll find yourself hoping to get up before the session is over. That's not meditation—that's clock watching. Don't look at the clock until you think the whole meditation period has passed. Actually, you don't need to consult the clock at all, at least not every time you meditate. In general, you should be sitting for as long as you want to sit. There is no magic length of time. It is best, however, to set yourself a minimum length of time. If you haven't predetermined a minimum, you'll find yourself prone to short sessions. You'll bolt every time something unpleasant comes up or whenever you feel restless. That's no good. These experiences are some of the most profitable a meditator can face, but only if you sit through them. You've got to learn to observe them calmly and clearly. Look at them mindfully. When you've done that enough times, they lose their hold on you. You see them for what they are: just impulses, arising and passing away, just part of the passing show. Your life smoothes out beautifully as a consequence.

"Discipline" is a difficult word for most of us. It conjures up images of somebody standing over you with a stick, telling you that you're wrong. But self-discipline is different. It's the skill of seeing through the hollow shouting of your own impulses and piercing their secret. They have no power over you. It's all a show, a deception. Your urges scream and bluster at you; they cajole; they coax; they threaten; but they really carry no stick at all. You give in out of habit. You give in because you never really bother to look beyond the threat. It is all empty back there. There is only one way to learn this lesson, though. The words on this page won't do it. But look within and watch the stuff coming up—restlessness, anxiety, impatience, pain—just watch it come up and don't get involved. Much to your surprise, it will simply go away. It rises, it passes away. As simple as that. There is another word for self-discipline. It is patience.

9. *Setup Exercises*

*I*n Theravada Buddhist countries, it is traditional to begin each meditation session with the recitation of a certain set of formulas. An American audience is likely to take one glance at these invocations and to dismiss them as harmless rituals and nothing more. These so-called rituals, however, have been devised and refined by a set of pragmatic and dedicated men and women, and they have a thoroughly practical purpose. They are therefore worthy of deeper inspection.

The Buddha was considered contrary in his own day. He was born into an intensely ritualized society, and his ideas appeared thoroughly iconoclastic to the established hierarchy of his own era. On numerous occasions, he disavowed the use of rituals for their own sake, and he was quite adamant about it. This does not mean that ritual has no use. It means that ritual by itself, performed strictly for its own sake, will not get you out of the trap. Indeed, such performance is a part of the trap. If you believe that mere recitation of words will save you, then you only increase your own dependence on words and concepts. This moves you away from the wordless perception of reality rather than toward it. Therefore, the formulae that follow must be practiced with a clear understanding of what they are and why they work. They are not prayers, and they are not mantras. They are not magical incantations. They are psychological cleansing devices that require active mental participation in order to be effective. Mumbled words without intention are useless. Vipassana meditation is a delicate psychological activity, and the mindset of the practitioner is crucial to its success. The technique works best in an atmosphere of calm, benevolent confidence. And these recitations have been designed to foster those attitudes. Correctly used, they can act as a helpful tool on the path to liberation.

THE THREEFOLD GUIDANCE

Meditation is a tough job. It is an inherently solitary activity. One person battles against enormously powerful forces, part of the very structure of the mind doing the meditating. When you really get into it, you will eventually find yourself confronted with a shocking realization. One day you will look inside and realize the full enormity of what you are actually up against. What you are struggling to pierce looks like a solid wall so tightly knit that not a single ray of light shines through. You find yourself sitting there, staring at this edifice, and you say to yourself, "That? I am supposed to get past that? But it's impossible! That is all there is. That is the whole world. That is what everything means, and that is what I use to define myself and to understand everything around me, and if I take that away the whole world will fall apart and I will die. I cannot get through that. I just can't."

It is a very scary feeling, a very lonely feeling. You feel like, "Here I am, all alone, trying to punch away something so huge it is beyond conception." To counteract this feeling, it is useful to know that you are not alone. Others have passed this way before. They have confronted that same barrier, and they have pushed their way through to the light. They have laid out the rules by which the job can be done, and they have banded together into a fellowship for mutual encouragement and support. The Buddha found his way through this very same wall, and after him came many others. He left clear instructions in the form of the Dhamma to guide us along the same path. And he founded the Sangha, the community of monks and nuns, to preserve that path and to keep each other on it. You are not alone, and the situation is not hopeless.

Meditation takes energy. You need courage to confront some pretty difficult mental phenomena and the determination to sit through various unpleasant mental states. Laziness just will not serve. In order to pump up your energy for the job, repeat the following statements to yourself. Feel the intention you put into them. Mean what you say.

"I am about to tread the very same path that has been walked by the Buddha and by his great and holy disciples. An indolent person cannot follow that path. May my energy prevail. May I succeed."

UNIVERSAL LOVING-FRIENDLINESS

Vipassana meditation is an exercise in mindfulness, that is, in egoless awareness. It is a procedure in which the ego will be eradicated by the penetrating gaze of mindfulness. The practitioner begins this process with the ego in full command of mind and body. Then, as mindfulness watches the ego function, it penetrates to the roots of the mechanics of ego and extinguishes ego piece by piece. There is a full-blown catch-22 in all this, however. Mindfulness is egoless awareness. If we start with ego in full control, how do we put enough mindfulness there at the beginning to get the job started? There is always some mindfulness present in any moment. The real problem is to gather enough of it to be effective. To do this we can use a clever tactic. We can weaken those aspects of ego that do the most harm so that mindfulness will have less resistance to overcome.

Greed and hatred are the prime manifestations of the ego process. To the extent that grasping and rejecting are present in the mind, mindfulness will have a very rough time. The results of this are easy to see. If you sit down to meditate while you are in the grip of some strong obsessive attachment, you will find that you will get nowhere. If you are all hung up in your latest scheme to make more money, you probably will spend most of your meditation period doing nothing but thinking about it. If you are in a black fury over some recent insult, that will occupy your mind just as fully. There is only so much time in one day, and your meditation minutes are precious. It is best not to waste them. The Theravada tradition has developed a useful tool that will allow you to remove these barriers from your mind at least temporarily, so that you can get on with the job of removing their roots permanently.

You can use one idea to cancel another. You can balance a negative emotion by instilling a positive one. Giving is the opposite of greed. Benevolence is the opposite of hatred. Understand clearly now: this is not an attempt to liberate yourself by autohypnosis. You cannot condition enlightenment. *Nibbana* is an unconditioned state. A liberated person will indeed be generous and benevolent, but not because she has been conditioned to be so. She will be so purely as a manifestation of her own basic nature, which is no longer inhibited by ego. So this is not conditioning. This is rather psychological medicine. If you take this medicine according to directions, it will bring temporary relief from the symptoms of the malady from which you are currently suffering. Then you can get to work in earnest on the illness itself.

You start out by banishing thoughts of self-hatred and self-condemnation. You allow good feelings and good wishes first to flow to yourself, which is relatively easy. Then you do the same for those people closest to you. Gradually, you work outward from your own circle of intimates until you can direct a flow of those same emotions to your enemies and to all living beings everywhere. Correctly done, this can be a powerful and transformative exercise in itself.

At the beginning of each meditation session, say the following sentences to yourself. Really feel the intention:

May I be well, happy, and peaceful. May no harm come to me. May I always meet with spiritual success. May I also have patience, courage, understanding, and determination to meet and overcome inevitable difficulties, problems, and failures in life. May I always rise above them with morality, integrity, forgiveness, compassion, mindfulness, and wisdom.

May my parents be well, happy, and peaceful. May no harm come to them. May they always meet with spiritual success. May they also have patience, courage, understanding, and determination to meet and overcome inevitable difficulties, problems, and failures in life. May they always rise above them with morality, integrity, forgiveness, compassion, mindfulness, and wisdom.

May my teachers be well, happy, and peaceful. May no harm come to them. May they always meet with spiritual success. May they also have patience, courage, understanding, and determination to meet and overcome inevitable difficulties, problems, and failures in life. May they always rise above them with morality, integrity, forgiveness, compassion, mindfulness, and wisdom.

May my relatives be well, happy, and peaceful. May no harm come to them. May they always meet with spiritual success. May they also have patience, courage, understanding, and determination to meet and overcome inevitable difficulties, problems, and failures in life. May they always rise above them with morality, integrity, forgiveness, compassion, mindfulness, and wisdom.

May my friends be well, happy, and peaceful. May no harm come to them. May they always meet with spiritual success. May they also have patience, courage, understanding, and determination to meet and overcome inevitable difficulties, problems, and failures in life. May they always rise above them with morality, integrity, forgiveness, compassion, mindfulness, and wisdom.

May all indifferent persons be well, happy, and peaceful. May no harm come to them. May they always meet with spiritual success. May they also have patience, courage, understanding, and determination to meet and overcome inevitable difficulties, problems, and failures in life. May they always rise above them with morality, integrity, forgiveness, compassion, mindfulness, and wisdom.

May all unfriendly persons be well, happy, and peaceful. May no harm come to them. May they always meet with spiritual success. May they also have patience, courage, understanding, and determination to meet and overcome inevitable difficulties, problems, and failures in life. May they always rise above them with morality, integrity, forgiveness, compassion, mindfulness, and wisdom.

May all living beings be well, happy, and peaceful. May no harm come to them. May they always meet with spiritual success. May they also have patience, courage, understanding, and determination to meet and overcome inevitable difficulties, problems, and failures in life. May they always rise above them with morality, integrity, forgiveness, compassion, mindfulness, and wisdom.

Once you have completed these recitations, lay aside all your troubles and conflicts for the period of practice. Just drop the whole bundle. If they come back into your meditation later, just treat them as what they are, distractions.

The practice of universal loving-friendliness is also recommended for bedtime and just after arising. It is said to help you sleep well and to prevent nightmares. It also makes it easier to get up in the morning. And it makes you more friendly and open toward everybody, friend or foe, human or otherwise.

The most damaging psychic irritant arising in the mind, particularly at the time when the mind is quiet, is resentment. You may experience indignation remembering some incident that caused you psychological and physical pain. This experience can cause you uneasiness, tension, agitation, and worry. You might not be able to go on sitting and experiencing this state of mind. Therefore, we strongly recommend that you should start your meditation with generating universal loving-friendliness.

You may wonder how we can wish: "May my *enemies* be well, happy, and peaceful; may no difficulties come to them; may no problem come to them; may they always meet with success. May they also have patience, courage, understanding, and determination to meet and overcome inevitable difficulties, problems, and failures in life."

You must remember that you practice loving-friendliness for the purification of your own mind, just as you practice meditation for your own attainment of peace and liberation from pain and suffering. As you practice loving-friendliness within yourself, you can behave in a most friendly manner without biases, prejudices, discrimination, or hate. Your noble behavior enables you to help others in a most practical manner to reduce their pain and suffering. It is compassionate people who can help others. Compassion is a manifestation of loving-friendliness in action, for one who does not have loving-friendliness cannot help others. Noble behavior means behaving in a most friendly manner. Behavior includes your thought, speech, and actions. If this triple mode of expression of your behavior is contradictory, then something is wrong, and contradictory behavior cannot be noble behavior. In addition, from a pragmatic perspective, it is much better to cultivate the noble thought "May all beings be happy minded" than the thought "I hate him." Our noble thought will one day express itself in noble behavior and our spiteful thought in evil behavior.

Remember that your thoughts are transformed into speech and action in order to bring the expected result. Thought translated into action is capable of producing a tangible result. You should always speak and do things with mindfulness of loving-friendliness. While speaking of loving-friendliness, if you then act or speak in a diametrically opposite way, you will be reproached by the wise. As mindfulness of loving-friendliness develops, your thoughts, words, and deeds should be gentle, pleasant, meaningful, truthful, and beneficial to you as well as to others. If your thoughts, words, or deeds cause harm to you, to others, or to both, then you must ask yourself whether you are really mindful of loving-friendliness.

Practically speaking, if all of your enemies were well, happy, and peaceful, they would not be your enemies. If they were free from problems, pain, suffering, affliction, neurosis, psychosis, paranoia, fear, tension, anxiety, etc., they would not be your enemies. The practical approach toward your enemies is to help them overcome their problems, so you can live in peace and happiness. In fact, if you can, you should fill the minds of all your enemies with loving-friendliness and make all of them realize the true meaning of peace, so you can live in peace and happiness. The more they are neurotic, psychotic, afraid, tense, and anxious, the more trouble, pain, and suffering they bring to the world. If you could convert a vicious and wicked person into a holy and saintly individual, you would perform a miracle. Let us cultivate adequate wisdom and loving-friendliness within ourselves to convert evil minds to saintly minds.

When you hate somebody, you think, "Let him be ugly. Let him lie in pain. Let him have no prosperity. Let him not be rich. Let him not be famous. Let him have no friends. Let him, after death, reappear in an unhappy state of deprivation in a bad destination for eternity." However, what actually happens is that your own body generates such harmful chemistry that you experience pain, increased heart rate, tension, change of facial expression, loss of appetite, deprivation of sleep, and you appear very unpleasant to others. You go through the same things you wish on your enemy. Also you cannot see the truth as it is. Your mind is like boiling water. Or you are like a patient suffering from jaundice to whom any delicious food tastes bland. Similarly, you cannot appreciate somebody's appearance, achievement, success, etc. And as long as this condition exists, you cannot meditate well.

Therefore, we recommend very strongly that you practice loving-friendliness before you start your serious practice of meditation. Repeat the preceding passages very mindfully and meaningfully. As you recite these passages, feel true loving-friendliness within yourself first and then share it with others, for you cannot share with others what you do not have within yourself.

Remember, though, these are not magic formulas. They don't work by themselves. If you use them as such, you will simply waste time and energy. But if you truly participate in these statements and invest them with your own energy, they will serve you well. Give them a try. See for yourself.

10. Dealing with Problems

You are going to run into problems in your meditation. Everybody does. Problems come in all shapes and sizes, and the only thing you can be absolutely certain about is that you will have some. The main trick in dealing with obstacles is to adopt the right attitude. Difficulties are an integral part of your practice. They aren't something to be avoided; they are to be used. They provide invaluable opportunities for learning.

The reason we are all stuck in life's mud is that we ceaselessly run from our problems and after our desires. Meditation provides us with a laboratory situation in which we can examine this syndrome and devise strategies for dealing with it. The various snags and hassles that arise during meditation are grist for the mill. They are the material with which we work. There is no pleasure without some degree of pain. There is no pain without some amount of pleasure. Life is composed of joys and miseries. They go hand in hand. Meditation is no exception. You will experience good times and bad times, ecstasies and fear.

So don't be surprised when you hit some experience that feels like a brick wall. Don't think you are special. All seasoned meditators have had their own brick walls. They come up again and again. Just expect them and be ready to cope. Your ability to cope with trouble depends upon your attitude. If you can learn to regard these hassles as opportunities, as chances to develop in your practice, you'll make progress. Your ability to deal with some issue that arises in meditation will carry over into the rest of your life and allow you to smooth out big issues that really bother you. If you try to avoid each piece of nastiness that arises in meditation, you are reinforcing the habit that has already made life seem so unbearable at times.

It is essential to learn to confront the less pleasant aspects of existence. Our job as meditators is to learn to be patient with ourselves, to see ourselves in an unbiased way, complete with all our sorrows and inadequacies. We have to learn to be kind to ourselves. In the long run, avoiding unpleasantness is a very unkind thing to do to yourself. Paradoxically, kindness entails confronting unpleasantness when it arises.

One popular human strategy for dealing with difficulty is autosuggestion: when something nasty pops up, you convince yourself it is not there, or you convince yourself it is pleasant rather than unpleasant. The Buddha's tactic is quite the reverse. Rather than hide it or disguise it, the Buddha's teaching urges you to examine it to death. Buddhism advises you not to implant feelings that you don't really have or avoid feelings that you do have. If you are miserable you are miserable; that is the reality, that is what is happening, so confront that. Look it square in the eye without flinching. When you are having a bad time, examine that experience, observe it mindfully, study the phenomenon and learn its mechanics. The way out of a trap is to study the trap itself, learn how it is built. You do this by taking the thing apart piece by piece. The trap can't trap you if it has been taken to pieces. The result is freedom.

This point is essential, but it is one of the least understood aspects of Buddhist philosophy. Those who have studied Buddhism superficially are quick to conclude that it is pessimistic, always harping on unpleasant things like suffering, always urging us to confront the uncomfortable realities of pain, death, and illness. Buddhist thinkers do not regard themselves as pessimists—quite the opposite, actually. Pain exists in the universe; some measure of it is unavoidable. Learning to deal with it is not pessimism, but a very pragmatic form of optimism. How would you deal with the death of your spouse? How would you feel if you lost your mother tomorrow? Or your sister or your closest friend? Suppose you lost your job, your savings, and the use of your legs, all on the same day; could you face the prospect of spending the rest of your life in a wheelchair? How are you going to cope with the pain of terminal cancer if you contract it, and how will you deal with your own death when that approaches? You may escape most of these misfortunes, but you won't escape all of them. Most of us lose friends and relatives at some time during our lives; all of us get sick now and then; and all of us will die someday. You can suffer through things like that or you can face them openly—the choice is yours.

Pain is inevitable, suffering is not. Pain and suffering are two different animals. If any of these tragedies strike you in your present state of mind, you will suffer. The habit patterns that presently control your mind will lock you into that suffering, and there will be no escape. A bit of time spent in learning alternatives to those habit patterns is time well invested. Most human beings spend all their energies devising ways to increase their pleasure and decrease their pain. Buddhism does not advise that you cease this activity altogether. Money and security are fine. Pain should be avoided whenever possible. Nobody is telling you to give away every possession or seek out needless pain, but Buddhism does advise you to invest time and energy in learning to deal with unpleasantness, because some pain is unavoidable. When you see a truck bearing down on you, by all means jump out of the way. But spend some time in meditation, too. Learning to deal with discomfort is the only way you'll be ready to handle the truck you didn't see.

Problems will arise in your practice. Some of them will be physical, some will be emotional, and some will be attitudinal. All of them can be confronted and each has its own specific response. All of them are opportunities to free yourself.

PROBLEM 1: PHYSICAL PAIN

Nobody likes pain, yet everybody has some at one time or another. It is one of life's most common experiences and is bound to arise in your meditation in one form or another.

Handling pain is a two-stage process. First, get rid of the pain, if possible, or at least get rid of it as much as possible. Then, if some pain lingers, use it as an object of meditation. The first step is physical handling. Maybe the pain is an illness of one sort or another, a headache, fever, bruises, or whatever. In this case, employ standard medical treatments before you sit down to meditate: take your medicine, apply your liniment, do whatever you ordinarily would do.

Then there are certain pains that are specific to the seated posture. If you never spend much time sitting cross-legged on the floor, there will be an adjustment period. Some discomfort is nearly inevitable. According to where the pain is, there are specific remedies. If the pain is in the leg or knees, check your pants. If they are tight or made of thick material, that could be the problem. Try to change it. Check your cushion, too. It should be about three inches in height when compressed. If the pain is around your waist, try loosening your belt. Loosen the waistband of your pants if that is necessary. If you experience pain in your lower back, your posture is probably at fault. Slouching will never be comfortable, so straighten up. Don't be tight or rigid, but do keep your spine erect. Pain in the neck or upper back has several sources. The first is improper hand position. Your hands should be resting comfortably in your lap. Don't pull them up to your waist. Relax your arms and your neck muscles. Don't let your head droop forward. Keep it up and aligned with the rest of the spine.

After you have made all these various adjustments, you may find you still have some lingering pain. If that is the case, try step two. Make the pain your object of meditation. Don't jump up and don't get excited. Just observe the pain mindfully. When the pain becomes demanding, you will find it pulling your attention off the breath. Don't fight back. Just let your attention slide easily over onto the simple sensation. Go into the pain fully. Don't block the experience. Explore the feeling. Get beyond your avoiding reaction and go into the pure sensations that lie below that.

You will discover that there are two things present. The first is the simple sensation—pain itself. Second is your resistance to that sensation. Resistance reaction is partly mental and partly physical. The physical part consists of tensing the muscles in and around the painful area. Relax those muscles. Take them one by one and relax each one very thoroughly. This step alone will probably diminish the pain significantly. Then go after the mental side of the resistance. Just as you are tensing physically, you are also tensing psychologically. You are clamping down mentally on the sensation of pain, trying to screen it off and reject it from consciousness. The rejection is a wordless "I don't like this feeling" or "go away" attitude. It is very subtle. But it is there, and you can find it if you really look. Locate it and relax that, too.

That last part is more subtle. There are really no human words to describe this action precisely. The best way to get a handle on it is by analogy. Examine what you did to those tight muscles and transfer that same action over to the mental sphere; relax the mind in the same way that you relax the body. Buddhism recognizes that body and mind are tightly linked. This is so true that many people will not see this as a two-step procedure. For them to relax the body is to relax the mind and vice versa. These people will experience the entire relaxation, mental and physical, as a single process. In any case, just let go completely until your awareness slows down past that barrier of resistance and relaxes into the pure flowing sensation beneath. The resistance was a barrier that you yourself erected. It was a gap, a sense of distance between self and others. It was a borderline between "me" and "the pain." Dissolve that barrier, and separation vanishes. You slow down into that sea of surging sensation, and you merge with the pain. You become the pain. You watch its ebb and flow and something surprising happens. It no longer hurts. Suffering is gone. Only the pain remains, an experience, nothing more. The "me" who was being hurt has gone. The result is freedom from pain.

This is an incremental process. In the beginning, you can expect to succeed with small pains and be defeated by big ones. Like most of our skills, it grows with practice. The more you practice, the more pain you can handle. Please understand fully: There is no masochism being advocated here. Self-mortification is not the point. This is an exercise in awareness, not in self-torture. If the pain becomes excruciating, go ahead and move, but move slowly and mindfully. Observe your movements. See how it feels to move. Watch what it does to the pain. Watch the pain diminish. Try not to move too much, though. The less you move, the easier it is to remain fully mindful. New meditators sometimes say they have trouble remaining mindful when pain is present. This difficulty stems from a misunderstanding. These students are conceiving mindfulness as something distinct from the experience of pain. It is not. Mindfulness never exists by itself. It always has some object, and one object is as good as another. Pain is a mental state. You can be mindful of pain just as you are mindful of breathing.

The rules we covered in chapter 4 apply to pain just as they apply to any other mental state. You must be careful not to reach beyond the sensation and not to fall short of it. Don't add anything to it, and don't miss any part of it. Don't muddy the pure experience with concepts or pictures or discursive thinking. And keep your awareness right in the present time, right with the pain, so that you won't miss its beginning or its end. Pain not viewed in the clear light of mindfulness gives rise to emotional reactions like fear, anxiety, or anger. If it is properly viewed, we have no such reaction. It will be just sensation, just simple energy. Once you have learned this technique with physical pain, you can then generalize it to the rest of your life. You can use it on any unpleasant sensation. What works on pain will work on anxiety or chronic depression as well. This technique is one of life's most useful and applicable skills. It is patience.

PROBLEM 2: LEGS GOING TO SLEEP

It is very common for beginners to have their legs fall asleep or go numb during meditation. They are simply not accustomed to the cross-legged posture. Some people get very anxious about this. They feel they must get up and move around. A few are completely convinced that they will get gangrene from lack of circulation. Numbness in the leg is nothing to worry about. It is caused by nerve pinch, not by lack of circulation. You can't damage the tissues of your legs by sitting. So relax. When your legs fall asleep in meditation, just mindfully observe the phenomenon. Examine what it feels like. It may be sort of uncomfortable, but it is not painful unless you tense up. Just stay calm and watch it. It does not matter if your legs go numb and stay that way for the whole period. After you have meditated for some time, that numbness will gradually disappear. Your body simply adjusts to daily practice. Then you can sit for very long sessions with no numbness whatsoever.

Problem 3: Odd Sensations

People experience all manner of varied phenomena in meditation. Some people get itches. Others feel tingling, deep relaxation, a feeling of lightness, or a floating sensation. You may feel yourself growing or shrinking or rising up in the air. Beginners often get quite excited over such sensations. Don't worry, you are not likely to levitate any time soon. As relaxation sets in, the nervous system simply begins to pass sensory signals more efficiently. Large amounts of previously blocked sensory data can pour through, giving rise to all kinds of unique sensations. It does not signify anything in particular. It is just sensation. So simply employ the normal technique. Watch it come up and watch it pass away. Don't get involved.

Problem 4: Drowsiness

It is quite common to experience drowsiness during meditation. You become very calm and relaxed. That is exactly what is supposed to happen. Unfortunately, we ordinarily experience this lovely state only when we are falling asleep, and we associate it with that process. So naturally, you begin to drift off. When you find this happening, apply your mindfulness to the state of drowsiness itself. Drowsiness has certain definite characteristics. It does certain things to your thought process. Find out what. It has certain bodily feelings associated with it. Locate those.

This inquisitive awareness is the direct opposite of drowsiness, and will evaporate it. If it does not, then you should suspect a physical cause of your sleepiness. Search that out and handle it. If you have just eaten a large meal, that could be the cause. It is best to eat lightly if you are about to meditate. Or wait an hour after a big meal. And don't overlook the obvious either. If you have been out hauling bricks all day, you are naturally going to be tired. The same is true if you only got a few hours of sleep the night before. Take care of your body's physical needs. Then meditate. Do not give in to sleepiness. Stay awake and mindful, for sleep and meditative concentration are diametrically opposed experiences. You will not gain any new insight from sleep but only from meditation. If you are very sleepy, then take a deep breath and hold it as long as you can. Then breathe out slowly. Take another deep breath again, hold it as long as you can, and breathe out slowly. Repeat this exercise until your body warms up and sleepiness fades away. Then return to your breath.

Problem 5: Inability to Concentrate

An overactive, jumping attention is something that everybody experiences from time to time. It is generally handled by the techniques presented in the chapter on distractions. You should also be informed, however, that there are certain external factors that contribute to this phenomenon. And these are best handled by simple adjustments in your schedule. Mental images are powerful entities. They can remain in the mind for long periods. All of the storytelling arts are direct manipulation of such material, and if the writer has done his job well, the characters and images presented will have a powerful and lingering effect on the mind. If you have been to the best movie of the year, the meditation that follows is going to be full of those images. If you are halfway through the scariest horror novel you ever read, your meditation is going to be full of monsters. So switch the order of events. Do your meditation first. Then read or go to the movies.

Another influential factor is your own emotional state. If there is some real conflict in your life, that agitation will carry over into meditation. Try to resolve your immediate daily conflicts before meditation when you can. Your life will run more smoothly, and you won't be pondering uselessly in your practice. But don't use this advice as a way to avoid meditation. Sometimes you can't resolve every issue before you sit. Just go ahead and sit anyway. Use your meditation to let go of all the egocentric attitudes that keep you trapped within your own limited viewpoint. Your problems will resolve much more easily thereafter. And then there are those days when it seems that the mind will never rest, but you can't locate any apparent cause. Remember the cyclic alternation we spoke of earlier. Meditation goes in cycles. You have good days and you have bad days.

Vipassana meditation is primarily an exercise in awareness. Emptying the mind is not as important as being mindful of what the mind is doing. If you are frantic and you can't do a thing to stop it, just observe. It is all you. The result will be one more step forward in your journey of self-exploration. Above all, don't get frustrated over the nonstop chatter of your mind. That babble is just one more thing to be mindful of.

Problem 6: Boredom

It is difficult to imagine anything more inherently boring than sitting still for an hour with nothing to do but feel the air going in and out of your nose. You are going to run into boredom repeatedly in your meditation. Everybody does. Boredom is a mental state and should be treated as such. A few simple strategies will help you to cope.

Tactic A: Reestablish true mindfulness

If the breath seems an exceedingly dull thing to observe over and over, you may rest assured of one thing: you have ceased to observe the process with true mindfulness. Mindfulness is never boring. Look again. Don't assume that you know what breath is. Don't take it for granted that you have already seen everything there is to see. If you do, you are conceptualizing the process. You are not observing its living reality. When you are clearly mindful of the breath or of anything else, it is never boring. Mindfulness looks at everything with the eyes of a child, with a sense of wonder. Mindfulness sees every moment as if it were the first and the only moment in the universe. So look again.

Tactic B: Observe your mental state

Look at your state of boredom mindfully. What is boredom? Where is boredom? What does it feel like? What are its mental components? Does it have any physical feeling? What does it do to your thought process? Take a fresh look at boredom, as if you have never experienced that state before.

PROBLEM 7: FEAR

States of fear sometimes arise during meditation for no discernible reason. It is a common phenomenon, and there can be a number of causes. You may be experiencing the effect of something repressed long ago. Remember, thoughts arise first in the unconscious. The emotional contents of a thought complex often leak through into your conscious awareness long before the thought itself surfaces. If you sit through the fear, the memory itself may bubble up to a point where you can endure it. Or you may be dealing directly with the fear that we all fear: "fear of the unknown." At some point in your meditation career you will be struck with the seriousness of what you are actually doing. You are tearing down the wall of illusion you have always used to explain life to yourself and to shield yourself from the intense flame of reality. You are about to meet ultimate truth face to face. That is scary. But it has to be dealt with eventually. Go ahead and dive right in.

A third possibility: the fear that you are feeling may be self-generated. It may be arising out of unskillful concentration. You may have set an unconscious program to "examine what comes up." Thus, when a frightening fantasy arises, concentration locks onto it, and the fantasy feeds on the energy of your attention and grows. The real problem here is that mindfulness is weak. If mindfulness was strongly developed, it would notice this switch of attention as soon as it occurred and handle the situation in the usual manner. No matter what the source of your fear, mindfulness is the cure. Observe the fear exactly as it is. Don't cling to it. Just watch it rising and growing. Study its effect. See how it makes you feel and how it affects your body. When you find yourself in the grip of horror fantasies, simply observe those mindfully. Watch the pictures as pictures. See memories as memories. Observe the emotional reactions that come along and know them for what they are. Stand aside from the process and don't get involved. Treat the whole dynamic as if you were a curious bystander. Most important, don't fight the situation. Don't try to repress the memories or the feelings or the fantasies. Just step out of the way and let the whole mess bubble up and flow past. It can't hurt you. It is just memory. It is only fantasy. It is nothing but fear.

When you let fear run its course in the arena of conscious attention, it won't sink back into the unconscious. It won't come back to haunt you later. It will be gone for good.

PROBLEM 8: AGITATION

Restlessness is often a cover-up for some deeper experience taking place in the unconscious. We humans are great at repressing things. Rather than confronting some unpleasant thought we experience, we try to bury it so we won't have to deal with the issue. Unfortunately, we usually don't succeed, at least not fully. We hide the thought, but the mental energy we use to cover it up sits there and boils. The result is that sense of unease that we call agitation or restlessness. There is nothing you can put your finger on. But you don't feel at ease. You can't relax. When this uncomfortable state arises in meditation, just observe it. Don't let it rule you. Don't jump up and run off. And don't struggle with it and try to make it go away. Just let it be there and watch it closely. Then the repressed material will eventually surface, and you will find out what you have been worrying about.

The unpleasant experience that you have been trying to avoid could be almost anything: guilt, greed, or other problems. It could be low-grade pain or subtle sickness or approaching illness. Whatever it is, let it arise and look at it mindfully. If you just sit still and observe your agitation, it will eventually pass. Sitting through restlessness is a little breakthrough in your meditation career. It will teach you a lot. You will find that agitation is actually rather a superficial mental state. It is inherently ephemeral. It comes and it goes. It has no real grip on you at all.

PROBLEM 9: TRYING TOO HARD

Advanced meditators are generally found to be pretty jovial people. They possess one of the most valuable of all human treasures, a sense of humor. It is not the superficial witty repartee of the talk show host. It is a real sense of humor. They can laugh at their own human failures. They can chuckle at personal disasters. Beginners in meditation are often much too serious for their own good. It is important to learn to loosen up in your session, to relax in your meditation. You need to learn to watch objectively whatever happens. You can't do that if you are tensed and striving, taking it all so very, very seriously.

New meditators are often overly eager for results. They are full of enormous and inflated expectations. They jump right in and expect incredible results in no time flat. They push. They tense. They sweat and strain, and it is all so terribly, terribly grim and solemn. This state of tension is the antithesis of mindfulness. Naturally, they achieve little. Then they decide that this meditation is not so exciting after all. It did not give them what they wanted. They chuck it aside. It should be pointed out that you learn about meditation only by meditating. You learn what meditation is all about and where it leads only through direct experience of the thing itself. Therefore the beginner does not know where he is headed because he has developed little sense of where his practice is leading.

The novice's expectation is naturally unrealistic and uninformed. Newcomers to meditation expect all the wrong things, and those expectations do no good at all. They get in the way. Trying too hard leads to rigidity and unhappiness, to guilt and self-condemnation. When you are trying too hard, your effort becomes mechanical, and that defeats mindfulness before it even gets started. You are well advised to drop all that. Drop your expectations and straining. Simply meditate with a steady and balanced effort. Enjoy your meditation and don't load yourself down with sweat and struggles. Just be mindful. The meditation itself will take care of the future.

Problem 10: Discouragement

The upshot of pushing too hard is frustration. You are in a state of tension. You get nowhere. You realize that you are not making the progress you expected, so you get discouraged. You feel like a failure. It is all a very natural cycle, but a totally avoidable one. Striving after unrealistic expectations is the source. Nevertheless, it is a common enough syndrome and, in spite of all the best advice, you may find it happening to you. There is a solution. If you find yourself discouraged, just observe your state of mind clearly. Don't add anything to it. Just watch it. A sense of failure is only another ephemeral emotional reaction. If you get involved, it feeds on your energy and it grows. If you simply stand aside and watch it, it passes away.

If you are discouraged over your perceived failure in meditation, that is especially easy to deal with. You feel you have failed in your practice. You have failed to be mindful. Simply become mindful of that sense of failure. You have just reestablished your mindfulness with that single step. The reason for your sense of failure is nothing but a memory. There is no such thing as failure in meditation. There are setbacks and difficulties. But there is no failure unless you give up entirely. Even if you have spent twenty solid years getting nowhere, you can be mindful at any second you choose. It is your decision. Regretting is only one more way of being unmindful. The instant that you realize that you have been unmindful, that realization itself is an act of mindfulness. So continue the process. Don't get sidetracked by an emotional reaction.

Problem 11: Resistance to Meditation

There are times when you don't feel like meditating. The very idea seems obnoxious. Missing a single practice session is scarcely important, but it very easily becomes a habit. It is wiser to push on through the resistance. Go sit anyway. Observe this feeling of aversion. In most cases it is a passing emotion, a flash in the pan that will evaporate right in front of your eyes. Five minutes after you sit down it is gone. In other cases it is due to some sour mood that day, and it lasts longer. Still, it does pass. And it is better to get rid of it in twenty or thirty minutes of meditation than to carry it around with you and let it ruin the rest of your day. At other times, resistance may be due to some difficulty you are having with the practice itself. You may or may not know what that difficulty is. If the problem is known, handle it by one of the techniques given in this book. Once the problem is gone, resistance will be gone. If the problem is unknown, then you are going to have to tough it out. Just sit through the resistance and observe it mindfully. It will pass. Then the problem causing it will probably bubble up in its wake, and you can deal with that.

If resistance to meditation is a common feature of your practice, then you should suspect some subtle error in your basic attitude. Meditation is not a ritual conducted in a particular posture. It is not a painful exercise or a period of enforced boredom. And it is not a grim, solemn obligation. Meditation is mindfulness. It is a new way of seeing and it is a form of play. Meditation is your friend. Come to regard it as such, and resistance will disappear like smoke on a summer breeze.

If you try all these possibilities and the resistance remains, then there may be a problem. Certain metaphysical snags that meditators sometimes encounter go beyond the scope of this book. It is not common for new meditators to hit these, but it can happen. Don't give up. Go and get help. Seek out qualified teachers of the vipassana style of meditation and ask them to help you resolve the situation. Such people exist for exactly that purpose.

PROBLEM 12: STUPOR OR DULLNESS

We have already discussed the sinking mind phenomenon. But there is a special route to that state you should watch out for. Mental dullness can result as an unwanted byproduct of deepening concentration. As your relaxation deepens, muscles loosen and nerve transmissions change. This produces a very calm and light feeling in the body. You feel very still and somewhat divorced from the body. This is a very pleasant state, and at first your concentration is quite good, nicely centered on the breath. As it continues, however, the pleasant feelings intensify and they distract your attention from the breath. You start to really enjoy the state and your mindfulness goes way down. Your attention winds up scattered, drifting listlessly through vague clouds of bliss. The result is a very unmindful state, sort of an ecstatic stupor. The cure, of course, is mindfulness. Mindfully observe these phenomena and they will dissipate. When blissful feelings arise accept them. There is no need to avoid them, but don't get wrapped up in them. They are physical feelings, so treat them as such. Observe feelings as feelings. Observe dullness as dullness. Watch them rise and watch them pass. Don't get involved.

You will have problems in meditation. Everybody does. You can treat them as terrible torments or as challenges to be overcome. If you regard them as burdens, your suffering will only increase. If you regard them as opportunities to learn and to grow, your spiritual prospects are unlimited.

11. Dealing with Distractions 1

At some time, every meditator encounters distractions during practice, and methods are needed to deal with them. Many useful strategies have been devised to get you back on track more quickly than that of trying to push your way through by sheer force of will. Concentration and mindfulness go hand in hand. Each one complements the other. If either one is weak, the other will eventually be affected. Bad days are usually characterized by poor concentration. Your mind just keeps floating around. You need a method of reestablishing your concentration, even in the face of mental adversity. Luckily, you have it. In fact, you can choose from an array of traditional practical maneuvers.

Maneuver 1: Time Gauging

The first technique has been covered in an earlier chapter. A distraction has pulled you away from the breath, and you suddenly realize that you've been daydreaming. The trick is to pull all the way out of whatever has captured you, to break its hold on you completely so you can go back to the breath with full attention. You do this by gauging the length of time that you were distracted. This is not a precise calculation. You don't need a precise figure, just a rough estimate. You can measure it in minutes, or by significant thoughts. Just say to yourself, "OK, I have been distracted for about two minutes," or "since the dog started barking," or "since I started thinking about money." When you first start practicing this technique, you will do it by talking to yourself. Once the habit is well established, you can drop that, and the action becomes wordless and very quick. The whole idea, remember, is to pull out of the distraction and get back to the breath. You pull out of the thought by making it the object of inspection just long enough to glean from it a rough approximation of its duration. The interval itself is not important. Once you are free of the distraction, drop the whole thing and go back to the breath. Do not get hung up in the estimate.

Maneuver 2: Deep Breaths

When your mind is wild and agitated, you can often reestablish mindfulness with a few quick deep breaths. Pull the air in strongly and let it out the same way. This increases the sensation inside the nostrils and makes it easier to focus. Make a strong act of will and apply some force to your attention. Concentration can be forced into growth, so you will probably find your full attention settling nicely back on the breath.

Maneuver 3: Counting

Counting the breaths as they pass is a highly traditional procedure. Some schools of practice teach this activity as their primary tactic. Vipassana uses it as an auxiliary technique for reestablishing mindfulness and for strengthening concentration. As we discussed in chapter 5, you can count breaths in a number of different ways. Remember to keep your attention on the breath. You will probably notice a change after you have done your counting. The breath slows down, or it becomes very light and refined. This is a physiological signal that concentration has become well established. At this point, the breath is usually so light or so fast and gentle that you can't clearly distinguish the inhalation from the exhalation. They seem to blend into each other. You can then count both of them as a single cycle. Continue your counting process, but only up to a count of five, covering the same five-breath sequence, then start over. When counting becomes a bother, go on to the next step. Drop the numbers and forget about the concepts of inhalation and exhalation. Just dive right in to the pure sensation of breathing. Inhalation blends into exhalation. One breath blends into the next in a never-ending cycle of pure, smooth flow.

Maneuver 4: The In-Out Method

This is an alternative to counting, and it functions in much the same manner. Just direct your attention to the breath and mentally tag each cycle with the words, "Inhalation . . . exhalation," or "In . . . out." Continue the process until you no longer need these concepts, and then throw them away.

Maneuver 5: Canceling One Thought with Another

Some thoughts just won't go away. We humans are obsessional beings. It's one of our biggest problems. We tend to lock on to things like sexual fantasies and worries and ambitions. We feed those thought complexes over years of time and give them plenty of exercise by playing with them in every spare moment. Then when we sit down to meditate, we order them to go away and leave us alone. It is scarcely surprising that they don't obey. Persistent thoughts like these require a direct approach, a full-scale frontal attack.

Buddhist psychology has developed a distinct system of classification. Rather than dividing thoughts into classes like "good" and "bad," Buddhist thinkers prefer to regard them as "skillful" versus "unskillful." An unskillful thought is one connected with greed, hatred, or delusion. These are the thoughts that the mind most easily builds into obsessions. They are unskillful in the sense that they lead you away from the goal of liberation. Skillful thoughts, on the other hand, are those connected with generosity, compassion, and wisdom. They are skillful in the sense that they may be used as specific remedies for unskillful thoughts, and thus can assist you in moving toward liberation.

You cannot condition liberation. It is not a state built out of thoughts. Nor can you condition the personal qualities that liberation produces. Thoughts of benevolence can produce a semblance of benevolence, but it's not the real item. It will break down under pressure. Thoughts of compassion produce only superficial compassion. Therefore, these skillful thoughts will not, in themselves, free you from the trap. They are skillful only if applied as antidotes to the poison of unskillful thoughts. Thoughts of generosity can temporarily cancel greed. They kick it under the rug long enough for mindfulness to do its work unhindered. Then, when mindfulness has penetrated to the roots of the ego process, greed evaporates and true generosity arises.

This principle can be used on a day-to-day basis in your own meditation. If a particular sort of obsession is troubling you, you can cancel it out by generating its opposite. Here is an example: If you absolutely hate Charlie, and his scowling face keeps popping into your mind, try directing a stream of love and friendliness toward Charlie, or try contemplating his good qualities. You probably will get rid of the immediate mental image. Then you can get on with the job of meditation.

Sometimes this tactic alone doesn't work. The obsession is simply too strong. In this case you've got to weaken its hold on you somewhat before you can successfully balance it out. Here is where guilt, one of man's most misbegotten emotions, finally serves a purpose. Take a good strong look at the emotional response you are trying to get rid of. Actually ponder it. See how it makes you feel. Look at what it is doing to your life, your happiness, your health, and your relationships. Try to see how it makes you appear to others. Look at the way it is hindering your progress toward liberation. The Pali scriptures urge you to do this very thoroughly indeed. They advise you to work up the same sense of disgust and humiliation that you would feel if you were forced to walk around with the carcass of a dead and decaying animal tied around your neck. Real loathing is what you are after. This step may end the problem all by itself. If it doesn't, then balance out the lingering remainder of the obsession by once again generating its opposite emotion.

Thoughts of greed cover everything connected with desire, from outright avarice for material gain, all the way to a subtle need to be respected as a moral person. Thoughts of hatred run the gamut from pettiness to murderous rage. Delusion covers everything from daydreaming to full-blown hallucinations. Generosity cancels greed. Benevolence and compassion cancel hatred. You can find a specific antidote for any troubling thought if you just think about it awhile.

MANEUVER 6: RECALLING YOUR PURPOSE

There are times when things pop into your mind, apparently at random. Words, phrases, or whole sentences jump up out of the unconscious for no discernible reason. Objects appear. Pictures flash on and off. This is an unsettling experience. Your mind feels like a flag flapping in a stiff wind. It washes back and forth like waves in the ocean. Often, at times like this, it is enough just to remember why you are there. You can say to yourself, "I'm not sitting here just to waste my time with these thoughts. I'm here to focus my mind on the breath, which is universal and common to all living beings." Sometimes your mind will settle down, even before you complete this recitation. Other times you may have to repeat it several times before you refocus on the breath.

These techniques can be used singly, or in combinations. Properly employed, they constitute quite an effective arsenal for your battle against the monkey mind.

12. Dealing with Distractions 2

So there you are, meditating beautifully. Your body is totally immobile, and your mind is totally still. You just glide right along following the flow of the breath, in, out, in, out . . . calm, serene, and concentrated. Everything is perfect. And then, all of a sudden, something totally different pops into your mind: "I sure wish I had an ice cream cone." That's a distraction, obviously. That's not what you are supposed to be doing. You notice that, and you drag yourself back to the breath, back to the smooth flow, in, out, in . . . And then: "Did I ever pay that gas bill?" Another distraction. You notice that one, and you haul yourself back to the breath. In, out, in, out, in . . . "That new science fiction movie is out. Maybe I can go see it Tuesday night. No, not Tuesday, got too much to do on Wednesday. Thursday's better . . ." Another distraction. You pull yourself out of that one, and back you go to the breath, except that you never quite get there, because before you do, that little voice in your head says, "My back is killing me." And on and on it goes, distraction after distraction, seemingly without end.

What a bother. But this is what it is all about. These distractions are actually the whole point. The key is to learn to deal with these things. Learning to notice them without being trapped in them. That's what we are here for. This mental wandering is unpleasant, to be sure. But it is your mind's normal mode of operation. Don't think of it as the enemy. It is just the simple reality. And if you want to change something, the first thing you have to do is to see it the way it is.

When you first sit down to concentrate on the breath, you will be struck by how incredibly busy the mind actually is. It jumps and jibbers. It veers and bucks. It chases itself around in constant circles. It chatters. It thinks. It fantasizes and daydreams. Don't be upset about that. It's natural. When your mind wanders from the subject of meditation, just observe the distraction mindfully.

When we speak of a distraction in insight meditation, we are speaking of any preoccupation that pulls the attention off the breath. This brings up a new, major rule for your meditation: When any mental state arises strongly enough to distract you from the object of meditation, switch your attention to the distraction briefly. Make the distraction a temporary object of meditation. Please note the word *temporary*. It's quite important. We are not advising that you switch horses in midstream. We do not expect you to adopt a whole new object of meditation every three seconds. The breath will always remain your primary focus. You switch your attention to the distraction only long enough to notice certain specific things about it. What is it? How strong is it? And how long does it last?

As soon as you have wordlessly answered these questions, you are through with your examination of that distraction, and you return your attention to the breath. Here again, please note the operant term, *wordlessly*. These questions are not an invitation to more mental chatter. That would be moving you in the wrong direction, toward more thinking. We want you to move away from thinking, back to a direct, wordless, and nonconceptual experience of the breath. These questions are designed to free you from the distraction and give you insight into its nature, not to get you more thoroughly stuck in it. They will tune you in to what is distracting you and help you get rid of it—all in one step.

Here is the problem: When a distraction, or any mental state, arises in the mind, it blossoms forth first in the unconscious. Only a moment later does it rise to the conscious mind. That split-second difference is quite important, because it is time enough for grasping to occur. Grasping occurs almost instantaneously, and it takes place first in the unconscious. Thus, by the time the grasping rises to the level of conscious recognition, we have already begun to lock on to it. It is quite natural for us to simply continue that process, getting more and more tightly stuck in the distraction as we continue to view it. We are, by this time, quite definitely thinking the thought rather than just viewing it with bare attention. The whole sequence takes place in a flash. This presents us with a problem. By the time we become consciously aware of a distraction, we are already, in a sense, stuck in it.

Our three questions, "What is it? How strong is it? And, how long does it last?" are a clever remedy for this particular malady. In order to answer these questions, we must ascertain the quality of the distraction. To do that, we must divorce ourselves from it, take a mental step back from it, disengage from it, and view it objectively. We must stop thinking the thought or feeling the feeling in order to view it as an object of inspection. This very process is an exercise in *mindfulness*, uninvolved, detached awareness. The hold of the distraction is thus broken, and mindfulness is back in control. At this point, mindfulness makes a smooth transition back to its primary focus, and we return to the breath.

When you first begin to practice this technique, you will probably have to do it with words. You will ask your questions in words, and get answers in words. It won't be long, however, before you can dispense with the formality of words altogether. Once the mental habits are in place, you simply note the distraction, note the qualities of the distraction, and return to the breath. It's a totally nonconceptual process, and it's very quick. The distraction itself can be anything: a sound, a sensation, an emotion, a fantasy, anything at all. Whatever it is, don't try to repress it. Don't try to force it out of your mind. There's no need for that. Just observe it mindfully with bare attention. Examine the distraction wordlessly, and it will pass away by itself. You will find your attention drifting effortlessly back to the breath. And do not condemn yourself for having been distracted. Distractions are natural. They come and they go.

Despite this piece of sage counsel, you're going to find yourself condemning anyway. That's natural too. Just observe the process of condemnation as another distraction, and then return to the breath.

Watch the sequence of events: Breathing. Breathing. Distracting thought arising. Frustration arising over the distracting thought. You condemn yourself for being distracted. You notice the self-condemnation. You return to the breathing. Breathing. Breathing. It's really a very natural, smooth-flowing cycle, if you do it correctly. The trick, of course, is patience. If you can learn to observe these distractions without getting involved, it's all very easy. You just glide through the distraction, and your attention returns to the breath quite easily. Of course, the very same distraction may pop up a moment later. If it does, just observe that mindfully. If you are dealing with an old, established thought pattern, this can go on happening for quite a while, sometimes years. Don't get upset. This too is natural. Just observe the distraction and return to the breath. Don't fight with these distracting thoughts. Don't strain or struggle. It's a waste. Every bit of energy that you apply to that resistance goes into the thought complex and makes it all the stronger. So don't try to force such thoughts out of your mind. It's a battle you can never win. Just observe the distraction mindfully and it will eventually go away. It's very strange, but the more bare attention you pay to such disturbances, the weaker they get. Observe them long enough and often enough with bare attention, and they fade away forever. Fight with them and they gain strength. Watch them with detachment and they wither.

Mindfulness is a function that disarms distractions, in the same way that a munitions expert might defuse a bomb. Weak distractions are disarmed by a single glance. Shine the light of awareness on them and they evaporate instantly, never to return. Deep-seated, habitual thought patterns require constant mindfulness repeatedly applied over whatever time period it takes to break their hold. Distractions are really paper tigers. They have no power of their own. They need to be fed constantly, or else they die. If you refuse to feed them by your own fear, anger, and greed, they fade.

Mindfulness is the most important aspect of meditation. It is the primary thing that you are trying to cultivate. So there is really no need at all to struggle against distractions. The crucial thing is to be mindful of what is occurring, not to control what is occurring. Remember, concentration is a tool. It is secondary to bare attention. From the point of view of mindfulness, there is really no such thing as a distraction. Whatever arises in the mind is viewed as just one more opportunity to cultivate mindfulness. Breath, remember, is an arbitrary focus, and it is used as our primary object of attention. Distractions are used as secondary objects of attention. They are certainly as much a part of reality as breath. It actually makes rather little difference what the object of mindfulness is. You can be mindful of the breath, or you can be mindful of the distraction. You can be mindful of the fact that your mind is still, and your concentration is strong, or you can be mindful of the fact that your concentration is in ribbons and your mind is in an absolute shambles. It's all mindfulness. Just maintain that mindfulness, and concentration eventually will follow.

The purpose of meditation is not to concentrate on the breath, without interruption, forever. That by itself would be a useless goal. The purpose of meditation is not to achieve a perfectly still and serene mind. Although a lovely state, it doesn't lead to liberation by itself. The purpose of meditation is to achieve uninterrupted mindfulness. Mindfulness, and only mindfulness, produces enlightenment.

Distractions come in all sizes, shapes, and flavors. Buddhist philosophy has organized them into categories. One of them is the category of hindrances. They are called hindrances because they block your development of both components of meditation, mindfulness and concentration. A bit of caution on this term: The word "hindrances" carries a negative connotation, and indeed these are states of mind we want to eradicate. That does not mean, however, that they are to be repressed, avoided, or condemned.

Let's use greed as an example. We wish to avoid prolonging any state of greed that arises, because a continuation of that state leads to bondage and sorrow. That does not mean we try to toss the thought out of the mind when it appears. We simply refuse to encourage it to stay. We let it come, and we let it go. When greed is first observed with bare attention, no value judgments are made. We simply stand back and watch it arise. The whole dynamic of greed from start to finish is simply observed in this way. We don't help it, or hinder it, or interfere with it in the slightest. It stays as long as it stays. And we learn as much about it as we can while it is there. We watch what greed does. We watch how it troubles us and how it burdens others. We notice how it keeps us perpetually unsatisfied, forever in a state of unfulfilled longing. From this firsthand experience, we ascertain at a gut level that greed is an unskillful way to run your life. There is nothing theoretical about this realization.

All of the hindrances are dealt with in the same way, and we will look at them here one by one.

Desire

Let us suppose you have been distracted by some nice experience in meditation. It could be a pleasant fantasy or a thought of pride. It might be a feeling of self-esteem. It might be a thought of love or even the physical sensation of bliss that comes with the meditation experience itself. Whatever it is, what follows is the state of desire—desire to obtain whatever you have been thinking about, or desire to prolong the experience you are having. No matter what its nature, you should handle desire in the following manner. Notice the thought or sensation as it arises. Notice the mental state of desire that accompanies it as a separate thing. Notice the exact extent or degree of that desire. Then notice how long it lasts and when it finally disappears. When you have done that, return your attention to breathing.

Aversion

Suppose that you have been distracted by some negative experience. It could be something you fear or some nagging worry. It might be guilt or depression or pain. Whatever the actual substance of the thought or sensation, you find yourself rejecting or repressing—trying to avoid it, resist it, or deny it. The handling here is essentially the same. Watch the arising of the thought or sensation. Notice the state of rejection that comes with it. Gauge the extent or degree of that rejection. See how long it lasts and when it fades away. Then return your attention to your breath.

Lethargy

Lethargy comes in various grades and intensities, ranging from slight drowsiness to utter torpor. We are talking about a mental state here, not a physical one. Sleepiness or physical fatigue is something quite different and, in the Buddhist system of classification, it would be categorized as a physical feeling. Mental lethargy is closely related to aversion in that it is one of the mind's clever little ways of avoiding those issues it finds unpleasant. Lethargy is a sort of turnoff of the mental apparatus, a dulling of sensory and cognitive acuity. It is an enforced stupidity pretending to be sleep.

This can be a tough one to deal with, because its presence is directly contrary to the employment of mindfulness. Lethargy is nearly the reverse of mindfulness. Nevertheless, mindfulness is the cure for this hindrance, too, and the handling is the same. Note the state of drowsiness when it arises, and note its extent or degree. Note when it arises, how long it lasts, and when it passes away. The only thing special here is the importance of catching the phenomenon early. You have got to get it right at its conception and apply liberal doses of pure awareness right away. If you let it get a start, its growth will probably outpace your mindfulness power. When lethargy wins, the result is the sinking mind, or even sleep.

Agitation

States of restlessness and worry are expressions of mental agitation. Your mind keeps darting around, refusing to settle on any one thing. You may keep running over and over the same issues. But even here, an unsettled feeling is the predominant component. The mind refuses to settle anywhere. It jumps around constantly. The cure for this condition is the same basic sequence. Restlessness imparts a certain feeling to consciousness. You might call it a flavor or texture. Whatever you call it, that unsettled feeling is there as a definable characteristic. Look for it. Once you have spotted it, note how much of it is present. Note when it arises. Watch how long it lasts, and see when it fades away. Then return your attention to the breath.

Doubt

Doubt has its own distinct feeling in consciousness. The Pali texts describe it very nicely. It's the feeling of a man stumbling through a desert and arriving at an unmarked crossroad. Which road should he take? There is no way to tell. So he just stands there vacillating. One of the common forms this takes in meditation is an inner dialogue something like this: "What am I doing just sitting like this? Am I really getting anything out of this at all? Oh! Sure I am. This is good for me. The book said so. No, that is crazy. This is a waste of time. No, I won't give up. I said I was going to do this, and I am going to do it. Or am I just being stubborn? I don't know. I just don't know." Don't get stuck in this trap. It is just another hindrance. Another of the mind's little smoke screens to keep you from actually becoming aware of what is happening. To handle doubt, simply become aware of this mental state of wavering as an object of inspection. Don't be trapped in it. Back out of it and look at it. See how strong it is. See when it comes and how long it lasts. Then watch it fade away, and go back to the breathing.

This is the general pattern you will use on any distraction that arises. By distraction, remember we mean any mental state that arises to impede your meditation. Some of these are quite subtle. It is useful to list some of the possibilities. The negative states are pretty easy to spot: insecurity, fear, anger, depression, irritation, and frustration.

Craving and desire are a bit more difficult to spot because they can apply to things we normally regard as virtuous or noble. You can experience the desire to perfect yourself. You can feel craving for greater virtue. You can even develop an attachment to the bliss of the meditation experience itself. It is a bit hard to detach yourself from such noble feelings. In the end, though, it is just more greed. It is a desire for gratification and a clever way of ignoring the present-moment reality.

Trickiest of all, however, are those really positive mental states that come creeping into your meditation. Happiness, peace, inner contentment, sympathy, and compassion for all beings everywhere. These mental states are so sweet and so benevolent that you can scarcely bear to pry yourself loose from them. It makes you feel like a traitor to humanity. There is no need to feel this way. We are not advising you to reject these states of mind or to become heartless robots. We merely want you to see them for what they are. They are mental states. They come, and they go. They arise, and they pass away. As you continue your meditation, these states will arise more often. The trick is not to become attached to them. Just see each one as it comes up. See what it is, how strong it is, and how long it lasts. Then watch it drift away. It is all just more of the passing show of your own mental universe.

Just as breathing comes in stages, so do the mental states. Every breath has a beginning, a middle, and an end. Every mental state has a birth, a growth, and a decay. You should strive to see these stages clearly. This is no easy thing to do, however. As we have already noted, every thought and sensation begins first in the unconscious region of the mind and only later rises to consciousness. We generally become aware of such things only after they have arisen in the conscious realm and stayed there for some time. Indeed we usually become aware of distractions only when they have released their hold on us and are already on their way out. It is at this point that we are struck with that sudden realization that we have been somewhere, daydreaming, fantasizing, or whatever. Quite obviously this is far too late in the chain of events. We may call this phenomenon catching the lion by his tail, and it is an unskillful thing to do. Like confronting a dangerous beast, we must approach mental states head on. Patiently, we will learn to recognize them as they arise from progressively deeper levels of our conscious mind.

Since mental states arise first in the unconscious, to catch the arising of the mental state, you've got to extend your awareness down into this unconscious area. That is difficult, because you can't see what is going on down there, at least not in the same way you see a conscious thought. But you can learn to get a vague sense of movement and to operate by a sort of mental sense of touch. This comes with practice, and the ability is another of the effects of the deep calm of concentration. Concentration slows down the arising of these mental states and gives you time to feel each one arising out of the unconscious even before you see it in consciousness. Concentration helps you to extend your awareness down into that boiling darkness where thought and sensation begin.

As your concentration deepens, you gain the ability to see thoughts and sensations arising slowly, like separate bubbles, each distinct and with spaces between them. They bubble up in slow motion out of the unconscious. They stay a while in the conscious mind, and then they drift away.

The application of awareness to mental states is a precision operation. This is particularly true of feelings or sensation. It is very easy to overreach the sensation. That is, to add something to it above and beyond what is really there. It is equally easy to fall short of sensation, to get part of it but not all. The ideal that you are striving for is to experience each mental state fully, exactly the way it is, adding nothing to it and not missing any part of it. Let us use pain in the leg as an example. What is actually there is a pure, flowing sensation. It changes constantly, never the same from one moment to the next. It moves from one location to another, and its intensity surges up and down. Pain is not a thing. It is an event. There should be no concepts tacked on to it and none associated with it. A pure unobstructed awareness of this event will experience it simply as a flowing pattern of energy and nothing more. No thought and no rejection. Just energy.

Early on in our practice of meditation, we need to rethink our underlying assumptions regarding conceptualization. For most of us, we have earned high marks in school and in life for our ability to manipulate mental phenomena, or concepts, logically. Our careers, much of our success in everyday life, our happy relationships, we view as largely the result of our successful manipulation of concepts. In developing mindfulness, however, we temporarily suspend the conceptualization process and focus on the pure nature of mental phenomena. During meditation we are seeking to experience the mind at the preconceptual level.

But the human mind conceptualizes such occurrences as pain. You find yourself thinking of it as "the pain." That is a concept. It is a label, something added to the sensation itself. You find yourself building a mental image, a picture of the pain, seeing it as a shape. You may see a diagram of the leg with the pain outlined in some lovely color. This is very creative and terribly entertaining but not what we want. Those are concepts tacked on to the living reality. Most likely, you will probably find yourself thinking: "I have a pain in my leg." "I" is a concept. It is something extra added to the pure experience.

When you introduce "I" into the process, you are building a conceptual gap between the reality and the awareness viewing that reality. Thoughts such as "me," "my," or "mine" have no place in direct awareness. They are extraneous addenda, and insidious ones at that. When you bring "me" into the picture, you are identifying with the pain. That simply adds emphasis to it. If you leave "I" out of the operation, pain is not painful. It is just a pure surging energy flow. It can even be beautiful. If you find "I" insinuating itself in your experience of pain or indeed any other sensation, then just observe that mindfully. Pay bare attention to the phenomenon of personal identification with pain.

The general idea, however, is almost too simple. You want to really see each sensation, whether it is pain, bliss, or boredom. You want to experience that thing fully in its natural and unadulterated form. There is only one way to do this. Your timing has to be precise. Your awareness of each sensation must coordinate exactly with the arising of that sensation. If you catch it just a bit too late, you miss the beginning. You won't get all of it. If you hang on to any sensation past the time when it has faded away, then what you are holding on to is a memory. The thing itself is gone, and by holding on to that memory, you miss the arising of the next sensation. It is a very delicate operation. You've got to cruise along right here in the present, picking things up and letting things drop with no delays whatsoever. It takes a very light touch. Your relation to sensation should never be one of past or future but always of the simple and immediate now.

The human mind seeks to conceptualize phenomena, and it has developed a host of clever ways to do so. Every simple sensation will trigger a burst of conceptual thinking if you give the mind its way. Let us take hearing, for example. You are sitting in meditation and somebody in the next room drops a dish. The sounds strike your ear. Instantly you see a picture of that other room. You probably see a person dropping a dish, too. If this is a familiar environment, say your own home, you probably will have a 3-D technicolor mind movie of who did the dropping and which dish was dropped. This whole sequence presents itself to consciousness instantly. It just jumps out of the unconscious so bright and clear and compelling that it shoves everything else out of sight. What happens to the original sensation, the pure experience of hearing? It gets lost in the shuffle, completely overwhelmed and forgotten. We miss reality. We enter a world of fantasy.

Here is another example: You are sitting in meditation and a sound strikes your ear. It is just an indistinct noise, sort of a muffled crunch; it could be anything. What happens next will probably be something like this. "What was that? Who did that? Where did that come from? How far away was that? Is it dangerous?" And on and on you go, getting no answers but your fantasy projection.

Conceptualization is an insidiously clever process. It creeps into your experience, and it simply takes over. When you hear a sound in meditation, pay bare attention to the experience of hearing. That and that only. What is really happening is so utterly simple that we can and do miss it altogether. Sound waves are striking the ear in a certain unique pattern. Those waves are being translated into electrical impulses within the brain, and those impulses present a sound pattern to consciousness. That is all. No pictures. No mind movies. No concepts. No interior dialogues about the question. Just noise. Reality is elegantly simple and unadorned. When you hear a sound, be mindful of the process of hearing. Everything else is just added chatter. Drop it. This same rule applies to every sensation, every emotion, every experience you may have. Look closely at your own experience. Dig down through the layers of mental bric-a-brac and see what is really there. You will be amazed how simple it is, and how beautiful.

There are times when a number of sensations may arise at once. You might have a thought of fear, a squeezing in the stomach, an aching back, and an itch on your left earlobe, all at the same time. Don't sit there in a quandary. Don't keep switching back and forth or wondering what to pick. One of them will be strongest. Just open yourself up, and the most insistent of these phenomena will intrude itself and demand your attention. So give it some attention just long

enough to see it fade away. Then return to your breathing. If another
one intrudes itself, let it in. When it is done, return to the breathing.

This process can be carried too far, however. Don't sit there looking for things to be mindful of. Keep your mindfulness on the breath
until something else steps in and pulls your attention away. When
you feel that happening, don't fight it. Let your attention flow naturally over to the distraction, and keep it there until the distraction
evaporates. Then return to breathing. Don't seek out other physical
or mental phenomena. Just return to breathing. Let them come to
you. There will be times when you drift off, of course. Even after
long practice you find yourself suddenly waking up, realizing you
have been off the track for some while. Don't get discouraged. Realize that you have been off the track for such and such a length of
time and go back to the breath. There is no need for any negative
reaction at all. The very act of realizing that you have been off the
track is an active awareness. It is an exercise of pure mindfulness
all by itself.

Mindfulness grows by the exercise of mindfulness. It is like exercising a muscle. Every time you work it, you pump it up just a little.
You make it a little stronger. The very fact that you have felt that
wake-up sensation means that you have just improved your mindfulness power. That means you win. Move back to the breathing
without regret. However, the regret is a conditioned reflex, and it
may come along anyway—another mental habit. If you find yourself
getting frustrated, feeling discouraged, or condemning yourself, just
observe that with bare attention. It is just another distraction. Give
it some attention and watch it fade away, and return to the breath.

The rules we have just reviewed can and should be applied
thoroughly to all of your mental states. You are going to find this
an utterly ruthless injunction. It is the toughest job that you will
ever undertake. You will find yourself relatively willing to apply this

technique to certain parts of your experience, and you will find yourself totally unwilling to use it on the other parts.

Meditation is a bit like mental acid. It eats away slowly at whatever you put it on. We humans are very odd beings. We like the taste of certain poisons, and we stubbornly continue to eat them even while they are killing us. Thoughts to which we are attached are poison. You will find yourself quite eager to dig some thoughts out by the roots while you jealously guard and cherish certain others. That is the human condition.

Vipassana meditation is not a game. Clear awareness is more than a pleasurable pastime. It is a road up and out of the quagmire in which we are all stuck, the swamp of our own desires and aversions. It is relatively easy to apply awareness to the nastier aspects of your existence. Once you have seen fear and depression evaporate under the hot, intense beacon of awareness, you will want to repeat that process. Those are the unpleasant mental states. They hurt. You want to get rid of those things because they bother you. It is a good deal harder to apply that same process to mental states that you cherish, like patriotism, or parental protectiveness, or true love. But it is just as necessary. Positive attachments hold you in the mud just as assuredly as negative attachments. You may rise above the mud far enough to breathe a bit more easily if you practice vipassana meditation with diligence. Vipassana meditation is the road to nibbana. And from the reports of those who have toiled their way to that lofty goal, it is well worth every effort involved.

13. *Mindfulness* (Sati)

$\mathcal{M}$indfulness is the English translation of the Pali word *sati. Sati* is an activity. What exactly is that? There can be no precise answer, at least not in words. Words are devised by the symbolic levels of the mind, and they describe those realities with which symbolic thinking deals. Mindfulness is presymbolic. It is not shackled to logic. Nevertheless, mindfulness can be experienced—rather easily—and it can be described, as long as you keep in mind that the words are only fingers pointing at the moon. They are not the moon itself. The actual experience lies beyond the words and above the symbols. Mindfulness could be described in completely different terms than will be used here, and each description could still be correct.

Mindfulness is a subtle process that you are using at this very moment. The fact that this process lies above and beyond words does not make it unreal—quite the reverse. Mindfulness is the reality that gives rise to words—the words that follow are simply pale shadows of reality. So it is important to understand that everything that follows here is analogy. It is not going to make perfect sense. It will always remain beyond verbal logic. But you can experience it. The meditation technique called vipassana (insight) that was introduced by the Buddha about twenty-five centuries ago is a set of mental activities specifically aimed at experiencing a state of uninterrupted mindfulness.

When you first become aware of something, there is a fleeting instant of pure awareness just before you conceptualize the thing, before you identify it. That is a state of awareness. Ordinarily, this state is short-lived. It is that flashing split second just as you focus your eyes on the thing, just as you focus your mind on the thing, just before you objectify it, clamp down on it mentally, and segregate it from the rest of existence. It takes place just before you start thinking about it—before your mind says, "Oh, it's a dog." That flowing, soft-focused moment of pure awareness is mindfulness. In that brief flashing mind-moment you experience a thing as an un-thing. You experience a softly flowing moment of pure experience that is interlocked with the rest of reality, not separate from it. Mindfulness is very much like what you see with your peripheral vision as opposed to the hard focus of normal or central vision. Yet this moment of soft, unfocused awareness contains a very deep sort of knowing that is lost as soon as you focus your mind and objectify the object into a thing. In the process of ordinary perception, the mindfulness step is so fleeting as to be unobservable. We have developed the habit of squandering our attention on all the remaining steps, focusing on the perception, cognizing the perception, labeling it, and most of all, getting involved in a long string of symbolic thought about it. That original moment of mindfulness is rapidly passed over. It is the purpose of vipassana meditation to train us to prolong that moment of awareness.

When this mindfulness is prolonged by using proper techniques, you find that this experience is profound and that it changes your entire view of the universe. This state of perception has to be learned, however, and it takes regular practice. Once you learn the technique, you will find that mindfulness has many interesting aspects.

THE CHARACTERISTICS OF MINDFULNESS

Mindfulness is mirror-thought. It reflects only what is presently happening and in exactly the way it is happening. There are no biases.

Mindfulness is nonjudgmental observation. It is that ability of the mind to observe without criticism. With this ability, one sees things without condemnation or judgment. One is surprised by nothing. One simply takes a balanced interest in things exactly as they are in their natural states. One does not decide and does not judge. One just observes. Please note that when we say, "One does not decide and does not judge," what we mean is that the meditator observes experiences very much like a scientist observing an object under a microscope without any preconceived notions, only to see the object exactly as it is. In the same way the meditator notices impermanence, unsatisfactoriness, and selflessness.

It is psychologically impossible for us to objectively observe what is going on within us if we do not at the same time accept the occurrence of our various states of mind. This is especially true with unpleasant states of mind. In order to observe our own fear, we must accept the fact that we are afraid. We can't examine our own depression without accepting it fully. The same is true for irritation and agitation, frustration, and all those other uncomfortable emotional states. You can't examine something fully if you are busy rejecting its existence. Whatever experience we may be having, mindfulness just accepts it. It is simply another of life's occurrences, just another thing to be aware of. No pride, no shame, nothing personal at stake—what is there is there.

Mindfulness is an impartial watchfulness. It does not take sides. It does not get hung up in what is perceived. It just perceives. Mindfulness does not get infatuated with the good mental states. It does not try to sidestep the bad mental states. There is no clinging to the pleasant, no fleeing from the unpleasant. Mindfulness treats all experiences equally, all thoughts equally, all feelings equally. Nothing is suppressed. Nothing is repressed. Mindfulness does not play favorites.

Mindfulness is nonconceptual awareness. Another English term for *sati* is "bare attention." It is not thinking. It does not get involved with thought or concepts. It does not get hung up on ideas or opinions or memories. It just looks. Mindfulness registers experiences, but it does not compare them. It does not label them or categorize them. It just observes everything as if it was occurring for the first time. It is not analysis that is based on reflection and memory. It is, rather, the direct and immediate experiencing of whatever is happening, without the medium of thought. It comes before thought in the perceptual process.

Mindfulness is present-moment awareness. It takes place in the here and now. It is the observance of what is happening right now, in the present. It stays forever in the present, perpetually on the crest of the ongoing wave of passing time. If you are remembering your second-grade teacher, that is memory. When you then become aware that you are remembering your second-grade teacher, that is mindfulness. If you then conceptualize the process and say to yourself, "Oh, I am remembering," that is thinking.

Mindfulness is nonegotistic alertness. It takes place without reference to self. With mindfulness one sees all phenomena without references to concepts like "me," "my," or "mine." For example, suppose there is pain in your left leg. Ordinary consciousness would say, "I have a pain." Using mindfulness, one would simply note the sensation as a sensation. One would not tack on that extra concept "I." Mindfulness stops one from adding anything to perception or subtracting anything from it. One does not enhance anything. One does not emphasize anything. One just observes exactly what is there—without distortion.

Mindfulness is awareness of change. It is observing the passing flow of experience. It is watching things as they are changing. It is seeing the birth, growth, and maturity of all phenomena. It is watching phenomena decay and die. Mindfulness is watching things moment by moment, continuously. It is observing all phenomena—physical, mental, or emotional—whatever is presently taking place in the mind. One just sits back and watches the show. Mindfulness is the observance of the basic nature of each passing phenomenon. It is watching the thing arising and passing away. It is seeing how that thing makes us feel and how we react to it. It is observing how it affects others. In mindfulness, one is an unbiased observer whose sole job is to keep track of the constantly passing show of the universe within.

Please note that last point. In mindfulness, one watches the universe within. The meditator who is developing mindfulness is not concerned with the external universe. It is there, but in meditation, one's field of study is one's own experience, one's thoughts, one's feelings, and one's perceptions. In meditation, one is one's own laboratory. The universe within has an enormous fund of information containing the reflection of the external world and much more. An examination of this material leads to total freedom.

Mindfulness is participatory observation. The meditator is both participant and observer at one and the same time. If one watches one's emotions or physical sensations, one is feeling them at that very same moment. Mindfulness is not an intellectual awareness. It is just awareness. The mirror-thought metaphor breaks down here. Mindfulness is objective, but it is not cold or unfeeling. It is the wakeful experience of life, an alert participation in the ongoing process of living.

Mindfulness is extremely difficult to define in words—not because it is complex, but because it is too simple and open. The same problem crops up in every area of human experience. The most basic concept is always the most difficult to pin down. Look at a dictionary and you will see a clear example. Long words generally have concise definitions, but short basic words like "the" and "be," can have definitions a page long. And in physics, the most difficult functions to describe are the most basic—those that deal with the most fundamental realities of quantum mechanics. Mindfulness is a presymbolic function. You can play with word symbols all day long and you will never pin it down completely. We can never fully express what it is. However, we can say what it does.

THREE FUNDAMENTAL ACTIVITIES

There are three fundamental activities of mindfulness. We can use these activities as functional definitions of the term: (a) mindfulness reminds us of what we are supposed to be doing, (b) it sees things as they really are, and (c) it sees the true nature of all phenomena. Let's examine these definitions in greater detail.

Mindfulness reminds you of what you are supposed to be doing

In meditation, you put your attention on one item. When your mind wanders from this focus, it is mindfulness that reminds you that your mind is wandering and what you are supposed to be doing. It is mindfulness that brings your mind back to the object of meditation. All of this occurs instantaneously and without internal dialogue. Mindfulness is not thinking. Repeated practice in meditation establishes this function as a mental habit that then carries over into the rest of your life. A serious meditator pays bare attention to occurrences all the time, day in, day out, whether formally sitting in meditation or not. This is a very lofty ideal toward which those who meditate may be working for a period of years or even decades. Our habit of getting stuck in thought is years old, and that habit will hang on in the most tenacious manner. The only way out is to be equally persistent in the cultivation of constant mindfulness. When mindfulness is present, you will notice when you become stuck in your thought patterns. It is that very noticing that allows you to back out of the thought process and free yourself from it. Mindfulness then returns your attention to its proper focus. If you are meditating at that moment, then your focus will be the formal object of meditation. If you are not in formal meditation, it will be just a pure application of bare attention itself, just a pure noticing of whatever comes up without getting involved— "Ah, this comes up . . . and now this, and now this . . . and now this."

Mindfulness is at one and the same time both bare attention itself and the function of reminding us to pay bare attention if we have ceased to do so. Bare attention is noticing. It reestablishes itself simply by noticing that it has not been present. As soon as you are noticing that you have not been noticing, then by definition you are noticing and then you are back again to paying bare attention.

Mindfulness creates its own distinct feeling in consciousness. It has a flavor—a light, clear, energetic flavor. By comparison, conscious thought is heavy, ponderous, and picky. But here again, these are just words. Your own practice will show you the difference. Then you will probably come up with your own words and the words used here will become superfluous. Remember, practice is the thing.

Mindfulness sees things as they really are
Mindfulness adds nothing to perception and it subtracts nothing. It distorts nothing. It is bare attention and just looks at whatever comes up. Conscious thought pastes things over our experience, loads us down with concepts and ideas, immerses us in a churning

vortex of plans and worries, fears and fantasies. When mindful, you don't play that game. You just notice exactly what arises in the mind, then you notice the next thing. "Ah, this . . . and this . . . and now this." It is really very simple.

Mindfulness sees the true nature of all phenomena

Mindfulness and only mindfulness can perceive that the three prime characteristics that Buddhism teaches are the deepest truths of existence. In Pali these three are called *anicca* (impermanence), *dukkha* (unsatisfactoriness), and *anatta* (selflessness—the absence of a permanent, unchanging entity that we call Soul or Self). These truths are not presented in Buddhist teaching as dogmas demanding blind faith. Buddhists feel that these truths are universal and self-evident to anyone who cares to investigate in a proper way. Mindfulness is that method of investigation. Mindfulness alone has the power to reveal the deepest level of reality available to human observation. At this level of inspection, one sees the following: (a) all conditioned things are inherently transitory; (b) every worldly thing is, in the end, unsatisfying; and (c) there are really no entities that are unchanging or permanent, only processes.

Mindfulness works like an electron microscope. That is, it operates on so fine a level that one can actually directly perceive those realities that are at best theoretical constructs to the conscious thought process. Mindfulness actually sees the impermanent character of every perception. It sees the transitory and passing nature of everything that is perceived. It also sees the inherently unsatisfactory nature of all conditioned things. It sees that there is no point grabbing on to any of these passing shows; peace and happiness cannot be found that way. And finally, mindfulness sees the inherent selflessness of all phenomena. It sees the way that we have arbitrarily selected a certain bundle of perceptions, chopped them off from the rest of the surging flow of experience, and then conceptualized them as separate, enduring entities. Mindfulness actually sees these things. It does not think about them, it sees them directly.

When it is fully developed, mindfulness sees these three attributes of existence directly, instantaneously, and without the intervening medium of conscious thought. In fact, even the attributes that we just covered are inherently unified. They don't really exist as separate items. They are purely the result of our struggle to take this fundamentally simple process called mindfulness and express it in the cumbersome and inadequate thought symbols of the conscious level. Mindfulness is a process, but it does not take place in steps. It is a holistic process that occurs as a unit: you notice your own lack of mindfulness; and that noticing itself is a result of mindfulness; and mindfulness is bare attention; and bare attention is noticing things exactly as they are without distortion; and the way they are is impermanent (*anicca*), unsatisfactory (*dukkha*), and selfless (*anatta*). It all takes place in the space of a few mind-moments. This does not mean, however, that you will instantly attain liberation (freedom from all human weaknesses) as a result of your first moment of mindfulness. Learning to integrate this material into your conscious life is quite another process. And learning to prolong this state of mindfulness is still another. They are joyous processes, however, and they are well worth the effort.

MINDFULNESS (SATI) AND INSIGHT (VIPASSANA) MEDITATION

Mindfulness is the center of vipassana meditation and the key to the whole process. It is both the goal of this meditation and the means to that end. You reach mindfulness by being ever more mindful. One other Pali word that is translated into English as mindfulness is *appamada,* which means nonnegligence or absence of madness. One who attends constantly to what is really going on in the mind achieves the state of ultimate sanity.

The Pali term *sati* also bears the connotation of remembering. It is not memory in the sense of ideas and pictures from the past, but rather clear, direct, wordless knowing of what is and what is not, of what is correct and what is incorrect, of what we are doing and how we should go about it. Mindfulness reminds meditators to apply their attention to the proper object at the proper time and to exert precisely the amount of energy needed to do that job. When this energy is properly applied, a meditator stays constantly in a state of calm and alertness. As long as this condition is maintained, those mind-states called "hindrances" or "psychic irritants" cannot arise— there is no greed, hatred, lust, or laziness.

But we all are human and we all err. Most of us err repeatedly. Despite honest effort, meditators let their mindfulness slip now and then and find themselves stuck in some regrettable, but normal, human failure. It is mindfulness that notices that change. And it is mindfulness that reminds us to apply the energy required to pull ourselves out. These slips happen over and over, but their frequency decreases with practice.

Once mindfulness has pushed these mental defilements aside, more wholesome states of mind can take their place. Hatred makes way for loving-friendliness, lust is replaced by detachment. It is mindfulness that notices this change, too, and that reminds the vipassana meditator to maintain that extra little mental sharpness needed to retain these more desirable states of mind. Mindfulness makes possible the growth of wisdom and compassion. Without mindfulness they cannot develop to full maturity.

Deeply buried in the mind, there lies a mechanism that accepts what the mind experiences as beautiful and pleasant and rejects those experiences that are perceived as ugly and painful. This mechanism gives rise to those states of mind that we are training ourselves to avoid—things like greed, lust, hatred, aversion, and jealousy. We choose to avoid these hindrances, not because they are evil in the normal sense of the word, but because they are compulsive; because they take the mind over and capture the attention completely; because they keep going round and round in tight little circles of thought; and because they seal us off from living reality.

These hindrances cannot arise when mindfulness is present. Mindfulness is attention to present-moment reality, and therefore, directly antithetical to the dazed state of mind that characterizes impediments. As meditators, it is only when we let our mindfulness slip that the deep mechanisms of our mind take over—grasping, clinging, and rejecting. Then resistance emerges and obscures our awareness. We do not notice that the change is taking place—we are too busy with a thought of revenge, or greed, whatever it may be. While an untrained person will continue in this state indefinitely, a trained meditator will soon realize what is happening. It is mindfulness that notices the change. It is mindfulness that remembers the training received and that focuses our attention so that the confusion fades away. And it is mindfulness that then attempts to maintain itself indefinitely so that the resistance cannot arise again. Thus, mindfulness is the specific antidote for hindrances. It is both the cure and the preventive measure.

Fully developed mindfulness is a state of total nonattachment and utter absence of clinging to anything in the world. If we can maintain this state, no other means or device is needed to keep ourselves free of obstructions, to achieve liberation from our human weaknesses. Mindfulness is nonsuperficial awareness. It sees things deeply, down below the level of concepts and opinions. This sort of deep observation leads to total certainty, a complete absence of confusion. It manifests itself primarily as a constant and unwavering attention that never flags and never turns away.

This pure and unstained investigative awareness not only holds mental hindrances at bay, it lays bare their very mechanism and destroys them. Mindfulness neutralizes defilements in the mind. The result is a mind that remains unstained and invulnerable, completely undisturbed by the ups and downs of life.

14. Mindfulness versus Concentration

Vipassana meditation is something of a mental balancing act. You are going to be cultivating two separate qualities of the mind—mindfulness and concentration. Ideally, these two work together as a team. They pull in tandem, so to speak. Therefore it is important to cultivate them side by side and in a balanced manner. If one of the factors is strengthened at the expense of the other, the balance of the mind is lost and meditation becomes impossible.

Concentration and mindfulness are distinctly different functions. They each have their role to play in meditation, and the relationship between them is definite and delicate. Concentration is often called one-pointedness of mind. It consists of forcing the mind to remain on one static point. Please note the word *force*. Concentration is pretty much a forced type of activity. It can be developed by force, by sheer unremitting willpower. And once developed, it retains some of that forced flavor. Mindfulness, on the other hand, is a delicate function leading to refined sensibilities. These two are partners in the job of meditation. Mindfulness is the sensitive one. It notices things. Concentration provides the power. It keeps the attention pinned down to one item. Ideally, mindfulness is in this relationship. Mindfulness picks the objects of attention, and notices when the attention has gone astray. Concentration does the actual work of holding the attention steady on that chosen object. If either of these partners is weak, your meditation goes astray.

Concentration could be defined as that faculty of the mind that focuses single-pointedly on one object without interruption. It must be emphasized that true concentration is a wholesome one-pointedness of mind. That is, the state is free from greed, hatred, and delusion. Unwholesome one-pointedness is also possible, but it will not lead to liberation. You can be very single-minded in a state of lust. But that gets you nowhere. Uninterrupted focus on something that you hate does not help you at all. In fact, such unwholesome concentration is fairly short-lived even when it is achieved—especially when it is used to harm others. True concentration itself is free from such contaminants. It is a state in which the mind is gathered together and thus gains power and intensity. We might use the analogy of a lens. Parallel waves of sunlight falling on a piece of paper will do no more than warm the surface. But if that same amount of light, when focused through a lens, falls on a single point, the paper bursts into flames. Concentration is the lens. It produces the burning intensity necessary to see into the deeper reaches of the mind. Mindfulness selects the object that the lens will focus on and looks through the lens to see what is there.

Concentration should be regarded as a tool. Like any tool, it can be used for good or for ill. A sharp knife can be used to create a beautiful carving or to harm someone. It is all up to the one who uses the knife. Concentration is similar. Properly used, it can assist you toward liberation. But it can also be used in the service of the ego. It can operate in the framework of achievement and competition. You can use concentration to dominate others. You can use it to be selfish. The real problem is that concentration alone will not give you a perspective on yourself. It won't throw light on the basic problems of selfishness and the nature of suffering. It can be used to dig down into deep psychological states. But even then, the forces of egotism won't be understood. Only mindfulness can do that. If mindfulness is not there to look into the lens and see what has been uncovered, then it is all for nothing. Only mindfulness understands. Only mindfulness brings wisdom. Concentration has other limitations, too.

Really deep concentration can only take place under certain specific conditions. Buddhists go to a lot of trouble to build meditation halls and monasteries. Their main purpose is to create a physical environment free of distractions in which to learn this skill. No noise, no interruptions. Just as important, however, is the creation of a distraction-free emotional environment. The development of concentration will be blocked by the presence of the five hindrances that we examined in chapter 12: desire for sensual pleasure, aversion, mental lethargy, agitation, and doubt.

A monastery is a controlled environment where this sort of emotional noise is kept to a minimum. Members of the opposite sex don't live together there. Therefore, there is less opportunity for lust to arise. Possessions aren't allowed, thereby eliminating ownership squabbles and reducing the chance for greed and covetousness. Another hurdle for concentration should also be mentioned. In really deep concentration, you get so absorbed in the object of concentration that you forget all about trifles. Like your body, for instance, and your identity, and everything around you. Here again the monastery is a useful convenience. It is nice to know that there is somebody to take care of you by watching over all the mundane matters of food and physical security. Without such assurance, one hesitates to go as deeply into concentration as one might.

Mindfulness, on the other hand, is free from all these drawbacks. Mindfulness is not dependent on any such particular circumstance, physical or otherwise. It is a pure noticing factor. Thus it is free to notice whatever comes up—lust, hatred, or noise. Mindfulness is not limited by any condition. It exists to some extent in every moment, in every circumstance that arises. Also, mindfulness has no fixed object of focus. It observes change. Thus, it has an unlimited number of objects of attention. It just looks at whatever is passing through the mind, and it does not categorize. Distractions and interruptions are noticed with the same amount of attention as the formal objects of meditation. In a state of pure mindfulness, your attention just flows along with whatever changes are taking place in the mind. "Shift, shift, shift. Now this, now this, and now this."

You can't develop mindfulness by force. Active teeth-gritting willpower won't do you any good at all. As a matter of fact, it will hinder progress. Mindfulness cannot be cultivated by struggle. It grows by realizing, by letting go, by just settling down in the moment and letting yourself get comfortable with whatever you are experiencing. This does not mean that mindfulness happens all by itself. Far from it. Energy is required. Effort is required. But this effort is different from force. Mindfulness is cultivated by a gentle effort. You cultivate mindfulness by constantly reminding yourself in a gentle way to maintain your awareness of whatever is happening right now. Persistence and a light touch are the secrets. Mindfulness is cultivated by constantly pulling yourself back to a state of awareness, gently, gently, gently.

Mindfulness can't be used in any selfish way, either. It is egoless alertness. There is no "me" in a state of pure mindfulness. So there is no self to be selfish. On the contrary, it is mindfulness that gives you real perspective on yourself. It allows you to take that crucial mental step backward from your own desires and aversions so that you can then look and say, "Aha, so that's how I really am."

In a state of mindfulness, you see yourself exactly as you are. You see your own selfish behavior. You see your own suffering. And you see how you create that suffering. You see how you hurt others. You pierce right through the layer of lies that you normally tell yourself, and you see what is really there. Mindfulness leads to wisdom.

Mindfulness is not trying to achieve anything. It is just looking. Therefore, desire and aversion are not involved. Competition and struggle for achievement have no place in the process. Mindfulness does not aim at anything. It just sees whatever is already there.

Mindfulness is a broader and larger function than concentration. It is an all-encompassing function. Concentration is exclusive. It settles down on one item and ignores everything else. Mindfulness is inclusive. It stands back from the focus of attention and watches with a broad focus, quick to notice any change that occurs. If you have focused the mind on a stone, concentration will see only the stone. Mindfulness stands back from this process, aware of the stone, aware of concentration focusing on the stone, aware of the intensity of that focus, and instantly aware of the shift of attention when concentration is distracted. It is mindfulness that notices that the distraction has occurred, and it is mindfulness that redirects the attention to the stone. Mindfulness is more difficult to cultivate than concentration because it is a deeper-reaching function. Concentration is merely focusing the mind, rather like a laser beam. It has the power to burn its way deep into the mind and illuminate what is there. But it does not understand what it sees. Mindfulness can examine the mechanics of selfishness and understand what it sees. Mindfulness can pierce the mystery of suffering and the mechanism of discomfort. Mindfulness can make you free.

There is, however, another catch-22. Mindfulness does not react to what it sees. It just sees and understands. Mindfulness is the essence of patience. Therefore, whatever you see must simply be accepted, acknowledged, and dispassionately observed. This is not easy, but it is utterly necessary. We are ignorant. We are selfish and greedy and boastful. We lust, and we lie. These are facts. Mind-fulness means seeing these facts and being patient with ourselves, accepting ourselves as we are. That goes against the grain. We don't want to accept it. We want to deny it. Or change it, or justify it. But acceptance is the essence of mindfulness. If we want to grow in mindfulness, we must accept what mindfulness finds. It may be boredom, irritation, or fear. It may be weakness, inadequacy, or faults. Whatever it is, that is the way we are. That is what is real.

Mindfulness simply accepts whatever is there. If you want to grow in mindfulness, patient acceptance is the only route. Mind-fulness grows only one way: by continuous practice of mindfulness, by simply trying to be mindful, and that means being patient. The process cannot be forced and it cannot be rushed. It proceeds at its own pace.

Concentration and mindfulness go hand in hand in the job of meditation. Mindfulness directs the power of concentration. Mind-fulness is the manager of the operation. Concentration furnishes the power by which mindfulness can penetrate into the deepest level of mind. Their cooperation results in insight and understanding. These must be cultivated together in a balanced manner. Just a bit more emphasis is given to mindfulness, because mindfulness is the center of meditation. The deepest levels of concentration are not really needed to do the job of liberation. Still, a balance is essential. Too much awareness without calm to balance it will result in a wildly over-sensitized state similar to abusing LSD. Too much concentra-tion without a balancing ratio of awareness will result in the "stone buddha" syndrome, where you get so tranquilized that you sit there like a rock. Both of these are to be avoided.

The initial stages of mental cultivation are especially delicate. Too much emphasis on mindfulness at this point will actually retard the development of concentration. When getting started in meditation, one of the first things you will notice is how incredibly active the mind really is. The Theravada tradition calls this phenomenon "monkey mind." The Tibetan tradition likens it to a waterfall of thought. If you emphasize the awareness function at this point, there will be so much to be aware of that concentration will be impossible. Don't get discouraged. This happens to everybody. And there is a simple solution. Put most of your effort into one-pointedness at the beginning. Just keep calling the attention from wandering over and over again. Tough it out. Full instructions on how to do this are in chapters 7 and 8. A couple of months down the track and you will have developed concentration power. Then you can start pumping your energy into mindfulness. Do not, however, go so far with concentration that you find yourself going into a stupor.

Mindfulness still is the more important of the two components. It should be built as soon as you comfortably can do so. Mindfulness provides the needed foundation for the subsequent development of deeper concentration. Most blunders in this area of balance will correct themselves in time. Right concentration develops naturally in the wake of strong mindfulness. The more you develop the noticing factor, the quicker you will notice the distraction, and the quicker you will pull out of it and return to the formal object of attention. The natural result is increased concentration. And as concentration develops, it assists the development of mindfulness. The more concentration power you have, the less chance there is of launching off on a long chain of analysis about the distraction. You simply note the distraction and return your attention to where it is supposed to be.

Thus the two factors tend to balance and support each other's growth quite naturally. Just about the only rule you need to follow at this point is to put your effort on concentration at the beginning until the monkey mind phenomenon has cooled down a bit. After that, emphasize mindfulness. If you find yourself getting frantic, emphasize concentration. If you find yourself going into a stupor, emphasize mindfulness. Overall, mindfulness is the one to emphasize.

Mindfulness guides your development in meditation because mindfulness has the ability to be aware of itself. It is mindfulness that will give you a perspective on your practice. Mindfulness will let you know how you are doing. But don't worry too much about that. This is not a race. You are not in competition with anybody, and there is no schedule.

One of the most difficult things to learn is that mindfulness is not dependent on any emotional or mental state. We have certain images of meditation. Meditation is something done in quiet caves by tranquil people who move slowly. Those are training conditions. They are set up to foster concentration and to learn the skill of mindfulness. Once you have learned that skill, however, you can dispense with the training restrictions, and you should. You don't need to move at a snail's pace to be mindful. You don't even need to be calm. You can be mindful while solving problems in intensive calculus. You can be mindful in the middle of a football scrimmage. You can even be mindful in the midst of a raging fury. Mental and physical activities are no bar to mindfulness. If you find your mind extremely active, then simply observe the nature and degree of that activity. It is just a part of the passing show within.

15. Meditation in Everyday Life

*E*very musician plays scales. When you begin to study the piano, that's the first thing you learn, and you never stop playing scales. The finest concert pianists in the world still play scales. It's a basic skill that can't be allowed to get rusty.

Every baseball player practices batting. It's the first thing you learn in Little League, and you never stop practicing. Every World Series game begins with batting practice. Basic skills must always remain sharp.

Seated meditation is the arena in which meditators practice their own fundamental skills. The game the meditator is playing is the experience of his own life, and the instrument upon which he plays is his own sensory apparatus. Even the most seasoned meditator continues to practice seated meditation, because it tunes and sharpens the basic mental skills he needs for his particular game. We must never forget, however, that seated meditation itself is not the game. It's the practice. The game in which those basic skills are to be applied is the rest of one's experiential existence. Meditation that is not applied to daily living is sterile and limited.

The purpose of vipassana meditation is nothing less than the radical and permanent transformation of your entire sensory and cognitive experience. It is meant to revolutionize the whole of your life experience. Those periods of seated practice are times set aside for instilling new mental habits. You learn new ways to receive and understand sensation. You develop new methods of dealing with conscious thought and new modes of attending to the incessant rush of your own emotions. These new mental behaviors must be made to carry over into the rest of your life. Otherwise, meditation remains dry and fruitless, a theoretical segment of your existence that is unconnected to all the rest. Some effort to connect these two segments is essential. A certain amount of carryover will take place spontaneously, but that process will be slow and unreliable. You are very likely to be left with the feeling that you are getting nowhere and to drop the process as unrewarding.

One of the most memorable events in your meditation career is the moment when you first realize that you are meditating in the midst of a perfectly ordinary activity. You are driving down the freeway or carrying out the trash and it just turns on by itself. This unplanned outpouring of the skills you have been so carefully fostering is a genuine joy. It gives you a tiny window on the future. You catch a spontaneous glimpse of what the practice really means. The possibility strikes you that this transformation of consciousness could actually become a permanent feature of your experience. You realize that you could actually spend the rest of your days standing aside from the debilitating clamoring of your own obsessions, no longer frantically hounded by your own needs and greeds. You get a tiny taste of what it is like to just stand aside and watch it all flow past. It's a magic moment.

That vision is likely to remain unfulfilled, however, unless you actively seek to promote the carryover process. The most important moment in meditation is the instant you leave the cushion. When your practice session is over, you can jump up and drop the whole thing, or you can bring those skills with you into the rest of your activities.

It is crucial for you to understand what meditation is. It is not some special posture, and it's not just a set of mental exercises. Meditation is the cultivation of mindfulness and the application of that mindfulness once cultivated. You do not have to sit to meditate. You can meditate while washing the dishes. You can meditate in the shower, or roller skating, or typing letters. Meditation is awareness, and it must be applied to each and every activity of one's life. This isn't easy.

We specifically cultivate awareness through the seated posture in a quiet place because that's the easiest situation in which to do so. Meditation in motion is harder. Meditation in the midst of fast-paced noisy activity is harder still. And meditation in the midst of intensely egoistic activities like romance or an argument is the ultimate challenge. Beginners will have their hands full with less stressful activities.

Yet the ultimate goal of practice remains: to build one's concentration and awareness to a level of strength that will remain unwavering even in the midst of the pressures of life in contemporary society. Life offers many challenges and the serious meditator is never bored.

Carrying your meditation into the events of your daily life is not a simple process. Try it and you will see. That transition point between the end of your meditation session and the beginning of "real life" is a long jump. It's too long for most of us. We find our calm and concentration evaporating within minutes, leaving us apparently no better off than before. In order to bridge this gulf, Buddhists over the centuries have devised an array of exercises aimed at smoothing the transition. They take that jump and break it down into little steps. Each step can be practiced by itself.

WALKING MEDITATION

Our everyday existence is full of motion and activity. Sitting utterly motionless for hours on end is nearly the opposite of normal experience. Those states of clarity and tranquility we foster in the midst of absolute stillness tend to dissolve as soon as we move. We need some transitional exercise that will teach us the skill of remaining calm and aware in the midst of motion. Walking meditation helps us make that transition from static repose to everyday life. It's meditation in motion, and it is often used as an alternative to sitting. Walking is especially good for those times when you are extremely restless. An hour of walking meditation will often get you through that restless energy and still yield considerable quantities of clarity. You can then go on to the seated meditation with greater profit.

Standard Buddhist practice advocates frequent retreats to complement your daily sitting practice. A retreat is a relatively long period of time devoted exclusively to meditation. One- or two-day retreats are common for laypeople. Seasoned meditators in a monastic situation may spend months at a time doing nothing else. Such practice is rigorous, and it makes sizable demands on both mind and body. Unless you have been at it for several years, there is a limit to how long you can sit and profit. Ten solid hours of the seated posture will produce in most beginners a state of agony that far exceeds their concentration powers. A profitable retreat must therefore be conducted with some change of posture and some movement. The usual pattern is to intersperse blocks of sitting with blocks of walking meditation. An hour of each with short breaks between is common.

To do the walking meditation, you need a private place with enough space for at least five to ten paces in a straight line. You are going to be walking back and forth very slowly, and to the eyes of most Westerners you'll look curious and disconnected from everyday life. This is not the sort of exercise you want to perform on the front lawn where you'll attract unnecessary attention. Choose a private place.

The physical directions are simple. Select an unobstructed area and start at one end. Stand for a minute in an attentive position. Your arms can be held in any way that is comfortable, in front, in back, or at your sides. Then while breathing in, lift the heel of one foot. While breathing out, rest that foot on its toes. Again while breathing in, lift that foot, carry it forward and while breathing out, bring the foot down and touch the floor. Repeat this for the other foot. Walk very slowly to the opposite end, stand for one minute, then turn around very slowly, and stand there for another minute before you walk back. Then repeat the process.

Keep your head up and your neck relaxed. Keep your eyes open to maintain balance, but don't look at anything in particular. Walk naturally. Maintain the slowest pace that is comfortable, and pay no attention to your surroundings. Watch out for tensions building up in the body, and release them as soon as you spot them. Don't make any particular attempt to be graceful. Don't try to look pretty. This is not an athletic exercise or a dance. It is an exercise in awareness. Your objective is to attain total alertness, heightened sensitivity, and a full, unblocked experience of the motion of walking. Put all of your attention on the sensations coming from the feet and legs. Try to register as much information as possible about each foot as it moves. Dive into the pure sensation of walking, and notice every subtle nuance of the movement. Feel each individual muscle as it moves. Experience every tiny change in tactile sensation as the feet press against the floor, and then lift again.

Notice the way these apparently smooth motions are composed of a complex series of tiny jerks. Try to miss nothing. In order to heighten your sensitivity, you can break the movement down into distinct components. Each foot goes through a lift, a swing, and then a down tread. Each of these components has a beginning, middle, and end. In order to tune yourself in to this series of motions, you can start by making explicit mental notes of each stage.

Make a mental note of "lifting, swinging, coming down, touching floor, pressing," and so on. This is a training procedure to familiarize you with the sequence of motions and to make sure that you don't miss any. As you become more aware of the myriad subtle events going on, you won't have time for words. You will find yourself immersed in a fluid, unbroken awareness of motion. The feet will become your whole universe. If your mind wanders, note the distraction in the usual way, then return your attention to walking. Don't look at your feet while you are doing all of this, and don't walk back and forth watching a mental picture of your feet and legs. Don't think, just feel. You don't need the concept of feet, and you don't need pictures. Just register the sensations as they flow. In the beginning, you will probably have some difficulties with balance. You are using the leg muscles in a new way, and a learning period is natural. If frustration arises, just note that and let it go.

The vipassana walking technique is designed to flood your consciousness with simple sensations, and to do it so thoroughly that all else is pushed aside. There is no room for thought and therefore no room for emotion. There is no time for grasping and none for freezing the activity into a series of concepts. There is no need for a sense of self. There is only the sweep of tactile and kinesthetic sensation, an endless and ever-changing flood of raw experience. We are learning here to escape into reality, rather than from it. Whatever insights we gain are directly applicable to the rest of our notion-filled lives.

POSTURES

The goal of our practice is to become fully aware of all facets of our experience in an unbroken, moment-to-moment flow. Much of what we do and experience is completely unconscious in the sense that we do it with little or no attention. Our minds are on something else entirely. We spend most of our time running on automatic pilot, lost in the fog of daydreams and preoccupations.

One of the most frequently ignored aspects of our existence is our body. The technicolor cartoon show inside our head is so alluring that we tend to remove all of our attention from the kinesthetic and tactile senses. That information is pouring up the nerves and into the brain every second, but we have largely sealed it off from consciousness. It pours into the lower levels of the mind, and it gets no further. Buddhists have developed an exercise to open the floodgates and let this material through to consciousness. It's another way of making the unconscious conscious.

Your body goes through all kinds of contortions in the course of a single day. You sit and you stand. You walk and lie down. You bend, run, crawl, and sprawl. Meditation teachers urge you to become aware of this constantly ongoing dance. As you go through your day, spend a few seconds every few minutes to check your posture. Don't do it in a judgmental way. This is not an exercise to correct your posture or to improve your appearance. Sweep your attention down through the body and feel how you are holding it. Make a silent mental note of "walking" or "sitting" or "lying down" or "standing." It all sounds absurdly simple, but don't slight this procedure. This is a powerful exercise. If you do it thoroughly, if you really instill this mental habit deeply, it can revolutionize your experience. It taps you into a whole new dimension of sensation, and you feel like a blind man whose sight has been restored.

Slow-Motion Activity

Every action you perform is made up of separate components. The simple action of tying your shoelaces is made up of a complex series of subtle motions. Most of these details go unobserved. In order to promote the overall habit of mindfulness, you can perform simple activities at very low speed—making an effort to pay full attention to every nuance of the act.

Sitting at a table and drinking a cup of tea is one example. There is much here to be experienced. View your posture as you are sitting, and feel the handle of the cup between your fingers. Smell the aroma of the tea, notice the placement of the cup, the tea, your arm, and the table. Watch the intention to raise your arm arise within your mind, feel your arm as it rises, feel the cup against your lip and liquid pouring into your mouth. Taste the tea, then watch the arising of the intention to lower your arm. The entire process is fascinating and beautiful, if you attend to it fully, paying detached attention to every sensation and to the flow of thought and emotion.

This same tactic can be applied to many of your daily activities. Intentionally slowing down your thoughts, words, and movements allows you to penetrate far more deeply into them than you otherwise could. What you find there is utterly astonishing. In the beginning, it is very difficult to keep this deliberately slow pace during most regular activities, but skill grows with time. Profound realizations occur during sitting meditation, but also profound revelations can take place when we really examine our own inner workings in the midst of day-to-day activities. This is the laboratory where we really start to see the mechanisms of our own emotions and the operations of our passions. Here is where we can truly gauge the reliability of our reasoning and glimpse the difference between our true motives and that armor of pretense that we wear to fool ourselves and others.

We will find a great deal of this information surprising, much of it disturbing, but all of it useful. Bare attention brings order into the clutter that collects in those untidy little hidden corners of the mind. As you achieve clear comprehension in the midst of life's ordinary activities, you gain the ability to remain rational and peaceful while you throw the penetrating light of mindfulness into those irrational mental nooks and crannies. You start to see the extent to which you are responsible for your own mental suffering. You see your own miseries, fears, and tensions as self-generated. You see the way you cause your own suffering, weakness, and limitations. And the more deeply you understand these mental processes, the less hold they have on you.

BREATH COORDINATION

In seated meditation, our primary focus is the breath. Total concentration on the ever-changing breath brings us squarely into the present moment. The same principle can be used in the midst of movement. You can coordinate the activity in which you are involved with your breathing. This lends a flowing rhythm to your movement, and it smoothes out many of the abrupt transitions. Activity becomes easier to focus on, and mindfulness is increased. Your awareness thus stays more easily in the present. Ideally, meditation should be a twenty-four-hour-a-day practice. This is a highly practical suggestion.

A state of mindfulness is a state of mental readiness. The mind is not burdened with preoccupations or bound in worries. Whatever comes up can be dealt with instantly. When you are truly mindful, your nervous system has a freshness and resiliency that fosters insight. A problem arises, and you simply deal with it, quickly, efficiently, and with a minimum of fuss. You don't stand there in a dither, and you don't run off to a quiet corner so you can sit down and meditate about it. You simply deal with it. And in those rare circumstances when no solution seems possible, you don't worry about that. You just go on to the next thing that needs your attention. Your intuition becomes a very practical faculty.

STOLEN MOMENTS

The concept of wasted time does not exist for a serious meditator. Little dead spaces during your day can be turned to profit. Every spare moment can be used for meditation. Sitting anxiously in the dentist's office, meditate on your anxiety. Feeling irritated while standing in a line at the bank, meditate on irritation. Bored, twiddling your thumbs at the bus stop, meditate on boredom. Try to stay alert and aware throughout the day. Be mindful of exactly what is taking place right now, even if it is tedious drudgery. Take advantage of moments when you are alone. Take advantage of activities that are largely mechanical. Use every spare second to be mindful. Use all the moments you can.

CONCENTRATION ON ALL ACTIVITIES

You should try to maintain mindfulness of every activity and perception through the day, starting with the first perception when you awake and ending with the last thought before you fall asleep. This is an incredibly tall goal to shoot for. Don't expect to be able to achieve this work soon. Just take it slowly and let your abilities grow over time. The most feasible way to go about the task is to divide your day up into chunks. Dedicate a certain interval to mindfulness of posture, then extend this mindfulness to other simple activities: eating, washing, dressing, and so forth. Some time during the day, you can set aside fifteen minutes or so to practice the observation of specific types of mental states: pleasant, unpleasant, and neutral feelings, for instance; or the hindrances, or thoughts. The specific routine is up to you. The idea is to get practice at spotting the various items, and to preserve your state of mindfulness as fully as you can throughout the day.

Try to achieve a daily routine in which there is as little difference as possible between seated meditation and the rest of your experience. Let the one slide naturally into the other. Your body is almost never still. There is always motion to observe. At the very least, there is breathing. Your mind never stops chattering, except in the very deepest states of concentration. There is always something coming up to observe. If you seriously apply your meditation, you will never be at a loss for something worthy of your attention.

Your practice must be made to apply to your everyday living situation. That is your laboratory. It provides the trials and challenges you need to make your practice deep and genuine. It's the fire that purifies your practice of deception and error, the acid test that shows you when you are getting somewhere and when you are fooling yourself. If your meditation isn't helping you to cope with everyday conflicts and struggles, then it is shallow. If your day-to-day emotional reactions are not becoming clearer and easier to manage, then you are wasting your time. And you never know how you are doing until you actually make that test.

The practice of mindfulness is supposed to be a universal practice. You don't do it sometimes and drop it the rest of the time. You do it all the time. Meditation that is successful only when you are withdrawn in some soundproof ivory tower is still undeveloped. Insight meditation is the practice of moment-to-moment mindfulness. The meditator learns to pay bare attention to birth, growth, and decay of all the phenomena of the mind. She turns from none of it and lets none of it escape. This includes thoughts and emotions, activities and desires, the whole show. She watches it all and watches it continuously. It matters not whether it is lovely or horrid, beautiful or shameful. She sees the way it is and the way it changes. No aspect of experience is excluded or avoided. It is a very thoroughgoing procedure.

If you are moving through your daily activities and you find yourself in a state of boredom, then meditate on your boredom. Find out how it feels, how it works, and what it is composed of. If you are angry, meditate on the anger. Explore the mechanics of anger. Don't run from it. If you find yourself sitting in the grip of a dark depression, meditate on that depression. Investigate depression in a detached and inquiring way. Don't flee from it blindly. Explore the maze and chart its pathways. That way you will be better able to cope with the next depression that comes along.

Meditating your way through the ups and downs of daily life is the whole point of vipassana. This kind of practice is extremely rigorous and demanding, but it engenders a state of mental flexibility that is beyond comparison. A meditator keeps his mind open every second. He is constantly investigating life, inspecting his own experience, viewing existence in a detached and inquisitive way. Thus, he is constantly open to truth in any form, from any source, and at any time. This is the state of mind you need for liberation.

It is said that one may attain enlightenment at any moment if the mind is kept in a state of meditative readiness. The tiniest, most ordinary perception can be the stimulus: a view of the moon, the cry of a bird, the sound of the wind in the trees. It's not so important what is perceived as the way in which you attend to that perception. That state of open readiness is essential. It could happen to you right now if you are ready. The tactile sensation of this book in your fingers could be the cue. The sound of these words in your head might be enough. You could attain enlightenment right now, if you are ready.

16. What's in It for You

You can expect certain benefits from your meditation. The initial ones are practical things; the later stages are profoundly transcendental. They run together from the simple to the sublime. We will set forth some of them here. Your own practice can show you the truth. Your own experience is all that counts.

Those things that we called hindrances or defilements are more than just unpleasant mental habits. They are the primary manifestations of the ego process itself. The ego sense itself is essentially a feeling of separation—a perception of distance between that which we call *me* and that which we call *other*. This perception is held in place only if it is constantly exercised, and the hindrances constitute that exercise.

Greed and lust are attempts to "get some of that" for me; hatred and aversion are attempts to place greater distance between "me and that." All the defilements depend upon the perception of a barrier between self and other, and all of them foster this perception every time they are exercised. Mindfulness perceives things deeply and with great clarity. It brings our attention to the root of the defilements and lays bare their mechanism. It sees their fruits and their effects upon us. It cannot be fooled. Once you have clearly seen what greed really is and what it really does to you and to others, you just naturally cease to engage in it. When a child burns her hand on a hot oven, you don't have to tell her to pull it back; she does it naturally, without conscious thought and without decision. There is a reflex action built into the nervous system for just that purpose, and it works faster than thought. By the time the child perceives the sensation of heat and begins to cry, the hand has already been jerked back from the source of pain. Mindfulness works in very much the same way: it is wordless, spontaneous, and utterly efficient. Clear mindfulness inhibits the growth of hindrances; continuous mindfulness extinguishes them. Thus, as genuine mindfulness is built up, the walls of the ego itself are broken down, craving diminishes, defensiveness and rigidity lessen, you become more open, accepting, and flexible. You learn to share your loving-friendliness.

Traditionally, Buddhists are reluctant to talk about the ultimate nature of human beings. But those who are willing to make descriptive statements at all usually say that our ultimate essence or buddha nature is pure, holy, and inherently good. The only reason that human beings appear otherwise is that their experience of that ultimate essence has been hindered; it has been blocked like water behind a dam. The hindrances are the bricks of which that dam is built. As mindfulness dissolves the bricks, holes are punched in the dam, and compassion and sympathetic joy come flooding forward. As meditative mindfulness develops, your whole experience of life changes. Your experience of being alive, the very sensation of being conscious, becomes lucid and precise, no longer just an unnoticed background for your preoccupations. It becomes a thing consistently perceived.

Each passing moment stands out as itself; the moments no longer blend together in an unnoticed blur. Nothing is glossed over or taken for granted, no experiences labeled as merely "ordinary." Everything looks bright and special. You refrain from categorizing your experiences into mental pigeonholes. Descriptions and interpretations

WHAT'S IN IT FOR YOU 167

are chucked aside, and each moment of time is allowed to speak for itself. You actually listen to what it has to say, and you listen as if it were being heard for the very first time. When your meditation becomes really powerful, it also becomes constant. You consistently observe with bare attention both the breath and every mental phenomenon. You feel increasingly stable, increasingly moored in the stark and simple experience of moment-to-moment existence.

Once your mind is free from thought, it becomes clearly wakeful and at rest in an utterly simple awareness. This awareness cannot be described adequately. Words are not enough. It can only be experienced. Breath ceases to be just breath; it is no longer limited to the static and familiar concept you once held. You no longer see it as a succession of just inhalations and exhalations, an insignificant monotonous experience. Breath becomes a living, changing process, something alive and fascinating. It is no longer something that takes place in time; it is perceived as the present moment itself. Time is seen as a concept, not an experienced reality.

This is a simplified, rudimentary awareness that is stripped of all extraneous detail. It is grounded in a living flow of the present, and it is marked by a pronounced sense of reality. You know absolutely that this is real, more real than anything you have ever experienced. Once you have gained this perception with absolute certainty, you have a fresh vantage point, a new criterion against which to gauge all of your experience. After this perception, you see clearly those moments when you are participating in bare phenomena alone, and those moments when you are disturbing phenomena with mental attitudes. You watch yourself twisting reality with mental comments, with stale images and personal opinions. You know what you are doing, when you are doing it. You become increasingly sensitive to the ways in which you miss the true reality, and you gravitate toward the simple objective perspective that does not add to or subtract from what is. You become a very perceptive individual. From this vantage point, all is seen with clarity. The innumerable activities of mind and body stand out in glaring detail. You mindfully observe the incessant rise and fall of breath; you watch an endless stream of bodily sensations and movements; you scan the rapid succession of thoughts and feelings; and you sense the rhythm that echoes from the steady march of time. And in the midst of all this ceaseless movement, there is no watcher, there is only watching.

In this state of perception, nothing remains the same for two consecutive moments. Everything is seen to be in constant transformation. All things are born, all things grow old and die. There are no exceptions. You awaken to the unceasing changes of your own life. You look around and see everything in flux, everything, everything, everything. It is all rising and falling, intensifying and diminishing, coming into existence and passing away. All of life, every bit of it from the infinitesimal to the Pacific Ocean, is in motion constantly. You perceive the universe as a great flowing river of experience. Your most cherished possessions are slipping away, and so is your very life. Yet this impermanence is no reason for grief. You stand there transfixed, staring at this incessant activity, and your response is wondrous joy. It's all moving, dancing, and full of life.

As you continue to observe these changes and you see how it all fits together, you become aware of the intimate connectedness of all mental, sensory, and affective phenomena. You watch one thought leading to another, you see destruction giving rise to emotional reactions and feelings giving rise to more thoughts. Actions, thoughts, feelings, desires—you see all of them intimately linked together in a delicate fabric of cause and effect. You watch pleasurable experiences arise and fall, and you see that they never last; you watch pain come uninvited and you watch yourself anxiously struggling to throw it off; you see yourself fail. It all happens over and over while you stand back quietly and just watch it all work.

Out of this living laboratory itself comes an inner and unassailable conclusion. You see that your life is marked by disappointment and frustration, and you clearly see the source. These reactions arise out of your own inability to get what you want, your fear of losing what you have already gained, and your habit of never being satisfied with what you have. These are no longer theoretical concepts—you have seen these things for yourself, and you know that they are real. You perceive your own fear, your own basic insecurity in the face of life and death. It is a profound tension that goes all the way down to the root of thought and makes all of life a struggle. You watch yourself anxiously groping about, fearfully grasping after solid, trustworthy ground. You see yourself endlessly grasping for something, anything, to hold on to in the midst of all these shifting sands, and you see that there is nothing to hold on to, nothing that doesn't change.

You see the pain of loss and grief, you watch yourself being forced to adjust to painful developments day after day in your own ordinary existence. You witness the tensions and conflicts inherent in the very process of everyday living, and you see how superficial most of your concerns really are. You watch the progress of pain, sickness, old age, and death. You learn to marvel that all these horrible things are not fearful at all. They are simply reality.

Through this intensive study of the negative aspects of your existence, you become deeply acquainted with *dukkha*, the unsatisfactory nature of all existence. You begin to perceive dukkha at all levels of our human life, from the obvious down to the most subtle. You see the way suffering inevitably follows in the wake of clinging; as soon as you grasp anything, pain inevitably follows. Once you become fully acquainted with the whole dynamic of desire, you become sensitized to it. You see where it rises, when it rises, and how it affects you. You watch it operate over and over, manifesting through every sense channel, taking control of the mind and making consciousness its slave.

In the midst of every pleasant experience, you watch your own craving and clinging take place. In the midst of unpleasant experiences, you watch a very powerful resistance take hold. You do not block these phenomena, you just watch them; you see them as the very stuff of human thought. You search for that thing you call "me," but what you find is a physical body and how you have identified your sense of yourself with that bag of skin and bones. You search further, and you find all manner of mental phenomena, such as emotions, thought patterns, and opinions, and see how you identify the sense of yourself with each of them. You watch yourself becoming possessive, protective, and defensive over these pitiful things, and you see how crazy that is. You rummage furiously among these various items, constantly searching for yourself—physical matter, bodily sensations, feelings, and emotions—it all keeps whirling round and round as you root through it, peering into every nook and cranny, endlessly hunting for "me."

You find nothing. In all that collection of mental hardware in this endless stream of ever-shifting experience, all you can find is innumerable impersonal processes that have been caused and conditioned by previous processes. There is no static self to be found; it is all process. You find thoughts but no thinker, you find emotions and desires, but nobody doing them. The house itself is empty. There is nobody home.

Your whole view of self changes at this point. You begin to look upon yourself as if you were a newspaper photograph. When viewed with the naked eyes, the photograph you see is a definite image. When viewed through a magnifying glass, it all breaks down into an intricate configuration of dots. Similarly, under the penetrating gaze of mindfulness, the feeling of a self, an "I" or "being" any-thing, loses its solidity and dissolves. There comes a point in insight meditation where the three characteristics of existence—impermanence, unsatisfactoriness, and selflessness—come rush-ing home with concept-searing force. You vividly experience the impermanence of life, the suffering nature of human existence, and the truth of no-self. You experience these things so graphically that you suddenly awake to the utter futility of craving, grasping, and resistance. In the clarity and purity of this profound moment, our consciousness is transformed. The entity of self evaporates. All that is left is an infinity of interrelated nonpersonal phenomena, which are conditioned and ever-changing. Craving is extinguished and a great burden is lifted. There remains only an effortless flow, without a trace of resistance or tension. There remains only peace, and blessed nibbana, the uncreated, is realized.

Afterword:
The Power of Loving-Friendliness

T he tools of mindfulness discussed in this book, if you choose to take advantage of them, can surely transform your every experience. In the afterword to this new edition, I'd like to emphasize the importance of another aspect of the Buddha's path that goes hand in hand with mindfulness: *metta,* or loving-friendliness. Without loving-friendliness, our practice of mindfulness will never successfully break through our craving and rigid sense of self. Mindfulness, in turn, is a necessary basis for developing loving-friendliness. The two are always developed together.

In the decades since this volume first appeared, much has happened in the world to increase people's feelings of insecurity and fear. In this troubled climate, the importance of cultivating a deep sense of loving-friendliness is especially crucial for our well-being, and it is the best hope for the future of the world. The concern for others embodied in loving-friendliness is at the heart of the promise of the Buddha—you can see it everywhere in his teachings and in the way he lived his life.

Each of us is born with the capacity for loving-friendliness. Yet only in a calm mind, a mind free from anger, greed, and jealousy, can the seeds of loving-friendliness develop; only from the fertile ground of a peaceful mind can loving-friendliness flower. We must nurture the seeds of loving-friendliness in ourselves and in others, help them take root and mature.

I travel all over the world teaching the Dhamma, and consequently I spend a lot of time in airports. One day I was in Gatwick Airport near London waiting for a flight. I had quite a bit of time, but for me having time on my hands is not a problem. In fact, it is a pleasure, since it means more opportunity for meditation! So there I was, sitting cross-legged on one of the airport benches with my eyes closed, while all around me people were coming and going, rushing to and from their flights. When meditating in situations like this, I fill my mind with thoughts of loving-friendliness and compassion for everyone everywhere. With every breath, with every pulse, with every heartbeat, I try to allow my entire being to become permeated with the glow of loving-friendliness.

In that busy airport, absorbed in feelings of metta, I was paying no attention to the hustle and bustle around me, but soon I had the sensation that someone was sitting quite close to me on the bench. I didn't open my eyes but merely kept on with my meditation, radiating loving-friendliness. Then I felt two tiny, tender hands reaching around my neck, and I slowly opened my eyes and discovered a very beautiful child, a little girl perhaps two years old. This little one, with bright blue eyes and a head covered in downy blond curls, had put her arms around me and was hugging me. I had seen this sweet child as I was people watching; she had had her hand grasped around her mother's little finger. Apparently, the little girl had loosened herself from her mother's hand and run over to me.

I looked over and saw that her mother had chased after her. Seeing her little girl with her arms around my neck, the mother asked me, "Please bless my little girl and let her go." I did not know what language the child spoke, but I said to her in English, "Please go. Your mother has lots of kisses for you, lots of hugs, lots of toys, and lots of sweets. I have none of those things. Please go." The child hung on to my neck and would not let go. Again, the mother folded her palms together and pleaded with me in a very kindly tone, "Please, sir, give her your blessing and let her go."

By this time, other people in the airport were beginning to notice. They must have thought that I knew this child, that perhaps she was related to me somehow. Surely they thought there was some strong bond between us. But I had never before that day seen this lovely little child. I did not even know what language she spoke. Again, I urged her, "Please go. You and your mother have a plane to catch. You are late. Your mother has all your toys and candy. I have nothing. Please go." But the little girl would not budge. She clung to me harder and harder. The mother then very gently took the little girl's hands off my neck and asked me to bless her. "You are a very good little girl," I said. "Your mother loves you very much. Hurry. You might miss your plane. Please go." But still the little girl would not go. She was crying and crying. Finally the mother carefully snatched her up. The toddler was kicking and screaming. She was trying to get loose and come back to me. But this time the mother managed to carry her off to the plane. The last I saw of her she was still struggling to get loose and run back to me.

Maybe because of my robes, this little girl thought I was a Santa Claus or some kind of fairy-tale figure. But there is another possibility: At the time I was sitting on that bench, I was practicing metta, sending out thoughts of loving-friendliness with every breath. Perhaps this little child felt this; children are extremely sensitive in these ways, their psyches absorb whatever feelings are around them. When you are angry, they feel those vibrations; and when you are full of love and compassion, they feel that too. This little girl may have been drawn to me by the feelings of loving-friendliness she felt. There was a bond between us—the bond of loving-friendliness.

THE FOUR SUBLIME STATES

Loving-friendliness works miracles. We have the capacity to act with loving-friendliness. We may not even know we have this quality in ourselves, but the power of loving-friendliness is inside us all. Loving-friendliness is one of the four sublime states defined by the Buddha, along with compassion, appreciative joy, and equanimity. All four states are interrelated; we cannot develop one without the other.

One way to understand them is to think of different stages of parenthood. When a young woman finds out she is going to have a child, she feels a tremendous outpouring of love for the baby she will bear. She will do everything she can to protect the infant growing inside her. She will make every effort to make sure the baby is well and healthy. She is full of loving, hopeful thoughts for the child. Like metta, the feeling a new mother has for her infant is limitless and all-embracing; and, like metta, it does not depend on actions or behavior of the one receiving our thoughts of loving-friendliness.

As the infant grows older and starts to explore his world, the parents develop compassion. Every time the child scrapes his knee, falls down, or bumps his head, the parent feels the child's pain. Some parents even say that when their child feels pain, it is as if they themselves were being hurt. There is no pity in this feeling; pity puts distance between others and ourselves. Compassion leads us to appropriate action; and the appropriate, compassionate action is just the pure, heartfelt hope that the pain stop and the child not suffer.

As time passes, the child heads off to school. Parents watch as the youngster makes friends, does well in school, sports, and other activities. Maybe the child does well on a spelling test, makes the baseball team, or gets elected class president. The parents are not jealous or resentful of their child's success but are full of happiness for the child. This is appreciative joy. Thinking of how we would feel for our own child, we can feel this for others. Even when we think of others whose success exceeds our own, we can appreciate their achievement and rejoice in their happiness.

To continue in our example: Eventually, after many years, the child grows up. He finishes school and goes out on his own; perhaps he marries and starts a family. Now it is time for the parents to practice equanimity. Clearly, what the parents feel for the child is not indifference. It is an appreciation that they have done all that they could do for the child. They recognize their limitations. Of course the parents continue caring for and respecting their child, but they do so with awareness that they no longer steer the outcome of their child's life. This is the practice of equanimity.

The ultimate goal of our practice of meditation is the cultivation of these four sublime states of loving-friendliness, compassion, appreciative joy, and equanimity.

The word *metta* comes from another Pali word, *mitra*, which means "friend." That is why I prefer to use the phrase "loving-friendliness" as a translation of metta, rather than "loving-kindness." The Sanskrit word *maitri* also refers to the sun at the center of our solar system that makes all life possible. Just as the sun's rays provide energy for all living things, the warmth and radiance of metta flows in the heart of all living beings.

THE SEED IS IN ALL OF US

Different objects reflect the sun's energy differently. Similarly, people differ in their ability to express loving-friendliness. Some people seem naturally warmhearted, while others are more reserved

and reluctant to open their hearts. Some people struggle to cultivate metta; others cultivate it without difficulty. But there is no one
who is totally devoid of loving-friendliness. We are all born with the
instinct for metta. We can see it even in young babies who smile
readily at the sight of another human face, any human face at all.
Sadly, many people have no idea how much loving-friendliness they
have. Their innate capacity for loving-friendliness may be buried
under a heap of hatred, anger, and resentment accumulated through
a lifetime—perhaps many lifetimes—of unwholesome thoughts and
actions. But all of us can cultivate our heart, no matter what. We
can nourish the seeds of loving-friendliness until the force of loving-
friendliness blossoms in all our endeavors.

In the Buddha's time, there was a man named Angulimala; this
man was, to use the language of today, a serial killer, a mass murderer. He was so wretched that he wore around his neck a garland
of fingers taken from the people he had slaughtered, and he planned
to make the Buddha his thousandth victim. In spite of Angulimala's
reputation and his gruesome appearance, the Buddha nonetheless
could see his capacity for loving-friendliness. Thus, out of love and
compassion—his own loving-friendliness—the Buddha taught the
Dhamma to this villainous murderer. As a result of the Buddha's
teaching, Angulimala threw away his sword and surrendered to the
Buddha, joining the followers of the Buddha and becoming ordained.

As it turned out, Angulimala started his vicious killing spree
many years earlier because a man whom Angulimala regarded as
his teacher had (for unwholesome reasons of his own) directed him
to do so. Angulimala was not by nature a cruel person, nor was he
an evil person. In fact, he had been a kind boy. In his heart, there
was loving-friendliness, gentleness, and compassion. As soon as he
became a monk, his true nature was revealed, and not long after his
ordination, he became enlightened.

The story of Angulimala shows us that sometimes people can appear very cruel and wicked, yet we must realize they are not that way by nature. Circumstances in their lives make them act in unwholesome ways. In Angulimala's case, he became a murderer because of his devotion to his teacher. For every one of us, not just violent criminals, there are countless causes and conditions—both wholesome and unwholesome—that make us act as we do.

In addition to the meditation offered earlier in this book, I'd like to offer another way to practice loving-friendliness. Again, you start out in this meditation by banishing thoughts of self-hatred and condemnation. At the beginning of a meditation session, say the following sentences to yourself. And again, really feel the intention:

May my mind be filled with the thoughts of loving-friendliness, compassion, appreciative joy, and equanimity. May I be generous. May I be gentle. May I be relaxed. May I be happy and peaceful. May I be healthy. May my heart become soft. May my words be pleasing to others. May my actions be kind.

May all that I see, hear, smell, taste, touch, and think help me to cultivate loving-friendliness, compassion, appreciative joy, and equanimity. May all these experiences help me to cultivate thoughts of generosity and gentleness. May they all help me to relax. May they inspire friendly behavior. May these experiences be a source of peace and happiness. May they help me be free from fear, tension, anxiety, worry, and restlessness.

No matter where I go in the world, in any direction, may I greet people with happiness, peace, and friendliness. May I be protected in all directions from greed, anger, aversion, hatred, jealousy, and fear.

When we cultivate loving-friendliness in ourselves, we learn to see that others have this kind, gentle nature—however well hidden it might be. Sometimes we have to dig very deep to find it, other times it might be nearer to the surface.

SEEING THROUGH THE DIRT

The Buddha told the story of a monk who finds a filthy piece of cloth on the road. The rag is so nasty, at first the monk does not even want to touch it. He kicks it with his foot to knock off some of the dirt. Disgusted, he gingerly picks it up with two fingers, holding it away from himself with contempt. Yet even as the monk does this, he sees potential in that scrap of dirty cloth, and takes it home and washes it—over and over and over. Eventually, the wash water runs clean, and from underneath the filth and grime, a useful piece of material is revealed. The monk sees that if he collects enough pieces, he could, perhaps, make this rag into part of a robe.

Likewise, because of a person's nasty words, that person may seem totally worthless; it may be impossible to see that person's potential for loving-friendliness. But this is where the practice of skillful effort comes in. Underneath such a person's rough exterior, you may find the warm, radiant jewel that is the person's true nature.

A person may use very harsh words for others, yet sometimes still act with compassion and kindness. In spite of her words, her deeds may be good. The Buddha compared this kind of person to a pond covered by moss. In order to use that water, you must brush the moss aside. Similarly, we sometimes need to ignore a person's superficial weaknesses to find her good heart.

But what if a person's words are cruel and her actions too are unkind? Is she rotten through and through? Even a person like this may have a pure heart. Imagine you have been walking through a desert. You have no water with you, and there is no water any-where around. You are hot and tired. With every step, you become thirstier and thirstier. You are desperate for water. Then you come across a cow's footprint. There is water in the footprint, but not much because the footprint is not very deep. If you try to scoop up the water with your hand, it will become very muddy. You are so thirsty, you kneel down and bend over. Very slowly, you bring your mouth to the water and sip it, very carefully so as not to disturb the mud. Even though there is dirt all around, the little bit of water is still clear. You can quench your thirst. With similar effort, we can find a good heart even in a person who seems totally without redemption.

The meditation center where I most often teach is in the hills of the West Virginia countryside. When we first opened our center, there was a man down the road who was very unfriendly. I take a long walk every day, and, whenever I saw this man, I would wave to him. He would just frown at me and look away. Even so, I would always wave and think kindly of him, sending him metta. I was not fazed by his attitude; I never gave up on him. Whenever I saw him, I waved. After about a year, his behavior changed. He stopped frown-ing. I felt wonderful. The practice of loving-friendliness was begin-ning to bear fruit.

After another year, when I passed him on my walk, something miraculous happened. He drove past me and lifted one finger off the steering wheel. Again, I thought, "Oh, this is wonderful! Loving-friendliness is working." And yet another year passed as, day after day, I would wave to him and wish him well. The third year, he lifted two fingers in my direction. Then the next year, he lifted all four fingers off the wheel. More time passed. I was walking down the road as he turned into his driveway. He took his hand completely off the steering wheel, stuck it out the window, and waved back to me.

One day, not long after that, I saw this man parked on the side of one of the forest roads. He was sitting in the driver's seat smoking a cigarette. I went over to him and we started talking. First we chatted just about the weather and then, little by little, his story unfolded: It turns out that, several years ago, he had been in a terrible accident—a tree had fallen on his truck. Almost every bone in his body had been broken, and he was left in a coma for some time. When I first started seeing him on the road, he was only beginning to recover. It was not because he was a mean person that he did not wave back to me; he did not wave back because he could not move all his fingers! Had I given up on him, I would never have known how good this man is. One day, when I had been away on a trip, he actually came by our center looking for me. He was worried because he hadn't seen me walking in a while. Now we are friends.

PRACTICING LOVING-FRIENDLINESS

The Buddha said, "By surveying the entire world with my mind, I have not come across anyone who loves others more than himself. Therefore one who loves himself should cultivate this loving-friendliness." Cultivate loving-friendliness toward yourself first, with the intention of sharing your kind thoughts with others. Develop this feeling. Be full of kindness toward yourself. Accept yourself just as you are. Make peace with your shortcomings. Embrace even your weaknesses. Be gentle and forgiving with yourself as you are at this very moment. If thoughts arise as to how you should be such and such a way, let them go. Establish fully the depth of these feelings of goodwill and kindness. Let the power of loving-friendliness saturate your entire body and mind. Relax in its warmth and radiance. Expend this feeling to your loved ones, to people you don't know or feel neutrally about—and even to your adversaries!

Let each and every one of us imagine that our minds are free from greed, anger, aversion, jealousy, and fear. Let the thought of loving-friendliness embrace us and envelop us. Let every cell, every drop of blood, every atom, every molecule of our entire bodies and minds be charged with the thought of friendliness. Let us relax our bodies. Let us relax our minds. Let our minds and bodies be filled with the thought of loving-friendliness. Let the peace and tranquility of loving-friendliness pervade our entire being.

May all beings in all directions, all around the universe, have good hearts. Let them be happy, let them have good fortune, let them be kind, let them have good and caring friends. May all beings everywhere be filled with the feeling of loving-friendliness—abundant, exalted, and measureless. May they be free from enmity, free from affliction and anxiety. May they live happily.

Just as we walk or run or swim to strengthen our bodies, the practice of loving-friendliness on a regular basis strengthens our hearts. At first it may seem as if you are only going through the motions. But by associating with thoughts of metta over and over, it becomes a habit, a good habit. In time, your heart grows stronger, and the response of loving-friendliness becomes automatic. As our hearts become stronger, even toward difficult people we can think kind and loving thoughts.

May my adversaries be well, happy, and peaceful. May no harm come to them, may no difficulty come to them, may no pain come to them. May they always meet with success.

"Success?" some people ask. "How can we wish our adversaries success? What if they're trying to kill me?" When we wish success for our adversaries, we don't mean worldly success or success in doing something immoral or unethical; we mean success in the spiritual realm. Our adversaries are clearly not successful spiritually; if they were successful spiritually, they would not be acting in a way that causes us harm.

Whenever we say of our adversaries, "May they be successful," we mean: "May my enemies be free from anger, greed, and jealousy. May they have peace, comfort, and happiness." Why is somebody cruel or unkind? Perhaps that person was brought up under unfortunate circumstances. Perhaps there are situations in that person's life we don't know about that cause him or her to act cruelly. The Buddha asked us to think of such people the same way we would if someone were suffering from a terrible illness. Do we get angry or upset with people who are ill? Or do we have sympathy and compassion for them? Perhaps even more than our loved ones, our adversaries deserve our kindness, for their suffering is so much greater. For these reasons, without any reservation, we should cultivate kind thoughts about them. We include them in our hearts just as we would those dearest to us.

May all those who have harmed us be free from greed, anger, aversion, hatred, jealousy, and fear. Let these thoughts of loving-friendliness embrace them, envelop them. Let every cell, every drop of blood, every atom, every molecule of their entire bodies and minds be charged with thoughts of friendliness. Let them relax their bodies. Let them relax their minds. Let the peace and tranquility pervade their entire being.

Practicing loving-friendliness can change our habitual negative thought patterns and reinforce positive ones. When we practice metta meditation, our minds will become filled with peace and happiness. We will be relaxed. We gain concentration. When our mind becomes calm and peaceful, our hatred, anger, and resentment fade away. But loving-friendliness is not limited to our thoughts. We must manifest it in our words and our actions. We cannot cultivate loving-friendliness in isolation from the world.

You can start by thinking kind thoughts about everyone you have contact with every day. If you have mindfulness, you can do this every waking minute with everyone you deal with. Whenever you see someone, consider that, like yourself, that person wants happiness and wants to avoid suffering. We all feel that way. All beings feel that way. Even the tiniest insect recoils from harm. When we recognize that common ground, we see how closely we are all connected. The woman behind the checkout counter, the man who passes you on the expressway, the young couple walking across the street, the old man in the park feeding the birds. Whenever you see another being, any being, keep this in mind. Wish for them happiness, peace, and well-being. It is a practice that can change your life and the lives of those around you.

At first, you may experience resistance to this practice. Perhaps the practice seems forced. Perhaps you feel unable to bring yourself to feel these kinds of thoughts. Because of experiences in your own life, it may be easier to feel loving-friendliness for some people and more difficult for others. Children, for example, often bring out our feelings of loving-friendliness quite naturally, while with others, it may be more difficult. Watch the habits in your mind. Learn to recognize your negative emotions and start to break them down. With mindfulness, little by little you can change your responses.

Does sending someone thoughts of loving-friendliness actually change the other person? Can practicing loving-friendliness change the world? When you are sending loving-friendliness to people who are far away or people you may not even know, of course, it is not possible to know the effect. But you can notice the effect that practicing loving-friendliness has on your own peace of mind. What is important is the sincerity of your own wish for the happiness of others. Truly, the effect is immediate. The only way to find this out for yourself is to try it.

Practicing metta does not mean that we ignore the unwholesome actions of others. It simply means that we respond to such actions in an appropriate way. There was a prince named Abharaja Kumara. One day he went to the Buddha and asked whether the Buddha was ever harsh to others. At this time the prince had his little child on his lap. "Suppose, Prince, this little child of yours were to put a piece of wood in his mouth, what would you do?" asked the Buddha. "If he put a piece of wood in his mouth, I would hold the child very tightly between my legs and put my crooked index finger in his mouth. Though he might be crying and struggling in discomfort, I would pull the piece of wood out even if he bleeds," said the prince.

"Why would you do that?"

"Because I love my child. I want to save his life," was his reply.

"Similarly, Prince, sometimes I have to be harsh on my disciples not out of cruelty, but out of love for them," said the Buddha. Loving-friendliness, not anger, motivated his actions.

The Buddha provided us with five very basic tools for dealing with others in a kindhearted way. These tools are the five precepts. Some people think of morality as restrictions on freedom, but in fact, these precepts liberate us. They free us from the suffering we cause ourselves and others when we act unkindly. These guidelines train us to protect others from harm; and, by protecting others, we protect ourselves. The precepts caution us to abstain from taking life, from stealing, from sexual misconduct, from speaking falsely or harshly, and from using intoxicants that cause us to act in an unmindful way.

Developing mindfulness through the practice of meditation also helps us relate to others with loving-friendliness. On the cushion, we watch our minds as liking and disliking arise. We teach ourselves to relax our mind when such thoughts arise. We learn to see attachment and aversion as momentary states, and we learn to let them go. Meditation helps us look at the world in a new light and gives us a way out. The deeper we go in our practice, the more skills we develop.

Dealing with Anger

When we are angry with someone, we often latch on to one particular aspect of that person. Usually it's only a moment or two, enough for a few harsh words, a certain look, a thoughtless action. In our minds, the rest of that person drops away. All that is left is the part that pushed our buttons. When we do this, we are isolating one miniscule fraction of the whole person as something real and solid. We are not seeing all the factors and forces that shaped that person. We focus on only one aspect of that person—the part that made us angry.

Over the years, I have received many letters from prisoners who are seeking to learn the Dhamma. Some have done terrible things, even murder. And yet they see things differently now and want to change their lives. There was one letter that was particularly insightful and deeply touched my heart. In it, the writer described how the other inmates shouted and jeered whenever the guard appeared. The inmate tried to explain to the others that this guard was also a human being, but the others were blinded by hatred. All they could see, he said, was the uniform, not the man inside it.

When we are angry with someone, we can ask ourselves, "Am I angry at the hair on that person's head? Am I angry at his skin? His teeth? His brain? His heart? His sense of humor? His tenderness?

His generosity? His smile?" When we take the time to consider all the many elements and processes that make up a person, our anger naturally softens. Through the practice of mindfulness, we learn to see both ourselves and others more clearly. Understanding helps us to relate to others with loving-friendliness. Within each of us is a core of goodness. In some, as in the case of Angulimala, we cannot see this true nature. Understanding the concept of "no-self" softens our heart and helps us forgive the unkind actions of others. We learn to relate to ourselves and others with loving-friendliness.

But, what if someone hurts you? What if someone insults you? You may want to retaliate—which is a very human response. But, where does that lead? "Hatred is never appeased by more hatred," it says in the *Dhammapada*. An angry response only leads to more anger. If you respond to anger with loving-friendliness, the other person's anger will not increase. Slowly it may fade away. "By love alone is anger appeased," continues the verse in the *Dhammapada*.

An enemy of the Buddha named Devadatta concocted a scheme to kill the Buddha. Having enraged an elephant with alcohol, Devadatta let him loose at a time and a place Devadatta knew the Buddha would be. Everyone on the road ran away. Everyone who saw the Buddha warned him to run away. But the Buddha kept on walking. His devoted companion, the Venerable Ananda, thought he could stop the elephant. When Ananda stepped in front of the Buddha to try to protect him, the Buddha asked him to step aside; Ananda's physical strength alone surely could not stop this elephant.

When the elephant reached the Buddha, his head was raised, his ears were upright, and his trunk was lifted in a mad fury. The Buddha simply stood in front of him and radiated loving, compassionate thoughts toward the animal—and the elephant stopped in his tracks. The Buddha gently raised his hand up with his palm toward the beast, sending him waves of loving-friendliness. The elephant knelt down before him, gentle as a lamb. With the power of loving-friendliness alone, the Buddha had subdued the raging animal.

The response of anger to anger is a conditioned response; it is learned rather than innate. If we have been trained from childhood to be patient, kind, and gentle, then loving-friendliness becomes part of our life. It becomes a habit. Otherwise anger becomes our habit. But even as adults, we can change our habitual responses. We can train ourselves to react in a different way.

There is another story from the Buddha's life that teaches us how to respond to insults and harsh words. The Buddha's rivals had bribed a prostitute named Cinca to insult and humiliate the Buddha. Cinca tied a bunch of sticks to her belly underneath her rough clothes in order to look like she was pregnant. While the Buddha was delivering a sermon to hundreds of people, she came right out in front of him and said, "You rogue. You pretend to be a saint preaching to all these people. But look what you have done to me! I am pregnant because of you." Calmly, the Buddha spoke to her, without anger, without hatred. With his voice full of loving-friendliness and compassion, he said to her, "Sister, you and I are the only ones who know what has happened." Cinca was taken aback by the Buddha's response. She was so shocked that on the way back she stumbled. The strings that were holding the bundle of sticks to her belly came loose. All the sticks fell to the ground, and everyone realized her ruse. Several people in the audience wanted to beat her, but the Buddha stopped them. "No, no. That is not the way you should treat her. We should help her understand the Dhamma. That is a much more effective punishment." After the Buddha taught her the Dhamma, her entire personality changed. She too became gentle, kind, and compassionate.

When someone tries to make you angry or does something to hurt you, stay with your thoughts of loving-friendliness toward that person. A person filled with thoughts of loving-friendliness, the Buddha said, is like the earth. Someone may try to make the earth disappear by digging at it with a hoe or an ax, but that is a futile act. No amount of digging—not in one lifetime or many lifetimes—makes the earth vanish. The earth remains, unaffected, undiminished. Like the earth, a person full of loving-friendliness is untouched by anger.

In another story from the Buddha's life, there was a man named Akkosana, whose name means "not getting angry." But in fact, this man was exactly the opposite: he was always getting angry. When he heard that the Buddha never got angry with anyone, he decided to visit him. He went up to the Buddha and scolded him for all sorts of things, insulting him and calling him awful names. At the end of his tirade, the Buddha asked this man if he had any friends and relatives. "Yes," he replied. "When you visit them, do you take them gifts?" "Of course," said the man. "I always bring them gifts." "What happens if they don't accept your gifts?" the Buddha asked. "Well, I just take them home and enjoy them with my own family." "And likewise," said the Buddha, "you have brought me a gift today that I don't accept. You may take that gift home to your family." With patience, wit, and loving-friendliness, the Buddha invites us to change how we think about the "gift" of angry words.

If we respond to insults or angry words with mindfulness and loving-friendliness, we are able to look closely at the whole situation. Perhaps that person did not know what he or she was saying. Perhaps the words were not meant to harm you. It may have been totally innocent or inadvertent. Perhaps it was your frame of mind at the time the words were spoken. Perhaps you did not hear the words clearly or misunderstood the context. It is also important to consider carefully what that person is saying. If you respond with anger, you will not hear the message behind the words. Perhaps that person is pointing out something you need to hear.

We all encounter people who push our buttons. Without mindfulness and loving-friendliness, we respond automatically with anger or resentment. With mindfulness, we can watch how our mind responds to certain words and actions. Just as we do on the cushion, we can watch the arising of attachment and aversion. Mindfulness is like a safety net that cushions us against unwholesome actions. Mindfulness gives us time; time gives us choices. We don't have to be swept away by our feelings. We can respond with wisdom rather than delusion.

UNIVERSAL LOVING-FRIENDLINESS

Loving-friendliness is not something we do sitting on a cushion in one place, thinking and thinking and thinking. We must let the power of loving-friendliness shine through every encounter with others. Loving-friendliness is the underlying principle behind all wholesome thoughts, words, and deeds. With loving-friendliness, we recognize more clearly the needs of others and help them readily. With thoughts of loving-friendliness we appreciate the success of others with warm feeling. We need loving-friendliness in order to live and work with others in harmony. Loving-friendliness protects us from the suffering caused by anger and jealousy. When we cultivate our loving-friendliness, our compassion, our appreciative joy for others, and our equanimity, we not only make life more pleasant for those around us, our own lives become peaceful and happy. The power of loving-friendliness, like the radiance of the sun, is beyond measure.

May all those who are imprisoned legally or illegally, all who are in police custody anywhere in the world meet with peace and happiness. May they be free from greed, anger, aversion, hatred, jealousy, and fear. Let their bodies and minds be filled with thoughts of loving-friendliness. Let the peace and tranquility of loving-friendliness pervade their entire bodies and minds.

May all who are in hospitals suffering from numerous sicknesses meet with peace and happiness. May they be free from pain, afflictions, depression, disappointment, anxiety, and fear. Let these thoughts of loving-friendliness embrace all of them, envelop them. Let their minds and bodies be filled with the thought of loving-friendliness.

May all mothers who are in pain delivering babies meet with peace and happiness. Let every drop of blood, every cell, every atom, every molecule of their entire bodies and minds be charged with these thoughts of friendliness.

May all single parents taking care of their children meet with peace and happiness. May they have the patience, courage, understanding, and determination to meet and overcome the inevitable difficulties, problems, and failures in life. May they be well, happy, and peaceful.

May all children abused by adults in numerous ways meet with peace and happiness. May they be filled with thoughts of loving-friendliness, compassion, appreciative joy, and equanimity. May they be gentle. May they be relaxed. May their hearts become soft. May their words be pleasing to others. May they be free from fear, tension, anxiety, worry, and restlessness.

May all rulers be gentle, kind, generous, and compassionate. May they have understanding of the oppressed, the underprivileged, the discriminated against, and the poverty-stricken. May their hearts melt at the suffering of their unfortunate citizens. Let these thoughts of loving-friendliness embrace them, envelop them. Let every cell, every drop of blood, every atom, every molecule of their entire bodies and minds be charged with thoughts of friendliness. Let the peace and tranquility of loving-friendliness pervade their entire being.

May the oppressed and underprivileged, the poverty-stricken and those discriminated against, meet with peace and happiness. May they be free from pain, afflictions, depression, disappointment, anxiety, and fear. May all of them in all directions, all around the universe, be well, happy, and at peace. May they have the patience, courage, understanding, and determination to meet and overcome the inevitable difficulties, problems, and failures in life. May these thoughts of loving-friendliness embrace all of them, envelop them. May their minds and bodies be filled with thoughts of loving-friendliness.

May all beings everywhere of every shape and form, with two legs, four legs, many legs, or no legs, born or coming to birth, in this realm or the next, have happy minds. May no one deceive another nor despise anyone anywhere. May no one wish harm to another. Toward all living beings, may I cultivate a boundless heart, above, below, and all around, unobstructed without hatred or resentment. May all beings be released from suffering and attain perfect peace.

Loving-friendliness goes beyond all boundaries of religion, culture, geography, language, and nationality. It is a universal and ancient law that binds all of us together—no matter what form we may take. Loving-friendliness should be practiced unconditionally. My enemy's pain is my pain. His anger is my anger. His loving-friendliness is my loving-friendliness. If he is happy, I am happy. If he is peaceful, I am peaceful. If he is healthy, I am healthy. Just as we all share suffering regardless of our differences, we should all share our loving-friendliness with every person everywhere. No one nation can stand alone without the help and support of other nations, nor can any one person exist in isolation. To survive, we need other living beings, beings who are bound to be different from us. That is simply the way things are. Because of the differences we have, the practice of loving-friendliness is absolutely necessary. It is what ties all of us together.

Appendix:
The Context of the Tradition

*T*he subject of this book is vipassana meditation practice. Repeat, practice. This is a meditation manual, a nuts-and-bolts, step-by-step guide to insight meditation. It is meant to be practical. It is meant for use.

There are many styles of meditation. Every major religious tradition has some sort of procedure that they call meditation, and the word is often very loosely used. Please understand that this volume deals exclusively with the *vipassana* style of meditation, as taught and practiced in South and Southeast Asian Buddhism. Vipassana is a Pali-language term often translated as "insight" meditation, since the purpose of this system is to give the meditator insight into the nature of reality and accurate understanding of how everything works.

Buddhism as a whole is quite different from the theological religions with which Westerners are most familiar. It is a direct entrance to a spiritual or divine realm, without assistance from deities or other "agents." Its flavor is intensely clinical, much more akin to what we might call psychology than to what we would usually call religion. Buddhist practice is an ongoing investigation of reality, a microscopic examination of the very process of perception. Its intention is to pick apart the screen of lies and delusions through which we normally view the world, and thus to reveal the face of ultimate reality. Vipassana meditation is an ancient and elegant technique for doing just that.

Theravada (pronounced "terra vada") Buddhism presents us with an effective system for exploring the deeper levels of the mind, down to the very root of consciousness itself. It also offers a considerable system of reverence and rituals, in which those techniques are contained. This beautiful tradition is the natural result of its 2,500-year development within the highly traditional cultures of South and Southeast Asia.

In this volume, we make every effort to separate the ornamental from the fundamental and to present only the plain truth. Those readers who are of a ritual bent may investigate the Theravada practice in other books, and will find there a vast wealth of customs and ceremony, a rich tradition full of beauty and significance. Those of a more pragmatic bent may use just the techniques themselves, applying them within whatever philosophical and emotional context they wish. The practice is the thing.

The distinction between vipassana meditation and other styles of meditation is crucial, and needs to be fully understood. Buddhism addresses two major types of meditation; they are different mental skills or modes of functioning, different qualities of consciousness. In Pali, the original language of Theravada literature, they are called *vipassana* and *samatha*.

Vipassana can be translated as "insight," a clear awareness of exactly what is happening as it happens. *Samatha* can be translated as "concentration" or "tranquility," and is a state in which the mind is focused only on one item, brought to rest, and not allowed to wander. When this is done, a deep calm pervades body and mind, a state of tranquility that must be experienced to be understood. Most systems of meditation emphasize the samatha component. The meditator focuses his or her mind on a certain item, such as a prayer, a chant, a candle flame, or a religious image, and excludes all other thoughts and perceptions from his or her consciousness. The result is a state of rapture, which lasts until the meditator ends the session of sitting. It is beautiful, delightful, meaningful, and alluring, but only temporary.

Vipassana meditation addresses the other component: insight. The vipassana meditator uses concentration as a tool by which his or her awareness can chip away at the wall of illusion that blocks the living light of reality. It is a gradual process of ever-increasing awareness into the inner workings of reality itself. It takes years, but one day the meditator chisels through that wall and tumbles into the presence of light. The transformation is complete. It's called liberation, and it's permanent. Liberation is the goal of all Buddhist systems of practice. But the routes to the attainment of that end are quite diverse.

There are an enormous number of distinct sects within Buddhism. They divide into two broad streams of thought: Mahayana and Theravada. Mahayana Buddhism prevails throughout East Asia, shaping the cultures of China, Korea, Japan, Nepal, Tibet, and Vietnam. The most widely known of the Mahayana systems is Zen, practiced mainly in Japan, Korea, Vietnam, and the United States. The Theravada system of practice prevails in South and Southeast Asia in the countries of Sri Lanka, Thailand, Myanmar, Laos, and Cambodia. This book deals with Theravada practice.

Traditional Theravada literature describes the techniques of both samatha (concentration) and vipassana (insight) meditation. There are forty different subjects of meditation described in the Pali literature. They are recommended as objects of concentration and subjects of investigation leading to insight. But this is a basic manual, and we will limit our discussion to the most fundamental of those recommended objects: breathing. This book is an introduction to the attainment of mindfulness through bare attention to, and clear comprehension of, the whole process of breathing. Using the breath as the primary focus of attention, the meditator applies participatory observation to the entirety of his or her own perceptual universe. The meditator learns to watch changes occurring in all physical experiences, feelings, and perceptions, and learns to study his or her own mental activities and the fluctuations in the character of consciousness itself. All of these changes are occurring perpetually and are present in every moment of our experiences.

Meditation is a living activity, an inherently experiential activity. It cannot be taught as a purely scholastic subject. The living heart of the process must come from the teacher's own personal experience. Nevertheless, there is a vast fund of codified material on the subject, produced by some of the most intelligent and deeply illumined human beings ever to walk the earth. This literature is worthy of attention. Most of the points given in this book are drawn from the Tipitaka, which is the three-section compendium of the Buddha's original teachings. The Tipitaka is comprised of the Vinaya, the code of discipline for monks, nuns, and laypeople; the Suttas, public discourses attributed to the Buddha; and the Abhidhamma, a set of deep psycho-philosophical teachings.

In the first century C.E., an eminent Buddhist scholar named Upatissa wrote the *Vimuttimagga (The Path of Freedom)*, in which he summarized the Buddha's teachings on meditation. In the fifth century C.E., another great Buddhist scholar, named Buddhaghosa, covered the same ground in a second scholastic thesis, the *Visuddhimagga (The Path of Purification)*, which remains the standard text on meditation today.

This book offers you a foot in the door. It's up to you to take the first few steps on the road to the discovery of who you are and what it all means. It is a journey worth taking.

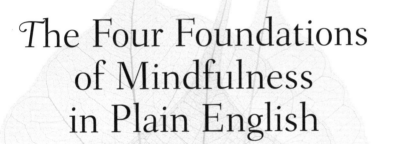

The Four Foundations
of Mindfulness
in Plain English

The Four Foundations of
Mindfulness Sutta

*B*efore we turn to a detailed consideration of each of the four foundations, let's look ahead to what we will be covering. As I mentioned, the teachings on the four foundations come down to us from a teaching talk given by the Buddha known as the *Satipatthana Sutta*. A summarized version of the sutta is given below. I have added headings not part of the original sutta to help you follow the sequence.

As you read this book, you may find it helpful to turn back to the sutta from time to time to refresh your memory about what's been covered and look ahead at what's to come. Try reading the sutta out loud when you turn to it. It's beneficial to hear the Buddha's words as if they were intended specifically for you—which, of course, they are!

A word of advice: This book is not meant to be read like a novel or digested like a university textbook. Rather, the teachings of the Buddha are to be explored and practiced, more like a piece of great music. As your familiarity grows, your experiential understanding of the Dhamma takes on a life of its own. In the beginning, mindfulness takes much effort, but eventually, it becomes second nature.

A Daily Mindfulness Practice

If you're already practicing meditation, or if reading this book inspires you to start, you can make reading the *Satipatthana Sutta* part of your meditation session.

I always recommend that people begin a session of meditation with thoughts of loving-friendliness for their parents, teachers, relatives, friends, strangers, adversaries, and ultimately, for all living beings. Starting your meditation session in this way helps develop your concentration and also avoid any resentment that may arise as you sit.

Then, before turning your attention to the breath or other point of focus, you may find it worthwhile to read aloud, recite, or even chant the version of the *Satipatthana Sutta* given below. Read or recite slowly, to give yourself time to review in your mind what you've learned or understood about each point. If you find that you cannot remember the Buddha's meaning or that you are confused about something, resolve to read more or to ask a more experienced meditator for help. If you read and think about the sutta every day, eventually the whole sequence of mindfulness practices will be at the tip of your tongue.

The Four Foundations of Mindfulness
Satipatthana Sutta

Bhikkhus, this is the direct path for the purification of beings,
for the surmounting of sorrow and lamentation,
for the disappearance of pain and grief,
for the attainment of the true way,
for the realization of nibbana—namely,
the four foundations of mindfulness.

1. Mindfulness of the Body
Mindfulness of the breath.
Mindfulness of the four postures: walking, standing, sitting, and lying down.
Mindfulness with clear comprehension: of what is beneficial, of suitability, of the meditator's domain, of nondelusion.
Reflection on the thirty-two parts of the body.
Analysis of the four elements.
Nine cemetery contemplations.

2. Mindfulness of Feelings
Pleasant, painful, and neither painful nor pleasant feelings, worldly and spiritual.
Awareness of their manifestation, arising, and disappearance.

3. Mindfulness of Mind
Understanding the mind as:
greedy or not greedy,
hateful or not hateful,
deluded or not deluded,
contracted or distracted,
not developed or developed,
not supreme or supreme,
not concentrated or concentrated,
not liberated or liberated.
Awareness of its manifestation, arising, and disappearance.

4. Mindfulness of Dhamma
FIVE MENTAL HINDRANCES
Sense desire, ill will, sloth and torpor, restlessness and worry, skeptical doubt.
Awareness of their manifestation, origin, and disappearance.

FIVE AGGREGATES OF CLINGING
Material form, feelings, perceptions,
mental formations, and consciousness.
Awareness of their manifestation, arising, and dissolution.

SIX INTERNAL AND SIX EXTERNAL SENSE BASES
Eye and visible objects, ear and sounds, nose and smells, tongue
and tastes, body and tangible objects, mind and mental objects.
Knowledge of them, and of the arising, abandoning, and
future nonarising of the fetters that originate dependent on both.

SEVEN FACTORS OF ENLIGHTENMENT
Mindfulness, investigation of Dhamma, energy,
joy, tranquility, concentration, and equanimity.
Knowledge of their presence, their arising, and their development.

FOUR NOBLE TRUTHS
Suffering, its origin, its cessation,
and the path that leads to the cessation of suffering.

NOBLE EIGHTFOLD PATH
Skillful understanding, thinking, speech, action, livelihood,
effort, mindfulness, and concentration.

Bhikkhus, if anyone should properly develop these four foundations of mindfulness for seven years . . . or even for seven days,
one of two fruits could be expected for that person:
either final knowledge here and now,
or, if there is a trace of clinging left, the state of nonreturning.

Part 1:

Mindfulness of the Body

1. Breath

Twenty years after the Buddha attained enlightenment, a senior monk by the name of Ananda became his personal attendant. One day he asked the Buddha, "Venerable sir, if people ask me whether you are still practicing meditation, what shall I tell them?"

The Buddha replied that, yes, he was still meditating.

"What kind of meditation do you practice, venerable sir?" Ananda asked.

"Mindfulness of breathing," the Buddha answered.

*M*editation on the breath is the ideal way to get started with mindfulness training. Breathing is our most constantly repeated physical action. The mind can always return to the breath as an object of focus because it is always with us. We don't need to be taught to breathe. Nor do we need long experience with meditation to place our attention on the breath. The breath is also our life force. No organ in the body can function without the supply of oxygen we get from the cycle of breathing in and breathing out.

Moreover, breathing is not exclusive. Living beings differ in appearance and behavior. They eat various kinds of food. They sleep in many types of beds. But all living beings breathe. Breathing does not differentiate among Buddhists, Christians, Hindus, Sikhs, Jews,

Muslims, and Zoroastrians. Nor does it distinguish between rich and poor, capitalists and socialists, or conservatives and liberals, for that matter. When we focus on the breath, we become mindful of the universal nature of all beings.

Although we have been breathing our entire life, until we pay attention to the process, we do not know what is really happening. But when we focus the mind on the breath, we discover everything related to the breath. Training in this way is so essential to our peace of mind and spiritual progress that the Buddha recommends that everyone practice meditation on the breath.

Even the Buddha used mindfulness of breathing to achieve his goal. After his enlightenment, the Buddha described how he had previously practiced extreme self-discipline by manipulating his breath in arcane and special ways. But he discovered that he could not get rid of impurities by holding his breath or altering his breathing. So he gave up breath-control exercises and followed his own middle way.

In the gathering dusk, on the night he would attain enlightenment, the Buddha asked himself, "What subject of meditation should I practice?" Then he remembered. "Ah! When I was a child, I used the breath. Let me use the breath again." So he focused his mind on the breath, just as it was. After long hours of unwavering mindfulness and deep concentration, everything became clear to him. The last of his negative mental habits disappeared, and he reached enlightenment—full and complete liberation from suffering.

THE BUDDHA'S INSTRUCTIONS

In one of the most important suttas, the Buddha explains in detail how to practice mindfulness of breathing. He suggests that people go to a quiet place, such as a forest or a house with few noises—somewhere they have undisturbed solitude and can withdraw from everyday concerns. There, he says, begin by establishing mindfulness "in front."

By these words he doesn't mean that we should place our attention on what is in front of us in space. Rather, we focus on the present moment. We cannot live in the past, nor can we live in the future. Even when we remember something that happened in the past, we understand that this memory is occurring now. The only place and time truly available to us is right here and right now. For this reason, we establish mindfulness by paying attention to this very instance of breathing in and breathing out.

Having established the mind in the present moment, the Buddha continues, sit in a comfortable posture, with the body straight—upright but not uptight. I explain more fully about comfortable postures for sitting meditation in the next chapter. Then focus the mind on the breath, going in and going out, in and out.

Among other things, we become aware that sometimes the breath is long and sometimes short. These variations are natural. If we watch a baby sleeping, we observe that the baby breathes for a while in a regular rhythm. Then she takes a long breath. Then she goes back to her previous rhythm.

As the Buddha explains, when we breathe in long, we understand, "I breathe in long," and when we breathe out long, we understand, "I breathe out long." Breathing in short, we understand, "I breathe in short." Breathing out short, we understand, "I breathe out short." This advice can be misinterpreted to mean that we should force ourselves to take long inhaling breaths and long exhaling breaths, or short inhaling breaths and short exhaling breaths. But when we deliberately alter the duration, our breathing does not follow its natural rhythm. Soon, we get tired. Meditation on the breath is not a breathing exercise. We are simply using the breath as a point of focus to cultivate mindfulness.

As we discover, when we pay attention to its natural rhythm, the breath becomes calm. Simultaneously, the mind quiets down. It all happens naturally. Mindfulness itself makes the breath relax. Any force is counterproductive. Agitation or extra effort makes our breathing speed up. When this happens, we pay attention to the fast breathing and notice the agitation. Then we relax the mind, and the agitation disappears by itself.

We also notice that when we inhale and exhale with mindfulness, we experience the feeling of each breath. The sensations change as the breath changes. So we observe the changing breath and the changing sensations. We find, for instance, that sometimes the breath is shallow; other times it is deep. Sometimes it is easy to breathe; other times, not so easy. We watch these variations.

Along with this, we notice another pattern of subtle feelings, a little bit of anxiety and relief of anxiety, pressure and release of pressure, for instance. Mindfulness helps us notice that when the lungs are full of air, we feel a slight pressure or tension in our lungs. As we breathe out, this tension is slowly released. But when there is no more air in our lungs, we experience a degree of anxiety because there is no air in our lungs. So we breathe in again, and this anxiety fades away. As it does, we experience a degree of pleasure but also the return of pressure.

Of course, we have to pay total attention to the cycle of breathing to notice these changes. We soon discover that there is no escape from them. We inhale and experience pleasure and then tension. We exhale and experience release but also anxiety. But even this pattern has much to teach us. When we experience tension, we remind ourselves not to be disappointed. When we experience pleasure, we remember not to attach to it.

So, as we breathe in and out, we strive to maintain equanimity, a balanced mind. We remind ourselves that our underlying preference for pleasant feelings often arises from desire, which can lead to greed for sensual pleasure. But when we crave pleasure, we always end up suffering, because like all impermanent things, pleasure eventually changes or disappears. We also remember that our underlying tendency to avoid unpleasant feelings often arises from resentment, which can lead to anger. We observe these tendencies, our greed and our anger, and then let them go, returning our attention to the breath.

THE BREATH-BODY

We also pay attention to how we feel at the beginning, the middle, and the end of each in-breath and out-breath. This awareness of the entire breathing cycle is called mindfulness of the breath-body. While the mind is engaged with the breath-body, the mind and the breath are relaxed. When they are relaxed, the rest of our body is also relaxed. This is so because the breath is part of the body. Paying attention to the breath-body is an aspect of being mindful of "the body in the body," as the Buddha recommends. Mindfulness helps us see that the breath and the body are not completely separate.

We experience the relationship between breath and body when we notice the rising and falling of the abdomen during the breathing cycle, as some meditation teachers suggest. When we breathe in, the abdomen expands, and when we breathe out, it contracts. But actually, the movement of the abdomen is the second stage of the body's rising and falling. The first stage occurs at the tip of the nose. Inhaling is rising and exhaling is falling. With mindfulness, we notice in a microscopic way our body's expansion or rising as we breathe in and contraction or falling as we breathe out.

While noticing these events, we also feel expansion, contraction, and other subtle movements in the entire body. These same motions occur in every material object. Even walls breathe! In summer, they expand; in winter, they contract. Astrophysicists tell us that the whole universe is actually expanding and contracting. To practice mindfulness of breathing, however, we need awareness only of the expansion and contraction in our own body.

INTERNAL AND EXTERNAL ELEMENTS

Another way we become aware of the relationship between the breath and the body is by noting that the breath is made up of four elements—earth, water, air, and heat. All material objects, including the body, are composed of these elements.

As we practice mindfulness of breathing, we recognize that it is the breath's earth element—its form or shape—that gives rise to pressure, release, and other sensations of touch in the nose, lungs, and abdomen. Similarly, we notice that the breath is dry when its water element is low. When we are aware of moisture in the breath, its water element is high.

The function of the air element is motion and energy. We experience the movement of the breath because of its air element. The temperature of the breath is due to its heat element. Heat fluctuates. When its heat element is high, we call the breath hot. When it goes down, we call the breath cold.

In addition to the four elements, the parts of the body—including the breath—are described as internal or external. The elements inside the body are internal; those outside are external. If we think about this distinction, it may occur to us that the breath that we have inhaled is internal. When we exhale, this internal breath mixes with the external air. Then the breath is external. We might also say that the internal body is inhaling, and the external body is exhaling.

In the *Maha Rahulovada Sutta*, the Buddha explains the meaning of the words "internal" and "external" as they apply to the four elements of the body. In terms of the air element, he says, "Whatever internally, belonging to oneself, is air . . . that is up-going winds, down-going winds, winds in limbs, in-breath and out-breath . . . this is called the internal air element."

Moreover, the Buddha explains, "Both the internal air element and the external air element are simply air element." This point is important because of our tendency to cling to things we perceive as belonging to us. But seen with "proper wisdom," we recognize that even the air we inhale—the internal air—"is not mine, this I am not, and this is not my self. When one sees it thus as it actually is . . . one becomes disenchanted with the air element and makes the mind dispassionate toward the air element."

Further, the Buddha continues, from time to time, the external air element is disturbed. It "sweeps away villages, towns, cities, districts, and countries," as it does in a hurricane or tornado. At other times, such as during the last month of the hot season, people "seek wind by means of a fan or bellows, and even the stands of straw in the drip-fringe of the thatch do not stir."

These seasonal changes in the external air, which we have all experienced, demonstrate vividly that the air element, "great as it is, is seen to be impermanent, subject to destruction, disappearance, and change." The same applies to the earth, water, and heat elements inside the body and outside the body. Since this is so, the Buddha asks, "What of this body, which is clung to by craving and lasts but a while?" Our body, too, he reminds us, is composed of four elements, which are always being destroyed, disappearing, or changing. Therefore, he concludes, "There can be no considering that as *I* or *mine* or *I am*."

BREATH AND THE AGGREGATES

As we see from our discussion of the four elements of the breath, mindfulness of breathing is instructive in many important ways. If we follow the Buddha's example and use the breath to examine our mind-body system as it is, we gain insight into a number of essential Dhamma points. As the Buddha explains, "All dhammas arise from attention." Among these, we gain firsthand knowledge of the five aggregates—form, feeling, perception, thought, and consciousness—the traditional constituents of the body and mind.

Let's look briefly at the five aggregates as they apply to the breath. The breath-body and all other material objects including the physical body belong to the *aggregate of form*. We have already noted that we experience the touch of the breath at the nose, lungs, and abdomen because the breath has a kind of form or shape. From moment to moment, the form of the breath changes, as we can see when we focus our attention at the nose or abdomen.

The other four aggregates describe our mental experience. The *aggregate of feeling* refers to our sensations of the breath and the emotions we experience as a result. The anxiety we feel when we sense that our lungs are empty and our feeling of relief when we inhale belong to this aggregate. Next is the *aggregate of perception*. We can use the breath as an object of meditation only because our minds perceive it.

The *aggregate of thought* includes all other mental activities, including ideas, opinions, and decisions. The thought "this is the feeling of the breath" and the decision to pay attention to the breath belong to this aggregate. The last of the five, the *aggregate of consciousness*, is the basis of all mental experience. We become aware of changes in the other four aggregates because of the aggregate of consciousness. But consciousness, too, is changing as the form of the breath and our feelings, perceptions, and thoughts change.

In the sutta on mindfulness of breathing, the Buddha tells us: "Mindful of impermanence breathe in, mindful of impermanence breathe out; mindful of dispassion breathe in, mindful of dispassion breathe out; mindful of cessation breathe in, mindful of cessation breathe out; mindful of relinquishing breathe in, mindful of relinquishing breathe out."

When we apply these words to the aggregates of the breath, we notice that all five consist of three very minor moments: the rising moment, the living or enduring moment, and the passing away moment. The same is true of all things that exist. This activity never stops. Such is the nature of impermanence. Forms, feelings, perceptions, thoughts, and even consciousness itself don't stick around. They cease without leaving a trace. Once they are gone, they are gone forever. New forms, feelings, perceptions, thoughts, and consciousness always appear. Observing these changes teaches us detachment and makes it easier for us to relinquish the habit of clinging to any part of the body or mind.

PATIENCE AND JOY

Below I suggest a basic technique for getting started with mindfulness meditation on the breath. Take time to work with the practice. Try not to be impatient or rush ahead to experience something new. Allow things to unfold naturally.

People these days are good at making things happen very quickly. Computers, email, and mobile telephones are fast. Washers and dryers, instant breadmaking machines, and instant coffeemakers are timesavers. But too many people don't have time to smile. They don't have time to allow joy to develop the natural way.

One day, a man who wanted to take my picture asked me to relax and be natural. When his camera was ready, he said, "Bhante, smile."

So I said to him, "First you ask me to be natural. Now you are asking me to smile. Do you want me to smile or be natural?"

When something is funny, smiling happens naturally. We also smile when our stress, tension, and fear disappear. Then our face becomes calm and peaceful, and we smile with our hearts without showing our teeth. That is the kind of smile the Buddha had all the time.

As we gain experience with mindfulness of breathing, we gradually overcome sleepiness, restlessness, and other obstacles to concentration. As our concentration deepens, we begin to smile with our hearts. It's not hard to understand why this happens. As we have seen, the breath is part of the body. When we relax the breath, the body becomes relaxed. The breath is free from greed, hatred, delusion, and fear. When the mind joins with the breath, the mind temporarily becomes free from greed, hatred, delusion, and fear. Relaxing the breath, breathe in. Relaxing the breath, breathe out. Then joy arises naturally.

With every small step of meditation, you gain a small degree of insight. Do your practice with patience. Don't rush. Let the insights unfold. Consider the analogy of an impatient hen who lays a few eggs. She wants to see chicks coming out of them quickly, so she turns them over very often to check. But she will never see chicks coming out of these eggs. Another hen lays a few eggs and sits on them patiently. When the eggs are properly hatched, the chicks break the eggshells with their little claws and bills. Then this mother hen sees good feathery results!

KEY POINTS FOR MEDITATION ON THE BREATH

- Go to a quiet place where you will be alone and not disturbed.

- Bring your attention to the present moment.

- Sit in a comfortable posture that allows your upper body to be straight and relaxed, upright but not uptight.

- Place your hands on the lap, palms upward, with the right hand on top of the left and the thumbs touching at the tips.

- Close your eyes or leave them half-open.

- Focus your attention on the breath, coming in and going out.

- To deepen your mindfulness, try counting:

  Inhale and exhale. Say silently, "One."
  Inhale and exhale. Say silently, "Two."
  Inhale and exhale. Say silently, "Three."
  Continue up to ten.
  Inhale and exhale. Say silently, "Ten."
  Inhale and exhale. Say silently, "Nine."
  Inhale and exhale. Say silently, "Eight."
  Continue down to one.

- When you complete this round of counting, settle on your primary object—breath, feeling, thought, rising and falling, or consciousness.

- If restlessness, agitation, or doubt occurs, don't intensify the distraction by following it. Instead, say to yourself, "Let me think how I started. I started from my breath. It is not difficult to find my breath." Breathe several times quickly and return your attention to the breath and its natural pace.

- If your mind wanders from its focus on the breath, don't get upset. Simply noticing that you have been thinking, daydreaming, or worrying is a wonderful achievement! Gently but firmly return your attention to the breath. And then do it again the next time, and the next time, and the time after that.

- If you feel sleepy or dull, try focusing with slightly more effort on the touch sensations of the in-breath and out-breath. If stronger focus does not help, stand up and continue meditating in a standing posture for a few minutes or try walking meditation. You'll find instructions for both postures in the next chapter.

- If you begin to feel pain, first try to address the situation as much as possible. Loosen your clothing and check your posture to make sure that you are not slouching. Move to a posture that's easier to maintain (as described in the next chapter). If these adjustments do not help, then work with the pain: try making the sensation of pain your object of meditation. Observe the sensation and watch how it changes over time.

- If questions arise, ask someone with more experience. Remind yourself that millions of people have used this practice to attain clarity and peace of mind.

- Keep practicing with patience.

2. Four Postures

For one entire night, Venerable Ananda practiced the four foundations of mindfulness. Because his mindfulness was pure, sharp, and
powerful, he perceived that each part of his body, each tiny physical movement, feeling, perception, thought, and even consciousness
itself is impermanent, unsatisfactory, and selfless.

At dawn, as he was beginning to lie down, he lifted his foot. In
that instant, he reached enlightenment.

Certainly, when the mind is perfectly clear and mindfulness is
strong, it is possible to attain enlightenment quickly, even while lifting
a foot.

We can develop mindfulness by paying complete attention
to any part of the body. We have already seen how mindfulness of breathing helps us become more calm and peaceful and
gain valuable insights into the Buddha's message. The same applies
to focusing on the body's positions and movements.

In the sutta on the four foundations of mindfulness, the Buddha
explains how mindfulness of four postures—sitting, standing, walking, and lying down—deepens our awareness. Most of the time we
talk about sitting and walking meditation, but we do not talk very
much about standing and lying down. Since all postures are equally

important, the Buddha never fails to mention all four in his instructions on mindfulness practice.

Venerable Ananda is not the only disciple of the Buddha to have achieved enlightenment through mindfulness of physical movements. Venerable Cakkhupala, another of the Buddha's followers, reached enlightenment while walking mindfully. I give complete instructions for walking as a mindfulness meditation later in this chapter. First, let's talk about mindfulness of sitting.

SITTING

When we sit to meditate, we adopt a posture and then make a contour survey of the body, checking to see that the upper body, the part above the waist, is upright and straight. The body should be held in a relaxed way, without being rigid. The hands are cupped with palms up and placed on the lap, right palm on the left and the thumbs touching. The eyes are closed or left half-open, especially if falling asleep is a problem.

So which posture is best for sitting meditation?

Full lotus. In the introduction to the *Four Foundations of Mindfulness Sutta*, no posture is mentioned other than full lotus. In this position, both knees touch the floor. The legs are crossed at the calf. The left foot rests on the right thigh, and the right foot rests on the left thigh. The soles of both feet are turned upward like the petals of a lotus.

When we sit correctly in this position, the body is very stable. The spine is straight, and the lungs expand and contract smoothly. Blood circulation is good, at least in the upper part of the body. Normally when the mind and body are relaxed, it is easy to fall asleep. But when we are sitting in full lotus, we fall asleep less often because the body remains securely upright.

For many people, full lotus is not an easy position. But any skill we try to learn can be difficult at the beginning. For instance, we probably fell many times when we were learning to ride a bicycle. By repeating the same activity day after day, gradually we gain proficiency. To get used to sitting in full lotus, try holding the position for one minute a day for several days. Don't expect to sit without pain. After a few days, increase the time to a couple of minutes, and continue to lengthen the time gradually day by day. Keep in mind that the posture won't be perfect immediately.

For many years, I sat in the half lotus posture I describe below. When I was sixty-five, one day I thought, "Let me try full lotus." I held the posture for only five minutes. It was really painful! I thought the blood circulation would be cut off in my legs, and I would get gangrene resulting in amputation! As soon as this thought arose in my mind, I changed my posture and sat in half lotus as usual. But the next day I tried again. This time I was able to sit for about eight minutes before the pain started. After ten minutes, the pain became unbearable. However, rather than changing my position immediately, I determined to sit a little longer. Although I had been sitting in half lotus for forty-five years, within three weeks I could sit in full lotus for half an hour.

Many healthy people can learn to sit in full lotus if they persist in their efforts as I did. However, people with physical problems should not force themselves to sit in this posture.

Half lotus. In this posture, both knees touch the floor. One leg lies flat on the floor from knee to foot. The foot of the other leg rests on top of the opposite thigh, with the sole turned upward. Many people can develop proficiency with the half lotus by the same gradual process I have described.

Burmese posture. In this posture, both legs lie flat on the floor from knee to foot. The lower legs are parallel, with one leg placed in front of the other and feet uncrossed. This posture is reasonably comfortable. Most people can learn to sit in this position without too much difficulty.

Easy style. The right foot is tucked under the left knee, and the left foot is tucked under the right knee. Many people can sit in this position for some time.

Using a meditation bench. If none of these postures are comfortable, it is also possible to kneel on a meditation bench. The feet are tucked under the bench, and the knees are on the floor. The bench goes across your shins, enabling you to sit comfortably in a kneeling posture without putting pressure on your feet.

Sitting in a chair. Some people find it impossible to sit comfortably in any of these postures. They may sit on a chair, placing the feet flat on the floor close to each other. In this posture, the back should be straight and not leaning against the back support of the chair.

MINDFULNESS OF SITTING

As we sit, we become aware of the feeling of the posture we have chosen and that the feeling changes over time. Changes actually begin the moment the body makes contact with the cushion, bench, or chair. When the body touches anything, we feel the touching. In that touch we notice the hardness or softness of the seat. Hardness and softness are characteristics of the earth element. The feeling that arises from contact with the seat is generally pleasant at first. But as it continues, the feeling often changes from pleasant, to neutral, to unpleasant or even painful.

We observe this. Then we notice that nobody is controlling these changes. They happen by themselves. The mind wants to remain calm and peaceful, experiencing the progress of our meditation. In spite of this wish, the feeling of the posture changes. Paying attention to these changes reminds us that the four elements are impermanent, as are our feelings and perceptions.

After we sit for a while, we feel the heat of our buttocks or thighs. As the heat radiates, the seat becomes warm. Soon the heat from our body and the heat from the seat make the whole body feel warm. Experiencing this, we are mindful of the heat element. On hot days, we may perspire. Sweat arises from the body's water element. So we are mindful of this element. We also experience movements associated with the breathing cycle, such as the rising and falling of the abdomen and chest. Sometimes we feel intestinal gas. These movements make us mindful of the air element.

To maintain whatever sitting posture we have adopted, we use mental energy that arises naturally from our knowledge that things are always changing. If this energy stops, we slouch, fall asleep, or lose our balance. As we watch these changes, we try not to become upset or disappointed. For instance, we avoid the thoughts "How can I meditate when I am in pain?" and "I'll never be able to sit in full lotus!"

We are also mindful of the five aggregates. The body is the form aggregate. The sensations that arise due to contact with the seat belong to the feeling aggregate. Our minds register changes that are occurring due to the perception aggregate. The thoughts that arise regarding our sitting, body, contact, feelings, and perceptions come from the thought aggregate, as does our attention to what is taking place. We become aware of all of these occurrences because of the consciousness aggregate.

We also become aware of the five aggregates cooperating with one another. When our posture changes, our feelings, perceptions, thoughts, and consciousness also change. No permanently existing entity causes these changes to happen. The aggregates change depending on each other, not independently or because *I* have caused the changes to happen.

The mind does not need to keep observing one object to see the completion of the three steps of change—rising moment, peak moment, and passing away moment. Mindfulness and concentration, working together, can notice countless changes taking place simultaneously. Deep mindfulness sheds light on the unmistaken nature of these changes. Sitting postures are best for gaining this insight.

STANDING

We can continue our meditation in a standing posture. Mindfully and slowly, we get up from sitting. We notice that mental activity generates sufficient physical energy to lift the body from its sitting position.

Standing, we relax our body and hands. The body is straight, the feet are parallel, and the spinal column is upright, just as it was when we were sitting. We breathe mindfully. We pay attention to the feeling of the posture and to the contact between the feet and the floor. We do not allow the body to sway. We have relaxed awareness of our breath, feelings, and consciousness.

We notice how the feeling of the standing position changes from comfortable to neutral and then to uncomfortable. We notice our

changing perception of these feelings. When thoughts arise regarding the body, feelings, and perceptions, we notice them with attention, which is also a thought. We notice how the thoughts change.
We are mindful of our conscious awareness of these changes. Thus,
while standing, we are aware of the five aggregates and their changes.

We are aware that whatever we are experiencing is impermanent,
unsatisfactory, and selfless. Our awareness of these factors reminds
us that "this is not *mine*, this is not *I*, this is not *myself*." Here "this"
means whatever we are experiencing at the moment. We realize that
it is neither some special being inside us nor some external being
that does the standing. Rather, standing takes place dependent on
various causes and conditions. One of these is our intention to stand
up and remain standing. Intention is also caused by something else.
Previously the sitting posture became uncomfortable. In order to
relieve this discomfort, a desire arose for us to stand up.

Energy is necessary to keep the body in a standing position. When
our energy is low, we cannot remain standing, as we have all experienced. The mind generates energy through intention. That energy
is an aspect of the air element created by our mental activities. We
also become aware of the air element through our breath going in
and out.

We are mindful of the other elements as well. The bones and
muscles holding us upright belong to the earth element. We also
experience the earth element in the touch of our feet on the floor.
When we stand in a particular place for a few minutes, friction
between the feet and the floor causes that spot to become warm,
and we feel the heat element under our feet. We feel the water element there, too, in the form of perspiration. Thus all four elements
are working together smoothly and dependently.

At the same time, we have to remain alert and not fall asleep.
Although we can stand habitually, if we are mindful, we become

aware of everything that is involved in standing. This awareness is what the Buddha means when he says, "When standing, understand standing." Although even children and animals know how to stand, they do not understand fully what is taking place.

We stand for maybe one minute, two minutes, three minutes, or as long as we feel comfortable in this position. We stand up while breathing. While we are standing, we are breathing. We never stop noticing the breath.

Walking

From the standing posture, if we choose, we can begin walking meditation. Mindfulness helps us notice that walking is really a sequence of nine actions:

1. We begin by standing for a couple of minutes, relaxing the hands and body and focusing on our breathing.

2. We lift the heel of one foot—let's say, the left foot.

3. We rest the left foot on its toes. We are mindful of the contact of the toes with the floor and the feeling arising from that contact. We notice how the feeling changes as the contact changes.

4. We lift the left foot.

5. We move the left foot forward. We notice that the feeling we had while standing is no longer there when we lift the heel of the left foot. Likewise, the feeling that we had while lifting the heel is no longer there when we rest the left foot on its toes. Now, new feelings arise as we lift the whole foot and move it forward. The thoughts "this is the foot; this is the movement;

this is the forward motion; this is the change" arise, remain briefly, and pass away. Until the left foot is placed on the floor and firmly settled, we balance the body on the right foot. If we become unmindful, we lose the balance.

6. The forward motion of the left foot stops.

7. We lower the left foot.

8. We touch the left foot to the ground.

9. Finally, we press the left foot against the ground.

10. Then the cycle of movements, feelings, perceptions, and thoughts begins again with the other foot.

In order to notice these tiny changes, we need to walk slowly. When our movements are deliberate and unhurried, we can observe each aspect of walking in detail. Walking slowly is like a slow-motion replay at a football game. Though the spectators might not see a penalty take place on the field because the players are moving too quickly, watching the replay slows down the action and allows the referee to make the correct call.

In the same way, when we walk at our usual rapid pace, it's hard to observe what's really happening. Slow and mindful walking gives the mind the opportunity to become aware of each small change in the body's position and in the other aggregates that alter as a result. It's relatively easier to notice these differences while we are sitting, because the body is not moving.

Only through mindful attention can we notice that every time we move a foot forward, new contact, feeling, thought, perception, and attention arise, and old contact, feeling, thought, perception, and attention pass away. We may not be aware of all these things when we first start to practice walking meditation, but with gradual training, we are able to see at least some of the things that are taking place.

MINDFULNESS OF WALKING

We walk slowly not only so that we can observe the details of the movements but also so that we can watch what is going on in our minds. The purpose of walking meditation is not training the body but rather, through using the physical activity of walking, to train the mind.

For this reason, though we are mindful of each movement as we walk, we do not verbalize silently what we are observing. Words come between our mental awareness and what is happening. Moreover, too many things are happening simultaneously to name them. And some of these things are so subtle that we will not find words for them, or we may be noticing things for the first time.

For instance, though we observe the movements of our feet, we don't have to say, "left, right, left, right," as if we were marching in the army. Nor should we say "lifting, lifting, lifting" when we lift each foot. We simply become aware of these movements directly, without words. The same is true of changes taking place in our feelings, perceptions, thoughts, and consciousness. We notice these without saying, "changing, changing, changing." When unintentional bodily activities flow smoothly, the mind is trained to be patient and develops deeper mindfulness.

However, we may need to verbalize some thoughts and emotions, especially those that distract us from focusing on what is happening. If a thought or emotion such as greed, anger, delusion, jealousy, fear, or worry arises, we use mindfulness to remove it as quickly as possible. For instance, if anger arises, we pay attention to it. But if the anger does not pass away by itself, we think in words to try to discover the cause of the anger. It is like having a silent conversation. Because we are mindful, we are careful not to blame anybody—neither ourselves nor someone else.

While we are walking, we are also mindful of our breathing. Coordinating the breath with the movement of the feet is possible only when we do not verbalize each event. With attention, we notice that the breath is flowing in and out and the feet are moving at the same time. Below I give detailed instructions for practicing walking meditation coordinated with the breath.

What We Learn

It's amazing how many activities of the body and mind we can train ourselves to notice while doing something we usually take for granted, like walking. These activities never stop. They have been going on and changing continually since the moment we were conceived. Observing the tiny changes that take place during each step helps us become aware that the body, the mind, and everything else are inescapably impermanent.

We also see that walking is an interdependently arising action that is made up of many other interdependent actions and events. At the speed of lightning, the intention to walk arises. Along with the intention, the heel lifts. The movement of the foot takes place so quickly that if we don't pay close attention, we nearly miss it. So we become aware that intention and attention seem to happen simultaneously.

Similarly, it is hard to notice intention apart from physical movements, such as lifting the heel. It all takes place so quickly, like the light that turns on when we flip the switch. However, with attention, we can learn to see the difference between the intention and the action that results. Very slowly, very mindfully, we notice the intention to breathe in, the intention to breathe out, the intention to lift one foot, the intention to move it forward, and so on. Since the mind is fully occupied by observing all this, it does not wander.

When we are mindful of walking as it actually is, it is also easier to understand that it is not a self or soul that does the walking. All of this activity has not been made possible by some permanent being inside us. It arises interdependently because of causes and conditions, which we can train ourselves to notice.

Key Points for Walking Meditation

Though you can practice walking meditation anywhere, a private place is best. Make sure there is enough space for you to walk at least five to ten paces in a straight line, though this is the bare minimum distance. Ideally, the walking distance should be much longer; some meditation centers have thirty-foot-long walking paths.

- Begin in the standing posture. Focus on your breathing.

- Inhale and lift the heel of one foot.

- Exhale and rest that foot on its toes.

- Inhale as you lift that foot and move it forward.

- Exhale as you bring that foot down and touch the floor.

- Repeat this sequence with the other foot.

- After five to ten paces, rest in standing posture for one minute, turn around, stand again for another minute, and repeat the sequence to walk back to where you started.

- As you walk, keep your head up and your neck relaxed. Walk slowly and naturally. Keep your eyes open to maintain balance, but avoid looking at anything in particular.

- Strive to be mindful of as many of the changes taking place in your body and mind as you can.

- Once you have grasped the technique of slow walking, you can speed up slightly. But don't walk too quickly. A good pace is one inhalation and one exhalation per step. Inhale while lifting the heel of one foot, resting it on its toes, lifting the whole foot, and moving it forward. Then, stop. While exhaling, lower the foot, touch the floor, and press it against the floor. Again, stop. Repeat the sequence with the other foot. After a while, the breath and the movement of the feet become almost automatic.

Lying Down

When the mind and body are relaxed, as they are during sitting mediation, it's easy to fall asleep. Imagine how easy it is to fall asleep while meditating in a lying down posture!

Nevertheless, I recommend this posture in a few circumstances. Most obviously, people who are so sick that they cannot sit up without pain can lie on their backs, with arms and legs extended, and meditate using the breath as the primary focus. The lying down posture can also be helpful for people who can't sleep because of a sinus condition or other painful problem. They may find relief by lying on their backs and meditating on how the uncomfortable sensations they are experiencing arise, remain, and pass away. While focusing on the impermanence of the sensations, they should take care to avoid feelings of resentment or depression.

I have suffered from difficulty sleeping because of sinus problems for many years. I lie on my back and meditate on the impermanence of the feelings. In ten or fifteen minutes, I fall asleep. Finally, even

232 THE FOUR FOUNDATIONS OF MINDFULNESS IN PLAIN ENGLISH

people with no physical problems can benefit from practicing mindfulness meditation on the breath while lying down in bed before going to sleep.

As is important in all postures, while lying down, we understand that we are lying down. We remember that there has been an intention to lie down and that the mind has generated the energy to do so. We are aware of the earth element in the contact between the body and the bed, the heat element that arises, as well as the water and air elements.

While lying down, as in every posture we have discussed, we use attention to build awareness that the five aggregates are impermanent, unsatisfactory, and selfless. We use mindfulness of everything that is taking place as a buffer against anger, resentment, lust, jealousy, fear, tension, and every other unwholesome thought and emotion. Of course, it is not easy to maintain clear awareness of lying down for very long, because this is the posture that we use most of the time to go to sleep. But until we fall asleep, we can remain mindful.

And like Ananda and many other followers of the Buddha, we can strive in every posture to have mindfulness that is so pure, sharp, and powerful that we progress toward liberation.

3. Clear Comprehension

When the Buddha was explaining the meaning of domain, one of the aspects of clear comprehension, he told the following story:

"In the Himalayas, the king of mountains, there are rugged and uneven zones where neither monkeys nor human beings can go, rugged and uneven zones where monkeys can go but not human beings, and flat and delightful regions where both monkeys and human beings can go. There, along the monkey trails, hunters set out traps of sticky pitch.

"A monkey who is not foolish sees the pitch and avoids it from afar. But a foolish monkey seizes the pitch with his hand and gets stuck there. Thinking, 'I will free my hand,' the monkey seizes the pitch with his other hand. Thinking, 'I will free both hands,' he seizes the pitch with his foot. Thinking, 'I will free both hands and my foot,' he seizes it with his other foot. Thinking, 'I will free both hands and feet,' he applies his muzzle to the pitch as well.

"Thus, bhikkhus, that monkey lies there screeching, trapped at five points. He has met with calamity and disaster, and the hunter can do with him as he wishes. So it is, bhikkhus, when one strays outside one's own domain into the domain of others. . . .

"What is the domain of others? It is the five cords of sensual pleasure. . . .

"And what is a bhikkhu's own domain? It is the four foundations of mindfulness."

(tr. Bhikkhu Bodhi)

. . . .

*T*his story illustrates an essential element of the Buddha's message: every calamity or disaster we experience begins with our own unwise actions. If we want to end our suffering, we must look carefully at the activities of our own body and mind. This is the laboratory where we must work very hard.

With the instruments of mindfulness and clear comprehension, we investigate our body, feelings, perceptions, thoughts, and consciousness—not as a biologist, chemist, or pathologist, but more profoundly, as a meditator, whose aims are morality, spiritual development, and deep insight. In every activity, whether we are sitting, standing, walking, lying down, talking, eating, or meditating, mindfulness and clear comprehension work together to help us see that whatever we are experiencing is temporary and thus can never bring us lasting satisfaction. Moreover, though we may think we understand perfectly what is happening, often we are confused and deluded.

So what is clear comprehension?

Traditionally, it has four aspects: purpose, suitability, domain, and nondelusion. In brief, *purpose* means that there is a good reason for us to engage in the activity. *Suitability* means that the activity fulfills that purpose. *Domain*, as we see from the story of the foolish monkey, means that the activity lies within appropriate boundaries. Finally, *nondelusion* means that while we are doing the activity, we are investigating whether we understand clearly what is really going on.

PURPOSE

When we do something, we generally have a purpose in mind. We go to a particular shop to buy an item that we need. We arrange to meet someone to conduct business or have a conversation or share a meal.

But when we engage in mindfulness meditation, our purpose is not an ordinary one, like going to the grocery store or the office. Instead, our goal is very specific and very special. According to the Buddha, we practice meditation

- to purify the mind,
- to overcome sorrow and lamentation,
- to end grief and despair,
- to progress on the path toward liberation, and
- to attain liberation and the end of suffering.

Let's look at each to understand the Buddha's meaning.

Purify the mind. The first purpose of meditation is purification. Very strong mindfulness can be compared to detergent. Just as we must wash a dirty plate before we can use it to eat healthy food, we must clear away impure mental states, such as hatred, greed, and delusion, before we can develop pure states, such as generosity, loving-friendliness, and wisdom.

The Buddha compared the process to what happens when we dye cloth: "O bhikkhus, just as an impure, stained cloth, when dyed blue, yellow, or red, takes a bad hue and an impure color because the cloth is impure and stained, in the same manner, when the mind is defiled, a bad state can be expected. Just as a pure, unstained cloth,

236 OF MINDFULNESS IN PLAIN ENGLISH

when dyed blue, yellow, or red, takes a pure color and a bright hue, so when the mind is pure, a good state can be expected." As the sutta tells us, when the householder Upali's mind had been purified so that it was ready, receptive, elated, and confident, the Buddha taught him the four noble truths:

> Just as a clean cloth with all marks removed would take dye evenly, so too, while the householder Upali sat there, the spotless immaculate vision of the Dhamma arose in him.
>
> (tr. Bhikkhu Bodhi)

The impure states that stain the mind include anger, lust, jealousy, skeptical doubt in the Dhamma, selfishness, stubbornness, and negligence. Mindfulness and clear comprehension help us eliminate these and similar unhealthy mental habits and replace them with knowledge of the Buddha's path and clarity about what we must do, and not do, to advance along it.

Overcome sorrow and lamentation. We don't meditate to weep or lament. When sad emotions arise, we might use mindfulness to look for the reason. We often find that our unhappiness is rooted in attachment to some person, position, place, or thing. Then we ask, "Why am I attached?" When we investigate carefully, we discover, "I am attached because I have forgotten that everything is impermanent. Foolishly, I think that the object of my attachment will bring me lasting happiness, pleasure, or security."

Other times we cry because we are remembering sad or traumatic events or someone else's suffering. In this case, we try to emulate the example of the Buddha. Though he saw very clearly the suffering of billions of living beings, he never wept, because he knew his sorrow could do nothing to relieve the suffering. Rather, he maintained unshakable mindfulness and perfect equanimity.

From a state of emotional balance, we can more easily see that the sad experiences of the past are no longer present. Moreover, anything we are attached to today will definitely change or pass away, without our control and without advance warning. The same is true of the joys and sufferings of others. Knowing this, our sorrow and lamentation slowly fade. Training ourselves to face this reality is the second purpose of mindfulness meditation.

End grief and despair. Grief and despair are more durable than sorrow and lamentation, so they take more effort to overcome. Sometimes, though we try to calm the mind through meditation, we cannot escape these emotions. We want to forget them; we honestly wish not to dwell on them, but they keep surfacing.

To end them, we use the same mental training I have described. We contemplate the impermanent nature of everything in life. Every past experience is already behind us. Nothing we have right now can bring us satisfaction forever. Everyone we hold dear, every attractive situation, and every pleasing moment will vanish someday. Nothing we do can prevent these changes from happening. These thoughts help us to see that our despair is a "dependent arising." It depends for its existence on causes and conditions that arise, remain for a time, and then disappear. When we use mindfulness to train the mind to accept this reality, these emotions, too, slowly fade away.

Progress on the path toward liberation. The fourth reason for practicing mindfulness is to follow the Buddha's noble eightfold path, the only sure road to freedom from sorrow, lamentation, grief, and despair. I say more about the eightfold path in the section on mindfulness of dhamma, but in brief, the eight steps are a comprehensive guide to a life based on right understanding, thinking, speech, action, livelihood, effort, mindfulness, and concentration.

In the context of the special purposes of meditation, it is important that we recognize that we cannot separate mindfulness practice from the Buddha's path to liberation. Though some people might say, "Vipassana and insight meditation have nothing to do with Buddhism," this is not correct. As our practice deepens and the mind becomes pure and clean, we cannot fail to see the connection between meditation and every step of the Buddha's noble eightfold path.

Attain liberation and the end of suffering. The final purpose of meditation is to free ourselves from the never-ending suffering of this life and future lives. Liberation is the supreme goal of mindfulness meditation; everything else is peripheral and ephemeral. A serious practitioner keeps this purpose in mind at all times—whether sitting, walking, standing, eating, drinking, talking, observing silence, taking a shower, or using the toilet!

Keeping the lofty goal of our practice of clear comprehension in mind keeps us from getting sidetracked by trivial concerns. Discussing whether some superficial aspect of our practice is or is not suitable wastes our time and distracts us from our real purpose. Since our goal is nothing short of liberation and the end of suffering, we must avoid the sticky traps of confusion and focus on the supreme goal of our practice. When we do, our mindfulness practice bears fruit very quickly.

Suitability

The second aspect of clear comprehension is making sure that our activities are morally wholesome and suitable for achieving our spiritual goals. We choose a job that gives us enough time to meditate and avoid associating with people who cause harm to themselves or others. We practice right speech and refrain from conversations that interfere with our ability to concentrate. We make healthy lifestyle choices, such as eating moderately and not sleeping too much.

We also make sure that our meditation practice is well suited to our temperament. If we habitually feel agitated or overly energetic, we choose a peaceful practice that calms the mind, such as sitting down to meditate and counting the breath. Conversely, if we tend to feel drowsy and lethargic, we engage in a practice that rouses our energy, such as walking meditation. We also assess continually how well our practice is working. For instance, we ask ourselves, "Am I really concentrating and gaining insights or just sleeping on the cushion?"

Similarly, we select subjects for contemplation that help us overcome unhealthy mental habits. For instance, a person who is troubled by jealousy might experiment to see whether thinking about generosity—open-handed giving with no expectation of return—or about appreciative joy—rejoicing in the good fortune of others—is the most effective way to counteract the jealousy. Since our time is limited and our spiritual aim is lofty, we must use good judgment and be selective. As the Buddha said, "Do not strive everywhere."

Domain

The third aspect of clear comprehension is practicing right thinking so that we remain within appropriate boundaries—our own domain or field. Allowing the mind to wander into "delightful regions" is dangerous, as illustrated by the story of the monkey trap told at the beginning of this chapter. If the foolish monkey had stayed within his proper domain, he would not have been tempted by the sticky pitch and would not have become trapped at five points and bound by five cords of sensual pleasure.

What are those points and those cords? They are the five kinds of sense consciousness and their five desirable objects: lovely forms cognizable by the eye, agreeable sounds cognizable by the ear, enticing smells cognizable by the nose, tantalizing tastes cognizable by the tongue, and pleasing touches cognizable by the body.

If the mind goes astray as we engage in meditation, we bring our focus back to the five aggregates as we are experiencing them right now—our body and posture, feelings, perceptions, thoughts, and consciousness. These are the appropriate fields of the four foundations of mindfulness. For example, if the thought of an attractive object arises, we reflect on it mindfully without getting involved in the details. We avoid emotional reactions, and mental or verbal commentaries, such as whether it is male or female, beautiful or ugly, enticing or disturbing. We think only that this is an impermanent object. We do the same with every other sight, sound, smell, taste, touch, and thought.

As the Buddha admonished his followers: "Monks, be islands unto yourselves; be a refuge unto yourselves with no other refuge. Let the Dhamma be your island . . . having put aside hankering and fretting for the world."

NONDELUSION

The fourth clear comprehension is nondelusion. This aspect is more difficult to understand. As we have noted, we are deluded when we think that the objects of our attachment will bring us permanent happiness and satisfaction. We are also deluded when we think that the people and situations that provoked our angry feelings will always infuriate us. However, it's harder to see that these delusions arise because of a deeper and more troublesome source of confusion—the notion of a permanently existing self.

At a conventional level, it is certainly true that *I* engage in many activities, such as walking forward and backward, eating, drinking, sleeping, wearing clothes, talking, and remaining silent. *I* also experience emotions, perceive sensations, and engage in many other activities with *my* body and mind. But as mindfulness meditation reveals, no activity takes places independently. Rather, everything and everyone that exists depends on a wide variety of simultaneous causes and conditions that come into existence, remain present, and then pass away.

Since everything arises interdependently, no separate self or soul causes an activity like walking to happen, as we see very clearly when we practice walking meditation. In the same way, there is no part of the body or mind that is inherently *me* and no possession or person that is permanently *mine*. Our feelings of attachment and anger start to fade when we recognize that there is no independently existing *I* to feel attached to *him* or angry with *her*.

We use terms like *I, we, self, soul, you, me, he, she, him, her* to make understanding easier. These are conventional terms coined by human beings to facilitate communication, but just because they are useful doesn't mean they refer to any independent and unchanging thing findable in the world.

Insight into this unmistaken truth about reality is known in Buddhism as "emptiness of self" or *sunnata*. Clear comprehension of this truth arises from our accumulated meditative experience of observing what is really happening from moment to moment in our body and mind. When we come to see that everything, including ourselves, is impermanent, unsatisfactory, and selfless, we have achieved clear comprehension of nondelusion.

Lost and Found Mindfulness

Another aspect of clear comprehension of nondelusion is very immediate and practical. Sometimes when we practice mindfulness, we delude ourselves with naive and foolish thinking. For instance, say we are practicing walking meditation. Suddenly we notice that twenty minutes have passed and we have walked two or three miles without mindfulness and clear comprehension. It may occur to us that we should go back to the point where we lost our mindfulness and pick it up!

That thought is deluded. Is mindfulness a tangible thing that we can drop at a certain time and place and then go back and pick up? Mindfulness is a mental state. Once a mental state is lost, we will never find it again. Lost mindfulness is gone forever. We were simply distracted. Probably we don't remember what distracted us or where or when this happened. Instead of returning to an imaginary point in time and space, the moment we remember that our mindfulness has been lost, we should begin again to be mindful.

The same is true any time we lose our mindfulness. Suppose a monk who is practicing mindfulness eats some food and then remembers that he has not been eating mindfully. He cannot take back the food that he has already consumed and start all over with mindfulness. The sensible solution for him is to continue eating, starting right now, with more diligence and mindfulness. (By the way, I explain more about mindful eating later in this chapter.)

We can also lose and find our mindfulness in a more subtle way. Sometimes, when we are practicing mindfulness, we suddenly experience a calm and peaceful feeling. Then it may occur to us that this calm and peaceful feeling is the self. As soon as this thought arises, we should be mindful of it. When we are mindful, we notice that the calm and peaceful feeling is also changing and fading away, expressing its impermanent nature. As it passes away, the notion of self also passes away. This is how we tackle the delusion of the existence of self and practice clear comprehension of nondelusion.

Always remember: becoming mindful of losing our mindfulness *is* mindfulness. Admitting that we have been unmindful is an honest and sincere way of practicing mindfulness. If regret or embarrassment arises, we notice these mental states without self-blame or self-hatred. Even mindfulness is impermanent. Becoming aware of the impermanence of mindfulness is mindfulness itself. Understanding this truth is clear comprehension of nondelusion.

Clear Comprehension in Daily Life

We develop clear comprehension by remaining mindful not only when we meditate but also in daily life during every kind of physical, verbal, and mental activity. The Buddha did not need to make any special effort to be mindful. His comprehension was also naturally clear. He performed every action with mindfulness and clear comprehension—walking, talking, bending, sitting down, wearing robes, eating, and drinking.

As a sutta tells us, the Buddha's mindfulness is like an elephant's neck. It is always connected to the elephant's head, a symbol of wisdom. Just as the elephant protects his vulnerable neck from the attack of a lion by using his huge body, the Buddha maintained his mindfulness by using clear comprehension, morality, concentration, wisdom, liberation, and knowledge of liberation—the qualities of his body of enlightenment. The Buddha advised us to follow his example and engage in all our activities with mindfulness and clear comprehension.

We have to eat, drink, wear clothes, and exercise to stay healthy. We need sleep and shelter. But we use clear comprehension to guard against attachment to these necessities and to avoid greed, hatred, delusion, competition, jealousy, and pride.

For instance, some people wear clothes to show off their wealth or beauty, which encourages pride and attachment to the notion of self. By contrast, when they get dressed, monks and nuns train themselves to think, "I wear these clothes to protect this body from cold, heat, mosquitoes, wind, and sun, and to cover my naked- ness." Similarly, when they lie down to sleep, they think, "I use this shelter and this bed to keep this body from cold, heat, mosquitoes, wind, and sun, to get rid of weariness, and to make the body com- fortable." We can do the same. In these very small ways, we purify the mind and begin to free it from greed and other unwholesome states.

Clear comprehension and mindfulness also help us make posi- tive choices concerning all other imaginable activities. For instance, someone once asked me, "Can I use my gun with clear comprehen- sion to shoot a deer?"

I answered, "No."

"Why not?" he asked.

So I explained further. "The Buddha divided thoughts into two categories—wholesome and unwholesome. When he saw that unwholesome thoughts were not suitable for achieving his goal of liberation, he abandoned them. When he saw that wholesome thoughts were suitable for achieving this goal, he cultivated them.

"The moment even the thought of a gun occurs, a person prac- ticing mindfulness realizes that any weapon is an instrument of cru- elty. The gun reminds him of violence, hatred, greed, and delusion. Violence begets violence. Hatred begets hatred. Greed begets greed. Delusion begets delusion.

"Then he thinks, 'I have suffered from these harmful thoughts long enough. Now I am trying to get rid of my greed, hatred, and delusion through the practice of mindfulness. I should not let my mind think of using any weapon.'"

We apply the same kind of reasoning to every other activity of body, speech, and mind. Doing so is the proper way to practice clear comprehension.

CLEAR COMPREHENSION OF EATING

Now, eating and drinking, chewing, munching, swallowing, tasting—how do we practice clear comprehension of these?

First, to remind ourselves of the appropriate purpose of eating, we recite at mealtime: "With mindful reflection, I eat this food, neither for amusement, nor for intoxication, nor for the sake of physical beauty and attractiveness, but only for the endurance and continuance of this body, for ending discomfort, and for assisting the holy life, considering, 'Thus I shall terminate old feelings without arousing new feelings. I shall be healthy and blameless and shall live in comfort.'"

Then, while we are eating, we observe a few simple disciplines that reinforce our mindfulness. We eat very slowly, moving our hands to the plate slowly and taking the food slowly. We also are mindful of what is happening in the mind. If greed arises because the food is so tasty, we clearly comprehend the greed and say to ourselves: "Ah! I must be mindful! All right, this food is delicious. But all of my actions must be suitable for my spiritual goals. I will not be greedy and overeat." Needless to say, we avoid junk food for the same mindful reasons.

In the same way, when we drink hot or cold liquids, we think, "I take this drink with mindful reflection to overcome pain caused by thirst, avoid sickness, and maintain the health of this body."

Monks and nuns train themselves to observe thirty rules concerning eating and drinking to maintain clear comprehension. Below are a few guidelines inspired by these rules that anyone can use to practice mindfulness of eating and drinking.

KEY POINTS FOR MINDFUL EATING

- I train myself to prefer healthy and nourishing food and drink.
- I train myself to eat moderately and to avoid junk food.
- I train myself to watch my mind while I am eating to avoid greed, hatred, and delusion.
- I train myself not to overfill my bowl or plate.
- I train myself to take whatever food is offered or available without being picky.
- I train myself not to look at others' food critically or with jealousy.
- I train myself to move my hands slowly.
- I train myself not to open my mouth before the food is carried to it.
- I train myself not to stuff my mouth with food.
- I train myself not to talk when I have food in my mouth.
- I train myself not to scatter food or be wasteful.
- I train myself not to smack my lips or make slurping sounds.
- I train myself not to lick my fingers.

4. Parts and Elements

A young monk was a student of Venerable Sariputta, one of the Buddha's senior bhikkhus. Since the young man was troubled by lust, Sariputta instructed him to go to the forest to meditate on the impurities of the body. Despite his devoted efforts, the monk found that his lust was increasing. So Sariputta took him to see the Buddha.

The Buddha handed the young monk a lily and told him to focus his mind on the flower's bright color. Using this method, the monk attained advanced states of concentration.

Because he was very pleased with the Buddha and the meditation he had suggested, the young monk developed tremendous attachment to the Buddha. As he was concentrating, he remembered the Buddha's handsome, radiant, serene, and majestic body, his sweet voice, and his wise-looking face.

Suddenly, the Buddha's image appeared in his mind, and he heard the Buddha's voice saying:

Destroy attachment to self,
As you could an autumn lily in your fist.
Cultivate the path to peace,
The Nirvana [Nibbana] taught by the Well-Gone-One.

When he opened his eyes, the young monk saw that the beautiful lily, once so bright, fresh, and lively, had withered away.

So he meditated on the impermanence of the beauty, freshness, and life of the lily. Reflecting that his own handsome, young, healthy, and strong body would grow old and wither just as the flower had, he attained liberation from attachment to his body, feelings, perceptions, thoughts, and consciousness.

. . . .

*W*hen we look at ourselves in the mirror, we normally feel proud of the parts of our body that appear handsome or beautiful and displeased by those that seem old or unattractive. Judgments like these lead to attachment to the parts that we like, such as our shiny hair, and hatred of those we dislike, such as our crooked teeth.

This chapter focuses on learning to look at the body differently. Through mindfulness, we train ourselves to see the body impartially, as a collection of thirty-two parts—not just the external parts we can see in the mirror, but also the internal parts, such as the bones, liver, and blood. As we discover, each of these parts is either solid like the earth element or liquid like the water element. Like all other material objects, each of these parts is always changing. In fact, they are all as impermanent as the "autumn lily" in the young monk's vision of the Buddha.

In practical terms, meditation on the body's parts and elements opens the mind to accepting our body as it is right now, without our usual emotional reactions. It helps us overcome pride and self-hatred and regard our body with the balanced mind of equanimity. The Buddha gave an example to illustrate this point:

Suppose there is a bag full of different types of grain—rice, hill rice, paddy rice, lentils, green peas, barley, sesame seed, and mustard seed. When a man with good eyesight looks into the bag, he identifies the various grains, saying, "This is rice, hill rice, paddy rice, lentils, green peas, barley, sesame seed, and mustard seed." He does not say, "This is barley. I hate barley." Nor does he say, "This is sesame seed. I love sesame seed."

We train in mindfulness so that we can see ourselves clearly, like the man with good eyesight. We discover that because every part of the body is subject to illness, injury, and death, no part can give us lasting satisfaction. Most important, we find that there is no being or person in any of the parts of the body or mind that we can identify as *me*. From this we learn that the body is selfless. With the Buddha's example in mind, we might call this method of meditation "going against the grain," as it runs counter to our ordinary way of viewing the body.

We should approach this subject of meditation cautiously, since meditating on our body or the bodies of others without proper mindfulness can lead to attachment, as happened to the student of Sariputta. Other emotions such as dislike, even hatred, can also occur if we are unmindful. Our intention should be to see the parts of the body as they are without distortion and to know that they are neither beautiful nor ugly but simply pieces of an ever-changing process.

THE FIRST FIVE PARTS

Traditionally, the body is divided into thirty-two parts. The whole list is given a little later in this chapter. To begin, we focus our mindfulness on just five parts: the head hairs, body hairs, nails, teeth, and skin. We start with these parts because they are so conspicuous; when we meet a person, these catch our eye first. We also spend a lot of money to decorate and improve these parts. We change our hair color, whiten our teeth, and get facial treatments to feel more attractive, but also, perhaps, to deceive others about our real appearance.

We can easily use these five parts to stand for the whole body, since every other part can be found between the hair on the head and the nails on the toes. Mindful contemplation of even one of these parts can be enough for some people to gain insight. So, for example, when we reflect with clear comprehension on our head hair, we see that it is always changing. We then apply this insight to all other parts of the body, recognizing that what happens to the visible parts happens to the invisible ones as well.

Here are some ways to begin meditating mindfully about the first five parts:

Head hair. Since hair is so visible and so present to our minds, it's easy to see the changes that take place in our hair day-by-day and year-by-year. On Monday, our hair may be soft and pretty looking, but by Tuesday, if we haven't washed it, it can be stringy or even smelly! Over the years, hair changes even more. Our dark brown hair turns gray or white, or it falls out, prematurely showing our scalp.

We can deepen this insight by thinking about how easily our attitude toward hair shifts, depending on where it is. Does it make sense to be proud of hair on the head given that we throw out a whole bowl of soup if one hair falls into it? And though we find hair in our food disgusting, hair can also be used for holy purposes. According to legend, a princess known as Hemamala hid the Buddha's tooth in her hair knot so that nobody could steal it and brought it to Sri Lanka. When we reflect on the nature of hair with clear comprehension, it doesn't matter whether the hair is on the head or in the bowl of soup or hiding a holy relic: our attitude toward it is the same.

Body hair. Our attitude toward hair on the body is similarly change-able. A man can be vain about his beard, cutting it, twisting it, grow-ing it, and shaving it to make it look attractive. But the same beard would be repulsive if it were separated from the body. Women also spend time and money changing the shape of their eyebrows and removing unwanted body hair. Considering these points, we recog-nize: "Hair is just hair. Wherever on the body it is, or isn't, it has no intrinsic meaning. Moreover, the hair on the body is not *mine*. It is not *I* and not my self. It is as impermanent as everything else in this body and mind. It vanishes. It is empty."

Nails. So long as nails are on our fingers and toes, they are attrac-tive. Some people decorate them colorfully to improve their appear-ance. Nails are useful because they protect our toes and fingertips. But toenail clippings are certainly not very beautiful! Fingernails collect dirt when we work with our hands and dead skin when we scratch our head, the soles of our feet, or our ears. Young, strong, and healthy-looking nails become old, yellowed, and brittle as we age. Fungus, ingrown nails, and other conditions are the source of pain and suffering. Thinking about the nails in this way, we recognize that they are impermanent and unsatisfactory. They are not *I* and not my self.

Teeth. Teeth are more useful than head hair, body hair, and nails. We are very happy when our teeth are strong and healthy. But teeth can make us very unhappy. Many people are afraid of going to the dentist. We can easily recall the last time we sat in the dentist's chair to have a tooth pulled. Once the tooth comes out, no matter how useful, strong, and beautiful it was, it becomes ugly and useless. Though the dentist puts the tooth in our palm, we don't want to

bring it home. Like every other part of the body, teeth are impermanent and unsatisfactory. Though it was once in *my* mouth, a tooth
is not *myself*.

Skin. Skin can be a sign of beauty, but only if it is a certain color
and is unwrinkled. Of course, the color that is considered beautiful changes depending on where we live! Skin is also useful. We
experience hardness, softness, roughness, and smoothness because
of touch information we receive through the skin. Skin also regulates
body temperature. When we are hot, the skin expands, and the body
cools itself through perspiration that pours through the skin. Skin-
to-skin contact is so important to newborn babies that they can die
if they are not touched.

But the skin is also a source of suffering. Rashes and other skin
diseases make us very uncomfortable. In spite of skin care treatments
and cosmetics, skin also wrinkles, sags, and darkens as we age. Every
day, our skin dries up and dies. Ordinary house dust is full of dead
skin! Many people experience discrimination because of their skin
color.

Considering these points, we conclude: "Like every other part
of the body, skin is neither beautiful nor ugly. It is useful but also a
cause of suffering. It is, therefore, impermanent and unsatisfactory.
It is not *mine. I* am not this. This is not my self."

Mindfulness of the Thirty-Two Parts

The parts of the body we have been considering so far are the first
five of thirty-two parts. These are traditionally divided into groups.
The first twenty parts belong to the body's earth element. These are
divided into four groups of five. The last twelve parts belong to the
body's water element. They are divided into two groups of six.

What follows is the traditional division. Below that, I suggest a method for getting started with mindfulness meditation on the thirty-two parts of the body.

Twenty Parts Belonging to the Body's Earth Element

- head hairs, body hairs, nails, teeth, skin
- flesh, sinews, bones, bone marrow, kidneys
- heart, liver, diaphragm, spleen, lungs
- large intestines, small intestines, contents of the stomach, feces, brain

Twelve Parts Belonging to the Body's Water Element

- bile, phlegm, pus, blood, sweat, fat
- tears, lymph, saliva, mucus, joint fluid, urine

KEY POINTS FOR MEDITATION
ON THE THIRTY-TWO PARTS OF THE BODY

Meditating on the parts of the body can help you take care of yourself calmly when things go wrong. Sometimes it is possible to accelerate healing by focusing your mind on a diseased part to send it positive body chemicals. To do so, you need strong attention, concentration, and visualization, which this meditation helps to develop. Another benefit is that when you understand the true nature of the body, you are not upset even by the thought of death.

- Begin meditating by cultivating loving-friendliness toward all beings.

- Remind yourself that your intention in meditating on the thirty-two parts of the body is to overcome pride and self-hatred for your own body and lust and loathing for the bodies of others. You want to regard all bodies and their parts with the balanced mind of equanimity.

- Meditate on the first five parts belonging to the earth element using thoughts similar to those I have suggested. Stay with these five until they become very clear in your mind.

- Then meditate on the next five parts. Contemplate these the same way. For instance, remember how important your bones are. They hold you upright when you stand and make walking and all other physical activities possible. But bones can also be the source of suffering, as anyone who has broken an arm or a leg has experienced.

- Next, combine the first two groups together and meditate on the first ten. Continue to add other groups until you complete the twenty parts of the body belonging to the earth element.

- Keep in mind that simply repeating the names of the body parts does not do any good. Use your imagination to visualize those parts that are hidden under the skin. Consider each with thoughts similar to those we used for the first five.

- Then add the first group of six liquid parts of the body and meditate on them until they become clear in your mind. Finally, add the remaining group of six.

- As you meditate on the last twelve parts, remember that none of them makes you especially proud or helps you make a good impression on others. However, like all other parts of the body, your liquid parts are essential and useful. Remembering this point helps you to overcome revulsion.

- If any part is not clear to you, drop it for the moment and focus on those parts that are clear. Once you have established mindfulness on the clear parts, go back to the hazy parts and meditate until they, too, become clear.

- How long you should meditate on each part or group varies. Some people take longer than others to achieve mindfulness and clear comprehension.

- Remember that your aim is to recognize that each of the thirty-two parts of the body is impermanent. Because it is subject to growth, decay, disease, and death, it cannot give you lasting satisfaction. Finally, recognize that each is "not *mine*, not *I*, and not my self."

MINDFULNESS OF THE BODY'S ELEMENTS

We have already mentioned the four elements—earth, water, heat, and air—in connection with mindfulness of breathing and mindfulness of postures. As I have explained, the thirty-two parts of the body are divided between the earth element and water element. The parts connected to these elements are tangible, which makes them easier to use to develop mindfulness. The heat element and air element are harder to visualize. However, meditating on these elements is also important to mindfulness of the body because they are responsible for essential life processes such as digestion and circulation.

The body's elements are not simply building blocks, like the particles studied by physicists. When the body's aggregates are attached to the elements, the body exists as a living, breathing being. Perhaps an example will help clarify this point.

Suppose a butcher kills a pig and cuts it up into four parts. When he sells the meat, the butcher no longer has the concept of pig.

He is simply selling pork—ham or bacon or butt or some other part. Before the pig became pork, it was a living being with form, feelings, perceptions, perhaps some thoughts, and consciousness. These aggregates were bound to the elements. But when the pig is no longer alive, just the four elements remain.

The same is true of human beings. In life, the aggregates are linked to the elements. Every activity—thinking, breathing, perceiving, willing, and becoming conscious of countless things—arises depending on the combination of aggregates and elements. The feelings, perceptions, thoughts, and consciousness of this life pass away with this body. Without these aggregates, the body is like a log or a rock. All that's left are the elements.

Thinking in this way, it is easy to see that there is no difference between the elements inside the body and those outside. Both are impermanent, suffering, and without self. Let's look more closely at the four elements to help us develop deeper mindfulness of the body and its processes.

Earth. The earth element occupies space. It is hard or soft. It can expand and contract. It is visible, tangible, and perceptible. It has shape, size, and color. That is all we can know of the earth element. Although we can see a body, we cannot see the earth element separately within that body.

Like all elements, the earth element is impermanent. No matter how large, strong, colorful, or powerful it is, the earth element is always changing. There is no way to stop this natural process. However, nobody can make the earth element disappear. Consider planet Earth: We may urinate on it, defecate on it, spit on it, dig into it, throw trash on it, or clean it. Still, the earth element is neither disappointed with us nor pleased with us. It goes on changing in its own way, in its own time, unconcerned about what we do to it. We should, however, emulate the earth element in one important way: we should be as firm as earth in our determination to develop mindfulness.

When we meditate mindfully on the earth element in connection with one of the parts of the body, we feel the touch of hardness or softness, expansion or contraction. This feeling can be pleasant, painful, or neutral. As we pay attention to a particular sensation, it fades away, and another feeling arises. This process repeats again and again. If we don't identify with any of these feelings, they pass away, leaving simple awareness. We are quiet and peaceful without emotional reactions. We have equanimity.

Water. The water element is liquid and soft. It flows downward. Every part of the body needs water to survive, as do all living things. Water is characterized by cohesion. Powdery substances like cement and sand will not stick together unless water is added. Because of this quality, the water element in the body cannot be separated totally from other elements. When water predominates in one part, we say that it belongs to the water element, but saliva, blood, and other liquid parts of the body contain the earth, heat, and air elements as well.

Water is powerful enough to wash away cities and penetrate even the strongest rocks. When this power is harnessed, it can cut through steel and produce electricity. We emulate the water element when we harness our concentration to penetrate a meditation subject, such as a part of the body, and recognize its impermanence, suffering, and selflessness. Water also washes away impurities, just as meditation cleans and purifies the mind. But the flow of water can also be soft and gentle. When we meditate, we should be as flexible as water to adapt to the environment without complaints, and flow with people and situations without friction—without compromising our moral, ethical principles and mindfulness to blend with people who are immoral, unethical, and unmindful.

When we meditate mindfully on the water element, we feel the moisture that has penetrated the earth element. This feeling can be pleasant, painful, or neutral. If we do not identify with them, these feelings fade away. We remain in a quiet and peaceful state of equanimity without emotional reactions.

Heat. Though none of the thirty-two body parts belongs to the heat element, the body needs the right proportion of heat to maintain good health. Heat digests our food, maintains body temperature, and causes the body to grow. We experience the heat element when we feel warmth, radiation, or a burning sensation in some part of the body.

Heat is extremely useful. We use fire to cook and to warm our homes. Fire also burns garbage and other unnecessary stuff, just as we use meditation to burn impurities in the mind. Fire can also be dangerous and destructive. It keeps burning until it reduces things to ashes. We put out a dangerous external fire with water. Similarly, when the internal fire of greed, lust, or anger threatens to destroy our peace of mind, we use mindfulness and concentration to extinguish it.

When we meditate on the heat element, we feel the touch of gentle heat, too much heat, or neither. This feeling can be pleasant, painful, or neutral. If we don't identify with these feelings, they pass away, leaving us with awareness, peace, and equanimity.

Air. The function of the body's air element is oscillation and movement. Air occupies any space in the body. It moves in and out of the nostrils as we breathe; it moves within the lungs, stomach, and intestines; it circulates blood and other substances; it exits the body when we burp or expel gas.

The external air element is very useful. It cools the body like a gentle breeze and blows away dust. When the Buddha was surveying the world for people to listen to his teachings, he thought, "There must be some people who have a little dust in their eyes. By getting in touch with the cool air of Dhamma, they would wipe the dust from their eyes and see the truth." We meditate with the aim of blowing away the dust of mental impurities. As the Buddha said to his son Rahula, "Meditate like air."

When we meditate mindfully on the air element, we feel the touch of gentle air, too much air, or neither. This feeling can be pleasant, painful, or neutral. As we pay attention to the particular feeling, we notice it fading away. Then another feeling arises. If we do not identify with any of these feelings, they pass away, leaving us to awareness and equanimity. We remain quiet and peaceful.

When we meditate on the thirty-two parts of the body, we consider as well their connections to the four elements. For instance, we recall that blood cleans the body of wastes because it flows like water and moves like air. As we meditate on the parts and elements, we keep in mind that every part and element is impermanent, unsatisfactory, and selfless. As the Buddha said in his sutta on the elements:

> Bhikkhu, "I am" is a conceiving; "I am this" is a conceiving; "I shall be" is a conceiving; "I shall not be" is a conceiving; "I shall be possessed of form" is a conceiving; "I shall be formless" is a conceiving. . . . By overcoming all conceptions, bhikkhu, one is called a sage at peace. And the sage at peace is not born, does not age, does not die; he is not shaken and is not agitated. For there is nothing present in him by which he might be born. Not being born, how could he age? Not aging, how could he die? Not dying, how could he be shaken? Not being shaken, why should he be agitated?

Deep awareness of this truth ends our suffering.

5. Death and Impermanence

Once the Buddha was speaking with his disciple Ananda about the causes of death.

The Buddha asked, "If there were absolutely no births of any kind anywhere—that is, of gods into the state of gods, of celestials into the state of celestials, of spirits, demons, human beings, quadrupeds, winged creatures, and reptiles each into their own state—if there were no births of beings of any sort into any state, then, in the complete absence of birth, would we discern aging and death?"

"Certainly not, venerable sir," Ananda replied.

"Therefore, Ananda, it is clear that there is one cause, source, origin, and condition for aging and death. Namely, birth!"

(tr. Bhikkhu Bodhi)

*W*e are born to die. Aging and death are our birthday gifts. As the Buddha taught, the cause of death is very simple . . . it is birth! We don't need to search for any other cause, since we are living with that cause within us. We cultivate mindfulness of death and impermanence so that we can accept this reality as it is.

Accepting the inevitability of death is healthier emotionally and spiritually than living in delusion. The Buddha said, "Beings who are subject to death often wish, 'May death never come to me!'"

But wishing for life cannot stop death. Since this is so, the Buddha taught us to meditate on death—and even to use a corpse as an object of contemplation—to train us to face our own mortality without fear or superstition.

It is said that if there were a world in which people live for a thousand years, a Buddha would not appear in that world, because its people would not grasp the meaning of impermanence. Even in our own world, in which only a few people live for a hundred years, it is difficult to be mindful that death is inevitable. A man who lives to a ripe old age in good health may become proud of his longevity and forget his mortal nature. But if he is mindful of the certainty of death, he will be less arrogant and find it easier to forgive other peoples' mistakes.

We should not wait until old age or until we find out that death is approaching to get ready. Practicing mindfulness of death is the best way to overcome fear and prepare for a peaceful death. In fact, mindfulness is the only way death can be defeated, as the sutta says:

> Mindfulness is the path to the deathless,
> Negligence is the path to death.
> The mindful do not die,
> The negligent are dead already.

THREE KINDS OF DEATH

Everything that comes into existence because of causes and conditions is impermanent. Since we are born as a result of causes and conditions, we are also impermanent. When we understand impermanence well, we understand death well. As we have discussed, everything that exists has three moments: a rising moment, a living or peaking moment, and a moment of cessation. Every cell of our

physical body, every feeling, perception, thought, and even consciousness itself, arises, reaches maturity, and then passes away. This
is the nature of all conditioned things.

The Buddha taught us to distinguish three kinds of death:
momentary death, conventional death, and eternal death. *Momentary death* is the kind of death that is occurring every moment. For
instance, the physical cells that make up the body are always dying.
Biologists tell us our bones produce 2.5 million red blood cells every
second to replace dying cells. At the same time, our feelings, perceptions, thoughts, and consciousness are also dying, and new feelings,
perceptions, thoughts, and consciousness arise to take their place.
Mental processes change even more rapidly than cells and other
physical things. We practice mindfulness to train ourselves to experience these inconceivably rapid mental changes.

By contrast, we become aware of the signs of decay of the physical
parts of the body only through the marks they leave behind. When a
storm is over, we see that trees are down, buildings have collapsed,
and water is running everywhere. In the same way, aging reveals
itself on the body through wrinkles, loss of teeth, hunched back,
slow walk, slow talk, dry throat, weak sight, inability to taste, poor
hearing, poor appetite, and gray hair. When we see these changes
over time, we recognize that we are born with a one-way ticket!

When this process of aging ends, we experience *conventional
death*. Normally this kind is what people have in mind when they
say the word "death." But conventional death is just the doorway to a
new life. Countless times we face conventional death, and countless
times we take rebirth. A full cycle of momentary deaths and rebirths
leading to conventional death is called one life. Another such series
is called another life. This repeating pattern causes us to suffer tremendously. The goal of Buddhist practice is to end this cycle once
and for all.

This ending is called *eternal death*. Both momentary death and conventional death are temporary. Both open a space and time for another birth. Again we have to go through the process of suffering—losing family and friends, growing old, facing death. But once we die the eternal death, our suffering dies forever. We do not have to endure another cycle of death and rebirth. Every death is a type of cessation, but eternal death is cessation with no further rebirth or what can be called cessation never to arise again. This cessation is nibbana, liberation, freedom from suffering. Nibbana is peace.

MY NEAR-DEATH EXPERIENCES

Every night when I go to bed I think, "Tonight in my sleep, I may die." That idea never bothers me, because I have spent the day doing Dhamma work. I am happy to die with the satisfaction of a day's good work. I have also had several near-death experiences. They taught me what death means and how it happens. This knowledge helped me overcome any fear of dying.

Several times when I was young I nearly drowned. When I was in primary school, my brother and I had to cross a little creek between our home and the school. Neither of us knew how to swim. My mother was petrified we would drown there. Every day, when she heard the school bell, she would stand in the doorway of our house and wait for us. She knew what a magnet the creek was and how my brother and I longed to throw down our books, tear off our sarongs, and jump into the cool water.

Some days, we did. My mother, ever vigilant, would scream at the top of her lungs, and we would climb out reluctantly. Once, though, we got away with it. Mother did not see us when we jumped into the water. Right away, I was trapped in a small whirlpool where the stream flowed under a stand of bamboo. I flailed my arms to stay afloat, but the eddy sucked me down with terrifying force. Somehow my brother managed to pull me out.

When I was a little older, another brother saved me from drowning in an irrigation creek that had been swollen by monsoon rains into a small river. We never told our parents; we feared what would happen if we did. But my most serious near drowning happened in 1945 when I was almost eighteen.

I was waiting for a train that would carry me to a school for young monks. A novice monk, maybe eight or nine years old, invited me to go swimming in the river near the station. Although I knew that I could not swim, how could I say no to this little novice? The novice tightened his under robe and jumped into the river. After swimming across, he saw me standing on the bank. "Jump!" he shouted. Swallowing my embarrassment, I tightened my under robe and jumped. Almost immediately, I realized that I had made a big mistake. I struggled for a few moments. Then I sank to the muddy bottom, drinking in lots of filthy water.

When the novice realized I could not swim, he swam back and tried to hold up my head. But he was too small to pull me out. I panicked and grabbed his under robe. Naked, he swam to the shallow water and shouted for help. A man jumped into the river right through the window of a restaurant! The novice shouted that I might be dead already, but pointed to the place where he had last seen me .

Meanwhile, I had gone down three times. The last time I bobbed to the surface, I saw the entire world like a red ball. When I went down for the last time, I remember squatting on the river bottom. Suddenly, I saw a man bending over my body. I thought, "What is he doing? I was swimming." When I opened my eyes, the man stopped giving me mouth-to-mouth resuscitation, smiled, and moved away.

Then I saw hundreds of people around me who had come to see my swimming adventure.

To this day, though I have traveled all over the world and crossed oceans countless times, I am uncomfortable around bodies of water! But these experiences and several other close brushes with death later in life have taught me not to be afraid. Having done my best to live by the principles the Buddha taught, I simply say to myself, "I have done what I could in my life."

Every day when I practice mindfulness meditation, I reflect on the impermanence of everything. This thought makes me feel very peaceful. In my view, this is how we all should die, with the knowledge that everything—including me—is always changing, disappearing, dying.

PREPARING FOR DEATH

Each day when we sit down to meditate, we should reflect on death as a part of our practice of mindfulness of the body. Contemplating death's inevitability is a good way for us to prepare for a peaceful death and fortunate rebirth. We remember that life is short, that death is certain, and that we cannot predict when this life will end. Doing so encourages us to practice generosity and loving-friendliness, strengthens our dedication to our practice, and arouses feelings of spiritual urgency.

When we meditate on death, we say to ourselves words such as the following:

> Perhaps tomorrow I will die. All those who lived in the past are dead, all those who are now living are dying, and all those who will come into existence in the future will die, without any exceptions. There is no certainty that I will live to

finish such and such a project or until such and such a date. Before I die, I must overcome my greed, disappointment, anger, fear, jealousy, restlessness, worry, sleepiness, conceit, deceptiveness, wish for false reputation, and other deluded states of mind.

The Buddha managed to defeat these inner obstacles. But even the Buddha, who attained full enlightenment, eventually succumbed to death. Only by understanding this point deeply and remembering it every day will I gain the courage to face death.

We can also reflect on these short sayings of the Buddha as part of our meditation:

"Death always comes along together with birth."

"Just as people who have achieved great success in the world have died, so, too, I must certainly die."

"I who am dying moment after moment can die in the blink of an eye."

"The life of mortals is signless; its length cannot be known in advance."

"As fruit, when ripe, has to fall, as a potter's earthen jars eventually must all break up, so, too, does the life of mortals eventually come to an end."

"Not the least bit stoppable, always going forward, life rushes toward its end like the rising sun to its setting."

CEMETERY CONTEMPLATION

Another important aspect of preparing for death is cultivating a realistic attitude. Traditional rituals to honor the dead are often based on fear and superstition or on attachment to the person who died. Superstitions are psychological and emotional outlets for our memories of a loved one who has passed away. Ancestor worship as practiced in many cultures likely originated from attachment. It is also possible to be attached to one's own dead body. Some people say, "I don't mind dying, but I am afraid of being buried or cremated." Because of fear, they leave elaborate instructions for what they want done to their body after death.

But strong attachment and superstitions make it hard for us to develop mindfulness of death and impermanence. Some people have told me that they find mindfulness of death very unpleasant and wish to skip this part of the meditation. They don't want to think that worms eat the decomposed bodies of their loved ones. But according to Theravada tradition, after the feelings, heat, and consciousness have left, a dead body is like a log. Practically speaking, it is worse than a log. At least a log can be used for fuel! Perhaps when its life force is gone, this body is useful only to medical students who can cut it up to gain knowledge about human diseases.

Perhaps one reason for our fear and superstition is that few people these days are lucky enough to see a dead body. Even if there is an opportunity, some people don't take it. They give orders to undertakers to do whatever they want with their dear ones' bodies. They say, "I don't want to look at the body of my mother or father. I want to remember my loved ones as they were, alive in good health." All they do is pay the undertakers' bills. That, in a sense, is a kind of superstition.

Actually, at the time of the Buddha, people wrapped dead bodies in a white cloth and deposited them unburied in an outdoor area so that animals could eat them. They wanted even their dead bodies to be of some use to living beings. Monks were instructed to go to these places and collect the shrouds in which corpses had been wrapped. The Buddha's own robe was made of shrouds collected from the cemetery. In addition, after they gained full understanding of mindfulness of the body, the Buddha instructed his monks to contemplate the corpse as an object of meditation. This practice is called cemetery meditation. It is the best way to overcome superstitions about death.

Though we may not be able watch dead bodies decay as was possible during the Buddha's lifetime, we can use our imagination to contemplate what happens to a body after death. Meditating on this subject is not meant to encourage sadness or other negative emotions. Rather, it is the most realistic way to develop mindfulness of the body's impermanence. However, meditation on the various stages of a corpse requires spiritual maturity and emotional stability.

Once you have meditated thoroughly on the other aspects of mindfulness of the body, you may be ready to practice cemetery contemplation. First, imagine a dead body in the cemetery, one, two, or three days after death. Then compare your living body with that body with thoughts such as these:

This is the nature of my body. It will become like this dead body. This result is unavoidable. Two, three, or four days after death, my body is bloated, discolored, festered, stinky. It has no feelings, perceptions, or thoughts. It rots. Animals eat it. The flesh disappears; the blood dries out; sinews break down; the bones separate. Bones also decay. They become

porous and slowly are reduced to powder and dust. One day,
when a big gust of wind blows, even this dust will disappear.

We can also reflect on these short sayings of the Buddha as part of
our meditation:

"When vitality, heat, and consciousness depart from this
physical body, then it lies there cast away, food for others,
without volition."

"Before long this body will lie cast away upon the ground,
bereft of all consciousness, like a useless block of wood."

KEY POINTS FOR MINDFULNESS OF DEATH

- The Buddha provided many examples to help you remember
  that life is short, death is inevitable, and the time of death is
  uncertain. For instance, he said, life is "like a flame blown out
  by the wind," "like lightening, a bubble, dewdrops, or a line
  drawn in the water." Meditating on these examples helps to
  develop mindfulness of death.

- Also keep in mind that no man or woman who has ever lived,
  no matter how successful, famous, powerful, or holy, has
  escaped death. Even the Buddha died.

- Recall as well that the cause of death is birth and that the
  moment you were born, you begin to die.

- The countless momentary deaths of this life lead inevitably to
  conventional death. Nothing you do can prevent death from
  happening.

- Using meditation to develop mindfulness of the impermanence of all things, including your body, feelings, thoughts, perceptions, and consciousness, helps you to think realistically about death.

- Mindfulness of death arouses feelings of spiritual urgency and is the best way to prepare for a peaceful death and a fortunate rebirth.

- Superstitious attachment to a dead body makes no sense. Mindfulness of death can help you overcome superstitions.

- If you have meditated thoroughly on other aspects of mindfulness of the body—breath, four postures, clear comprehension, thirty-two parts, and four elements—and you are emotionally stable and spiritually mature, you should meditate on the stages of the corpse.

Part 2:

Mindfulness
of Feelings

6. Sensations and Emotions

. Burdened with years, the householder Nakulapita went to see the Buddha. He said, "I am aged, venerable sir, come to the last stage, afflicted in body, often ill. Let the Blessed One instruct me."

"So it is, householder," the Buddha replied. "If anyone carrying around this body of yours were to claim to be healthy even for a moment, what is that other than foolishness? You should train yourself thus: 'Even though I am afflicted in body, my mind will not be afflicted.'"

Nakulapita delighted in the Blessed One's words. He paid respect to the Buddha and left. Then he approached the Venerable Sariputta and asked him to explain in detail the meaning of the Buddha's brief statement.

Venerable Sariputta said, "A person who is unfamiliar with the teaching of the Buddha regards the five aggregates as his self. With the change and decay of these aggregates, there arises in him sorrow, lamentation, pain, grief, and despair. Thus, he is afflicted both in body and in mind.

"A noble disciple who has heard the Dhamma, on the other hand, does not regard the aggregates as his self. The aggregates may change, but sorrow, lamentation, pain, grief, and despair do not arise in him. Thus, though he may still be afflicted in body, he is not afflicted in mind."

Nakulapita rejoiced, since this wise advice would lead to his welfare and happiness for a long time.

....

We can say that the entire teaching of the Buddha is based on feelings. Toward the end of his life, after forty-five years of teaching, the Buddha said, "Bhikkhus, I have taught only two things: suffering and the end of suffering." The story of Nakulapita points to the essence of the Buddha's teaching on ending the feeling of suffering. Because of our untrained body, senses, and consciousness, we suffer physical pain, such as that caused by illness and aging, and emotional pain, such as sorrow and grief.

Our suffering arises, as Venerable Sariputta explained to Nakulapita, because we regard the five aggregates—body, feelings, perceptions, thoughts, and consciousness—as being in our self or our self as being in them. In fact, the feeling we all have of "I am" or "I exist"—what Western psychology calls the "ego"—arises from clinging to these aggregates and regarding them as *mine* or *me*.

But through training in the second foundation of mindfulness—mindfulness of feelings—we can train our minds to use life's inevitable pains, such as illness and aging, as objects of meditation. However, we should not wait till we become old and ill like Nakulapita. If we build the habit now, when we experience painful feelings, we will understand that, like everything else, pain is impermanent. Moreover, there is no permanent self or *me* who is experiencing the pain! When we develop spiritually and realize this truth, neither physical pain nor mental unhappiness can cause us to suffer.

As we begin work on developing mindfulness of feelings, we should keep two points in mind. First, in English, we use the word "feeling" in two ways. It means both physical sensations that arise as a result of contact with external objects and inwardly generated emotions that are primarily mental or psychological. But in the Buddha's teaching, the word "feeling" (*vedana* in Pali and Sanskrit) includes both physical sensations and mental emotions. For clarity, I use the word "sensations" to refer to feelings that arise from external sensory contact and "emotions" to refer to nonsensory feelings that are generated internally. When I use the word "feelings," I mean to include both sensations and emotions.

Second, we must recognize that pain, sadness, and other unpleasant sensations and emotions are not the only feelings that cause us to suffer. Pleasurable feelings, such as attachment, desire, and clinging, also cause suffering. As the *Dhammapada* says: "As a great flood carries away a sleeping village, so death seizes and carries away the man with a clinging mind, doting on his children and cattle." Clinging to anything—children, cattle, or really any persons, places, sounds, smells, tastes, touches, or ideas—is like sleeping. When we are attached, even pleasantly so, we are not mindful, and thus we are vulnerable to suffering. When we are free from desire, although the entire universe continues to change, we do not suffer.

THREE KINDS OF FEELINGS

The first step in developing mindfulness of feelings is distinguishing among the various kinds. Sometimes the Buddha says that there are two kinds of feelings—pleasant and unpleasant. Other times, he mentions three kinds—pleasant, unpleasant, and neutral. Neutral feelings are neither pleasant nor unpleasant.

When we have a pleasant feeling, we should be mindful that we are having a pleasant feeling. That's pretty straightforward. Whenever we feel pleasure, we know that it is pleasure. Similarly when we have a painful feeling, we know that it is painful feeling and can be mindful of that. People understand pleasant and unpleasant feelings naturally without too much explanation. The third category, neutral feelings, may be slightly more confusing for people who do not pay much attention to feelings. It helps to remember that in the Dhamma, there is no category called "mixed feeling."

Maintaining mindfulness of the three kinds of feelings is relatively easy, because when we pay attention, we notice that when we are experiencing a pleasant feeling, no unpleasant or neutral feeling is present. The same is true of an unpleasant and a neutral feeling. In other words, we experience one emotion or sensation at a time.

Moreover, when we are mindful, we notice very quickly that our feelings are always changing without any conscious control. Say, for instance, we are in a happy mood. The sun is shining, and we've finished our work and are heading home to a good dinner. But after a while, even though we might wish to hold on to that pleasant feeling, it disappears and a neutral feeling arises. Then, perhaps, we recall an argument we had with a friend during the day, and our neutral feeling changes to an unpleasant one. So from our experience we know very well that every feeling—pleasant, painful, or neutral—is impermanent.

Watching how quickly our feelings change, without any effort on our part, we realize another important truth. We begin to see that feelings are just feelings, not *my* feelings or parts of *me*. We realize that we often identify so closely with our feelings that they seem to be part of our basic identity. We say, "*My* knee hurts whenever *I* sit down to meditate" or "*I* am angry about the government," as if these feelings were unchanging parts of a self that is also permanent, everlasting, and immutable. But if our feelings were identical with the self, and the self were permanent, then our feelings of pain or anger should also be permanent. Experience tells us that this is not the case. Feelings change and our so-called self has no control over the changes. Observing this, we see very clearly that the self cannot be a permanent entity.

Dealing with Pain

Of the three basic kinds of feelings we have been discussing—pleasant, unpleasant, and neutral—the unpleasant feeling of pain is likely the most difficult for us to manage. So long as we have a body and consciousness, we have pain. Even enlightened beings have pain. Once Devadatta, the Buddha's enemy, hurled a rock at the Buddha. A splinter hit the Buddha's foot. His personal physician, Jivaka, applied some medicine to the spot where the Buddha had bruises. That night the Buddha experienced excruciating pain. But using mindfulness, he endured the pain.

Unlike the Buddha, when painful sensations arise, we often become anxious, angry, or depressed. We react this way because we don't know how to deal with pain. The Buddha's basic instruction to his monks is very clear on this point: "When [a monk] is feeling a painful feeling, he becomes mindful that he is feeling a painful feeling." So the first step is simply to notice that we are feeling pain. But this instruction also tells us that the sensation of pain has both a physical and a psychological dimension.

Physical pain can often be overcome by medical treatment. So, of course, first we should do whatever we can to alleviate the pain, such as consulting a doctor or taking medicine. However, some ailments cause pain that persists no matter how much medicine we take. In such cases, we should follow the Buddha's example and use the pain as an object of meditation.

When we mindfully pay attention to a sensation of pain, the first thing we notice is that the sensation is always changing. For instance, a sharp stabbing pain changes to tingling pain, which changes to burning pain. In other words, like all feelings, pain is impermanent. As we become absorbed in watching these changing sensations, we start to relax and drop our resistance to the pain. As the barrier between *me* and the pain dissolves, and we watch the sensations ebb and flow, we may be surprised to observe that we are no longer suffering. The pain may still be there as a flow of sensations, but the *me* that was being hurt by the pain has disappeared!

The same technique can be used to deal with painful emotions, such as sadness, grief, or depression. When painful emotions arise, we pay attention to them. We notice that they are always changing. We watch them ebb and flow. For instance, we mindfully pay attention as grief changes to anger and then to anxiety or depression. We keep in mind that no permanently existing self is experiencing these emotions and that no painful emotion is permanent. This recognition in itself brings a measure of relief.

MANY KINDS OF FEELINGS

Once we understand the three basic kinds of feeling, we can begin to make more detailed distinctions. For instance, we are all familiar with pleasant and unpleasant feelings that arise through our five senses, such as the pleasant agreeable form of a beautiful flower or the unpleasant disagreeable smell of garbage. As the Buddha explained, when we consider the five types of sense consciousness and the objects they perceive—eyes and forms, nose and smells, ears and sounds, tongue and tastes, and skin and touches—we can distinguish fifteen types of feelings: pleasant, unpleasant, and neutral feelings linked to each sense.

We can also add a sixth sense, mind and mental objects such as thoughts, memories, imaginings, and daydreams. These can also be pleasant, unpleasant, or neutral. So now we have eighteen kinds of feelings. When we consider that each of these eighteen kinds can arise as either a physical sensation or an internally generated emotion, we have thirty-six. Multiplying these thirty-six by past, present, and future, we can distinguish 108 kinds of feelings!

You may be wondering, "What's the point of all these categories?" To answer this question, we remember that the Buddha's basic instruction on mindfulness of feelings is "contemplate the feeling in feelings . . . in order to know feelings as they really are." The Dhamma teaches us about 108 kinds of feelings to underscore that there are, indeed, many different kinds of "feeling in feelings."

In addition, when we start paying attention to feelings, at first we notice them only superficially. We practice being mindful of experiencing pleasant, unpleasant, and neutral feelings. As our mindfulness deepens, we begin to make further distinctions. So, for instance, we are mindful of the difference between sensations and emotions and of which sense consciousness is linked to the feeling. Only through practice can we distinguish among all 108 categories.

HOW FEELINGS ARISE

So how do feelings arise? Understanding a little bit about this process helps us to develop mindfulness because we see that even a simple feeling, such as our pleasure when we see the form of a beautiful flower, arises from a series of interdependent steps. In brief, feelings arise dependent upon contact. Contact arises dependent on three other factors—the senses, an object, and consciousness. Here is how the process works:

Things that can be known by the mind through the senses, like a flower, are called mental objects. Each object has a certain quality or function. The senses are like the tentacles of an octopus. The tentacles make initial contact with the object and pass this contact along to the mind. However, the real contact takes place in the mind. Simultaneously with the exposure of the senses to an object, consciousness arises. The mind must be conscious to receive the contact passed along by the senses and interpret it correctly.

When the mind contacts an object, a mental impression arises in the mind that brings out the function of the object. This impression is feeling. Feeling can be compared to a hand that squeezes an orange to get orange juice. When pleasure is squeezed out of the object, we experience a pleasant feeling. When pain is squeezed out of the object, we experience an unpleasant feeling. This feeling can be either a physical sensation or a mental emotion.

The intensity and clarity of a particular feeling depends on many conditions. For example, if our eyes are healthy, the beautiful flower we are looking at is illuminated by bright sunlight, and we are standing close by and paying attention, our visual contact with the flower will be sharp and clear. As a result, the pleasant feeling arising from the eye contact will also be sharp and clear. But if our eyesight is poor, the light is dim, we are far away, or our consciousness is distracted, the flower will not make strong contact. In that case, the feeling that arises dependent on these conditions will be weak and subtle. The same applies to the other external senses.

In the same way, if the mind is clear, the thoughts arising in the mind are clear, and the feeling arising from the mind contact is strong. The feeling we get also depends on our mental state. An object may generate a pleasant feeling in one person and an unpleasant feeling in someone else, depending on the person's state of mind.

Meditating on Mindfulness of Feelings

When we meditate on mindfulness of feelings, we keep in mind that feeling arises dependent upon contact. As contact changes, the feelings also change. When we experience a pleasant feeling, we think, "This is a pleasant feeling. It has arisen depending on these factors. When these factors disappear, this pleasant feeling will also disappear." We do the same for an unpleasant feeling or a neutral feeling. We don't do anything to control our feelings or make them change. We only notice that our feelings are changing. Each feeling arises due to causes and conditions and then slips away. The mind cannot hold on to what we are experiencing and naturally lets it go. What else can it do? Nothing!

As we observe this process, we should not try to put our feelings into words. Labeling our sensations and emotions can actually distort them or disguise them as something else. Each person's feelings of pain or pleasure are totally personal. Feelings cannot really be conveyed in words exactly as they were experienced. We simply let the breath flow in and out. We stay fully awake and alert, paying total attention to each feeling as it arises, peaks, and passes away.

As we meditate, certain special feelings may arise. One of these is called "spiritual urgency." We see clearly that pain arises and pain disappears; pleasure arises and pleasure disappears. As we watch this repeating pattern, an insight arises that as long as we take birth in any form, we will continue to suffer. This insight inspires us to accelerate our spiritual practice and find a way to end this vicious cycle of birth and death right now, once and for all.

We may also experience a special feeling of pleasure as we meditate that does not have an underlying tendency toward desire. Our body becomes calm, our mind becomes calm, and there is no agitation, no excitement. We experience very deep peace. This pleasurable feeling, arising from knowing that this pleasurable feeling and everything else is impermanent, unsatisfactory, and selfless, does not arouse any attachment. We simply experience it. We see the reality.

Key Points for Mindfulness of Feelings

- You can practice mindfulness of feelings within your regular meditation on mindfulness of breathing.

- When feelings arise, notice whether they are pleasant, unpleasant, or neutral. Watch as each feeling arises, peaks, and passes away. You do not need to do anything to control these feelings or make them change. Simply observe and then return your attention to the breath.

- When feelings arise, notice whether they are sensations that result from contact with an external object or emotions that arise internally. Watch as each arises, peaks, and passes away; then return your attention to the breath.

- As you observe your sensations, notice which sense and sense consciousness is the source of the sensation. For example, are you feeling warmth arising from the touch contact between your skin and the cushion, or the sound of a bird outside the window, or the smell of the soup cooking in the kitchen? Don't verbalize these sensations or try to label them. Simply notice that you are experiencing a sensation and then return your attention to the breath.

- For instance, say that the sensation is the agreeable sound of a bird. Pay attention only to the process that allows you to hear the sound—sound waves making contact with your ear and being transmitted to your brain, which analyzes the contact, giving rise to a mental impression of feeling. Remind yourself, "This is a pleasant feeling. It has arisen depending on these factors. When these factors disappear, this pleasant feeling will also disappear." Return your attention to the breath.

- If a sensation of physical pain arises, watch how the sensation changes. Watch its intensity ebb and flow without rejecting or resisting it. Remember that pain is not a thing, but an event. Pain is impermanent. There is no permanent I who is experiencing this sensation.

- If you feel an internally generated emotion, notice it without value judgment. Don't help it, hinder it, or interfere with it in the slightest. Simply watch as the emotion rises, peaks, and passes away. Then return your attention to the breath.

- For instance, if you experience a pleasant fantasy while you are meditating, notice that you have been distracted by a fantasy, notice how strong it is and how long it lasts. Notice the mental state of desire that accompanies the fantasy. Watch as it passes away and return your attention to the breath.

7. Harmful and Beneficial Feelings

Once there was a Brahmin named Akkosana, a person of high rank and authority. He had a habit of getting angry with everyone, even for no reason. When Akkosana heard that the Buddha never got angry, he went to see the Buddha and abused him with insults.

The Buddha listened patiently and compassionately. Then he asked Akkosana, "Do you have friends or relatives?"

"Yes, I have many relatives and friends," Akkosana replied.

"Do you visit them periodically?" the Buddha asked.

"Of course. I visit them often," said Akkosana.

"Do you bring gifts for them when you visit?" the Buddha continued.

"Surely. I never go to see them without a gift."

Then the Buddha asked, "When you give them gifts, suppose they do not accept. What would you do with the gifts?"

"I would take them home and enjoy them with my family."

Then the Buddha said, "Similarly, friend, you gave me a gift of your insults and abuse. I do not accept it. It is all yours. Take it home and enjoy it with your family."

Akkosana was deeply embarrassed. He understood and admired the Buddha's advice.

*A*s we have discussed, we experience 108 different kinds of feelings. Both sensory contact with external objects through the eyes, ears, nose, tongue, and body and nonsensory contact with internal objects within the mind give rise to sensations and emotions. These feelings can be pleasant, unpleasant, or neutral. Some depend on past contact; others on present contact; still others on imagination of future contact. Feelings can be intense and clear or weak and subtle.

As we improve our ability to recognize the variety of sensations and emotions within the aggregate of feelings, we can also become mindful of the habits or tendencies that are their underlying causes. Three are essential: Some pleasant feelings have greed, desire, or craving as their underlying tendency. Some unpleasant feelings have anger or hatred as their underlying tendency. And some neutral feelings are rooted in ignorance or confusion.

Feelings that are activated by any of these negative tendencies are called "worldly." Worldly feelings arise most often when we are engaged in everyday pursuits, such as seeking wealth, companionship, a better job, or more power and recognition. Becoming aware of our tendencies toward anger and attachment and using mindfulness to subdue these habits gives us the opportunity to experience "spiritual" feelings, such as letting go, spiritual urgency, and the special joy we experience when we meditate. As our mindfulness deepens, we enjoy spiritual pleasant feelings more frequently.

Overcoming our negative tendencies takes hard work! Like Akkosana, we may have the habit of getting angry, even when there is no reason. Akkosana's habit was so strong that if a man who had been wronged did not get angry, Akkosana would get angry because the man did not! However, like Akkosana, when we become aware that anger has become a habit, we're often embarrassed. Anger is an unpleasant emotion that feels awful. Though it may take effort to become mindful of our anger and learn to control it, it's relatively easy for us to see that anger is harmful.

Desire and craving are much more difficult to recognize and eliminate. Pleasure generally feels good and makes us feel happy. It's easy to wish to hold on to our good feelings. Our habit is to cling to the pleasure we have, to want more, and to want to experience the pleasure again in the future. However, as we all know very well, whenever we try to hold on to a pleasurable feeling, we end up disappointed. Though it's less easy to remember that desire is harmful, when we think carefully, we see that to end our suffering, we must end our craving.

The third tendency is delusion. Ordinarily, we experience this feeling as confusion with regard to our self and how we exist. Sometimes when we experience a feeling that is neither painful nor pleasurable, we grab on to it with the thought, "Aha, this is real. Let me hold on to it!" We believe that there must be something real and permanent called *I* or *me* that is experiencing this feeling. When we look for this eternal self, it seems to be identical with the five aggregates or within the five aggregates. Only wise and diligent mindfulness can root out this harmful misconception.

In regard to these three, the Buddha's instructions are clear:

> Bhikkhus, the underlying tendency to lust should be abandoned in regard to pleasant feeling. The underlying tendency to aversion should be abandoned in regard to painful feeling. The underlying tendency to ignorance [delusion] should be abandoned in regard to neither painful nor pleasant feeling. When a bhikkhu has abandoned [these] underlying tendencies, then he is one who sees rightly. He . . . has made an end to suffering.
>
> (tr. Bhikkhu Bodhi)

Let's look more closely at these three harmful feelings so that we can recognize them when they arise. We also consider beneficial feelings, such as loving-friendliness, joy, and equanimity, that can help us to overcome them. Our aim is to strengthen our mindfulness of feelings so that we, too, can see rightly and end our suffering.

Anger and Hatred

Anger often starts with a feeling of annoyance or irritation. The trigger can be anything: a work colleague gets a promotion we feel we deserve, a friend makes an unkind remark, a neighbor forgets again to put out the trash. If we ignore these feelings, they can grow into resentment, contempt, even hatred. The underlying tendency of these feelings is aversion—the feeling of disliking something and wanting to be separated from it.

When we pay attention, we see how miserable anger makes us feel. Our mind is cloudy, and our thoughts are tangled. We feel restless and agitated. We lose our appetite and cannot appreciate anything pleasurable. When we burn with what the Buddha calls the "fire of hatred," we are like a pot of boiling water—all hot and confused. Even meditation makes us irritated!

To control anger, the first step is becoming aware of it. With practice, we can learn to recognize the signs and take action before our feelings escalate. As soon as we notice that we are getting angry, we pay total attention to the feeling without trying to justify it. Anger grows when we remember past events, dwell on present situations, and imagine what might happen in the future. Instead, we use what we have learned about mindfulness to put out the fire. We think, "Anger is an unpleasant feeling. It has arisen in dependence on causes and conditions. Everything is impermanent.

When these factors disappear, this unpleasant feeling will also disappear."

Here are some other ways to use mindfulness to overcome anger.

KEY POINTS FOR DEALING WITH ANGER

- Practice mindfulness of breathing. Take a few deep breaths. Inhale, exhale, and count one. Repeat up to ten. Then do the same, counting down from ten to one. Continue until you feel calm.

- Practice restraint. If a conversation seems likely to become an argument, simply stop talking. During the pause, use mindfulness to investigate whether jealousy, stinginess, vengefulness, or some other unwholesome feeling is hiding behind your words. Practice patience to buy time so that you can say the right thing at the right time.

- Avoid blaming. When you say, "It is not my fault. He always does something to make me angry," you sound just like a child saying, "He started it!" Don't blame yourself, either. It takes two to have an argument.

- Talk to a warm-hearted friend. Your friend might remind you, "You cannot know what is going on in someone else's mind. There may be reasons for this behavior that you can't see."

- Cultivate gratitude. When you are angry, it is easy to forget the good things someone has done for you. Being grateful softens your heart.

- Practice generosity. Change the atmosphere between you and a person with whom you are angry by offering a gift or other favor. Doing so may give both of you a chance to apologize.

- Listen to the Dhamma. Find a Dhamma talk on the Web or read a Dhamma article or book. Even if the subject does not pertain to anger, when you hear the Dhamma, your anger fades.

- Avoid angry people. Spending time with people prone to anger can make you tense and anxious. Eventually, you may become angry as well.

- Make a commitment. In the morning, when your mind is fresh, say words such as, "Something might happen today to make me angry. A conversation, a person, or a situation I cannot anticipate may irritate me. Whatever comes up, today I am going to do my best to be mindful and not get angry."

- Remember that you do not want to die with anger. If your mind is confused at the time of death, you may be reborn in a painful state. Life is short. Live yours in peace and harmony, without anger.

Using mindfulness in this way is a type of skillful effort. First, we try to prevent anger from arising. If it does arise, we take steps to overcome it. These two activities work together to make us calm. One day we will say, "Ah, it is wonderful. I am a different person now. I can handle my anger. This has become possible because of my mindfulness."

When the mind is calm, it is easy to cultivate loving-friendliness (*metta* in Pali and *maitri* in Sanskrit). This beneficial feeling is a natural sense of interconnectedness with all beings. Because we want peace, happiness, and joy, we know that all others—including anyone with whom we have had difficulties—must also wish for these qualities. The daily mindfulness practice I suggest on pages 201–4 is a good way to begin. Loving-friendliness heals the wounds of anger. We feel comfortable, secure, and so relaxed that we can talk with anybody without getting angry. Even if someone insults us, we respond with patience and compassion, as the Buddha did to Akkosana.

DESIRE AND CRAVING

Desire is everywhere. Every living thing has the desire to stay alive. Even plants "strive" to propagate themselves. Craving is our creator. Our parents' craving for each other and our craving for rebirth combined to create us. Even painful feelings give rise to craving. When a painful feeling arises, we do not like it. We wish to get rid of the pain, and we wish to enjoy some pleasure. Both wishes are craving.

Surely, we think, desire is necessary. Without it, there would be no birth. Life as we know it would end. In a way, we are right. Desire *is* the underlying motivation for the continuation of life in samsara, the cycle of uncontrolled death and rebirth. As the sutta tells us, "All dhammas converge in feeling."

Of course there are moments of pleasure or enjoyment in our life. We are not suffering all the time. Sixty such moments are mentioned in the *Four Foundations of Mindfulness Sutta*. Enjoyment is the reward we get for all this suffering. That is why we live. But we must work very hard to get this pleasure, because pain comes along with it. As our growing understanding of mindfulness teaches us, whenever we experience a pleasant feeling, we wish to hold on to it. If someone suggests that clinging is a problem, we get upset and try to justify it: "How can I live without clinging to my family, my house, my country?"

The truth is, we don't really want to be free from desire or to admit that clinging to the pleasures of the senses—the taste of delicious food; the sound of music, gossip, or a joke; the touch of a sexual embrace—ends unavoidably in disappointment and suffering. We don't have to deny that pleasant feelings are pleasurable. But we must remember that like every other feeling, pleasure is impermanent. Wishing to keep any person, place, possession, or experience with us forever is hopeless!

Moreover, the wish for sensory pleasure distracts us from our mindfulness. When we are sitting on the cushion, the desire might arise in us to eat a piece of chocolate or to feel the touch of our partner. If we allow this feeling to grow, our mindfulness vanishes. Desire takes over and we reflect: "This is a beautiful feeling. It gives me pleasure. This taste, smell, touch, or sound gives me pleasure . . . this is all I need in my life. It makes me happy, comfortable; it makes me healthy and strong. It gives me full satisfaction."

But then, perhaps, we recognize, "I have this desire in me." We remember that sensory pleasure binds us to this life and future lives. It disrupts our mindfulness and blocks our ability to attain higher states of concentration. What we really want is to enjoy the profound pleasure of deep meditation that leads to liberation from the cycle of suffering. When we are bound to sensory pleasure, liberation is impossible.

So we use mindfulness to penetrate the superficiality of our desire and reflect: "If I cling to this object, I will end up in pain. . . . I can't hold on to it forever; I have no way of controlling it. If I get involved in it, I'll lose my mindfulness. I have enjoyed many things in life . . . where are they now? Why should I sacrifice this precious moment for the sake of superficial satisfaction? . . . let me not think of it." Because of mindfulness, our desire fades away, at least for the moment. When it disappears, we notice that it is gone. We reflect, "That desire is no longer in my mind." We remain mindful to make sure that it does not come back.

Pleasure without pain is possible only as we progress toward higher states of mindfulness. Unlike sensory pleasure that leads only to an instant of temporary happiness, the joy we feel when we achieve deep concentration brings peace and tranquility. This beneficial feeling is accompanied by energy and focus, along with the wholesome desire to experience the wonderful feeling of joy again and again. (I explore this topic in much more detail in *Beyond Mindfulness in Plain English*.)

DELUSION

Delusion is the confused way we regard all objects, including *me*, as permanent and as possessing a self or soul. Because of this confusion, we believe that objects and our feelings about them—pleasant, unpleasant, or neutral—can bring us permanent happiness or cause us permanent misery.

We often notice this confusion when we experience a neutral feeling. Even though we are healthy and have done our meditation as well as we can, we have some kind of nagging feeling in our mind. This feeling is neutral, neither pleasant nor unpleasant, but its underlying tendency is confusion. We think, "*I* exist. This is how my self works. This feeling and all other feelings are part of *me*."

What causes this confusion? For one thing, when we remember our childhood, we believe the same *I* existed then as now, ignoring the many ways our body, feelings, and other aggregates have changed since *I* was a child. We also believe that this same *I* will live into our old age and even into the next life, ignoring all of the changes that will happen between now and then.

The information we get from our senses seems to support this mistaken view. When we see our current body, hear our current voice, smell our current smell, taste food and drink, and touch physical objects, we think, "These are the senses that *I* had yes-terday, last week, last month, eighty years ago. *I* still remember the conversation I had with him or with her. This same *I* existed then and will continue to exist through time."

But even a basic understanding of impermanence reveals that this belief is mistaken. All forms, feelings, perceptions, thoughts, and even consciousness itself are impermanent—arising, existing for a time, and then passing away. Happily, all of our confused habits of mind are also impermanent, even delusion itself. Like anger and craving, delusion arises dependent on causes and conditions. When these causes and conditions change, as they can as a result of our practice of mindfulness, delusion itself vanishes.

EQUANIMITY

The beneficial feeling we hope to cultivate through our mind-fulness practice is equanimity. When we rest in equanimity, our feelings are in perfect balance. We neither push away unpleasant feelings nor grasp at pleasant ones. We are not confused by igno-rance and see everything very clearly. Since we don't identify our self with our feelings, they pass quietly away, leaving us at peace. As a feeling, equanimity is both neutral and spiritual. It is neither pleasant nor unpleasant, but it is not indifferent. We are awake and alert and can continue our observation of our body, feelings, thoughts, and other experiences without being pushed and pulled by desire or aversion.

As the sutta tells us, when we are in a state of equanimity and see a pleasant, unpleasant, or neutral sight, we recognize that it is condi-tioned, gross, and dependently arisen. Then we return to equanimity as quickly as we might open or shut our eyes. The same is true for each of the other senses:

When [meditators] hear a pleasant, unpleasant, or neutral sound, they understand that it is conditioned, gross, and dependently arisen. Then they turn their minds to equanimity just as quickly as a man snaps his fingers.

When they smell a pleasant, unpleasant, or neutral smell, they understand that it is conditioned, gross, and dependently arisen. Then they turn their minds to equanimity just as quickly as drops of water roll off a sloping lotus leaf. . . .

Similarly, when they experience an idea with their minds and a pleasant, unpleasant, or neutral sensation arises, they understand that it is conditioned, gross, and dependently arisen. Then, just as when two or three drops of water fall onto an iron plate that has been heated for a whole day, the falling of the drops might be slow, but they quickly evaporate and disappear. In the same way sensations arisen due to ideas are replaced quickly and easily with equanimity.

With equanimity, we are no longer troubled by the ups and downs of pleasure and pain. Mind and body are in balance. We are free of restlessness, agitation, and worry. Confusion has ended and we rest in harmony with reality. Even the subtle desire for a beautiful experience to continue has disappeared. Instead, we feel immeasurable loving-friendliness and boundless compassion.

Having completely let go of what the Buddha calls "low quality" pleasant feelings—the pleasures of family, friends, good health, prosperity—we experience "high quality" pleasant feelings—the profound joys of higher states of meditative concentration. With each higher state, our enjoyment increases until we attain what the Buddha calls "the cessation of feeling and perception." From there we can move to the highest quality pleasure of all, nibbana, total liberation from suffering.

Part 3:

Mindfulness
of Mind

8. Mind and Consciousness

The Buddha was explaining to his bhikkhus what he had done to overcome unwholesome thoughts that arose in his mind while he was still an unenlightened bodhisatta.

"It occurred to me," the Buddha said, "suppose I divide my thoughts into two classes. On one side, I set thoughts of sensual desire, ill will, and cruelty. On the other side, I set thoughts of renunciation, loving-friendliness, and compassion.

"As I abided thus, diligent, ardent, and resolute, a thought of sensual desire arose in me. When I considered that this thought leads to my own affliction and the affliction of others, it subsided in me. When I considered that this thought obstructs wisdom, causes difficulties, and leads away from nibbana, it subsided in me. Thus I abandoned it, did away with it, removed it. . . .

"Whatever a bhikkhu frequently thinks upon, that will become the inclination of his mind. If he ponders renunciation, if he has abandoned the thought of sensual desire to cultivate the thought of renunciation, then his mind inclines to thoughts of renunciation."

These words, taken from the *Two Kinds of Thought Sutta*, illustrate the most important practical lesson in the Buddha's teachings on the third foundation of mindfulness, mindfulness of mind:

whatever thoughts we cultivate frequently become a mental habit. Just as the Buddha abandoned thoughts of wishing for sensual pleasure by cultivating thoughts of renunciation, he did away with thoughts of anger by thinking of compassion and thoughts of cruelty by thinking of loving-friendliness. What simple good sense this advice is!

But the Buddha's advice goes one step further, as the sutta tells us. He also warned his monks that too much thinking—even beneficial thoughts such as renunciation, compassion, and loving-friendliness—tires the body and strains the mind. "When the mind is strained," the Buddha explained, "it is far from concentration." So rather than thinking at all, he "steadied his mind internally, quieted it, brought it to singleness, and concentrated it." "Meditate, bhikkhus," the Buddha concluded, "do not delay, or else you will regret it later." With this, "the bhikkhus were satisfied and delighted in the Blessed One's words."

As we work toward the state of single-pointed, concentrated meditation that the Buddha encourages in this sutta, we encounter a formidable obstacle—our own mind or consciousness. In Buddhist writings, the untamed mind is often described using animal metaphors. Sometimes it is a newly captured "wild elephant" that screams and tramples and pulls against the rope of mindfulness. Other times it is the "wandering monkey mind" that roams all over the universe through imagination. We have all experienced this mind. We are trying to meditate or even to fall asleep, but thoughts distract us. We remember injustices, wars, problems, places, situations, books we have read, people we met long ago, our job, house, family, friends, relatives, and many other things.

Clearly, we need more of the Buddha's good advice so that we can convince this monkey to settle down! As a first step, let's look more closely at what the Buddha says about the nature of mind so that we can move ahead with better understanding.

MIND OR CONSCIOUSNESS

So what is consciousness? Is it the same as mind? Where is it? And how does it function? These are difficult questions, but let's do our best to look at them in a way that helps to deepen our practice of mindfulness. As you already know, consciousness is one of the five aggregates, along with the body, feelings, perceptions, and thoughts. As is true of all the aggregates, consciousness is always changing. In fact, it changes much faster than anything else. Not knowing how consciousness arises, how it ends, and what leads to that end is called ignorance. That is why consciousness is so difficult to understand.

The function of the aggregate of consciousness is basic awareness. When we speak about this function, we sometimes use the word "mind." Mind is a nonphysical phenomenon that perceives, thinks, recognizes, experiences, and reacts. It is clear and formless, which means that thoughts and other mind objects can arise in it. It is also described as luminous, which means "able to shine light on things"—in other words, "knowing."

There is no single place in the body where mind is stored. Some people say that the mind resides in the heart. The Pali word *citta* means both mind and heart. Others say that it exists in the brain. Still others believe that the mind is located all over the body and operates through the brain and central nervous system. The Buddha did not mention a particular place as the home of mind. He simply used the phrase "cave of the body."

Though consciousness is present in every thought, perception, and feeling, it does not have independent existence. In fact, we don't notice consciousness at all until it meets with an object. Consciousness arises dependent on the six senses and their contact with objects. It even has different names according to the sense through which it arises—sight consciousness, smell consciousness, touch consciousness, and so on. For instance, when the ear contacts the sound of a train whistle or a woman singing, sound consciousness arises. When the mind contacts internal objects, such as thoughts and memories, mind consciousness arises.

Thus, there is no such thing as mere mind or mere consciousness. We know mind only by its contents. It is always hanging on to a thought, feeling, perception, the body, or some mental object. In itself, the consciousness that arises as a result of contact with objects is pure. But almost simultaneously with consciousness, desire ("I want this"), hatred ("I don't want that"), delusion ("This is me"), or some related confusion arises. The mind wants to shine by itself, but its mental contents don't allow it. They conceal the mind's luminosity and distort our ability to know things as they really are.

The best we can say is that mind is an impermanent and dependent phenomenon. It arises as a result of causes and conditions. Understood in this way, instead of the word "mind," it makes more sense to talk about the "body-mind complex"—the combination of mental factors (including contact, feeling, perception, attention, concentration, life force, and volition) that work together in each instant of consciousness.

Since consciousness arises as a result of causes and conditions, the consciousness of this life must also have come from causes and conditions.

So what is our role in this process? Did we select our present life? And can we choose where this stream of consciousness will arise next? Unfortunately, the answer to both questions is no, or at least, not directly.

As the Buddha has explained, at the time of death, we have already made all the arrangements for the next life—not by writing a will, but by engaging in countless actions of body, speech, and mind.

These thoughts, words, and deeds are causes, the first half of the universal principle of cause and effect known as *kamma* (or karma). Our present life is the second half of the principle—the result of the causes we created in previous lives. Thus the consciousness that arises in this life can be called a stream of "result consciousness." Our kamma, combined with our craving for rebirth and our ignorance, propel us to start the process of birth, aging, and death all over again.

The kamma we have created determines the nature of our rebirth: good actions lead to a fortunate rebirth; bad actions, to an unfortunate one.

Of course, the good news is that there is one thing we can do immediately to make sure that our next life is a fortunate one. Right now, while we are alive, we can use mindfulness to train ourselves to avoid thoughts, words, and deeds motivated by sensual desire, anger, cruelty, and other causes of bad kamma and to cultivate beneficial actions motivated by renunciation, compassion, loving-friendliness, and other causes of good kamma!

Cleansing the Mind

So how do we practice mindfulness of mind? Since we know mind only by its contents, we cannot contemplate or focus on just the mind. In a nutshell, the practice consists of cleansing the mind so that the harmful tendencies toward desire, hatred, and ignorance—the same tendencies that caused us to take rebirth—do not have the opportunity to manifest as actions. If they do arise, we make the effort to overcome them. And when they are overcome, we make the effort to replace them with beneficial states of mind.

Desire, hatred, delusion, and other poisons are able to pollute the mind because of the harmful tendencies or inclinations we created

306 THE FOUR FOUNDATIONS OF MINDFULNESS IN PLAIN ENGLISH

by our previous actions. As the Buddha explained in the *Two Kinds of Thought Sutta* mentioned at the beginning of this chapter, whatever thoughts we cultivate frequently become a habit. For instance, when we are accustomed to angry thoughts, it is easier to entertain angry thoughts in the future.

These harmful tendencies hide within the mind until they are activated by contact with external objects and situations. That's why, for example, spending time with angry people can activate our own tendency to anger. However, once the mind is purified, we no longer have to guard our senses against external situations that can stimulate deluded thoughts. A person who insults us does not make us angry; a person who craves wine and offers us some does not make us want to get drunk ourselves. As the sutta explains:

> As rain gets into an ill-thatched house, so craving gets into an untrained mind. As rain does not get into a well-thatched house, so craving does not get into a well-trained mind.

Worrying over or dwelling upon harmful actions we have done in the past is a waste of time and energy. Instead, we should put our efforts into cultivating beneficial thoughts to overcome and replace harmful ones. In fact, we must cultivate thoughts of generosity, compassion, loving-friendliness, and equanimity again and again in order to weaken and destroy harmful inclinations and create beneficial ones.

We do this most effectively by practicing mindfulness meditation. As I have mentioned, our practice consists of two types of meditation: concentration meditation or *samatha* and insight meditation or *vipassana*. Concentration meditation suppresses the hindrances and makes the mind calm, peaceful, and luminous. Hindrances are negative tendencies that obstruct our spiritual progress and interfere with our ability to concentrate. I explain more about the hindrances in chapter 10. Insight meditation, which we have been calling mindfulness, eradicates the hindrances and all other negative tendencies. It helps us to overcome ignorance so that we can be liberated from samsara, the cycle of repeated births and deaths.

Key Points for Practicing Mindfulness of Mind

- If you are sitting on your meditation cushion and a craving arises in your mind, like lust, what should you do? First, acknowledge that if there were no tendency toward craving in your mind, craving would have not arisen. Although your mind is luminous, it is not totally pure.

- Next, recognize the possibility of liberating your mind from craving. Observe your thoughts without following them until the craving thoughts fade away.

- When the craving ends, recognize that it has gone. You think, "This is wonderful! This mind was full of craving before. Now there is none. That means even I have the chance to liberate this mind from craving."

- Reflect on the nature of a craving-free mind. It is generous, gentle, compassionate, and happy to renounce thoughts of sensual pleasure. With this confidence you proceed.

- Another time, while you are meditating, you hear a sound. Somebody is walking loudly. Somebody coughs. Somebody sneezes. Somebody is snoring. And aversion or anger arises.

- You get irritated and begin to question: "Why doesn't this person walk quietly? Why doesn't this person take some cough medicine? Why doesn't this person stay in a cabin alone and meditate there without troubling us? Why doesn't the person sitting next to this snoring person wake him up?"

- These questions and many more thoughts bother you. You get angry. Hateful thought can arise in any of the four postures, sitting, standing, walking, or lying down.

- When hate arises, you recognize, "Hateful thoughts have arisen in me." Hate arises depending on previous experiences. It arises depending on causes or conditions. You cannot predict when hate will arise.

- So you use the techniques of mindfulness you have been practicing to overcome these thoughts. Pay attention to the thought without following it. Observe the impact of hatred on your consciousness. Don't think of any incident, any situation, or any person. Don't verbalize by saying, "My mind is full of hatred." Words block awareness of what is going on in your mind. Just pay attention and recognize what has arisen as having arisen.

- Reflect on the nature of a hate-free mind. It is beautiful, peaceful, relaxed, and loving-friendly.

- Suddenly, thoughts of friendliness and compassion arise. These have no particular object and are focused on no particular person. Recognize them, feel them, delve into them, accept them—simply be with them.

- The mind must be free from delusion to understand that it is free from delusion. Before delusion arose in your mind, it was clear, just as before you fell asleep, you were awake. All you need do at that moment is to pay attention to the fact that your mind is clear.

- When you pay attention, the clouds of delusion slowly fade away and the clear blue sky-like mind appears again. You see that consciousness is always changing. Thoughts arise and disappear. They are impermanent. When delusion arises you pay attention to it, knowing that it is a delusion. Then it slowly fades away. Then you know mind as clear, aware, luminous.

9. Mental States

One day, someone brought a delicious dish of fish to offer to the monks at a temple. In that temple lived one monk and one temple boy. When the monk sat down to eat, the boy offered him the whole dish. In it were eight small pieces of fish. The monk took three at once.

As the monk ate, the temple boy watched attentively. He said to himself, "Well, he is the monk and the head of the temple. Let him have three pieces. There are five more. That is enough for my lunch and dinner."

When the monk finished eating, he stretched out his hand to pick up more fish.

The temple boy thought, "Surely, he is the monk and the head of the temple. He deserves half of this dish. Let him have one more."

This time the monk took two pieces.

Then the boy thought, "Never mind, let him have five pieces. There are three more. That is plenty for me."

After eating the two pieces, the monk helped himself to two more, leaving only one small piece of fish in the dish.

Then the boy thought, "Never mind. I am small. He is big. One piece is enough for me."

When the monk reached for the last piece, the boy's patience ran out. "Venerable sir," he cried. "Are you going to eat this last piece of fish without leaving anything for me?"

In his greed for fish, the monk was so unmindful that he had totally forgotten the faithful temple boy, waiting patiently to have his meal. The monk was so embarrassed that, ever after, he refrained from eating greedily.

. . . .

*D*eveloping mindfulness of greed and other states of mind is hard work. As we have noted, because we see mind only by its contents, we cannot contemplate the mind by itself. When consciousness with greed arises in the mind, instead of looking at the mind, we quickly do what the greedy mind demands, as we see clearly in the traditional story of the greedy monk and the temple boy. We follow our instinct, acting blindly and impulsively, even if we suspect we may regret our actions later. Once the mind is obsessed, we seldom have enough discipline to be mindful. We speak, think, and act in bewildered haste.

Mindfulness training teaches us to pause and look at the mind. First, we practice while sitting on the cushion. As thoughts come and go, we watch them arise, peak, and pass away. Since we are not engaging in immediate action based on our impulses, we are able to assess our mental states calmly. The *Four Foundations of Mindfulness Sutta* recommends that we watch particularly for eight pairs of mental states. Our goal is learning to recognize whether the mind is:

1. greedy or not greedy,
2. hateful or not hateful,
3. deluded or not deluded,
4. contracted/distracted or not contracted/distracted,
5. developed or not developed,
6. supreme or not supreme,

7. concentrated or not concentrated,

8. liberated or not liberated.

The first four pairs of mental states can be experienced both during meditation sessions and while we are engaging in everyday activities. After practicing awareness of them on the cushion, we often find it easier to be mindful of them at other times. The last four pairs focus on states we achieve only through dedicated meditation practice. Knowing about these states inspires us to try to attain them. To begin, let's look briefly at each pair to help us recognize them.

Greedy or not. We have all acted on impulse like the greedy monk. Suppose we see a dish of food on a buffet table that we like very much. Our greedy mind becomes active. We scoop deeply into the dish and serve up a big portion without thinking about the people lined up behind us eyeing the same dish. The goal of mindfulness training is becoming aware of our mental states so that we can take steps to short-circuit our impulsive actions. The moment we realize that our mind is obsessed, we think about the discomfort we might cause others who are waiting their turn. Like the greedy monk in the story, we apply the discipline of mindfulness in a practical way to change our behavior.

When our greed disappears, even for a short period, we immediately feel more comfortable. We notice that easy state of mind and also recognize that greed can arise any time, any place, and in any situation. When we pay attention, we find many opportunities to reflect on our mental state and to practice self-control.

I walk as much as I can every day. Often I see deer that have been shot by hunters. Sometimes the hunters cannot find them, and the carcasses rot by the roadside. I also see trash thrown by the road—beer cans, liquor bottles, TV antennas, refrigerators, tables, and other household junk. Throughout the spring and summer, this garbage also rots.

Because I desire to see a clean environment, these sights sometimes disturb my mind. But then mindfulness intervenes. I remind myself that desire does me more harm than good. Even the wholesome wish for people to stop hunting or to dispose properly of their trash unsettles my mind and causes me to suffer. So, instead of being attached to my environmental principles, I remind myself that I cannot fix the whole world and let go of my desire. I may not be able to remove the world's greed, but I can get rid of my own. The moment I do, I begin to relax. Then and there I experience peace.

Hateful or not. In its natural state, the mind is like cool, calm, and clear water. Hateful thoughts overheat the mind. Under their influence, the mind boils like a pot of water, distorting our ability to think clearly or see things as they are. Our relaxed, calm, and peaceful state of mind dissolves, and the mind simmers with jealousy, vengefulness, malicious thoughts, thoughts of cruelty. We want to cause harm to someone. If we do not intervene with mindfulness, the mind orders the tongue to become active and we wound others with harsh words.

Mindfulness suffocates anger by taking away the fuel it needs to keep burning. When hate fills our mind, we should think: "Hate makes me sick. My thinking is confused. A sick mind defeats the purpose of my meditation. Only with a calm and peaceful mind can I see myself clearly and reach my goal." The Buddha described the relief we feel when we overcome hate-filled thoughts in this way:

Suppose that a man were to become sick, afflicted, gravely ill, so that he could not enjoy his food and his strength declined. After some time, he recovered from that illness so that he could enjoy his food and regain his bodily strength. He would reflect on this, and as a result he would become glad and experience joy.

Deluded or not. Recognizing delusion is tricky. The mind must be free from delusion to understand that it is free from delusion! So how can we tell that we are deluded? The secret is remembering that, by nature, the mind is clear and luminous. We have experienced this clarity many times—perhaps during a peaceful session of meditation, or just before falling asleep, or when we first wake up in the morning. We should make a habit of noticing this clarity when it occurs. Then, when delusion arises, it is easier to recognize it.

Delusion most often manifests as confusion about who we are and how we exist. When strong greed or hatred grips the mind, we think, "I must have that" or "I despise that." The *I* that arises at that time feels very solid and very needy. It's as if the mind is locked in jail by that powerful need. We feel that if this need cannot be met, *I* will die! But, remember, before the mind was imprisoned, it was free. That memory of freedom helps us to become mindful.

The key is impermanence. When we pay attention to deluded thoughts, the cloud of confusion slowly fades. Soon the clear, blue sky-like mind appears again. When we recognize delusion as delusion, delusion ends—at least temporarily. When we attain the liberation of nibbana, freedom from delusion becomes permanent.

Contracted/distracted or not. A contracted mind is depressed or withdrawn. This mental state, related to displeasure, can occur at any time. Sometimes we experience it when we are sitting on the cushion and the thought arises that we are not making any progress in our meditation. We think, "Nothing works for me. Everyone else is happy and peaceful. I'm the only one who never gets it right!" This mind also shows up during ordinary activities. We think, "Nobody loves me. I am so old, so fat, so ugly. I always say the wrong thing, do the wrong thing."

When we become mindful that the mind is contracted in this way, the only thing to do is to keep watching and watching. Don't rationalize or justify. Don't allow one thought to lead to another. Don't hold on at all. Just pay attention. This state of mind is also impermanent. Like any other, it slowly fades away.

The opposite of a contracted mind is a distracted one. The mind expands beyond all boundaries. The whole universe seems open and welcoming. We feel that we are really someone special. This mental state is also an obstacle. If we don't rein it in with purposeful attention, it escapes like the "monkey mind" and travels all over the universe through imagination.

Developed or not developed. In everyday consciousness, we do not experience the developed mental state. Some translators use the word "exalted" to describe it. We reach this calm, peaceful, and tranquil state only as a result of deep concentration meditation. The mind has gone beyond normal consciousness. We feel as if we are floating a few feet above the ground. The mind is harmonious, relaxed, serene, bright, and balanced. Even accomplished meditators do not achieve this state every time they practice.

When the meditation session ends and the mind returns to normal awareness, we experience the mental state that is not developed. Our ordinary consciousness with its sense experiences returns. We become aware that the mind is not anything special.

Supreme or not supreme. The next pair of mental states also refers to the attainments of deep concentration meditation. "Supreme" means that we have reached "the highest state." After the Buddha became enlightened, he said that his mind had attained an unsurpassable, peerless, or transcendent state. An accomplished meditator can also achieve this kind of mental experience. The mind is pure, soft, steady, and imperturbable. Although it is wonderful, this state is temporary. Only when we achieve liberation does it become permanent. Any other mental state achieved during meditation is not supreme. This term acknowledges that we know that it is possible for us to achieve a state that is superior.

Concentrated or not concentrated. Sometimes when we meditate, the mind is able to concentrate on one thing without interruption. When we achieve this level of single-pointed focus, we train ourselves to be mindful of it, recognizing concentrated mind as concentrated mind. When the mind is contracted or distracted, we recognize that our mental state is not concentrated.

Sometimes when people have distracted mind, rather than cultivating simple awareness, they complain, "My mind is jumping all over the place. I can't concentrate." Thinking along these lines leads only to more grumbling and more worry. Instead, we should follow the Buddha's advice and simply notice. Soon, the mind that is not concentrated fades and it becomes possible to achieve concentration once again. The key is observing with mindfulness.

Liberated or not liberated. A liberated mind is free of all problems. It is not greedy, hateful, deluded, contracted, or distracted. It is developed, supreme, and concentrated. In the highest states of concentration meditation, it is possible to achieve temporary liberation. But even temporary liberation from harmful mental states is an extraordinarily beneficial experience. If we follow the steps of mindfulness very closely, eventually the mind may become fully liberated.

WORKING WITH MENTAL STATES

The pairs of mental states we have been considering do not always arise in the mind in the order given in the sutta. However, it is certain that when one half of a pair is present in consciousness, the other half is not. So, for instance, when greed fades away, we enjoy the state of "not" greed. In the *Removal of Distracting Thought Sutta*, the Buddha presents a series of vivid comparisons that illustrate ways to overcome a negative mental state so that we experience its opposite. The methods are listed in order of increasing forcefulness. If one fails, we try the next.

- Replace it: Say that greed, hate, or delusion arises because you pay unwise attention to some aspect of an object. Then pay attention instead to some wholesome aspect, just as a skilled carpenter assembling furniture might tap out a coarse peg by hammering in a fine one.

- Remember the suffering it causes: If the mental state does not go away, examine the danger in it. Contemplate that such thoughts are reprehensible and result in suffering, just as a young man or woman who is fond of ornaments would be horrified, humiliated, and disgusted by the carcass of a snake hung around the neck.

- Ignore it: If the thought persists, try to forget it. Pay no attention, just as a man with good eyes who did not want to see something bad would shut his eyes or look away.

- Remember that it is impermanent: If the thought still stays, remind yourself that every mental state arises and passes away. Then leaving the first state, the mind goes to the next, just as a man who is walking fast might think, "Why am I walking fast? What if I walk slowly?" Then he walks slowly. Later he might think, "Why am I walking slowly? What if I stand?" Then he stands. Later he might think, "Why am I standing? What if I sit?" Then he sits. Later he might think, "Why am I sitting? What if I lie down?" Then he lies down.

- Overpower it: If the thought still remains in your mind, then with teeth clenched and tongue pressed against the roof of your mouth, use all your energy to overcome it. Crush mind with mind, just as a strong man might seize a weaker man by the head or shoulders and beat him down, constrain him, and crush him.

Though negative states of mind are more troublesome and thus require strong measures to overcome them, we should also use mindfulness to encourage states that are wholesome and beneficial. For instance, when thoughts of generosity, loving-friendliness, appreciation, and equanimity arise, we should ask ourselves, "Is my mindfulness strong enough to maintain them? If not, what else can I do?" For instance, we can make changes to our lifestyle, such as living in a suitable place, keeping the house clean, getting together with like-minded friends, reading inspiring books, and developing a diligent daily mindfulness practice.

With mindfulness and effort, we can develop wonderful states of mind, including confidence, patience, concentration, attention, thoughts of service, thoughts of simplicity, determination to good things, thoughts of contentment, and thoughts of wisdom.

Key Points for Meditation on Mental States

- To practice mindfulness of mind, begin every day with meditation, using your breath as the primary focus. As the breath becomes calm, subtle, and relaxed, the mind becomes calm and relaxed.

- Practice awareness of your mental states by watching them arise, peak, and pass away. Practicing awareness on the cushion helps you to be mindful of mental states in everyday life.

- Awareness of impermanence also is impermanent. That is why the mind, while watching mental states arise, peak, and pass away, drifts from this awareness. While you are mindful of the changes of one mental state, another arises. Then leaving the first state, your mind goes to the second. This means that the mind watching impermanence is also changing.

- If mindfulness of the impermanence of a harmful mental state is not sufficient to overcome it, try a more forceful method.

- When greed, hatred, delusion, and other harmful states are abandoned, the mind is steadied internally and quieted. In this state, it can be brought to singleness and concentrated.

- Mindfulness and concentration working together in unison and stability notice countless changes taking place in the mind simultaneously.

- Apply mindfulness and attention without concepts. Ideas or thoughts are impediments. Without them, you can focus the mind like a laser beam on the five aggregates. Then the mind can see that *I* exists only when the body, feelings, perceptions, thoughts, and consciousness exist. They, in turn, exist dependent on causes and conditions. They are impermanent. You can't find any self or soul or *I* in any of the aggregates.

- Each moment is a new moment. Each moment is a fresh moment. Each moment brings you new insight and new understanding.

- Nothing is static. Everything is dynamic. Everything is changing. Everything is appearing and disappearing. Feeling arises and passes away. Thought arises and passes away. Perception arises and passes away. Consciousness arises and passes away. You experience only change.

- In the mental state of deep concentration, you see things as they really are.

Part 4:

Mindfulness of Dhamma

10. *Hindrances*

Once when the Venerable Anuruddha was meditating in seclusion, seven thoughts occurred to him. Knowing Anuruddha's thoughts, the Buddha appeared in front of him.

The Blessed One sat down on a prepared seat and said, "Good, Anuruddha, very good. It's good that you think these seven thoughts of a great person: This dhamma is for one who is modest, not one who is boastful; for one who is content, not one who is discontent; for one who is reclusive, not one who is entangled in society. This dhamma is for one who is energetic, not one who is lazy; for one who is mindful, not one who is unmindful; for one whose mind is centered, not one whose mind is distracted; for one who is discerning, not for one who is heedless.

"Now then, Anuruddha, think the eighth thought of a great person: This dhamma is for one who is wise, not for one who delights in delusion." Then the Buddha gave Anuruddha instructions for using his insights to reach states of deep concentration. . . .

Dwelling alone, secluded, heedful, ardent, and resolute, Anuruddha followed the Buddha's instructions and in a short time attained liberation, the supreme goal of the holy life. On becoming one of the arahants, Anuruddha recited this verse:

Knowing my thoughts, the Teacher came to me.

He taught in line with my thoughts, and then further,

Delighting in nondelusion, he taught wisdom.
Knowing his Dhamma, I delighted in doing his bidding.
Knowledge has been obtained; the Buddha's bidding done.

. . . .

Now we come to the last section of the *Four Foundations of Mindfulness Sutta*, mindfulness of dhamma. It gives instructions and practical advice to help us overcome things that hold us back from making progress in our meditation. As the story of Anuruddha illustrates, it takes outstanding qualities of mind and heart to reach our spiritual goals. We must be modest, content, reclusive, mindful, centered, discerning, and wise. If we already have these noble qualities, the Dhamma benefits us by leading us toward liberation. If we do not yet have these qualities, the Dhamma helps us to develop them. In practical terms, our mindfulness practice gradually helps us to grow the attributes of enlightenment.

To begin, we remove the habits of mind that block our progress on the path. Our task is like preparing a plot of ground to grow a garden. First, we clear away the brush, weeds, and other obvious obstructions. In the Dhamma, we call these impediments "hindrances." In this chapter, we consider five hindrances and what we can do to remove them.

Once the ground has been cleaned up, at least on the surface, we can begin work at a deeper level. In chapter 11, we dig down to the underlying root system of the hindrances: the five aggregates of clinging, the contact of the senses with sensory objects, and the ten fetters that arise from that contact.

Only when we have uprooted these deep causes can seven positive qualities, called the factors of enlightenment, start to grow. We explore these qualities in chapter 12. Finally, in chapter 13, we look at the Buddha's road map of the Dhamma path, the four noble truths and eight mindful steps. It outlines the journey we must take to travel from suffering to freedom.

THE FIVE HINDRANCES

When we practice mindfulness meditation, it doesn't take long for us to discover that it's not always easy to concentrate. Whether we are trying to focus on the breath or to observe the changes in our body, feelings, or thoughts, distractions have a way of pulling us off track. The most powerful of these distractions are called the "hindrances." They interfere with our ability to concentrate both during meditation and in everyday life.

We have already mentioned some of the hindrances. For instance, we noted that our *desire* for pleasure and *hatred* for pain hide behind many of our feelings. Other hindrances to progress on the path are *restlessness and worry*, laziness (also called *sloth and torpor*), and *doubt*. Mindfulness helps us to know five important things about the hindrances: when they are present, when they are absent, how they arise, what to do to make them go away, and how to keep them from coming back.

When the hindrances have been overcome, the mind automatically becomes calm, bright, and clear. This clarity is essential to insight into the impermanent, suffering, and selfless nature of everything that exists.

Desire

As a hindrance, desire means more than just "clinging." In Pali, the word used at this point in the *Four Foundations of Mindfulness Sutta* is *chanda*, which means "willingness to have sense pleasure." As we have noted, the willingness to experience delightful sights, sounds, smells, tastes, and touches often distracts us when we are trying to meditate. As we have all experienced, sense desire also disturbs our concentration at work or when we are trying to finish some household task. How often have we lost focus because we are suddenly hungry for ice cream or because of physical desire for our boyfriend or girlfriend? Distractions like these are chanda, desire for physical pleasure arising from the senses.

Desire can also arise in the sixth sense, the mind. So, while meditating, sometimes the sound of a song we like starts running through our mind. Then, instead of paying attention to its arising and vanishing, we want to keep enjoying that sound. If we're not careful, soon our attention is focused on the song rather than on the breath or other meditation subject.

The first step to overcoming the hindrance of desire is recognizing that we have it. So when the wish to see a movie distracts us from our focus, we recognize, "I have this desire in me." Next, rather than feeding our desire by indulging in imaginary enjoyment of it, we use mindfulness to understand its source and suppress it. For instance, we remember that the pleasure that arises from sense contact exists for an instant and disappears just as quickly, leaving us disappointed. We can also reflect about how unattractive or harmful our desire is. For instance, "Ice cream is terrible for me. My face breaks out and it makes me fat!" Or perhaps, "This desire is disrupting my concentration and holding me back from making progress in my meditation. Let me not think of it!"

When the desire is gone, we notice that it is gone. Finally, we use vigilant effort to make sure that it does not return, at least for the remainder of this meditation session. Unfortunately, these measures are only a temporary solution. Until we destroy the roots of desire through deep concentration meditation, it keeps coming back again and again.

Ill Will

Ill will includes every kind of aversion from mild irritation to violent hatred. As we have discussed, even ordinary anger makes us feel awful and destroys our ability to concentrate. The story is told about a monk who spent years in solitude meditating in a cave. When he finally emerged and went down to the village, a passerby brushed against him by mistake and stepped on his toe. Immediately the monk cried out in anger, "Get out of my way!" Of course, we have to assume that this unfortunate monk did not meditate correctly using mindfulness and concentration to remove the hindrances and destroy their roots.

The method for overcoming the hindrance of ill will is the same as we discussed for desire. When irritation arises, we try to notice it immediately so that we can take action to overcome it before it escalates. The practical suggestions for overcoming anger given on pages 290–93 are a good place to start. Keep in mind that every kind of ill will arises from the wish to be physically separated from something that causes us discomfort or pain. Remember also that ill will and its causes are impermanent. Looking back, we often feel embarrassed that we got angry over some trivial thing. Over time, like everything else, anger fades away.

Until it does, we practice patience to keep us from reacting in ways that we may regret later on. The profound practice of patience calms the mind and makes us peaceful. Of course, patience does not mean allowing someone to abuse us. Rather, it is buying time so that our overheated emotions cool down and we can respond kindly and appropriately. If ill will arises while we are trying to meditate, we should remember that anger makes it impossible to think clearly and hinders our progress on the path.

The most powerful way to get rid of anger is to cultivate the mind of loving-friendliness, or *metta*. No matter what someone does to make us angry, we can always find a reason to feel compassion. Perhaps the person who offended us was sincerely trying to help us, or was physically ill or emotionally disturbed. Metta softens the heart and helps us to feel sorry for someone who has acted unskillfully. Rather than lashing out, we think, "How can I help this person?"

When such thoughts have helped us to overcome ill will, we notice that it is gone. We use mindfulness and diligence to keep this hindrance from returning.

Sloth and Torpor

In everyday life, physical laziness, or sloth, arises for many reasons. For some, laziness is just a bad habit. For others, it's a way of escaping from feelings of discontent or depression. When we have eaten too much rich food, had too much to drink, or exercised too vigorously, we often feel drowsy. When it becomes a regular occurrence, physical laziness is a problem because we have no drive or energy. It is impossible to get any work done. All we want to do is lie down and take a nap.

Mental laziness, or torpor, is an even bigger obstacle to concentration. The mind becomes sluggish and cloudy, like water covered by mossy plants. Everything we try to focus on seems indistinct and very far away. We can't read, we can't think, we can't speak clearly, and even the simplest question is confusing. We have no idea what is happening around us or inside us. This dull state is very close to ignorance, which is sometimes called eternal slumber.

When we meditate, the breath, mind, and body become so relaxed that it's easy to slide into drowsiness or dullness. Although sleepiness is very sweet and we welcome it at the right time, the joys of deep concentration do not arise from laziness. We must not confuse the pleasurable feeling of physical or mental relaxation with the attainment of high meditative states. Insight requires energy, vigor, and sharpness.

When we recognize that we are under the influence of laziness, we pay attention to it. We remember that sloth and torpor hinder our mindfulness and apply remedies to overcome it. For instance, we remember the stories of diligent meditators like Anuruddha who attained liberation by practicing with persistent dedication, not by taking a nap! As Anuruddha realized and the Buddha confirmed, "This Dhamma is for the energetic, not for the lazy."

It also helps to talk to our laziness. For instance, we say silently, "I have been born a human being. To be born as a human is rare. The best use of human life is not indulging in the pleasures of dullness and doing nothing. My mind must be clear so that I can free myself from fear, tension, and worry. My ultimate goal is to be free from greed, hatred, and delusion. A lazy person cannot achieve real peace and happiness." In a sutta, an internal pep talk like this is compared to a cowherd who guides cows with a stick. Whenever one of them goes astray, he taps her and makes her come back to the herd. When laziness disappears, we notice that it is gone. We use mindfulness to make sure it does not return.

Here are a few other simple suggestions for overcoming sloth and torpor and for making sure it does not come back:

- Open your eyes and roll your eyeballs for a few seconds. Close your eyes and go back to your mindfulness meditation.

- Visualize a bright light, a sunny sky, or a dazzling white field of snow. Focus your mind on this image for a few seconds. As you are visualizing, the sleepiness fades away.

- Take a deep breath and hold it as long as you can. Then slowly breathe out. Repeat this several times until your body warms up and perspires. Then return to your mindfulness practice.

332 THE FOUR FOUNDATIONS OF MINDFULNESS IN PLAIN ENGLISH

- Stand up and do standing meditation for a few minutes until sleepiness goes away. If it does not, follow the instructions for walking meditation given on pages 230–31 until sleepiness disappears. Then return to your sitting practice.

- Wash your face with cold water. Or pinch your earlobes hard with thumbs and index fingers and really feel the pinch.

- Remember the outstanding qualities of the Buddha and allow his example to inspire you.

- If sleepiness or dullness occurs frequently, change the time of your meditation session. Some people are most alert in the early morning; others meditate best before bed. Experiment with various times and find one that works best for you.

- Consider what other helpful lifestyle changes you might make, such as not eating a meal before you meditate.

- If none of these techniques work, practice loving-friendliness for yourself and nap for a few minutes.

Restlessness and Worry

This hindrance is the opposite of sloth and torpor. Instead of shutting down and going to sleep, the mind becomes unsettled and hyperactive. It is like water rippled by the wind. We worry about the things that we have not done or have not done properly. We worry about security. We worry that something may go wrong at home, or with our job, or with the family, or with our health, or with the economy. We worry about events in the city, in the country, or on the other side of the world. When this mind gets going, we can always find one thing or another to worry about!

Physical restlessness can also be a problem. We are filled with nervous anxiety and find it impossible to sit still. We pace the floor, pick up the phone and put it down, open the refrigerator even though we're not hungry. We don't know why we are so restless; perhaps there is no reason. Of course, in this state, accomplishing any practical task, let alone sitting down to meditate, is out of the question.

As with the other hindrances, the first step is simply becoming aware that we are restless or worried. We acknowledge that these states make it impossible to concentrate and take action to overcome them. The best remedy is meditation on the breath. As we have noted, when we focus on the breath, our breathing naturally becomes calm. When the breath becomes calm, the mind and body also become calm.

We use the counting technique we have talked about. Breathe in and out. Then count "one." Breathe in and out. Then count "two." Breathe in and out. Then count "three." Go on, counting up to ten. Then do the same, counting down from ten to one. Repeat this cycle, this time counting from one to nine and back down. The third time, count up to eight and back to one. Continue until mind and body settle down.

To keep restlessness and worry from returning, cultivate a feeling of confidence in the Buddha and in his teachings, the path so many people just like us have followed to overcome hindrances and free themselves from suffering.

Doubt

Having doubts is natural. Intelligent doubt—using our own experience and best judgment to make sure that we are on the right course—is actually helpful to progress on the spiritual path. But when doubts take over the mind and prevent us from practicing mindfulness, they are a hindrance. For instance, sometimes we sit down to meditate and immediately start to wonder why we are doing this. We are not sure that the method we are following will work or whether it's the right method for us. We wonder whether we have understood the instructions of our meditation teacher or even if we're the right kind of person for meditation. Once doubt gets going, it gets bigger and bigger. We wonder whether there is any such thing as enlightenment or whether the whole system of meditation makes any sense.

Again, first notice that doubt has arisen. Simply watch until doubt fades away. If it does not, we take stronger measures. Reflect mindfully on the qualities of the Buddha and his Dhamma teachings. Remember other people who have followed these teachings and become inspiring role models. Remember past successes, such as peaceful and focused meditation sessions, times when hindrances such as sleepiness or restlessness were overcome, or other ways we have changed for the better as a result of our practice. Have a talk with doubt. Be gentle but firm. Say, for instance, "Life is short. I cannot allow doubts to keep me from making progress toward my spiritual goals."

When doubt disappears, notice that it is gone. Stay mindful to keep doubt from coming back.

What We Gain

When we overcome the hindrances, even temporarily, it's a great victory. We have cleared the ground, and good qualities—such as faith, effort, mindfulness, concentration, and wisdom—can begin to grow. In a sutta, the Buddha described how good this victory feels:

> Suppose a man with wealth and possessions were traveling along a deserted road where food was scarce and dangers were many. After some time he crossed over the desert and

arrived at a village that is safe and free from danger. He would reflect on this, and as a result, he would become glad and experience joy.

In the same way, when a bhikkhu sees that these five hindrances . . . have been abandoned within himself, he regards that as freedom from debt, as good health, as release from prison, as freedom from slavery, as a place of safety. . . . Gladness arises. When he is gladdened, rapture arises. When his mind is filled with rapture, his body becomes tranquil. Tranquil in body, he experiences happiness. Being happy, his mind becomes concentrated.

(tr. Bhikkhu Bodhi)

11. *Clinging and the Fetters*

Once Venerable Sariputta and Venerable Mahakotthita were living in the Deer Park near Varanasi. In the late afternoon, Mahakotthita left his seclusion and went to Sariputta. After exchanging courteous greetings, Mahakotthita said, "Now tell me, friend Sariputta, is the eye the fetter of visible objects, or are visible objects the fetter of the eye? Similarly, is this so for the ear and sounds, the nose and smells, the tongue and tastes, the body and tangible objects, and the mind and mental objects?"

"Friend Kotthita," Sariputta replied, "the eye is not the fetter of visible objects, nor are visible objects the fetter of the eye. Rather, the desire and craving that arise in dependence on both, that is the fetter."

Then Sariputta gave the following example: "Suppose, friend, a black ox and a white ox were yoked together by a single harness. If a man were to say, 'The black ox is the fetter of the white ox, and the white ox is the fetter of the black ox,' would he be speaking rightly?

"No, friend," Sariputta continued. "The black ox is not the fetter of the white ox, nor is the white ox the fetter of the black ox. Rather the single harness by which the two are yoked together, that is the fetter.

"So, too, friend, the eye is not the fetter of visible objects . . . nor are mental objects the fetter of the mind. Rather, the desire and craving that arises in dependence on both, that is the fetter. . . .

337

"By this line of reasoning, friend," Sariputta concluded, "it may be understood why the Blessed One proclaimed this holy life for the complete destruction of suffering."

"How so?" asked Mahakotthita.

"In this manner," Sariputta replied. "There is an eye in the Blessed One. The Blessed One sees forms with the eye. Yet there is no desire and craving. Thus it is, also, for the ear, nose, tongue, body, and mind. Because the Blessed One is well liberated in mind, there is the complete destruction of suffering."

(tr. Bhikkhu Bodhi)

. . . .

*A*s we discussed, hindrances are like weeds in a garden. To grow healthy plants, first we must clear away these obvious obstructions. The roots of the hindrances are the fetters. As anyone who has cultivated a garden knows, the root system of a weed is often much larger than the part of the plant aboveground. These roots, underlying tendencies in the mind, arise directly from the contact of our senses with sensory objects and consciousness.

As we noted, there are two types of contact, external and internal. An argument with a friend is an example of external contact. As soon as it begins, we think, "*I* am angry. You have said such and such to *me*. You have done this or that with something that is *mine*." Let's call this underlying tendency "I, Me, Mine." It has confused our mind for many lifetimes. "I, Me, Mine" can also arise from internal contact with mental objects, such as the memory of some unkind thing this friend did in the past or the fantasy of what she might do in the future.

Sometimes it feels as if this "I, Me, Mine" exists within the five aggregates of body, feeling, perception, thought, and consciousness. Other times, "I, Me, Mine" seems to be the container of the five aggregates. Or we may think that "I, Me, and Mine" and the aggregates are identical. This fetter—belief in a permanent self—traps us in the cycle of death and rebirth. It causes us to suffer tremendously. Only when this fetter and nine others are uprooted by the special kind of insight known in the Dhamma as "wisdom" can we know without doubt or hesitation that the five aggregates are impermanent, unsatisfactory, and selfless. As Sariputta explained to Mahakotthita, well liberated in mind by wisdom, we attain the complete destruction of suffering.

THE FIVE AGGREGATES OF CLINGING

In our ordinary state, the five aggregates are all we know. Eat a meal, take a shower, talk to somebody, listen to something, read a book, and the five aggregates are activated. When we remember the past or imagine the future, we are thinking of the five aggregates. In the present, we sit, stand, walk, talk, eat, drink, and sleep only with the five aggregates.

So which aggregate arises first? It's hard to say because the aggregates are so interlinked. We drink a glass of orange juice. It has citrus acid, citrus oil, vitamin C, sour and sweet taste, orange color, and water. Which of these ingredients do we drink first? The answer is obvious: all of them simultaneously.

However, when we observe our actions carefully, we notice that the intention to do something actually arises first. Intention belongs to the aggregate of thought. But no aggregate works alone. The moment we reach out a hand to pick up the glass, all five aggregates are activated: neurons in brain cells, muscles and tendons, feelings, perceptions, mental energy, contact with some object, and consciousness. If we restrain the hand from picking up the glass, the aggregates linked to the intention to drink the juice stop as well.

As the word "aggregate" reminds us, each of the five aggregates is made up of many parts. Form has many millions of physical particles composed of subatomic particles. Feeling is a collection of 108 kinds of feelings. Feelings arise from contact through the eye, ear, nose, tongue, body, and mind. A feeling can be pleasant, unpleasant, or neutral. It can arise dependent on past experience of contact, present experience of contact, or imagination of future contact. It can be physical or mental. It can be gross or subtle. In the same way, perception, thought, and consciousness arise from various types of contact and have countless minute subdivisions.

So why is this important? Ordinarily, we forget that the aggregates are composed of parts and that these parts are always changing. Moreover, we habitually confuse the aggregates with the fetter we are calling "I, Me, Mine." Since the body is *mine*, we cling to it. We do the same with feelings, perceptions, thoughts, and consciousness. Then they are the "aggregates of clinging." When the aggregates change, as they inevitably do, we suffer. Then they are also the "aggregates of suffering."

The aggregates themselves are neutral. They become aggregates of clinging only when *I* perceive them with *my* senses and make them *my* objects. The difference is our mental state. If we don't cling, the Buddha tells us again and again, we don't suffer. Then they are just the five aggregates—coming into being, existing, and passing away. In a way, we can say that all of the Buddha's teachings are for the purpose of explaining the five aggregates and how to be liberated from them!

FETTERS

The source of our confusion is the fetters, deep-rooted habits in the unenlightened mind. Fetters are triggered by contact between the six senses and six sense objects: the eye and visible objects, the ear and sounds, the nose and smells, the tongue and tastes, the body and tangible objects, and the mind and mental objects. As we work with the fetters, we need to keep the example of the white ox and black ox in mind. The fetter is not the eye, nor is it the visible forms that the eye perceives. Rather, fetters arise as a result of contact between the two and consciousness.

When the senses make contact with external objects—a woman walking down the street, a cup of tea, a yellow flower—or internal objects—a memory, thought, idea, or fantasy—pleasant, unpleasant, or neutral feelings arise in the mind, as do thoughts, such as names, ideas, memories, and imagination, and many other conceptions. Because of desire and ignorance, which are also fetters, powerful negative habits lying dormant in the mind come to the forefront of consciousness. A sutta explains the process this way:

> Dependent on the eye and forms, eye-consciousness arises. The meeting of the three is contact. With contact as condition, there is feeling. What one feels, that one perceives. What one perceives, one thinks about. What one thinks about, on that, one mentally proliferates. With what one has mentally proliferated about as the source, perceptions and notions born of mental proliferation beset a man with respect to past, future, and present forms cognizable through the eye.
>
> (tr. Bhikkhu Nanamoli and Bhikkhu Bodhi)

This sequence hints at the origin of the whole parade of suffering that makes up a human life. Depending on feeling, craving arises—either to hold on to pleasant feelings or to get away from unpleasant ones. Depending on craving, clinging arises. Depending on clinging, becoming arises. Dependent on becoming, birth arises. And following birth arise growth, decay, death, sorrow, lamentation, pain, grief, and despair!

The good news is that the fetters are not always present. There are many moments in daily life when no fetter has been triggered. When the fetters are absent, we are glad about it. When a fetter arises, we are mindful of it and take steps to overcome it. When it has been overcome, we use mindfulness to protect the mind against fetters that might arise in the future.

Here are the ten fetters. Some of these harmful mental tendencies also arise as hindrances, though there are subtle differences that I will point out as we go along. In general, fetters are embedded more deeply in the mind and are less obvious than hindrances. As a result, it takes more effort and deeper levels of mindfulness and concentration to root them out.

Belief in a permanent self. Earlier, we called this fetter "I, Me, Mine." It commonly appears as the belief that we have a permanent self or soul that was born into this life from a previous one and that will go on to whatever life comes next. It also shows up as the feeling that the person who said or did something yesterday, or last year, or in first grade, is the same person who is reading this book in the present. Mindfulness weakens this fetter. When we experience how often, even within a few minutes, our breath, body, posture, feelings, thoughts, and perceptions change, we begin to see that there is no such thing as a permanent *I*, only a collection of aggregates that are always changing.

Skeptical doubt. As a hindrance, doubt focuses on our practice of mindfulness. We doubt that we're doing it correctly or that it will lead to good results. As a fetter, doubt always refers to the self. We doubt whether the Buddha is correct that there is no such thing as a permanent self or soul. We doubt the principle of kamma. We wonder where the self came from, how it exists in the present, and what will happen to it after death. Healthy doubt is fine because it prompts us to use our intelligence and experience to ponder important questions. But when doubt paralyzes and confuses us, it is harmful and should be abandoned.

Clinging to rituals. In the time of the Buddha, some ascetics stood on one foot until they fell down. Others went naked or rolled in the dust. They did these things because they believed that ritual observances would somehow lead to liberation. Clinging to such beliefs is a fetter. If rituals such as offering incense and flowers to a Buddha image become our main or only practice, and if everybody does that, eventually the Buddha's mindfulness teachings will disappear, and only rituals will remain.

Sensory craving. As a hindrance, desire for sensory pleasure can be suppressed temporarily through deep concentration meditation. But when our meditation ends, desire comes back. That happens because attachment to sensory pleasure is also a fetter that remains latent in the mind. As a fetter, sensory craving traps us in the cycle of suffering lives. One definition of the word "dhamma" is "whatever our minds can remember, imagine, think, create, or produce by way of mental processes." If these phenomena happen to be pleasant, we like them and wish to repeat them, now and in the future. We cherish the pleasant feelings that arise from them so strongly that we even crave rebirth so that we can enjoy them again!

Hatred. The opposite of sensory pleasure is hatred. If we cannot enjoy some pleasure, or if something goes against our wishes, hatred arises in us. For this reason wise people realize that love and hate are two sides of the same coin. Like sensory craving, hatred or ill will can arise as a hindrance during concentration meditation. When we pay attention and reflect properly, it fades away temporarily. However, like desire, the root of hate remains in the mind as a fetter that comes back again and again.

Craving for fine material existence. Craving for fine material existence arises primarily during deep concentration meditation. Because we experience profound peace, we may wish to dwell in that state even after death. Mistakenly, we believe that being reborn in a realm without feeling, perception, thoughts, and consciousness guarantees us permanent happiness. However, even beings born in fine material existence are not exempt from the suffering of death.

Craving for immaterial existence. Similarly, we may mistakenly believe that we can achieve permanent happiness in a realm in which only mind exists. Unfortunately, even subtle immaterial existence comes to an end after many thousands of eons.

Conceit. This fetter arises as the subtle feeling, "This I am." We take pride in our achievements. We are proud of our health, youthful appearance, long life, wealth, family, friends, country, prestige, beauty, power, skill, or strength. Sometimes people are even proud of their spiritual attainments. So long as we have proud thoughts, even very subtle ones, we can never attain full enlightenment.

Restlessness. As a hindrance, restlessness arises because of unfinished business or because of things that we have not done or not done properly. We can overcome it temporarily through deep concentration. As a fetter, restlessness arises in a very subtle way when we are close to attaining enlightenment. We are so tired of everything; we wish to leave the cycle of existence behind. We are restless because we wish to reach enlightenment as quickly as possible.

Ignorance. Ignorance is not knowing the Buddha's teachings, especially the four noble truths. In essence, not recognizing suffering, its cause, its end, and the path leading to that end.

THE TEN PERCEPTIONS

Cutting through the confusion caused by the fetters takes hard work. In the suttas, the Buddha calls the process "uprooting all conceiving." Through mindfulness and meditation, we train ourselves to regard sense perceptions and the feelings and thoughts that arise from them with a certain detachment.

Detachment from our ordinary way of perceiving comes in stages. We cannot expect to get there all at once. Impermanence is the key. Working with our own experience, we cultivate the awareness that everything is always changing—the six senses, the six objects of the six senses, contact, consciousness, and the feelings and thoughts that arise as a result. Using mindfulness, we replace our ordinary confused way of looking at the world with ten very special perceptions.

KEY POINTS FOR MINDFULNESS OF THE TEN PERCEPTIONS

- *Perception of impermanence.* You become mindful of impermanence by experiencing it. You ask yourself, "How long have I been reading this book? What changes do I perceive in that time? Are my eyes tired? Is my body uncomfortable? Have I changed my posture? Am I hungry or thirsty? Is my concentration the same as before? Have the ideas in the book changed my mind?" All these and many more are perceptions of impermanence. You do not learn about impermanence from books or teachers or even from the Buddha. You simply pay attention to the changes in your own body and mind.

- *Perception of the absence of self.* Perceiving the impermanence of your own aggregates convinces you that nothing within you endures. This perception is not mere imagination. It is your genuine experience. It helps you accept yourself as you are—always changing as a result of causes and conditions. You remember, "What I felt this morning is gone now. What I feel now will not be there tomorrow. Nothing in life gives me permanent self-identity." Perceiving this truth gives you emotional stability.

- *Perception of impurities.* When you meditate on the parts of the body, some parts are quite repulsive, for instance bile, phlegm, and pus. You meditate on these impure parts not to make you hate your body or any other body. Rather, you wish to perceive the body realistically. Your aim is clear comprehension and the balanced perception of equanimity. So you meditate on the body until you perceive its parts clearly. Then you apply the same clarity to your perception of feelings, thoughts, perceptions, and consciousness.

- *Perception of danger.* Like all human beings, you enjoy pleasure, and pleasure leads to dangerous situations. Divorce, quarrels, greed, jealousy, fear, anxiety, worry, nervous breakdowns—anything can happen because of your attachment to pleasure. Abstaining from pleasure does not free you from danger, but restraining the senses can lessen the danger somewhat. The perception of danger does not mean that you are afraid to get out of bed in the morning. It simply means that you are mind-ful. When something happens, you are not devastated. You carry on your daily business with awareness.

- *Perception of abandoning.* Abandoning is giving up and get-ting rid of anything unwholesome or unskillful. You think, "I refuse to tolerate the thought of sense desire. I cannot endure the feeling of hatred. I abandon anything that harms me or someone else." The perception of abandoning requires effort. It is not enough simply to perceive what is happening. You must be proactive and nip every wrong feeling or thought in the bud, before it has the chance to bear fruit.

- *Perception of dispassion.* Attachment to impermanent things causes suffering. The opposite of attachment is dispassion. Mindful that everything that arises as a result of causes and conditions is impermanent, unsatisfactory, and selfless, you become dispassionate toward everything. You abandon all conceptions. The perception of dispassion arises in a state of calm bliss. Being dispassionate, you gain insight into reality. Insight liberates you from suffering.

- *Perception of cessation.* Cessation means "ending." When hin-drances such as desire, hatred, and ignorance end as a result of deep concentration meditation, you are free from suffering temporarily. Meditating in this state, you understand: "This is calm; this is excellent. I have given up craving for any kind of rebirth. All conceptions have been extinguished." This very thought of calming all conceptions brings peace and bliss, equal to the peace and bliss of nibbana. You perceive this state of cessation with calmness and tranquility.

- *Perception of nondelight in the whole world.* Normally you do everything possible to be delighted in the world. Nondelight sounds awful and rather crazy. But eventually, through deep meditation, you see the impurity of the aggregates, the danger of sense pleasures, and the peace and tranquility of dispassion. Free from hindrances, you become receptive, elated, confident, and ready. You realize, "All that is subject to arising is subject to cessation." Crossing over doubt, you do away with perplexity and gain the courageous perception of nondelight in the whole world.

- *Perception of impermanence in all thoughts and conceptions.* When you see that all thoughts and conceptions are impermanent, unsatisfactory, and selfless, you no longer wish to entertain them. You see that rebirth in any form, in any place, brings suffering. You are tired of it all. Your mind is focused on total liberation.

- *Perception of breathing in and breathing out.* When you breathe mindfully, you see the arising, existing, and passing away of the form of the breath, or breath-body, immediately as it happens. In the same way, as you breathe in and breathe out, you perceive that feeling, perception, thought, and consciousness are arising, existing, and passing away. When the mind is fully engaged with this "participatory observation," there is no room in the mind for clinging to the aggregates.

Through mindfulness of these perceptions, we eventually realize that the eye, the woman walking down the street, the eye-consciousness that arises as a result of contact, the feeling of desire or hatred, and any thoughts, plans, fantasies, and other conceptions that arise in the mind as a result of this perception come into being due to a combination of causes and conditions. They exist for a moment and then pass away. When we see things as they really are, craving diminishes, and we find peace. As the sutta tells us:

When one abides not inflamed by lust, unfettered, uninfatuated, contemplating danger, then the five aggregates affected by clinging are diminished for oneself in the future. One's craving . . . is abandoned. One's bodily and mental troubles are abandoned. One's bodily and mental torments are abandoned. One's bodily and mental fevers are abandoned, and one experiences bodily and mental pleasure.

(tr. Bhikkhu Nanamoli and Bhikkhu Bodhi)

12. Factors of Enlightenment

Once when the Buddha was living at Rajagaha, the Venerable Mahakassapa, who was living in Pipphali Cave, became very ill. In the evening, the Buddha left his solitude to pay a visit to the Venerable Mahakassapa.

After taking his seat, the Buddha said, "How is it with you, Kassapa? How are you bearing your illness? Are your pains decreasing?"

Mahakassapa replied, "Lord, I am not bearing my illness well. My pain is very great, and it shows no sign of decreasing."

Then the Buddha said, "Kassapa, I have taught seven factors of enlightenment. When these factors are cultivated and carefully developed, they lead to realization and perfect wisdom—in other words, to nibbana.

"What seven?" the Buddha continued. "Mindfulness, investigation into phenomena, energy, joy, tranquility, concentration, and equanimity."

Hearing these words, Kassapa rejoiced. "O Blessed One," he said, "these seven are indeed factors of enlightenment. I welcome the utterance of the Worthy One."

Then and there, Mahakassapa rose from his sickness and his ailment vanished.

*T*he seven factors of enlightenment are the qualities we need to achieve the goal of our practice. As our meditation deepens and the fetters subside, these seven positive qualities arise in us. With mindfulness as their crown jewel, the seven factors help us defeat the forces of delusion that disturb our concentration and delay our progress on the path to liberation. The suttas tell a number of stories like that of Mahakassapa in which even hearing someone speak the names of the factors provides relief from pain, disease, and adversity. Once when the Buddha himself was ill, the Venerable Mahacunda recited the names of the seven factors, and the Buddha's grievous sickness disappeared.

It is easy to memorize the list of the factors of enlightenment, and some people do. But it is not enough just to know what the factors are. We must understanding the meaning of each factor and use our mindfulness to see when it is present, how it arises, and how to develop and maintain it.

In Pali, the seven factors are known as *bojjhangas*. The word comes from *bodhi*, which means "enlightenment," and *anga*, which means "limb." The seven factors we discuss in this chapter are the limbs—the arms and legs of enlightenment. Without them, we cannot walk the path to freedom from suffering. They arise in the same order for everyone. In fact, each marks a stage in our progress along the path. We cannot skip any stage because each develops naturally out of the one before. Let's look more closely at each factor.

Mindfulness

Everything we have been discussing so far pertains to mindfulness. All progress on the path starts with this quality. As the Buddha said, "Mindfulness is the chief of all the dhammas." But in order for our mindfulness to become a factor leading to enlightenment, it has to be strong, focused, and specific. Here is how the Buddha describes this special kind of mindfulness:

> Bhikkhus, on whatever occasion a bhikkhu abides contemplating the body as a body, ardent, fully aware, and mindful, having put away covetousness and grief for the world—on that occasion unremitting mindfulness is established in him. On whatever occasion unremitting mindfulness is established in a bhikkhu—on that occasion the mindfulness enlightenment factor is aroused in him, and he develops it, and by development, it comes to fulfillment in him.
>
> (tr. Bhikkhu Nanamoli and Bhikkhu Bodhi)

What can we learn from these words? First, to become a factor of enlightenment, our mindfulness must have a clear focus, such as the body as a body. We can also focus on feelings, thoughts, or phenomena. These four, of course, are the four foundations of mindfulness we have been considering.

Next, we must be ardent and alert. That means that we meditate with effort and enthusiasm. Third, we must put aside covetousness and grief with reference to the world. In other words, we do not allow feelings and thoughts about ordinary day-to-day concerns to disturb our concentration. Actually, we should put aside greed and distress about the world all the time, not only when we are sitting on the cushion!

Finally, our mindfulness must be unremitting. In other words, we must practice mindfulness all the time, not just while we are meditating. In fact, we should practice mindfulness during all activities, whether we are talking, eating, drinking, or waiting for the bus! Because of mindfulness, even ordinary activities are wholesome and beneficial. If we remember our mindfulness only occasionally, or practice it only during meditation sessions, it will take a very long time to develop to the level necessary to liberate us from the fetters. Mindfulness becomes a factor of enlightenment only when we are fully engaged in being mindful every waking moment.

As we have been discussing, mindfulness requires a specific kind of awareness. In each instant of mindfulness, we are conscious of the changing nature of everything that happens to us. We recognize that none of it can make us permanently happy. Most important, we understand that there is no permanent self or soul who is experiencing any of this.

When mindfulness is established as our constant attitude, we discover that we have been practicing the seven factors of enlightenment all along. When we meditate on mindfulness of the body as a body, we naturally use the factors of investigation, effort, joy, tranquility, concentration, and equanimity. The same is true when we meditate on mindfulness of feelings, thoughts, and phenomena. Our task now is to make our mindfulness even more steady and strong so that mindfulness itself becomes the focus of our meditation. As we continue to meditate in this way, mindfulness becomes a factor of enlightenment and speeds our progress on the path toward liberation.

INVESTIGATION

Wise people are inquisitive. Using our deeply cultivated mindfulness, we investigate the dhammas or phenomena in our own mind and body. Turning inward in this way happens naturally when the mindfulness factor is strong and clear. The focus of our investigation is the five aggregates. Our mindfulness inquires everywhere into our form, feelings, perceptions, thoughts, and consciousness. We see the arising of the breath, postures, clear comprehension, parts of the body, four elements, 108 types of feelings, five hindrances, six senses, and ten fetters that arise depending on the senses and their objects. We see their disappearing nature. We investigate all of them with powerful mindfulness.

How do we investigate? The process is the same for us as it was in the Buddha's time: we listen to the Dhamma, remember what we have heard, and then examine the meaning of the Dhamma we have learned. If anything is unclear or doubt arises, we ask questions, we think, we discuss. We focus our mindfulness on every aspect of our life and activities, on and off the cushion.

For instance, when a thought arises, we investigate to see whether it is spiritually beneficial. We ask, "Does this thought reduce my greed and hatred or increase them? Does it minimize my confusion or add to it? Does it make me, and others, peaceful?" If we discover that the thought increases greed, hatred, and delusion, and destroys peace and happiness, we ask, "What can I do to eliminate it?" If we discover that the thought is wholesome, we ask, "What can I do to maintain it? Is my mindfulness sufficient? If not, how can I improve it?"

We use the same method to investigate the other aggregates. For instance, we inquire into our feelings by asking, "Am I attached to pleasant feelings? Do I reject unpleasant feelings? How many times have I been distracted from my mindfulness by desire for pleasant objects or hatred for unpleasant ones?"

We also investigate how well we understand essential Dhamma concepts, such as impermanence. We ask, "Does it occur to me that the body is mine? What makes me think that it is mine? Do I see that the body's parts and elements are always changing?" Perhaps we discover that our understanding of impermanence is not very clear. We suspect that this confusion may be why the thought that "the body is mine" keeps coming back. As a result, we resolve, "I will spend more time meditating on the body's impermanence."

We also examine our everyday actions and attitudes. We ask, "How many times have I gotten angry when somebody pointed out my faults? How many times have I enjoyed criticizing others? How many times have I taken pleasure in gossiping or quarreling?" If we find that our actions and attitudes are healthy, we investigate how to maintain and strengthen them. If we find that they need to be improved, we figure out what to do to change them.

As we can see from these examples, it is our job to make sure we understand the four foundations of mindfulness and apply this understanding to our meditation and our life. No one can do this hard work for us. We have to manage our own body, mind, and actions every moment of our waking life. No one can walk the path on our behalf. We use mindfulness and intelligent investigation to check whether what we are doing is holding us back or helping us move toward our spiritual goals.

The attitude we should adopt is called "come and see." Nobody has invited us to investigate the Dhamma. There is no place we have to go to engage in this investigation. And there is nothing we can see with our eyes. Rather, the truth of what we experience all the time invites our attention. This truth is called Dhamma. It invites us, saying, "If you want to be free from trouble, look at me." As the sutta tells us, "the Dhamma is directly visible, immediate, inviting one to come and see, to be personally experienced by the wise."

ENERGY

As we continue our investigation of the five aggregates, we become more and more interested in what we are doing. That interest arouses the energy to make even greater effort to stay the course. We experience enthusiasm, along with the determination never to give up. This combination is the energy factor of enlightenment.

A simple example illustrates how investigation arouses energy. When we watch with mindfulness and attention, anything we experience seems to follow a trajectory similar to the motion of a stone thrown into the air. The stone rises as strongly as the power we use to throw it. But as it moves upward, the rising energy reduces, and the speed slows down. Eventually the upward motion stops. Finally the stone reverses course and falls to the ground. Seeing this, we become interested in checking to see whether every instant of feeling, thought, perception, and consciousness follows this pattern. This interest generates the determination to be even more mindful, and the energy factor leading to enlightenment develops within us.

When mindfulness combines with the enlightenment factor of energy, we are increasingly able to use skillful effort to keep from getting caught in greed, hatred, and delusion. Skillful effort helps us distinguish between thoughts and feelings we should welcome and those we must avoid. When harmful impulses arise, we close the doors of our senses to suffocate them. Then we use effort to replace them with beneficial impulses such as generosity, loving-friendliness, and wisdom. Because our energy is aroused, we are not lenient. We do not let down our guard for even an instant. As the sutta tells us, "Realizing that this body is as fragile as a clay pot, and fortifying this mind like a well-defended city, drive out [delusion] with the sword of wisdom."

Until the final battle is won, we use energetic effort to safeguard, secure, and maintain what we have gained. But our energy is calm and focused rather than hyperintense. Skillful mindfulness, skillful investigation, and skillful effort work together like a well-trained team to purify the mind. We recognize that life is as brief as a flash of lightening, but there is still a chance to liberate ourselves from the cycle of suffering. As the Bodhisatta, the Buddha-to-be, exclaimed with profound determination, "Let my blood dry up, my flesh wither away, my body be reduced to a skeleton; I will not give up what humanly can be attained."

Joy

When the energy factor of enlightenment is strong, joy arises as a factor of deep concentration meditation. The stages of deep concentration meditation, called the *jhanas*, take us "beyond" the ordinary mindfulness that we have been talking about into a series of deeply tranquil, harmonious, and powerful states. As mentioned earlier, I describe the jhana states in detail in *Beyond Mindfulness in Plain English*.

As we progress through the successive stages of jhana, the five hindrances are put to sleep and the ten fetters are neutralized, making our concentration even stronger. When the hindrance of ill will is overcome, our meditation becomes joyful. This emotion relaxes the body and mind, generating a feeling of serenity and peace.

As our concentration deepens further, we experience five increasingly intense feelings of joy: minor joy, momentary joy, showering joy, uplifting joy, and all-pervading joy. Minor joy makes our body hair stand on end. Momentary joy is like lightning flashing moment after moment. Showering joy descends on the body and then disappears, like waves breaking on the seashore. Uplifting joy is able to lift the physical body—actually, to move it. A sutta tells the story of a young girl who aroused uplifting joy while contemplating the thought of a shrine. Carried by uplifting joy, the girl traveled to the shrine through the air, arriving before her parents who went there on foot! All-pervading joy suffuses every part of the body.

It's important to keep in mind that the joy we experience in the initial stages of jhana is not the same as the pleasurable feelings of everyday life. And even within the jhana states, the joy that is one of the seven factors of enlightenment arises only as a result of the development of three previous factors—mindfulness, investigation, and energy. Mindfulness combined with investigation shines light into dark areas of the mind. Energy drives our tireless effort to see reality as it is, removing additional obstacles to the attainment of enlightenment.

As obstacles subside, the special kind of joy that is a factor of enlightenment arises in the mind. This joy is more durable than the joy that we experience in the initial stages of jhana. Because it comes from understanding, enlightenment joy never becomes weak or fades. When we reach this state, we remain joyful all the time!

TRANQUILITY

When enlightenment joy is developed and perfected, the factor of tranquility arises. Tranquility is a mental state in which the mind and body are calm, relaxed, and peaceful. There is no part of us that is not steady, still, and tranquil. Desire, grief, and delusion have disappeared. We feel satisfied, safe, and secure. We do not feel like moving the body. Nor do we feel thirsty, hungry, tired, bored, or lazy. Everything is serene and perfect. Although we have not yet achieved the final goal of our practice, for the moment, we enjoy profound peace and happiness.

CONCENTRATION

In this state of joy and tranquility, concentration becomes noticeably stronger and more focused. In earlier stages of mindfulness meditation, our concentration is unsteady. Moments of clear focus alternate with moments in which we are aware of our internal dialogue and of sounds, smells, and other sense impressions. Increasingly, these distractions fade to the background, and we are able to concentrate exclusively on the breath or other object for longer and longer periods. This improved ability to focus is called "access concentration." It marks the boundary between ordinary meditation and the jhana states of deep concentration.

As we progress through the stages of jhana, concentration becomes a factor of enlightenment. Using concentration as a powerful tool, we focus the mind like a laser beam on the five aggregates. Our concentration penetrates to the three universal characteristics of all conditioned things: the reality of constant change, the unsatisfactory nature of everything that exists, and the complete absence of a permanent self or soul. These characteristics are no longer a theory. We recognize them as essential truths. In jhana, mindfulness and concentration work together to dissolve all barriers to achieving realization.

Equanimity

Equanimity is like the center point on an old-fashioned balance scale. On one side of the scale, we place a heap of rice. On the other side, we place a metal weight. We adjust the quantity of rice until the pointer on the scale is exactly perpendicular. Then we know that we have the correct measurement. This balancing point is equanimity. In the states of jhana, we use equanimity like a balance scale to fine-tune our cultivation of the other enlightenment factors. If we find that the mind is sluggish, we intensify our mindfulness and investigation in order to rouse our energy and restore balance. If the mind is overexcited, we focus on increasing our joy, tranquility, and concentration so that we become more calm.

The equanimity that we experience in the jhana states differs from the type we use in mindfulness meditation to balance harmful and beneficial feelings. Equanimity based on sensual objects—forms, sounds, smells, tastes, and touches—is called "equanimity based on diversity." In the jhana states, the equanimity that arises as a factor of enlightenment is called "equanimity based on unity" because it focuses on a single internal object.

At this late stage of the path, all of the components of the body and mind—the five aggregates in the past, present, and future—are exactly the same. There is no such thing as good, bad, or indifferent. It is all simply reality, impermanent, unsatisfactory, and selfless. In this state of perfect balance, the sutta tells us, "clinging to the material things of the world ceases utterly without remainder."

KEY POINTS FOR DEVELOPING CONCENTRATION

The concentration that arises in the jhana states as a factor of enlightenment develops out of the concentration you begin to cultivate the very first time you sit down to meditate. Concentration is like a muscle that strengthens as you exercise it. Here are some ways to build concentration to support every step in your practice of mindfulness:

- First make sure that your concentration is wholesome and free of hindrances, such as greed, hatred, and delusion. For instance, concentration motivated by greed for advanced states so that you can travel through the air is not wholesome.

- Use skillful effort to put aside feelings and thoughts about ordinary day-to-day concerns. Remind yourself that life is as brief as a flash of lightening. Resolve to use this session of meditation to liberate yourself from the cycle of suffering.

- Focus your mind on your chosen object of meditation, such as the breath, postures, parts of the body, four elements, three types of feelings, five hindrances, or ten fetters.

- Keep your mind in the present moment. Use unremitting effort to maintain focus on your chosen object. If you find that your mind has wandered from your object, gently but firmly bring it back.

- Be ardent and alert. If you find that your mind is sluggish or sleepy, use effort to arouse enthusiasm. If you find that your mind is over-excited or jumpy, focus on your breathing until it calms down.

- Be especially alert for any of the five hindrances—desire, hatred, worry, laziness, and doubt. If any hindrance is present, cultivate its opposite. For instance, overcome greed with thoughts of generosity and hatred with thoughts of loving-friendliness. Once the hindrance is gone, refocus the mind on your chosen object.

- Your goal is to use concentration as a powerful tool to penetrate to the three universal characteristics of every experience: constant change, the unsatisfactory nature of all conditioned things, and the absence of a permanent self or soul that is aware of any of this.

- As your concentration deepens, the mind gradually loses interest in other things and is able to focus on the object of meditation for longer and longer periods.

- At this point, you should not investigate the details of your experience. Simply focus mindfully on your chosen object.

- Each time you practice wholesome concentration, it is easier to maintain your focus. No matter how briefly you were able to concentrate, you should feel happy about what you have accomplished. Working together as a team, concentration and mindfulness purify the mind and help keep the hindrances suppressed.

- Concentration helps you gain firsthand experience of the truth of the Buddha's message. This motivates you to develop more profound states of concentration so that you can attain deeper insights.

13. Four Truths and Eight Steps

After he attained enlightenment, the Buddha reflected on the profound Dhamma truths he had realized. He saw that most beings were so immersed in ignorance that even if he revealed these truths, people might not understand. So he resolved to maintain silence.

But then he thought to himself, "Well, there are some beings with a little dust in their eyes. They are like lotuses in a pond. Some are tiny buds hidden deep in the muddy water. Others are halfway to the surface. Others have emerged from the water, though they are still not ready to bloom. But there are a few that are ready to flower. For their benefit, let me teach the Dhamma."

In his first teaching after attaining enlightenment, delivered at the Deer Park near Varanasi, the Buddha presented what has come to be known as the four noble truths. In his forty-five years of teaching, the Buddha explained these four ideas many times. Mindfulness of them and of the eight steps of the Buddha's path is the key to our own attainment of inner peace and liberation.

So what are these truths? In brief, the first is *suffering*, the dissatisfaction or unhappiness we inevitably feel in our lives. The second is the origin or *cause* of this suffering, our own undisciplined, grasping mind. The third is *cessation*, the truth that by eliminating desire and craving, it is possible to end our suffering. The fourth is the *path*, the eight mindful steps we must take to reach this goal.

MINDFULNESS OF THE FOUR NOBLE TRUTHS

Many people find it easier to think about other people's problems than about their own. "Look at the state of the world," they say. "It is full of diseases, starvation, joblessness, divorce, war, disasters, and other terrible things." Problems like earthquakes and epidemics seem so real and immediate, it is easy to feel compassion for the victims. Of course, it wonderful to feel moved by the suffering of others and to do what we can to help. But sometimes our concern is a way to forget or ignore the suffering we experience ourselves every day.

The message of the Buddha's *first noble truth* is that every being experiences suffering. Not all suffering is catastrophic. Most is quite ordinary. The *Four Foundations of Mindfulness Sutta* lists many examples. We suffer because we experience aging, illness, and death. We suffer physically and emotionally because of misfortunes of all kinds. We regularly experience sadness and distress. In essence, we suffer whenever we encounter anything or anyone that is unpleasant or harmful and whenever we are separated from anything or anyone that is pleasant or comforting.

With a moment's reflection, we can all list many personal examples. Whether we call it stress, anxiety, depression, chronic illness, fear, or nervousness, the Buddha's first truth reminds us that in our unenlightened state, suffering is unavoidable.

Mindfulness helps us to recognize that underlying all of these kinds of suffering is desire or clinging. All five aggregates fall sick, grow old, and die every moment. Because we cling to the body, when it ages or becomes ill, we suffer physical pain and emotional distress. Because we wish to hold on to pleasant feelings and to avoid painful ones, life's inevitable ups and downs cause us to feel depressed and unhappy. Every perception of beauty and even the most brilliant or delightful thought arises for an instant and then passes away. If we cling to any aggregate, it becomes an aggregate of clinging—and the cause of suffering. The truth is, it's up to us. When we do not cling, we do not suffer. Mindfulness of this recognition is the *second noble truth*.

However, suffering can end, as the Buddha promised us in his *third noble truth*. As the Buddha has explained, happiness is the peace we experience when our mind is free of negative states— greed, hatred, delusion, birth, growth, decay, death, sorrow, lamentation, pain, grief, and despair. When we give up our thirst for the pleasures of the senses, we stop suffering in its tracks. The eye and sight, the ear and sounds, the nose and smells, the tongue and tastes, the body and touches, and the mind and mental phenomena of all kinds set in motion the train of events that lead to craving and other negative states. But when our mindfulness helps us to recognize that every experience, however delightful or horrible, lasts for only an instant, we short-circuit this process. Suffering ceases, and we remain at peace, knowing reality as it is—impermanent, unsatisfactory, and selfless.

MINDFULNESS OF THE EIGHTFOLD PATH

The *fourth noble truth* is the Buddha's eight-step path. In the *Four Foundations of Mindfulness Sutta*, the four noble truths are mentioned at the end of the seven factors of enlightenment. This placement makes excellent sense. When we experience the last of the seven factors, the balanced mind of equanimity, we can see our own suffering clearly. We stop getting caught up in the story line. We also see how we cause our suffering and understand that our suffering can end. These realizations are the foundation of our practice of the eight steps of the Buddha's path. The eight steps are easy enough to list, but each is a profound and comprehensive subject that requires an understanding of many related aspects of the Buddha's teachings. I discuss each step in detail in my book *Eight Mindful Steps to Happiness*. In brief, here is the list:

Skillful understanding: We see that every action we take is a cause leading to an effect. We accept that it is up to us to create the causes for the good life we wish to have now and in the future.

Skillful thinking: We cultivate positive thoughts, such as generosity or letting go, loving-friendliness, and compassion.

Skillful speech: We tell the truth and avoid harsh or malicious talk and idle gossip.

Skillful action: We lead moral lives, abstaining from killing, stealing, sexual misconduct, and intoxication.

Skillful livelihood: We choose an ethical profession and conduct ourselves at work with honesty and integrity.

Skillful effort: We are unrelenting in preventing and overcoming negative states of mind and cultivating and maintaining positive states.

Skillful mindfulness: We practice mindfulness meditation daily and cultivate mindfulness as our approach to everyday living.

Skillful concentration: We train our minds in single-pointed focus so that we can attain the jhana states of deep concentration.

Only through diligent practice of these eight steps can we attain the states leading to enlightenment.

THE FRUITS OF THE PATH

As the *Four Foundations of Mindfulness Sutta* tells us, "If anyone should properly develop these four foundations for seven years . . . or even for seven days, one of two fruits could be expected for that person: either final knowledge here and now or, if there is a trace of clinging left, the state of nonreturning." The word "properly" tells us that practicing the Buddha's path requires effort. It is certainly easier to continue our comfortable bad habits. But mindfulness of our own experiences teaches us that as we reduce greed, hatred, and other negative states, we also reduce our dissatisfaction and unhappiness. Mindfulness motivates us to work harder and to strive for the ultimate goal of ending our suffering once and for all.

As our ability to engage in concentration meditation strengthens, we begin to attain the fruits of the path. First, we harmonize the four bases of accomplishment—desire, effort, mind, and investigation. In essence, our desire to end our suffering and the energetic effort we devote to our meditation must be in perfect balance. Our ability to concentrate so that we can investigate phenomena must be neither too tense nor too slack. When these factors are in perfect balance, the mind becomes increasingly open, clear, and luminous, and we develop *iddhipada*, spiritual powers. These help us to destroy the fetters as we progress to higher and higher states.

The path to enlightenment has four concluding stages: stream-enterer, once-returner, nonreturner, and arahant. As our practice of the noble eightfold path becomes more and more profound, we progress through these levels of accomplishment.

Stream-enterer. The first milestone we reach is called stream entry.

Once the Buddha said to Venerable Sariputta, "Sariputta, this is said: 'The stream, the stream.' What now, Sariputta, is the stream?"

"This noble eightfold path, venerable sir, is the stream," Sariputta replied.

"Good, good, Sariputta," the Buddha said. "Now, Sariputta, this is said: 'A stream-enterer, a stream-enterer.' What now, Sariputta, is a stream-enterer?"

"One who possesses this noble eightfold path, venerable sir, is called a stream-enterer."

This is an extremely important passage. The noble eightfold path is the "stream we enter" that carries us to enlightenment. When we have meditated for a considerable length of time, our mind gradually becomes clear. Doubts fade away. We see the connection between greed and suffering very clearly. In fact, the two seem almost identical.

Now we practice the noble eightfold path with confirmed confidence. Good morality becomes second nature. We abstain from any destruction of life, from taking what is not given, and from engaging in sexual misconduct. We abandon false speech, divisive speech, harsh speech, and idle gossip. We cultivate positive thoughts and are unrelenting in overcoming negative states of mind and cultivating positive states.

As a result of these good actions of body, speech, and mind, the first three fetters are destroyed—belief in a permanent self, skeptical doubt, and clinging to rituals. We understand that all five aggregates are the same nature, arising and passing away. We have no wish to experience the sorrow of birth, aging, and death ever again. Our only goal is liberation from samsara and freedom from its cycle of suffering. We can honestly declare to ourselves, "I am finished with hell, finished with the animal realm, finished with the domain of ghosts, finished with the plane of misery, the bad destinations, the nether world. I am a stream-enterer, no longer bound to the nether world, fixed in destiny, with enlightenment as my destination" (tr. Bhikkhu Bodhi).

Once-returner. Next, mindfulness helps us to be more and more aware of each instant of change in the five aggregates. As a result, the most obvious or gross part of the next two fetters, craving for sensory experience and hatred, are destroyed. We become a "once-returner." This term means that we will take rebirth in the human realm at most one more time before we achieve enlightenment.

Nonreturner. At the third stage, our deep concentration meditation destroys the remaining subtle aspects of craving and hatred. We become a "nonreturner." We will never be reborn in the human realm again. Instead, we will take rebirth in a Pure Abode, which some traditions call a Pure Land. Here we continue our practice toward complete liberation.

Arahant. At the final stage of the path, the five remaining fetters are destroyed by our advanced concentration meditation. We no longer crave rebirth in a fine material realm or an immaterial realm. We overcome conceit and restlessness. The mind is so sharp, clear, and luminous that we can see all four noble truths operating as one unit—suffering, its cause, its end, and the path leading to its end.

Finally, our mind rejects completely the notion that self can be found anywhere in the five aggregates. The last shreds of ignorance of the four noble truths are destroyed, and we become an arahant— one who is completely liberated from suffering. We have achieved the goal of the path. We know, "Birth is finished, the holy life has been led, done is what had to be done, there is nothing further here."

As the Venerable Sariputta explained, "For the arahant, friend, there is nothing further that has to be done and no repetition of what he has already done." The suffering of this life and all future lives is ended, as Sariputta stated: "When these things are developed and cultivated, they lead to a pleasant dwelling in this very life and to mindfulness and clear comprehension."

There is only one doorway to these attainments—dedicated practice of the four foundations of mindfulness.

KEY POINTS FOR PRACTICING THE PATH

- The best way to review the main points of the *Four Foundations of Mindfulness* is to read or recite the short version of the sutta given on pages 202–4.

- Mindfulness gives you insight into the characteristics of everything that exists: impermanence, dissatisfaction, and selflessness.

- You gain this insight by using mindfulness to investigate your body, feelings, thoughts, and phenomena.

- The best way to begin mindfulness training is to meditate on the breath, as the breath is always present and easy to observe. When the mind is united with the breath, your mind is in the present moment.

- Mindfulness and clear comprehension reveal that the body's thirty-two parts are composed of four elements that are always changing. Because it is subject to growth, decay, disease, and death, the body cannot give you lasting satisfaction. Most important, the body is "not mine, not I, and not my self."

- Mindfulness of feelings helps you become aware that suffering arises from the mind's habitual reactions to three kinds of feelings—craving pleasant feelings, rejecting unpleasant feelings, and experiencing a confused sense of "self" in neutral feelings. Like everything else, feelings arise, peak, and pass away.

- Mindfulness of mind helps you become aware that your thoughts and mental states are also always changing.

- When you cultivate mindfulness of dhammas, or phenomena, you become aware of the arising and disappearing of the five hindrances, ten fetters, five aggregates, six senses and their objects, seven factors of enlightenment, four noble truths, and eights steps of the Buddha's path.

- Properly practicing mindfulness of the four foundations leads to nibbana, liberation, complete freedom from suffering. The Buddha has promised that you can achieve this goal within this very life. Proper mindfulness also alleviates suffering right now and makes this life more pleasant.

Beyond Mindfulness
in Plain English

1. The Concentration Path

How Much Faith Do You Need?

Though Buddhism is quite different from most religions, and is in some ways more akin to a kind of practical philosophy, the practices and teachings we will be exploring do come from a religious context, namely from Theravadan Buddhism. All you need to do is render the hindrances dormant. All religion depends on some kind of faith, which at heart is nothing more than the willingness to accept provisionally something without yet having proved or verified it for oneself. And this is true with this material as well. But you don't have to be a Buddhist, in any religious sense whatsoever, to gain absorption concentration. Anybody can do it.

So, how much faith do you need? Do you need to convert to Buddhism? Do you need to abandon the tradition in which you were raised or the ideals to which you have deep commitment? Do you need to cast aside anything that your intellect or understanding of the world tells you is true?

Absolutely not. You can retain your current frame of reference and accept only what you are prepared to accept, a piece at a time, and only what you in fact find helpful. Yet you do need *some* faith.

You need the same kind of faith that you need to read a good novel or conduct a scientific experiment. You need "a willing suspension of disbelief." I invite you to, as an experiment, put any automatic rejection you may have on hold long enough to see if this path works for you, to see if you yourself can verify what generations of people just like you have verified for millennia.

That temporary suspension of disbelief is all you need here—but even that is not easy. Our conditioned preconceptions are deep and often unconscious. We frequently find ourselves rejecting something without really inspecting that judgment, without even knowing that we have made a judgment. And indeed, this is one of the beauties of the concentration path that we'll be exploring together. It trains us to look at our own minds, to know when we are judging and simply reacting. Then we can decide how much of that instantaneous reaction we wish to accept. You are completely in control of that process.

There is, of course, a snag. You need to be able to suspend your disbelief deeply enough and long enough to give concentration meditation a real, honest, best-effort try, and the deep results are not instantaneous. Do not expect that you can give this a half-hearted effort and two weeks later the heavens will open and the golden sunbeam of inspiration will pour down upon your head. This will almost certainly lead to disappointment.

We are dealing with the deepest forces in the mind, and epiphany is seldom immediate.

WHY DEEP CONCENTRATION IS IMPORTANT

There is no concentration without wisdom, no wisdom without concentration. One who has both concentration and wisdom is close to peace and emancipation.

The wisdom referred to in this passage is of two varieties. First, there is ordinary wisdom, the kind that can be expressed in words, the kind we know with our ordinary minds. Then there is the wisdom of knowing things at the deepest level, a knowing beyond words and concepts. This book presents you with wisdom of the first kind so that you can seek and find the higher wisdom on your own.

To seek this deep understanding we must quest into the basic nature of the mind itself. In the following passage from the Pali scriptures, the Buddha speaks to his primary disciples and explains the nature of the mind, what makes it ill, and what we have to do to correct that.

> This mind, O monks, is luminous, but it is corrupted by adventitious defilements. The uninstructed worldling does not understand this as it really is. Therefore, for him, there is no mental development.
>
> This mind, O monks, is luminous, but it is free from adventitious defilements. The instructed noble disciple understands this as it really is. Therefore, for him, there is mental development.

In this passage, *"This mind"* is mentioned twice, once for the "uninstructed worldling" and once for the "instructed noble disciple." Yet whether we are ordinary people or advanced meditators, we all have the same kind of mind. The deep mind is constant and luminous, but its light is not light as we ordinarily understand it. The mind, by its very nature, is not dark, murky, or turbulent. In its essential character, it has light; it is bright, filled with a shining, open, nonconceptual intelligence and a deep tranquility.

But all of us have something that keeps it from shining properly. A few of us succeed in removing what is referred to above as "adventitious defilements"— obscurations not inherent to the mind's true nature—and gain "mental development." In the sutta above, "mental development" refers to the deep concentration described in this book. The Buddha says that the mind is luminous, but that uninstructed people do not know this. They do not know it, in short, because they do not practice concentration, and they do not practice concentration because they do not know that there is a pure and luminous mind to be experienced.

To achieve concentration we must remove something, and the class of things we must remove are called "defilements." A "defilement" is a corruption, an adulteration, or a contaminant. It is something that muddies the mind. But it is also like a kind of mental toxin. It makes the mind sick. It gives rise to much suffering. But fortunately, these defilements are "adventitious," added from the outside, not part of the deep mind's basic structure.

So: these "adventitious defilements" are qualities of mind we must remove. To attain the benefits of mental development, we must learn what they are and how to get rid of them. This removal operates by cultivating mindfulness and leads to seeing the "luminous" character of the mind.

Sounds interesting, right?

It is.

Sounds like something good to do, right?

It is.

But it is tricky. There are lots of pitfalls along the way and there is plenty to know. But you're holding the right book!

FOLLOWING THE BUDDHA'S EXAMPLE

After his enlightenment, the Buddha went to Banares and delivered his first discourse to a group of disciples known as the Five Ascetics. These men knew him well. Indeed, they had been practicing self-mortification with him for six long years—until the Buddha realized the shortcoming of the ascetic path and set out toward the Middle Way. As he approached the Five Ascetics, they did not pay him any special respect. They simply called him "friend," just as they had when he was one of them. They did not think he was anybody special. They did not know that he had attained enlightenment.

The Buddha told them of his attainments and that they might now learn from him; he told them outright that he had, in fact, attained enlightenment. They did not believe him. Seeing their skepticism, the Buddha asked them a question:

> "Bhikkhus, have I ever said to you before that I had attained enlightenment?" "No, sir." "So long bhikkhus, as my knowledge and vision of these four noble truths, as they really are, in their three phases and twelve aspects, was not thoroughly purified, I did not claim to have awakened to the unsurpassed perfect enlightenment."

The Buddha was forthright. He knew who he was and what had happened to him. The four noble truths are the cornerstone of all his teaching. Each is understood and practiced in three phases. That constitutes what are called the twelve aspects. The three phases are theory, practice, and realization. You must first understand something as a *theory*. Then you put it into *practice* so that you actually experience it taking place. Then you *realize*, that is to say "make real," the result. That is the process by which one verifies a theory as reality. In this usage, the word *realization* means both "understanding" and "final attainment."

The Buddha employed this three-phase method when he uncovered the four noble truths:

The first noble truth is that suffering exists. The Buddha knew that suffering was real before he saw it deeply. That is the theory. Actually experiencing the nature of suffering was the Buddha's practice. From his own meditation practice he came to know that suffering is real life and that it should be understood. The Buddha experienced suffering at all conceivable levels. And he learned how to work to overcome it. Finally, the Buddha's realization became perfected. He knew he could end his suffering—and he did it.

The second noble truth is that suffering has a specific cause. The Buddha understood the causes of suffering, exactly as they are, as a theory. His prior practice had led him to this intellectual understanding, but he had not yet realized it fully, experientially. When he did, the Buddha understood that the cause of suffering can be eliminated by eradicating its causes, by ripping it out by the roots. That was the Buddha's practice. He actually did what he said should be done. He attacked the issue at its fundamental layer by eradicating the underlying causes. When he eliminated the causes of suffering fully, the Buddha gained his freedom. That constituted his realization.

The third noble truth is that suffering actually does cease. In theory, the Buddha knew that there is an end to suffering somewhere. As he put this theory into *practice*, he understood that the end of suffering should be attained. He gained the full result of the cessation of suffering as his realization.

The fourth noble truth is that there is a path that leads to the end of suffering. First the Buddha figured out in theory that the path exists. He figured out the steps he needed to take to gain liberation. He put the theory into practice in his own life. And as a result, he was able to clarify the path to liberation as his realization.

The point here is simple. You need to really understand each point of what you are doing, actually *put each step into practice* and actually personally *see the full results* within your own mind. Nothing less will do the job—the ultimate job, the job of becoming free from suffering. Yet this kind of liberation requires full commitment, much work and much patience, and taking the process all the way to perfect realization.

The Buddha gave us the Dhamma, his teachings, so that we can practice. He himself gained the knowledge from his own practice. He did not just come up with an idea, rush out and tell it to the world when it was still just a theory. He waited until he had it all, the theory, the practice, and the full realization. The Buddha gave us a beautiful plan, just the way an architect draws a plan for a building. And, just as builders must diligently follow an architect's careful plans in order to bring the building into being, we too must follow the Buddha's plan to bring liberation into being.

The Buddha gave us a really good, detailed plan. You need to follow it exactly. Other people propose other plans—from the Buddha's time right down to the twenty-first century—but they may not work; they have not been tested by generation after generation for two thousand years.

The Buddha's plan even includes a guarantee: If you follow the instructions given in these discourses exactly, you can attain full enlightenment in as few as seven days. If you cannot get rid of all your defilements, you will attain at least the third stage of enlightenment within seven years.

It's like an extended warranty. Of course, there are a few extra clauses and requirements in the contract, a few ways you can, regrettably, void the warranty. In order to for warranty to be valid, you must:

- Have faith and place that faith in the Buddha, who is free from illness and afflictions.

- Have adequate health and be able to bear the strain of striving.

- Be honest and sincere. Show yourself as you actually are to the teacher and your companions in the holy life.

- Be energetic in abandoning unhealthy states of mind and behavior and in undertaking healthy states.

- Be unfaltering, launching your effort with firmness and persevering doggedly in cultivating wholesome states of mind.

- Be wise. Possess wisdom regarding the rising and disappearance of all phenomena that is noble and penetrative and leads to the complete destruction of suffering.

This book will give you the theory, piece by piece, for how to do all those things. The practice and the realization are up to you. The Buddha reached this perfection of realization of the four noble truths and attained enlightenment by combining concentration and mindfulness in perfect balance.

You can do the same.

THE JHANA ROAD MAP

Traveling along the concentration path takes practice. We begin right here, in the world as we know it through our physical senses and our conceptual thinking. If you envision the concentration path as a road map, you could say that we all start in pretty much the same geographical region, but each in a slightly different location. That is because we are different personalities and we have accumulated different proportions of the "defilements" that need to be removed through our efforts. We start by performing slightly different cleansing actions, putting the accent on whatever is holding us back the most. Then as we go, our paths converge. What we are doing becomes more and more similar until we are traveling pretty much the same road.

The beginning of the path lies in identifying and deactivating a class of things called *hindrances*. They are the gross aspects of our negative mental functioning and we can spot them easily. To do this we attain and move through special meditative states called the *jhanas*. I'll introduce these in more detail in the next chapter, but for our purposes here it's sufficient to note that in the higher jhanas we temporarily neutralize a class of things called the *fetters*. These are the more subtle factors in the mind that give rise to the hindrances.

Once we have temporarily removed the roadblocks, concentration becomes strong. Then we point it at certain very fruitful objects and look for the characteristics of those objects that lead to freedom.

This is not really as much of a 1-2-3 operation as it sounds. In fact we are doing many of these steps together. Success in each area permits further development in the other areas.

Way down the road, ever-strengthening concentration drops us suddenly into a new landscape. The world of the senses and thinking recedes and we experience four successive stages of joy, happiness, and ever more subtle kinds of experience. These are the *material jhana* states. They are still on the map of our ordinary world, but just barely.

After that come four more stages that have almost nothing whatever to do with the world we know right now, through a mind that has not yet experienced such special meditative states. These are the *immaterial jhanas*. They are pretty much off the map of reality as we experience it now.

After that come states called the *supramundane jhanas*. They are, in an important way, clean off the continent of the familiar.

This is the road we will cover together in coming chapters.

2. Concentration and the Jhanas

*C*oncentration is a gathering together of all the positive forces of the mind and tightly focusing them into an intense beam. Mastering concentration means learning to aim that beam and keep it directed where we want it. This kind of concentration is strong and energetic, yet gentle, and it does not wander away. Building concentration is primarily a matter of removing certain mental factors that hinder its application. We then learn to point the beam at the right things, the really fruitful things within the mind. When we study these things carefully, they cease to bind us and we become free. Concentration, along with awareness, allows the mind to look at itself, to examine its own workings, to find and dissolve the things that impede its natural flow.

How Do We Get There?

We move toward concentration slowly, primarily by weakening certain bothersome factors in the mind and then putting them "in suspension." These things to be weakened are just little things, really—things like terror and anxiety and rage and greed and shame. Just little habits of the mind that are so deeply embedded we think they are natural, that they belong there, that they are somehow *right*, somehow accurate and appropriate responses to the world.

Even further, we think they *are* us; we believe they are somehow embedded in our basic nature and we *identify* with them.

These kinds of things are the basic ways we live, the only way we know how to perceive the world. And we think we absolutely *need* them to survive in the world, that someone who did not think his way through everything would have to be foolish, that someone who was not driven by emotion would have to be a soulless robot at best, and dead at worst.

But all these obscurations and hindrances are just habits. We can learn about them and learn certain skills that put them to sleep for a while. Then, while the hindrances are sleeping, we wakefully can experience directly the shining, joyous, luminous nature of the basic mind that lies below.

When we have experienced how the mind really is, underneath all the mental junk we carry, we can begin to bring pieces of that luminous calm back into our daily lives. Those pieces allow us to carry further the work of undermining the habits we want to remove. This allows deeper concentration, which allows more bliss to seep into our lives. This in turn allows deeper understanding of the habits, which then weakens them further.

And so it goes. It is an upward spiral into peace and joy and wisdom.

But we have to start *here*, right where we are now.

What Are the Jhanas?

The heart of this book is a guide to the jhanas. The jhanas are states of mental function that can be reached through deep concentration meditation. They are beyond the operation of the ordinary, conceptual mind, the mind with which you are reading this book right now. For most of us, this conceptual functioning is all we have ever known and the only thing we can conceptualize. Right now, it's unlikely we can even imagine what it would be like to be beyond thinking, beyond sensory perception, and beyond our enslavement to emotion. This is because the level of the mind that is trying to do the imagining is made up solely of sensing and thinking and emoting. And that is all we may know. Yet the jhanas lie beyond all that. They are challenging to describe because the only words we know are pinned to these concepts, sense impressions, and emotions that have us mesmerized.

The word *jhana* derives from *jha* (from the Sanskrit *dyai*), meaning to "burn," "suppress," or "absorb." What it means in experience is difficult to express. Generally it is translated into English as "a deeply concentrated meditative state" or "absorptive concentration" or even just "absorption."

Translating *jhana* as "absorption" can be misleading, however. You can be absorbed in anything—paying your taxes, reading a novel, or plotting revenge, just to name a few such things. But that is not jhana. The word "absorption" can also connote that the mind becomes like a rock or a vegetable, without any feeling, awareness, or consciousness. When you are totally absorbed in the subject of your meditation, when you merge with or become one with the subject, you are completely unaware. That too is not jhana, at least not what Buddhism considers "right jhana." In right jhana, you may be unaware of the outside world, but you are completely aware of what is going on within.

Right jhana is a balanced state of mind where numerous wholesome mental factors work together in harmony. In unison, they make the mind calm, relaxed, serene, peaceful, smooth, soft, pliable, bright, and equanimous. In that state of mind, mindfulness, effort, concentration, and understanding are consolidated. All these factors work together as a team.

And since there is no concentration without wisdom, nor wisdom without concentration, jhana plays a very important role in meditation practice.

RIGHT CONCENTRATION AND WRONG CONCENTRATION

Right concentration is awake and aware. Mindfulness and clear comprehension are its hallmarks. The mind may be paying no attention to the exterior world, but it knows exactly what is going on within the state of jhana. It recognizes the wholesome mental factors of jhana, without processing them in words, and it knows what they are and what they mean. Mindfulness is the precursor to right concentration. Jhana comes about through restraint of the hindrances. You must have mindfulness to recognize that a hindrance is present in the mind so that you can overcome it. Mindfulness *before* jhana carries over into mindfulness *within* jhana. In addition to mindfulness, clarity, purity, faith, attention, and equanimity must be present in right concentration.

Wrong concentration is absorption concentration without mindfulness. It is dangerous, because you may become attached to the jhanic state. If you realize that what you are doing is wrong concentration, you should come out of it as quickly as possible. The habit is alluring and deepens easily. It is best not to attain wrong concentration at all.

How do you know your concentration is wrong concentration? One indication is that you lose all feeling. There is still feeling in right jhana. It is subtle, but it is present. You lose all feeling only when you have attained the highest jhana known as the attainment of "cessation of perception and feelings." Until such time you certainly have feelings and perceptions.

There are false states in which it appears that you have attained this level. If, when you sit to meditate, your body becomes relaxed and peaceful, you lose the sensation of your breath, you lose the sensations of your body, you cannot hear anything—you should realize that these are sure signs of heading toward sleepiness, not toward the bright wakefulness of jhana. In a moment you will be snoring away, figuratively if not literally too. If you don't feel anything at all, you are not in right concentration.

You can stay in such incorrect absorptions for quite a long time.

> Not only Alarakalama has faith, energy, mindfulness, concentration, and wisdom. I too have faith, energy, mindfulness, concentration, and wisdom.

The Buddha said this to Alarakalama and repeated it to Uddakaramaputta. These two men were his former teachers. They had faith, energy, mindfulness, concentration, and wisdom, but not the right kind.

What is the difference between the right kind and the wrong kind? His teachers' qualities were not based on right understanding. They had a strong faith in their own tradition. They had faith in joining their soul with the creator. They used their effort, mindfulness, concentration, and wisdom toward realizing this goal. These are goals that promote a further sense of self and therefore more clinging and more suffering. Therefore their faith, effort, mindfulness, concentration, and wisdom are considered to be of the wrong type.

Ordinarily, when the mind is not concentrated or gains wrong concentration, the notion of self arises. The Buddha's former teachers got stuck in this problem. And this was the breaking-away point for the Buddha. He had been going from place to place and from teacher to teacher in search of truth. He ended up with Alarakalama and Uddakaramaputta. Both of them taught him to meditate and gain the highest immaterial jhana. Fortunately for us all, he decided for himself that more was possible.

These two highly attained meditation teachers could not proceed beyond the highest level of immaterial jhanic concentration into complete liberation. Their concentration did not have right mindfulness or right understanding. They thought what they saw was an entity, a soul, a self, which they thought was eternal, everlasting, imperishable, immutable, and permanent. Right mindfulness would have shown them the truth of selflessness. Concentration without right mindfulness and right understanding is wrong concentration.

CONCENTRATION AND MINDFULNESS

There is an essential relationship between concentration and mindfulness practice. Mindfulness is the prerequisite and the basis of concentration. Concentration is developed and strengthened through "serenity [and] nonconfusion, and mindful reflection upon them." Stated somewhat simplistically, you develop concentration through mindful reflection within a serene and unconfused state of mind. And what are you mindful of? You are mindful of the state itself, the very fact that it is serene and unconfused. As jhana practice is developed, mindfulness gradually increases.

Mindfulness is used to develop your concentration and it is used within the concentrated states to lead to liberation. The most important results of right concentration are the four mundane jhanas, without which right concentration is not complete. Right effort and right mindfulness join together to allow right concentration to reach completion. It is this kind of right concentration that shows things as they really are.

Once you see things as they really are, you become disenchanted with the world of suffering and with suffering itself. This disillusionment with suffering thins down desire and some amount of dispassion arises. Withdrawn from passion, the mind is liberated from desire. This leads to experiencing the bliss of emancipation. Right concentration and right mindfulness always grow together. One cannot be separated from the other.

Both concentration and mindfulness must work together to see things as they really are. One without the other is not strong enough to break the shell of ignorance and penetrate the truth. You may start with concentration and gain jhana, and then use the concentration to purify insight or mindfulness to see things as they are. Or, you may start with mindfulness, then gain concentration to purify mindfulness, so that you can use this purified mindfulness to see things as they really are.

CLEAR COMPREHENSION

Clear comprehension means remaining fully awake and conscious in the midst of any activity, everything your body is doing, and everything you are perceiving. It is a turned-within monitoring of everything going on in the mind and body. Clear comprehension requires "bare attention" ("bare" in the sense of stripped down or nothing added over top) to assure that you are mindful of the right things and mindful in the right way. It is a quality-control factor that monitors what is being noticed and how the noticing is taking place.

You must direct this full, clear, bare attention especially to four things:

The purpose of concentration: You do it for liberation through seeing the *anicca* (pronounced "ah-NI-chah"; impermanence), *dukkha* (suffering), and *anatta* (no-fixed-self/selfless nature) of all we experience (we will explore these three "marks of existence" in much more detail in chapter 7). You make mindful effort to grasp the purpose of gaining concentration. You are trying to gain concentration in order to understand things as they really are. You are not doing it for pleasure or mental or psychic power.

The suitability of your concentration practice: Are you carrying out your concentration in the right way, paying attention in a mindful way without greed, hatred, and delusion? Or are you dwelling on unwholesome objects and feeding the hindrances? You make mindful effort to understand that all your preparatory works for gaining concentration should be correct to achieve your goal. Many things are necessary for the practice to succeed and you must make them all work for you.

The domain of concentration: What are you concentrating *on?* The proper domain of your concentration is the four objects given in the four foundations of mindfulness—specifically, mindfulness of the body, mindfulness of feelings, mindfulness of consciousness, and mindfulness of mental objects. You will learn more about these points in chapter 10. Your domain in gaining concentration is the particular subject of meditation that you have selected to focus your mind upon until finally the mind gains concentration.

The nondelusion of right concentration as opposed to wrong concentration: Are you actually seeing what is there—impermanence, suffering, and selflessness? Is your attention bright, alert, and penetrating the veils of illusion? Or are you seeing what appear to be solid, enduring things with the potential to make you permanently happy or sad?

In truth, the value of clear comprehension goes beyond just the jhanas; you must bring clear comprehension to everything you do. Eat mindfully with clear comprehension; drink, walk, sit, lie down, and answer the call of nature the same way. Mindfully and with clear comprehension, wear your clothes, work, drive and attend to traffic safety, talk, be silent, write, cook, wash dishes. Do it all completely awake to the doing. Try to know everything going on in the mind and body.

These activities, performed with mindfulness and clear comprehension, prepare your mind to attain jhana. When you are truly ready, you attain it without difficulty.

THE BENEFITS OF JHANA

Some teachers say that the jhanas are unnecessary, perhaps that they are rather like playthings for advanced meditators. It may be technically true that some can attain final release from craving, delusion, and suffering without jhanic meditation, but there are many benefits to achieving the jhanas.

First, there is the incredible peace and joy you experience. That feeling is wonderful in itself, and you also bring some of that back with you into your daily life. The vast calm of the jhanas begins to pervade your daily existence.

Even more important is their encouragement to the rest of your practice. The jhanas taste like liberation, a total freedom from all the mental and emotional woes that plague us. But the jhanas themselves are *not* that total freedom; they are temporary states that eventually end, and when they do then your normal world and the suffering-causing way you relate to it creeps back in. But still, they give you the absolute assurance that more is possible, that *your* mind too holds the seeds of complete freedom; through the jhanas you can be assured experientially that liberation is not just a theory, it is not something that could maybe happen to other people but never happen to *you*. In this way, attaining the jhanas gives you incredible energy and encouragement for your practice.

The jhanas teach you the true, strong concentration that is essential for vipassana, the path of insight meditation. The jhanas, especially the fourth jhana (which we will explore in detail in chapter 12), can be used to see impermanence, suffering, and selflessness. Seeing this true nature of reality is the goal of meditation and the jhanas can be used in the service of that goal.

THE POTENTIAL PITFALLS OF JHANA

It's important to know that there are, in fact, certain "dangers" associated with incorrect practice of the jhanas, and a prudent person should be fully informed of the hazards and take them seriously. Here are the two main dangers:

A practitioner of jhana can get "trapped" in jhanic ecstasy.

A practitioner of jhana can build pride around the attainment.

These must be taken seriously. The ego can pervert and co-opt *anything*—even the Buddha's path to liberation—to its own selfish purposes.

Ecstasy is the prime goal of many non-Buddhist contemplative systems. You concentrate on something—an image, a scripture, a sacred stone—and you flow into it. The barrier between self and other dissolves and you become one with your object of contemplation. The result is ecstasy. Then the meditation ends and you are back to the same old you, in your same old life, and same old struggles. That hurts. So you do it again. And again. And again and again and again.

Buddhist meditation is aimed at a goal beyond that—a piercing into the truth of your own existence that dispels the illusion and gives you total, permanent freedom. It is a bit like a railroad track. There is a well-defined track that leads to full emancipation. Incorrect jhana, jhana without mindfulness, can lure you off the track and into a dead-end cul-de-sac. The challenge comes from the fact that this cul-de-sac is in a very attractive location. You can sit there forever enjoying the view. After all, what could possibly be better than profound ecstasy? The answer, of course, is a lasting liberation that frees you from all suffering, not just for the brief period you are maintaining your ecstatic state.

The second danger is also perilous. The jhana states are rare accomplishments. When we attain them we begin to conceptualize ourselves as very special people. "Ah, look how well I am doing! I am becoming a really advanced meditator. Those other people cannot do this. I am *special*. I am Becoming Enlightened!" Some of this may, in fact, be true to a greater or lesser degree. You *are* special. And you *are* becoming an advanced meditator. You are also falling into an ego trap that will stall your progress and create discouragement for everyone around you.

You must take these cautions seriously! The ego is subtle and clever. You can fall into these traps without knowing you are doing so. You can engage in these harmful ways of being with the full conviction that you are *not* doing so!

This is where the teacher enters the picture, someone who has walked the full path her- or himself, and can shepherd the process and keep you from fooling yourself too badly. The value of a true teacher, especially in the middle and later stages of jhana practice, cannot be overstated.

Do please seek one out.

3. Getting Ready for Jhana Meditation

*T*he Pali literature mentions certain preliminaries for meditation—though in an important way they should not be considered preliminary at all. For most of us this will be our full-time
occupation for quite some time to come.

Our ability to concentrate is hindered at present because our
minds are filled with distractions. They are so common and so constant that we think this condition is normal, that it is the way we
really are. We think that it is just "the human condition" and that
nothing can be done about it. Yet, although it is the current condition of most human minds, it can be changed. A great number of
marvelous minds have done it, and they have laid out a series of
principles and steps by which we can do it too.

You cannot attain jhana without peace of mind. You cannot
have peace without a calm and settled life. You must pave the way
with decent behavior and a certain degree of noninvolvement in
the hectic and alluring things all around you. In this chapter, we'll
explore the way to live the kind of settled life that can be a foundation for jhana practice.

Morality

The first preliminary is practicing morality. This is the most steady and durable foundation for Buddhist spiritual practice. But Buddhist morality does not mean following rules blindly; there are not a series of *Thou Shalt Nots*. Even so with understanding and determination, you must follow moral and ethical principles. Determination alone does not produce jhana—although you absolutely do need determination to remove obstacles while preparing for the attainment of jhana.

You must apply a *fourfold effort* to get rid of unwholesome habitual practices that hamper your attainment of jhana: With unremitting mindful effort, you try to prevent the formation of any harmful habits that are not currently present. You make the same kind of effort to overcome the unhealthy, harmful habits you already have. You cultivate new, beneficial, wholesome habits that you don't yet have. With the same firm determination, you maintain these new positive habits and perfect them.

Gradually, you build momentum with wholesome thoughts, words, and deeds. When you are mindful and really make an effort to build this momentum, the mind turns naturally toward peace. You find yourself looking for a suitable place and time to develop jhana. You seek out the right posture, subject, and environment.

When you begin the jhana meditation practice, you avoid anything not conducive to gaining concentration. On the cushion, you avoid the hindrances, the reactions that would pull you away from your meditation subject. Off the cushion, you practice the same skills by avoiding the thoughts, words, and deeds that perpetuate the hindrances.

The simplest and most basic moral practice for laypeople is the five precepts. You have to enact two sides of each precept.

One side is to abstain from: killing; taking anything that is not freely given; engaging in any misconduct with regard to sense pleasures; speaking falsely; taking intoxicants.

The other side is to practice the seven forms of virtuous conduct: friendliness; compassion; generosity; truthfulness; appreciative joy (taking joy in others' good fortune and good qualities); maintaining a sober state of mind; equanimity.

You must apply energy to beginning your program, continuing it and never giving up. You cannot attain jhana without a sense of peace and contentment with your life as it is. Striving to make your life radically other than it actually and presently is will interfere with steady movement toward jhana. Such striving is a form of living for the imagined future; jhana grows out of living in the now. You have to find your present conditions suitable and sufficient or you will always be yearning. You must be content with your food, clothing, and lodging. You need to find contentment in all the situations that arise in your life.

Meditators find from their own experience that, when they practice meditation following moral and ethical principles, their greed, hatred, and delusion slowly diminish. As your meditation makes progress, you see the advantage of morality. Seeing this result, you do not become proud and praise yourself or disparage others. With a humble and impartial mind, you simply recognize that a clean mind—with mindfulness, friendliness, appreciative joy, and equanimity—does make progress in gaining concentration more easily than a mind that is unclean, impure, biased, unsteady, and disturbed.

CONTENTMENT

Contentment means not becoming too greedy for food, clothing, shelter, medicine, or anything else beyond all your other basic requisites.

The life of one who is content is very easy. The practice of meditation also becomes easy. This Dhamma practice, the practice of jhanas, is for one who is content, not one who is fundamentally discontent.

Practicing mindfulness with clear comprehension makes the mind fully engaged in all the activities you do. You practice mindfulness and clear comprehension while walking forward, backward, looking around, standing, sitting, wearing clothes, and any other mental and physical activities. Everything is included—every action, every thought. Then there is no room in the mind to think of acquiring any material thing or situation. The mind withdraws from the very thought of obtaining something. This is contentment. You need nothing more than the moment provides.

Contentment is being satisfied with wholesome thoughts, words, and deeds. You are content with your friends, relatives, and family members. You are content with your food and eat moderately. You are content with your clothes. You acquire them and wear them moderately. You do everything moderately without being greedy, hateful, or confused. One who is full of contentment feels full all the time. One who is discontented feels something is missing all the time.

One day Mahapajapati Gotami, the Buddha's stepmother, asked him to give her some very brief instruction on Dhamma. One of the things he taught was to cultivate contentment:

> Contentment is the highest wealth. What use is there for
> a well if there is water everywhere? When craving's root is
> severed, what should one go about seeking?

RESTRAINING THE SENSES

Observing moral and ethical principles is essential for the successful practice of jhana. This includes restraining the senses.

You should restrain your senses and avoid unwholesome food, unwholesome speech, and unwholesome activities. Restraint of the senses does not mean shutting your eyes when visual objects are present in front of you, or plugging your ears when you hear something. It does not require pinching your nose when there is something to smell. You can still taste your food and touch physical objects.

If shutting off the senses to prevent perceiving any sensory object made a mind clean and pure, then the blind and deaf would have clean and pure minds all the time! Unfortunately, this is not so. We are all human.

In this context, restraint means that, when sensory objects present themselves to your senses, you should focus in a certain way. As a diligent meditator, when you meet a person, do not focus the mind with distorted perception on the general signs of gender, or on the detailed signs of color, height, eyes, ears, nose, lips, hair, legs, or hands. Do not use the mind to enhance or fasten on the person's movements, the sound of the voice, the way the person speaks, looks, or walks.

There are beautiful things all around, beautiful visual objects, sweet sounds, sweet smells, delicious tastes, delightful touches, and compelling thoughts. They are the objects of craving. Our six senses are like hungry animals. They always look for something outside us to consume.

So what do you do instead? You pay mindful attention to your own body and simply mentally note the arising of sense contact. The existence of objects in the world does not cause craving to arise in your mind until you encounter them and reflect on them in an unwise manner.

Craving is one of the most powerful of the unwholesome forces of the mind. It is nourished by the injudicious consideration of these objects. The principal cause of suffering is craving. Once craving is eliminated, much suffering will be eliminated. Still more suffering will be eliminated once ignorance is eliminated. Both craving and ignorance are equally powerful defilements that cause suffering.

In the famous teaching called the "Fire Sermon," the Buddha likens craving to fire. All our senses are on fire, burning with the flames of craving. When one starts meditation, one begins by over-coming covetousness and disappointment. There is a difference between covetousness and greed or desire. With greed and desire, we want things for ourselves. In covetousness, if others have some-thing, we think we should have it.

We begin the practice by overcoming this envious craving and our disappointment in what the world gives us. Here "the world" means our *internal* world. We watch the mind attempting to glue onto something or hold on to something, and we keep that in mind-ful reflection until it fades away.

SECLUSION

A suitable place for the practice of jhana meditation is strongly rec-ommended. Since we cannot find a place without any noise at all we should find a place with very little noise, with very little sound, and by and large with an absence of human beings, suitable to hide away from human beings and conducive for the practice of solitude.

For jhana practice—for the periods of time you set aside to really do this work—it is very important to leave behind all work, all people, all meetings, all working on new construction or repairing old build-ings, all office work, and all family concerns. In other words, all your normal worries and unease. This is physical separation and it is essential. And this is the value of a retreat, of physical seclusion.

You need mental seclusion too. Don't carry all your mental bag-gage with you on retreat. Don't bring your work, your office, mental games, business plans, internal wars and fights with you when you go away. Say goodbye to all of them for a while. Tell them, kindly but firmly, "Don't trouble me now. I will take care of you later on. I know you will be there when I come back."

Another form of seclusion separation is called *liberation from attachment*. This is a real luxury. Gone to a solitary place, you must also separate from the very habit of grasping and clinging. Only then is jhana attainment possible. This kind of mental seclusion is pretty difficult to achieve but absolutely necessary to attain jhana. However, the benefits are enormous. When you don't put energy into thinking about the things that seem so very important, they do gradually disappear from your mind. On the other hand, whatever you often do with your mind, whatever you think about frequently and mentally grab on to, stays in the mind, coming back again and again.

In order to give your mind a little rest, you need to "forget" things deliberately from time to time. This is like draining all the energy from your batteries in order to fully recharge them. When you drain all the energy from the battery of your electronic device and recharge it, the battery lasts longer. Give some rest to your mind. Cease to think about all those duties and responsibilities for a little while. Give the mind full rest by not thinking about anything. When you practice jhana, the mind becomes fresh, clean, pure, and strong. Then you can use that mind to practice vipassana even better. And to take care of your life even more skillfully.

You don't have to go to a cave to attain seclusion. You can do it in a group if all the group members agree to create the physical atmosphere that promotes the state. This is exactly what we do when we attend a retreat. But you don't even need to do that.

You might, for instance, set up a place and time where you can be alone, silent, and undisturbed for at least one hour, a place that is like your own private cave or retreat center. Maybe it is just a closet or a corner of your bedroom. It does not need to be fancy or ornate. It just needs to be somewhere special, withdrawn from the world. It is someplace that you reserve for meditation only, someplace where you can drop everything you are carrying and just do your practice.

A little altar with a statue of the Buddha and some candles is very common, though, of course, not essential. A little bell to start and end your sessions is nice. It can be ornate or starkly simple. Use whatever really reminds you of your own dedication to the practice.

Be prepared to sit solidly for at least an hour. Even if pain arises, try not to move.

Somebody who is really serious in the practice of jhana meditation should make an effort to practice every single day, several times a day. You cannot gain jhana while driving (nor should you try!), or while working in your office, attending meetings, or attending a dinner party. You need a quiet time and a quiet place with reasonably comfortable sitting. The only thing that produces that degree of comfort is consistent, frequent practice.

MINDFUL REFLECTION

Before the mind is purified, there are unwholesome tendencies underlying the mind; therefore, greed, hatred, or delusion can arise. You see a form, hear a sound, smell a smell, taste food or drink, and there is an emotional reaction deep in the mind. You touch a tangible object, and there is a reaction. When you even think of some previously conceived image of one of these objects, craving, hatred, or delusion usually arise.

These sensory objects are neither beautiful nor ugly in their own nature. They are simply neutral sensory objects. But when you perceive something with the notion that it is pleasant, yearning arises. If you perceive something with the notion that it is ugly, resentment arises. If your mind is deluded by something's presence, delusion dominates the mind.

Suppose you wear colored glasses and look at objects. You see them according to the color of the lenses you are wearing. If you wear blue lenses, for instance, you see objects as blue. Instead simply look at each arising phenomenon with no lenses at all. Just be mindful of the fact that you have just seen an impermanent object, that you heard a voice, smelled a scent, or saw the movement of a person. Having completed this mindful awareness of the sensory object, you return to your subject of meditation. You should be mindful of what is seen purely as something seen, and what is heard only as something heard. You must simply note anything smelled purely as an instance of smelling, something tasted only as a pure tasting sensation. Something touched is experienced as just a touching. Thoughts and concepts are perceived as just mental objects perceived.

See objects, hear sounds, smell smells, taste food and drink, touch tangible things, and think thoughts *mindfully*, with mindful reflection. Mindful reflection means reflecting on something without greed, hatred, and delusion. It means relating to your environment without notions of "I," "me," and "mine." It means thinking about what is happening without thoughts like, "I am this way or that way," "I love or hate or care nothing about this or that."

When seeing an object, mindfully reflect that it arises depending on a particular sense and a particular object. When the eye, for instance, meets the object you are looking at, there is contact. Then there is a split second of pure wordless recognition and a particular type of consciousness arises. Depending on the combination of these three—senses, consciousness, and contact—other things arise: feeling, perception, deciding, and thinking.

Then come concepts, labeling, feeling, thought, craving, and detailed thinking. Then comes deliberation or perhaps more elaborate thinking. All of this arises spontaneously and in progression. Most of it is without any conscious will on your part. But all of these are impermanent, unsatisfactory, and selfless. Because they are impermanent, they have already vanished before you blink your eyes, before you can take a single inhalation or exhalation.

Seeing these things is called mindful reflection. When your concentration becomes pure, sharp, clear, and steady, it can penetrate all these veils of distortion and show you things as they really are.

Then the mind opens to penetrate reality more deeply.

Practicing the Noble Eightfold Path

Undisciplined meditators find it very difficult to gain concentration. Discipline, or *shila*, both physical and mental, is absolutely necessary. All those who have attained jhana have practiced shila. There are two sets of disciplinary rules of conduct. One is for the monastic community and the other is for the lay community. The monastic rules are relatively difficult for laypeople to practice. For this reason the Buddha has recommended a stepped-down version for them. It is outlined in the noble eightfold path.

The noble eightfold path constitutes the backbone of how we need to train ourselves in order to attain liberation. The eight steps create the container within which meditation can do its job. The eight steps can be divided into three overarching categories—moral conduct, right concentration, and wisdom. Jhana is included in the concentration group. The eight steps of the noble eightfold path must all be in place in your life in order to create the peaceful, settled atmosphere you need to cultivate jhana.

Right view. Jhana must be pursued and practiced within the context of an overall understanding of what the Buddhist path is all about.

Without that view, use of jhana can foster the purposes of ego, rather than eroding them. All use of jhana must be liberation-oriented and supported by mindfulness.

Right resolve. If you do not have firm and clear intentions of what you should be doing and why, you will accomplish nothing or get the wrong result. Three types of right resolve are considered essential. They are the intentions *toward* renunciation (letting go) and *away from* ill will and harm.

Right speech. You need to set up habits of speech conducive to your practice. Speaking is important. Every word you say colors your mind. Things like lying and frittering away your time talking about trifles will not help you at all. And moreover, speech can reinforce habits of mind: speaking coarsely and unkindly, for instance, actually strengthens the hindrances of anger and aversion.

Right action. What we do comes back to us. What we put out into the world creates the emotional environment in which we live. Robbing a bank is clearly not conducive to the depth of calm and tranquility necessary to achieve jhana. Even eating your neighbor's apple agitates the mind. Tiny misdeeds accumulate to create enough tension in the mind to keep you from the goal.

Right livelihood. Making your living as a thief or a drug dealer obviously does not promote peace, but those are only gross examples. Even small, dubious business practices disturb the mind. Does your job harm someone or something, even indirectly? You either carry the tension and guilt of your deeds or you deaden yourself to them. Neither will allow you to achieve jhana. Bringing care and consideration to the means by which you make your livelihood are essential.

Right effort. Obtaining jhana is not easy. We have to make certain efforts to create the conditions that allow it to manifest. We must honestly generate an aspiration to achieve it or it won't happen. Then we have to actually try. Then, once we have it, we have to foster it, preserve it, and maintain it. This is a matter of genuine intention and doing some real work.

Right mindfulness. Mindfulness cannot become strong without concentration. Concentration cannot become strong without mindfulness. To achieve jhana we keep the hindrances dormant. It is mindfulness that notices the nature of the content of each moment of hindrance so that we can surmount it.

Right concentration. Right concentration is using the mind in the direction of jhana. You don't need to succeed at that in order to make progress on the path, but the benefits of doing so are considerable.

Anyone who is interested in practicing meditation to attain jhana should, without exception, practice these ethical principles. But don't wait until your morality is perfect to start the practice for attaining jhana. When you meditate with imperfect morality, soon you will realize that it is very difficult to attain concentration. One hindrance or another gets in your way. Then you make mindful effort to understand and overcome that hindrance. You repeat this trial and error method and one day you will attain jhana. Yet it takes time and patience and the willingness to simply start again each time you slip.

MINDFULNESS

Mindfulness, as we have seen, is your first and most important tool for starting to build the foundation of jhana and jhana itself. You must make a mindful effort to understand unwholesome things as unwholesome and wholesome things as wholesome. You must make a mindful effort to overcome the unwholesome and to cultivate every wholesome thought, word, and deed that you can. When you practice jhana, you must make mindful effort to understand what you are doing, to prepare the mind to attain jhana.

All of us from time to time encounter people who "push our buttons." Without mindfulness, we respond automatically with anger or resentment. With mindfulness, we can watch how our mind responds to certain words and actions. Just as you do on the cushion, you can watch the arising of attachment and aversion. Mindfulness is like a safety net that cushions you against unwholesome action. Mindfulness gives you time. Time gives you choices. Choices, skillfully made, lead to freedom. You don't have to be swept away by your feeling. You can respond with wisdom and kindness rather than habit and reactivity.

When you engage in your activities mindfully, you realize for yourself that certain thoughts, like greed, hatred, and confusion, trouble your mind and you don't gain even a little concentration, let alone jhanic concentration. Then, from your own experience, you come to know, "Well, I need a break from all these negative thoughts." At that point you deliberately begin to cultivate wholesome and positive thoughts.

Since greed and ignorance work as a team to generate suffering, you cannot eliminate suffering without eliminating both greed and ignorance. The Buddha pointed out how the practice of meditation can bring an end to your suffering and allow you to experience the bliss of peace.

If you respond to insults or angry words with mindfulness, you can look closely at the whole situation. Perhaps the person who harmed you was not paying mindful attention to what he or she was saying. Perhaps he or she did not mean to hurt you. The person might have said what he or she said totally innocently or inadvertently. Perhaps you were not in the right mood at the time the words were spoken. Perhaps you did not hear the words clearly or you misunderstood the context.

It is also important to really consider carefully what that person is saying. If you respond with anger, you will not hear the message behind the words. Perhaps that person was pointing out something you needed to hear. Actually listen to what the person is saying and do not get angry while doing so. Anger opens your mouth and seals your ears.

Development of mindfulness helps us relate to others with loving-friendliness. On the cushion, you watch your mind as liking and disliking arise. You teach yourself to relax your mind when such thoughts arise. You learn to see attachment and aversion as momentary states and you learn to let them go. Meditation helps you look at the world in a new light and gives you a way out of anger. The deeper you go in your practice, the more skills you develop. The ultimate use for mindfulness is seeing impermanence in action. Everything else is a steppingstone toward that goal.

Mindfulness is always present in right jhana or indeed in any wholesome activity. So, all the way along the path, you should endeavor to do everything with mindfulness. Then it becomes a habit. It becomes simply the way the mind functions most of the time. That way, when you attain jhana, mindfulness will be present in your jhana.

THE FIVE SPIRITUAL FACULTIES

The five spiritual faculties are *mindfulness, wisdom, energy, faith*, and *concentration*. In truth, you cannot practice right concentration by itself in the absence of the other faculties.

When you try to gain *concentration*, hindrances arise. In order to overcome hindrances you must use *mindfulness*. Whatever method you employ to overcome hindrances must be employed with mindfulness to make it work. One such method, the cultivation of loving-friendliness, is explored in the next chapter.

The *energy* factor is needed too. It boosts your practice. When you practice mindfulness and concentration, they work well only if you have adequate energy. Without energy you will be sluggish and lazy. You will not be able to make much progress.

Faith, as we have seen, is also an important factor. You will not have any initiative to practice if you don't have faith in the Buddha, Dhamma, and Sangha. In this context this means trusting that someone (the Buddha) has indeed attained what you yourself are trying to attain, that there exists a road map (the Dhamma) that will help you attain it, and that there are people (the Sangha) who can guide you and accompany you on the path to liberation.

Wisdom comes into play too. You must be wise enough to really understand why you are launching yourself on this path. What are your real goals? Which ones do you really believe in and which are just something you read in a book or heard from someone else?

All the five spiritual faculties must work together in order for you to proceed smoothly with the practice.

People sometimes ask me to tell them more about what I mean by this word "wisdom." Here is one answer that I give.

As you keep paying total undivided attention to everything you experience in your body, feelings, perceptions, volitional formations, and consciousness, all you can honestly see with your mental eye is that everything is constantly changing. Certain things you experience are pleasant; certain things are unpleasant; and certain things

414 BEYOND MINDFULNESS IN PLAIN ENGLISH

are neither pleasant nor unpleasant. But all of them, without any exception, are constantly changing.

Your ordinary state of mind is not aware of these changes. So, in spite of their changes, your mind, even without your awareness, does three things: clings to the pleasant; rejects the unpleasant; and gets sucked into the neither-pleasant-nor-unpleasant.

This last is especially important. This neither-pleasant-nor-unpleasant business is tricky. It is ordinary, everyday experience. It is so familiar that you think this neither-pleasant-nor-unpleasant state is the experience of your soul or permanent self, the "real me."

This clinging to the pleasant, rejecting the unpleasant, and confusing the neither-pleasant-nor-unpleasant experiences with "reality" is a naturally built-in system.

This clinging, rejecting, and getting confused changes too. With meditation your intuition tells you that this repetition of changing—the arising and passing away of all your experiences, the pleasant, unpleasant, and neither pleasant nor unpleasant—is not satisfactory, is not a happy situation.

Seeing this frustrating situation, your mind gets tired of all experience, even the pleasant ones. Then your mind lets go of clinging to any pleasant experience; it lets go of any unpleasant experience; it lets go of any neither-pleasant-nor-unpleasant experience.

Then you experience peace within yourself. Then your mind becomes free from greed, hate, and delusion. This particular skill, power, or faculty, or the strength of liberating the mind from these three poisons, three weapons, or three kinds of fire, is what Buddhists called true wisdom.

Each of the six senses is sometimes called "ocean." Each ocean is full of dangers of sharks, demons, waves of greed, hatred, and delusion. The clear vision of using them skillfully is wisdom. The Buddha summarizes this like this:

One who has crossed this ocean so hard to cross, with its dangers of sharks, demons, waves, the knowledge-master who has lived the holy life, reached the world's end, is called one gone beyond.

4. *Wishing the Best for Yourself and Others*

*T*he force of loving-friendliness within the mind is called *metta* in Pali. It means wishing the best for yourself and others. Metta is also used to refer to mental exercises we use to cultivate this loving-friendly state of mind. We say specific words and think specific thoughts in order to generate a pure feeling. Generating metta is one of the principal routes *to* jhana. It is also a specific remedy for states of mind that keep us *from* jhana.

In fact, metta makes the perfect preparation for jhana-oriented meditation. It clears away the hindrances so that concentration may arise.

Loving-Friendliness in Thought and Action

Practicing loving-friendliness meditation can change your habitual negative thought patterns and reinforce your positive ones. When you practice loving-friendliness meditation, your mind will become filled with peace and happiness. You will be relaxed. You will gain concentration.

But loving-friendliness is not limited to your thoughts. You must manifest it in your words and your actions, too. And it involves others, not just yourself. You cannot cultivate loving-friendliness in isolation.

You can start by thinking kind thoughts about everyone you have contact with every day. If you have mindfulness, you can do this every waking minute with everyone you deal with. Whenever you see someone, consider that, like yourself, that person wants happiness and wants to avoid suffering. We are all the same. We all feel that way. All beings feel that way. Even the tiniest insect recoils from harm.

When you recognize that common ground, you see how closely we are all connected. The woman behind the checkout counter, the man who cuts you off on the expressway, the young couple walking across the street, the old man in the park feeding the birds, and the birds themselves. Whenever you see another being, any being, keep this in mind. Wish that one happiness, peace, and well-being. It is a practice that can change your life and the lives of those around you.

The meditation center where I teach is in the hills of the West Virginia countryside. When we first opened our center, there was a man down the road who was very unfriendly. I encountered him regularly on the long walk I take every day. It is a quiet forest road with little traffic and I always wave at everyone who goes by. Whenever I saw this man, I would wave to him. He would just frown at me and look away. Even so, I would always wave and think kindly of him, sending him loving-friendliness. I was not disappointed by his attitude. I never gave up on him. Whenever I saw him, I waved just as I did with other people. After about a year, his behavior changed. He stopped frowning. I felt wonderful. The practice of loving-friendliness was bearing fruit.

After another year, when I passed him on my walk, something miraculous happened. He drove past me and lifted one finger off the steering wheel. Again, I thought, "Oh, this is wonderful.

Loving-friendliness is working." Another year passed. Day after day, when I took my walk, I would wave to him and wish him well. The third year, he lifted two fingers in my direction. Then the next year, he lifted *all four fingers* off the wheel. More time passed. One day I was walking down the road as he turned into his driveway. He took his hand off the steering wheel, stuck it out the window, and waved to me.

One day, not long after, I saw him parked on the side of one of the forest roads. He was sitting in the driver's seat smoking a cigarette. I went over to him and started talking. First we chatted just about the weather and then, little by little, his story unfolded. It turns out that he had been in a terrible accident. A tree had fallen on his truck. Almost every bone in his body was broken. He had been in a coma. When I first started seeing him on the road, he was only beginning to recover. He did not refrain from waving because he was a mean person. He did not wave because *he could not move all his fingers.* Had I given up on him I would never have known how good this man is.

To top it all off, one day, when I had been away on a trip, he actually came by our center looking for me. He was worried because he hadn't seen me walking in a while.

Now we are friends.

Cultivating Friendliness toward Different Types of People

You need to find reasons to develop loving-friendliness toward those you have problems with. A few traditional analogies describing five different types of people may help guide you here.

The first type of person is someone whose deeds are rotten. He does bad things and has a very base manner. He does not know how to behave. He is not polite. His manners are rough. He does not show respect to anybody.

Venerable Sariputta compared such a person to a dirty rag. Suppose a traveling monk sees a dirty rag on the road in front of him. It is so dirty that he cannot even pick it up with his hands. He holds it by one foot and kicks it with the other foot and dusts it off. He cleans it off that way—only with his feet. Then he picks it up with two fingers and shakes it off with contempt. Then he takes it home, washes it neatly, and puts it to some use. He might use it to patch up a robe or make a doormat. He puts that piece of cloth to work.

This metaphor teaches us, when you want to cultivate loving friendship for such a person, you find one reason or another.

The layers of dirt on the rag are like the layers of conditioning on this person that have made him so rough and impolite. Maybe he has acquired this from his parents, his teachers, his associates, his education, and his upbringing. Maybe he has been discriminated against. Maybe he has been mistreated and abused and intimidated in his childhood. Maybe he is not an educated person. All kinds of things you do not know about may be contributing to his rough behavior. These are his history. You do not know about these things, but it is best to forgive him for all his misdeeds. Practice metta toward him.

He is suffering from his own hatred and he deserves our compassion. He does not know how to deal with his own suffering. Perhaps he has lost his friends, his home, his job, his relatives, due to his own hatred. Maybe he has had a terrible divorce. All we can see is that he is suffering. All we can do is practice compassion.

Maybe this helps to reduce his hatred and make him happy, maybe it doesn't. If it doesn't, we practice equanimity toward him. This is a balanced state of mind, but it doesn't mean we just give up. We think of other ways to help him.

You may discover a second kind of person with bad words whose deeds are good. This is someone who has no polite words in his vocabulary, only foul language, yet he or she nonetheless does something good for you or for the world.

This person might see you frustrated at doing things improperly. He may come up to you and say, "You fool! You idiot! You don't know how to do this. You're going to kill yourself if you do it that way. Here, let me do it!" Then maybe he does the whole job for you. That is a good reason for you to develop loving-friendliness toward that person.

This person, in spite of his filthy language, may do something wonderful. For that, you must respect him, admire him, and you share loving-friendliness with him. Help him change his way of talking. When you associate with him and show your loving friendship for him, he will perhaps gradually change. You arouse loving-friendliness within yourself for that person, and that, in turn, can arouse it in him.

This second person is compared to a pond covered with algae. When you want to dive into it or get water out of it, you have to remove the moss by hand, and only then can you dive in and swim properly. Similarly, you learn to ignore such an algae-covered person's superficial weaknesses. You watch and you find out that her heart opens to compassion and loving friendship from time to time. She develops a pure heart from time to time. That is a good reason for you to develop loving-friendliness toward this second person.

A third person may have both bad words *and* bad deeds, yet a flickering impulse toward kindness within. This person is like a puddle on the road. Suppose you are walking on a road where there is no water, no well. You are thirsty and tired. You are hungry and thirsty, desperately looking for some water to drink. You are almost dehydrated. At that time, you find a little water in a cow's footprint. There is not too much water because a cow's footprint is not too deep, but there is a little water in it. If you try to take that water by hand, you make it muddy. So, what do you do? You bend down, kneel down, and slowly bring your mouth close to that bit of water. Then sip it without disturbing the mud. Even though it is dirty and muddy, you may still quench your thirst for a moment. You sip the water gently and leave the mud behind. In this way we can see at least the *potential*, from time to time, for even such a person bad in word and deed to, in certain circumstances, open his heart to noble things, friendly things, and compassionate things. You should practice loving-friendliness toward such a person, in spite of all his weaknesses.

You meet another person, a fourth person. This person's words are bad, his behavior is bad, and his heart does not open at all for anything noble. This person is like a patient, a sick man, walking on a road where there is no hospital, no village, and no humans around, no one to help him. There is no water, no house to rest in, no tree to give shelter, just the hot sun and his burning thirst. This person is afflicted and suffering from a severe sickness. He really needs medical attention; otherwise he will surely die. You see him and you feel very sorry for him. Your heart melts. You think, "How can I help this suffering being? What can I do for him? He needs water, medicine, and clothes. He needs somebody to help him. How can I help him?" In spite of all those difficulties, and despite the fact that you will almost certainly receive no gratitude, you nonetheless resolve to be of service.

When I meet such a person I think thoughts like this, "With bad bodily conduct and bad verbal conduct like this, he is committing many unwholesome and unskillful acts. He is suffering from that now and he will suffer from it in the future. Let me help him get rid of his hatred."

A fifth person's thoughts are sweet and wonderful. His words are beautiful and friendly. His deeds are friendly, beautiful, and pure. Everything is ideal. It is, of course, very easy for us to cultivate loving-friendliness toward that person. Even so, doing this mindfully can be of great value.

You must try to cultivate loving-friendliness equally toward all these five people without discrimination. This is not very easy. You have to make a great sacrifice—a sacrifice of your comfort, a sacrifice of your thoughts, a sacrifice of your feelings and your attitudes. You have to sacrifice many things in order to cultivate loving-friendliness. You must remember that the overall purpose of what you are doing here is to make *yourself* calm and peaceful, to make your mind and body healthy, and to make your surroundings healthy. You are trying to make others feel comfortable in associating with you. To make them comfortable, you first make yourself comfortable with them. When you feel comfortable to associate with others, you carry on your conversations and activities harmoniously. You have to take the initiative to lay the groundwork and prepare yourself to practice loving-friendliness.

When you come to truly understand suffering, your heart opens to the hidden nature of your own loving-friendliness. Then you feel so much love and compassion for all living beings that your mind naturally wishes them all to live in peace and harmony.

Over the years, I have received many letters from prisoners who are seeking to learn the Dhamma. Some have done terrible things, even murder. They see things differently now and want to change their lives. There was one letter that was particularly insightful and deeply touched my heart. In it, the writer described how the other inmates shouted and jeered whenever the guard appeared. The inmate tried to explain to the others that this guard was also a human being. But the others were blinded by hatred. All they could see, he said, was the uniform, not the man inside it. This man was putting loving-friendliness into action and it altered his perceptions.

424 BEYOND MINDFULNESS IN PLAIN ENGLISH

Loving-friendliness is not something you do by just sitting on a cushion, thinking and thinking and thinking. You must let the power of loving-friendliness shine through your every encounter with others. Loving-friendliness is the underlying principle behind all wholesome thoughts, words, and deeds. With loving-friendliness, you recognize more clearly the needs of others and help them readily. With thoughts of loving-friendliness you appreciate the success of others with warm feeling. You need it in order to live and work with others in harmony. It protects you from the suffering, fear, and insecurity caused by anger and jealousy. When you cultivate your loving-friendliness, your compassion, your appreciative joy for others, and your equanimity, you not only make life more pleasant for those around you, your own life becomes peaceful and happy. The power of metta is like the radiance of the sun, beyond measure.

Loving-friendliness goes beyond all boundaries of religion, culture, geography, language, and nationality. It is a universal and ancient law that binds all of us together—no matter what form we may take. Loving-friendliness should be practiced unconditionally. My enemy's pain is my pain. His anger is my anger. His loving-friendliness is my loving-friendliness. If he is happy, I am happy. If he is peaceful, I am peaceful. If he is healthy, I am healthy. Just as we all share suffering regardless of our differences, we should all share our loving-friendliness with every person everywhere.

No one nation can stand alone without the help and support of other nations, nor can any one person exist in isolation. To survive, you need other living beings, beings that are bound to be different from yourself. That is simply the way things are. Because of the differences we all have, the practice of loving-friendliness is absolutely necessary. It is the common denominator that ties all of us together.

WHY METTA IS IMPORTANT FOR JHANA

You cannot practice mindfulness without loving-friendliness, nor can you practice loving-friendliness without mindfulness. These two always go hand in hand. When you are flowing metta to all living beings, radiating it outward in all directions, with your whole mind, on every sense channel, when you are doing it sincerely, there is simply no room for the hindrances. You cannot radiate good will and be greedy at the same time. You cannot be fearful or angry. You cannot have doubts, restlessness, boredom, or dullness.

When you practice loving-friendliness you build up a very powerful spiritual magnet that pulls people toward you. You feel very comfortable wherever you go. You feel that everybody around you is friendly toward you. You feel secure thinking that everybody around you is friendly. You can trust them. You can leave home knowing that your friends protect your home. You feel comfortable that your friends protect your family.

Your metta practice makes you so relaxed and peaceful that you are pleasing to all around you. You can sleep well. You will not have nightmares. You can get up with a fresh feeling. You can talk to anybody without anger. You like them, and they often like you in response.

The practice of loving-friendliness is also a healing meditation for the one who does it. It heals all the wounds of anger. When the power of loving-friendliness repels anger, you are very relaxed and joyful.

Remember, it is crucial to extend loving-friendliness to yourself as well as to others. Your practice will not succeed if you harbor animosity or indifference toward yourself. Practicing loving-friendliness toward yourself first makes you peaceful and happy. Resting in that experience, you can wish others the same peace and happiness by cultivating loving-friendliness toward them. You send it out from a calm, peaceful, compassionate center and that must start with yourself.

MEDITATIONS ON LOVING-FRIENDLINESS

This section presents six formal meditations on metta. The metta practice has three levels. The first is the verbalizing level, the second is the thinking level, and the third is the feeling level. When you are in jhana, you experience the feeling level of metta.

General Instructions

Start with the words and ideas. Say the formal words given below, or some variant of them. These are just examples provided here to show the progression of beings involved and how to extend your metta outward. You start with yourself as a focal point for peace and good wishes; then expand your area of focus outward by stages until it includes the entire universe of beings.

If the formal words do not resonate with you, you can use words that are truly meaningful to you.

Envision *specific* people or animals in each category. Hold them clearly in mind. Make the feelings real and personal. Some categories and types of people are more challenging than others. Work on each category until you can do it fluidly and sincerely.

Explore the physical feelings associated with metta. Find out, deeply and with mindfulness, exactly what is going on in your body, exactly where it is happening and precisely how it feels.

Focus on the physical feelings until they become a pure distillation of all the thoughts and physical sensations. It is a feeling beyond sensation, almost an emotional coloring in the mind. It is often accompanied by sensations of warmth and swelling in the area of the heart.

Drop the words, the images, the beings, the physical feelings, and the stages. Move deeply into the pure feeling of metta as an intangible thing, beyond simple thought, emotion, and physical feelings. Get the living essence of the thing.

Use yourself as a kind of radiator to pump the pure feeling of friendliness and kindness out to the whole universe. Stay with that.

Metta meditation has the potential to carry you into jhana. The pure feeling of metta as an experience can be used to carry you across the barrier into the wordless. It is very close to the feelings that predominate in the first jhana and it can be used as a tool to reach them.

Metta Meditation 1

May *I* be well, happy, and peaceful. May no harm come to me. May I always meet with spiritual success. May I also have patience, courage, understanding, and determination to meet and overcome inevitable difficulties, problems, and failures in life. May I always rise above them with morality, integrity, forgiveness, compassion, mindfulness, and wisdom.

May *my parents* be well, happy, and peaceful. May no harm come to them. May they always meet with spiritual success. May they also have patience, courage, understanding, and determination to meet and overcome inevitable difficulties, problems, and failures in life. May they always rise above them with morality, integrity, forgiveness, compassion, mindfulness, and wisdom.

May *my teachers* be well, happy, and peaceful. May no harm come to them. May they always meet with spiritual success. May they also have patience, courage, understanding, and determination to meet and overcome inevitable difficulties, problems, and failures in life. May they always rise above them with morality, integrity, forgiveness, compassion, mindfulness, and wisdom.

428 BEYOND MINDFULNESS IN PLAIN ENGLISH

May *my relatives* be well, happy, and peaceful. May no harm come to them. May they always meet with spiritual success. May they also have patience, courage, understanding, and determination to meet and overcome inevitable difficulties, problems, and failures in life. May they always rise above them with morality, integrity, forgiveness, compassion, mindfulness, and wisdom.

May *my friends* be well, happy, and peaceful. May no harm come to them. May they always meet with spiritual success. May they also have patience, courage, understanding, and determination to meet and overcome inevitable difficulties, problems, and failures in life. May they always rise above them with morality, integrity, forgiveness, compassion, mindfulness, and wisdom.

May *all people to whom I am indifferent* be well, happy, and peaceful. May no harm come to them. May they always meet with spiritual success. May they also have patience, courage, understanding, and determination to meet and overcome inevitable difficulties, problems, and failures in life. May they always rise above them with morality, integrity, forgiveness, compassion, mindfulness, and wisdom.

May all *unfriendly persons* be well, happy, and peaceful. May no harm come to them. May they always meet with spiritual success. May they also have patience, courage, understanding, and determination to meet and overcome inevitable difficulties, problems, and failures in life. May they always rise above them with morality, integrity, forgiveness, compassion, mindfulness, and wisdom.

May *all living beings* be well, happy, and peaceful. May no harm come to them. May they always meet with spiritual success. May they also have patience, courage, understanding, and determination to meet and overcome inevitable difficulties, problems, and failures in life. May they always rise above them with morality, integrity, forgiveness, compassion, mindfulness, and wisdom.

Metta Meditation 2

Having seen that all beings, like yourself, have a desire for happiness, you should methodically develop loving-friendliness toward all beings.

May I be happy, and free from suffering! And, always, like my self, may my friends, neutral persons, and hostile ones be happy too.

May all beings in this town, in this state, in other countries, and in the world systems be ever happy.

May all persons, individuals, beings, and creatures in all world systems be ever happy.

So too, may all women, men, noble ones, nonnoble ones, gods, humans, and beings in the lower worlds be happy.

May all beings in every direction and every place be happy.

Metta Meditation 3

May I be free from hatred. May I be free from affliction. May I be free from worry. May I live happily.

As I am, so also may my parents, teachers, preceptors, and friendly, indifferent, and hostile beings be free from hatred. May they be free from affliction! May they be free from worry. May they live happily! May they be released from suffering. May they not be deprived of their fortune, duly acquired.

May all beings . . . all living things . . . all creatures . . . all persons . . . all those who have arrived at a state of individuality, all women . . . all men . . . all noble ones . . . all nonnoble ones . . . all gods . . . all humans . . . all nonhumans . . . all those who are in the hell, and in this home, village, town, this country, in this world, in this galaxy, may all of them without any exception be free from worry. May they live happily. May they be released from suffering. May they not be deprived of their fortune, duly acquired.

Metta Meditation 4

May those with no feet receive my love. May those with two feet receive my love. May those with four feet receive my love. May those with many feet receive my love.

May those with no feet not hurt me. May those with two feet not hurt me. May those with four feet not hurt me. May those with many feet not hurt me.

May all beings, all those with life, be happy.

May suffering not come to anyone.

May those suffering be free from suffering. May the fear-struck be free from fear. May the grieving be free from grief.

So too may all beings be.

From the highest realm of existence to the lowest, may all beings arisen in these realms, with form and without form, with perception and without perception, be released from all suffering and attain to perfect peace.

Metta Meditation 5

May all beings be happy and secure. May all beings have happy minds.

Whatever living beings there may be without exception—weak or strong, long, large, medium, short, subtle, or gross, visible or invisible, living near or far, born or coming to birth—may all beings have happy minds.

Let no one deceive another nor despise anyone anywhere. Neither from anger nor ill will should anyone wish harm to another.

As a mother would risk her own life to protect her only child, even so toward all living beings one should cultivate a boundless heart.

One should cultivate for all the world a heart of boundless loving-friendliness above, below, and all around, unobstructed, without hatred or resentment.

Whether standing, walking, or sitting, lying down or whenever awake, one should develop this mindfulness; this is called divinely dwelling here.

Metta Meditation 6

Let me direct my mind in the eastern direction and wish all living beings in that direction to be free from greed, anger, aversion, hatred, jealousy, and fear. Let these thoughts of loving-friendliness embrace all of them, envelop them. Let every cell, every drop of blood, every atom, every molecule of their entire bodies and minds be charged with these thoughts of friendliness. Let their bodies and minds be relaxed and filled with the peace and tranquility of loving-friendliness. Let the peace and tranquility of loving-friendliness pervade their entire bodies and minds.

Let me direct my mind to the southern direction and wish all living beings in that direction to be free from greed, anger, aversion, hatred, jealousy, and fear. Let these thoughts of loving-friendliness embrace all of them, envelop them. Let every cell, every drop of blood, every atom, every molecule of their entire bodies and minds be charged with these thoughts of friendliness. Let their bodies and minds be filled with the thought of loving-friendliness. Let the peace and tranquility of loving-friendliness pervade their entire bodies and minds.

Let me direct my mind to the western direction and wish all living beings in that direction to be free from greed, anger, aversion, hatred, jealousy, and fear. Let these thoughts of loving-friendliness embrace all of them, envelop them. Let every cell, every drop of blood, every atom, every molecule of their entire bodies and minds be charged with these thoughts of friendliness. Let their bodies and minds be relaxed and filled with the peace and tranquility of loving-friendliness. Let the peace and tranquility of loving-friendliness pervade their entire bodies and minds.

Let me direct my mind to the northern direction and wish all living beings in that direction to be free from greed, anger, aversion, hatred, jealousy, and fear. Let these thoughts of loving-friendliness embrace all of them, envelop them. Let every cell, every drop of blood, every atom, every molecule of their entire bodies and minds be charged with these thoughts of friendliness. Let their bodies and minds be relaxed and filled with the peace and tranquility of loving-friendliness. Let the peace and tranquility of loving-friendliness pervade their entire bodies and minds.

Let me direct my mind to the celestial direction and wish all living beings in that direction to be free from greed, anger, aversion, hatred, jealousy, and fear. Let these thoughts of loving-friendliness embrace all of them, envelop them. Let every cell, every drop of blood, every atom, every molecule of their entire bodies and minds be charged with these thoughts of friendliness. Let their bodies and minds be relaxed and filled with the peace and tranquility of loving-friendliness. Let the peace and tranquility of loving-friendliness pervade their entire bodies and minds.

Let me direct my mind to the animal realm and hell realms and wish all living beings in that direction to be free from greed, anger, aversion, hatred, jealousy, and fear. Let these thoughts of loving-friendliness embrace all of them, envelop them. Let every cell, every drop of blood, every atom, every molecule of their entire bodies and minds be charged with these thoughts of friendliness. Let their bodies and minds be relaxed and filled with the peace and tranquility of loving-friendliness. Let the peace and tranquility of loving-friendliness pervade their entire bodies and minds.

May all beings in all directions, all around the universe be beautiful; let them be happy; let them have good fortune; let them have good friends; let them after death be reborn in heavens.

May all beings everywhere be filled with the feeling of loving-friendliness, abundant, exalted, measureless, free from enmity, free from affliction and anxiety. May they live happily.

May all those who are imprisoned legally or illegally, all who are in police custody anywhere in the world awaiting trials, be met with peace and happiness. May they be free from greed, anger, aversion, hatred, jealousy, and fear. Let these thoughts of loving-friendliness embrace all of them, envelop them. Let every cell, every drop of blood, every atom, every molecule of their entire bodies and minds be charged with these thoughts of friendliness. Let their bodies and minds be relaxed and filled with the peace and tranquility of loving-friendliness. Let the peace and tranquility of loving-friendliness pervade their entire bodies and minds.

May all of them in all directions, all around the universe be beautiful; let them be happy; let them have good fortune; let them have good friends; let them after death be reborn in heavens.

May all children abused by adults in numerous ways be free from pain, afflictions, depression, disappointment, dissatisfaction, anxiety, and fear. Let these thoughts of loving-friendliness embrace all of them, envelop them. Let every cell, every drop of blood, every atom, every molecule of their entire bodies and minds be charged with these thoughts of friendliness. Let their bodies and minds be relaxed and filled with the peace and tranquility of loving-friendliness. Let the peace and tranquility of loving-friendliness pervade their entire bodies and minds.

May all of them in all directions, all around the universe be beautiful; let them be happy; let them have good fortune; let them have good friends; let them after death be reborn in heavens.

May all rulers be gentle, kind, generous, compassionate, considerate, and have best understanding of the oppressed, the underprivileged, the discriminated against, and the poverty-stricken. May their hearts melt at the suffering of the unfortunate citizens. May the oppressed, the underprivileged, the discriminated against, and the poverty-stricken be free from pain, afflictions, depression, free from disappointment, dissatisfaction, anxiety, and fear. Let these thoughts of loving-friendliness embrace all of them, envelop them. Let every cell, every drop of blood, every atom, every molecule of their entire bodies and minds be charged with these thoughts of friendliness. Let their bodies and minds be relaxed and filled with the peace and tranquility of loving-friendliness. Let the peace and tranquility of loving-friendliness pervade their entire bodies and minds.

May all of them in all directions, all around the universe be beautiful; let them be happy; let them have good fortune; let them have good friends; let them after death be reborn in heavens.

5. Breath Meditation

*I*n addition to the loving-friendliness meditations we have just explored, there is another kind of meditation of inestimable value to building the foundation of jhana practice: breath meditation.

How to do breath meditation is a large topic. It has been thoroughly covered in the first book in this collection, *Mindfulness in Plain English*. If you are uncertain of the technique, please see that book or any other well-respected primer on the subject (the recommendations for further reading offer suggestions). But for our purposes now, I will offer just a brief recap. This section just lays out some simple pointers on applying breath meditation toward the goal of achieving deep concentration.

First, fasten the mind on the breath and hold it there. You may start with the rise and fall of the abdomen and the chest, but then you should switch over to the breath at the nostrils or the upper lip. This is where you will get a single, distinct point of sensation.

Stay with that single point of sensation. When other thoughts, feelings, or perceptions pull you away, notice them just enough to see their impermanence, their fleetingness. They rise, stay a bit, and then fade away. Just see that, over and over. In this way, every distraction from your object of focus acts as a steppingstone toward your process of liberation. Seeing the impermanence in every distraction—just that, all by itself—may be enough to lead you into genuine concentration.

If distractions refuse to go away or keep coming back, analyze which hindrance is present. Then apply one or more of the remedies presented in the next chapter.

Also bear in mind that sometimes your mind is like a cup of muddy water. How can you get clear water from a cup of muddy water? All you have to do is to set the cup on flat ground. Then the sediment settles down and the clear water stays on top. Similarly, when the mental sediment has settled down, your mind becomes clear. Then you should be able to sit, ideally, for one solid hour. Even if you have aches and pains, you should not move (though don't sit in a position that needlessly causes you excruciating pain). Let the physical sensations move into the background.

When you want to gain concentration, don't go into the details of the breath—rising, falling, and so forth. If you happen to notice the rising and falling of breath, the movement of the abdomen, and so forth, don't worry about it. Just go ahead and notice them until your mind settles down. Do not investigate or elaborate. Stay with the overall feeling of breath as a single, flowing process. Don't think or categorize or conceptualize. Then the mind switches over to pure concentration all by itself.

VIPASSANA AWARENESS OF THE BREATH

Sometimes when you begin to meditate, your mind is restless. It's very hard to center on the breath and stay there. You need something interesting to hold your attention. But what could possibly be interesting about the breath? You've had it all your life and you take it for granted. Isn't breath the most boring thing in the world?

There *is* something going on. In fact, there are, by traditional reckoning, *twenty-one* things going on, over and over. They are things you can notice, things you can make the subject of your vipassana awareness. You can notice each of them as a separate event if that helps you keep your attention on the meditation object.

Twenty-one points of repetition occur with every inhaling and exhaling.

Inhaling has: a beginning, a middle, an end, a brief pause.

Exhaling has the same four events. That is eight points.

We can also identify the following four points: *Pressure*—When the lungs are full with inhaled breath we experience pressure; *Release*—There is a release of pressure when we breathe out; *Anxiety or urgency*—When you breathe out and the lungs are empty of breath, there is a small degree of anxiety or urgency; *Relief of anxiety or urgency*—When you breathe in, the anxiety fades away and you experience relief.

The *four elements* are there, too: *Earth element*—The breath touches your nostrils, the tip of your nose or the upper lip, and inside the nose between the eyes. This touch is sometimes hard and sometimes soft. That is an expression of the earth element. *Water element*—Sometimes breath is dry and sometimes moist. This is due to the presence of the water element in the air we breathe in and out. *Heat element*—Sometimes breath is warm and sometimes cool. *Air element*—The air itself is, of course, present in the breath.

You can also observe the *five aggregates*, the traditional constituents of your body and mind. The five aggregates are form, feeling, perceptions, volitional formations, and consciousness: *Aggregate of form*— Breath has a kind of a shape to it. Because of the presence of the four elements in the breath, the ancient texts refer to breath as *a body*: the body of breath. *Aggregate of feeling*—We must feel the breath to notice that it is there for us to use as an object of meditation. *Aggregate of perception*—We must mentally perceive the breath in order to identify its presence. This cognitive function belongs to the perception aggregate. *Aggregate of volitional formation*—We intentionally pay attention to our breath, feeling, and perception. *Aggregate of consciousness*—And, last but not least, we cannot do any of them without consciousness.

These twenty-one points are always repeatedly present, and mindful breath meditation can bring them all into awareness.

Notice especially the points about anxiety or urgency, its coming and its going. Anxiety motivates much of our behavior, especially the parts we would be better off without. There is much to be learned here about the function of your own emotional life. Full-blown anxiety often manifests as constant recurring thoughts about your situation, some sensation in the area of the heart, lungs, and stomach, plus an almost undetectable "flavor" in the mind. Here is your chance to study how small anxiety manifests for you so that later, when anxiety is strong, you will be able to study it further. This is an excellent practical application of your vipassana skills.

The Four Elements

The four elements is an analytical system to help you develop mindfulness. It works very well with the practice of mindfulness of breathing meditation. This is an ancient categorization scheme for looking at the nature of our own experience. It analyzes every experience we have in terms of symbolic qualities that are like some of the primary things we see in the normal world: earth, water, air, and fire.

Please keep in mind that these are not mere words, nor are they some highly philosophical or mystical qualities only available to deep thinkers and spiritual supermen. These are things you are experiencing right now. It is just a different way of analyzing the experience you are having at this very moment. Each of the four elements manifests in the single practice of mindfulness of breathing.

The *earth* element represents the property of solidity, heaviness, solidness, compactness. Its characteristics are hardness or softness.

Just feel yourself sitting. Place your attention on that solid feeling where your body touches whatever you are sitting on. Feel your feet pressing against the floor. Those are hard sensations. Feel the light touch of the air against your skin. That is a soft sensation. This is the earth element.

The breath itself shows you the earth element. The breathing can be hard or soft. You would not feel anything unless there were solid flesh doing the feeling and you can feel that solidity. You feel whatever part of the body the air contacts as hard. You feel the solidness of the abdomen as it rises and falls. You feel the solidity of the nostrils as the air passes over them. Sometimes the breath has a roughness to it. Sometimes a gentle breath is so soft you can scarcely feel it.

It's a very simple concept, really. It's so simple that we totally overlook it unless somebody points it out to us.

Mindfulness of breathing shows us the *hard*, *soft*, and *solid* qualities of our experience.

The *water* element has a moist or flowing quality. The blood pumps through your veins. Your stomach pulses and gurgles with digestion. There are various squishing and swishing feelings happening within you right now. And most of the time you ignore them. When you get quiet in meditation they stand revealed. Any sensation that is damp, humid, or clammy in nature is in this category too.

Breath has a flowing quality. Sometimes you feel the moisture as humid air comes in. When the external air is dry, you can feel that it is more moist as it goes out. As you concentrate on the breath, other sensations from the rest of the body intrude. Some of them have this flowing quality too.

Mindfulness of breathing shows us the *liquid*, *moist*, and *flowing* qualities of our experience.

The *air* element is experienced primarily as motion or stillness. The moving quality of anything is the air element expressed through that thing. You experience little tinglings and vibrations in the skin. It feels like something is moving. There may be deep grinding feelings inside that have a moving quality. The flow of blood, the same sensation that revealed the liquid factor, can also show you the air element if you open up to it as pure movement.

The air element can also be experienced as space—the space within which movement of breathing takes place. Sometimes the body feels like an empty house, a vacant space, a mere shell within which all kinds of things are taking place. Maybe nothing is taking place. You still have the element of air present as the feeling of an empty locality within which there is absence or stillness.

The breath is constantly moving. The abdomen fills; it rises and falls. The physical air moves in and out. Even in the pauses there is a feeling of hollowness or vacuum within which it all happens.

Mindfulness of breathing shows us the *moving, still,* or *spacious* quality of our experience.

The *fire* element manifests as heat or cold or any sense of temperature in between. It also manifests as the dry sensation that goes with heat. When you feel hot and want to be cooler, the pure feeling that precedes the thought is the fire element manifesting. The temperature in the room drops and you feel cold. That is the fire element manifesting. The temperature feels neutral and you have to really seek to feel any temperature at all. That is the fire element too.

Any sensation within the body that has an energetic or burning or chilling quality is the fire element at work. There are feelings that go *zing* and *zoom.* They vibrate very fast. There are burnings and acidic stingings.

The air often feels cool against the nostrils on the in-breath, warmer on the out-breath. That is the fire element. You become distracted by the temperature around you. You feel the temperature of the physical air against your skin. That is fire manifesting.

Mindfulness of breathing shows us the *hot-cold* or *energetic* quality of our experience.

So . . . what is the point of this four elements category scheme?

We contemplate the *four elements of the breath body* as a meditation exercise to examine our own experience with precision. With every passing material experience that we see in meditation we silently ask, "Which of the four qualities predominates here?" The whole purpose is to push us, almost against our will, into contact with the pure, experiential essence of sensory reality. Training the mind to see the impingements of material experience as simply elemental vibrations helps to break down our usual mental habits. It frees us from the concepts that usually arise and the mental reactions to those concepts.

And, like all other vipassana meditation, when the intense examination carries you into the wordless, nonconceptual observation of what is happening, you drop the words, drop the labels, and just sit in the midst of change.

DEVELOPING A DAILY MEDITATION PRACTICE

The most effective daily regimen I have found is to combine the two primary practices presented here. You use metta meditation to prepare the mind for jhana and then use either the breath or the pure feeling of metta to carry you into the jhana state.

The advantage of using the breath is that it is a habit that most of us have developed and cultivated throughout our meditation career. It is something we already have. For most of us, when the mind is quiet it swings naturally to the breath. We have trained it to do that. The advantage of metta is the similarity between the pure feeling of metta, with its calm and joy, and the feelings that predominate in the jhana state.

Which you choose is a matter partly of your own personality. You use the one that works best for you. But remember to start with metta and, if you are going to switch to the breath, let metta make the mind still. Quite often the mind swings to the breath naturally out of habit. The switch should be gentle, if possible, occurring by itself.

You might begin with a formal recitation of your intentions. You want to really feel it in a personal way. It is often very effective when expressed in your own thoughts, your own private internal language, the way you normally talk to yourself inside your head. I often use something like this:

Let me clear my mind of all resentment, anger, and hatred. Let me banish all want and need and agitation. Let my mind be bright and awake and aware. Let it be filled with friendly feeling.

Let the clear mind experience clear Dhamma. Let my mind be filled with compassion. Let me have metta so that I can feel other people's suffering and my own joy. Let me have strength to practice without difficulties. Let me find peace and joy and give them to everyone.

I want to keep my mind alert throughout this session. I want to attain concentration. I honestly want to understand the Dhamma so that I can share my understanding of Dhamma with everybody. I don't have any ulterior motive. I do it for myself and everybody else. We all benefit.

I want my mind to be clear. I want everyone's mind to be clear. I want to find peace and joy for myself and everyone everywhere.

I am doing this for myself and everybody. I am clearing my mind to taste the peace and joy that lies down at the roots of my mind, down under the thoughts. I want peace and joy for myself and everyone. I want to see impermanence happening before the eye of wisdom so that I can be free and help everybody else become free too.

You may use any words you like to generate the friendly, peaceful thoughts in your mind. Make it real. The formal recitations are a good place to start, but your own thoughts often work better.

Remember your goal: to see the impermanence in all experience. Keep mindfulness bright and clear. Spot every hindrance that arises. Know which hindrance it is and see it when it is present. Use the tools presented in the next chapter to overcome each one. Watch it. Know when it is present and when it is no longer there. See its impermanence.

When the mind becomes quiet and still and joyous, let the attention glide to the breath or ride the pure feelings of peace and contentment and good will into jhana.

Stay with your object of attention. Rest the mind on it. Watch it. Watch for "the sign" to arise. (We will have more to say later about what exactly this means.) Watch yourself watching for it and notice your own desire or any other reaction. Stay with the object. Know peace.

Remember, jhana happens when it happens. It cannot be forced or rushed. Every apparent failure is a step toward success. When it doesn't happen as you want it to, use mindfulness to notice the feelings of frustration that arise. Every time you do that, you are strengthening your mindfulness and moving one step closer to the goal.

You cannot lose unless you give up.

6. Why Can't We Concentrate Strongly Right Now?

Why do we have to learn to concentrate? Why do we have to practice to develop a skill that, theoretically, should be a natural, built-in characteristic of the mind? The simple fact of the matter is that we have to do it because distractions arise to pull us off the track. These distractions get in our way and impede our progress along the path.

Our minds are filled with thoughts and emotions that we think are normal. They are powerful and alluring, even in small doses. They suck us right in and dominate our attention. They are distractions. The mind cannot focus in the presence of these disturbances.

Try not to think of a dinosaur.

Just for one minute, sit right there and do not think about a pink dinosaur. Think about a jet aircraft instead. Stop reading and do that right now.

Doesn't work very well, does it? The power of suggestion pulls us back to that pink dinosaur image pretty strongly, doesn't it? And, for most of us, a pink dinosaur is not something with which we are really obsessed. But how about paying the bills when your bank account is empty? How about sex and romance and your job and that guy who hates you? Those things are much more powerful. Have you ever tried to study or meditate after a tough day, when everything has gone wrong and you feel exhausted and confused? Very difficult.

The Pali suttas list five things that are the most powerful distractions for all of us. These hindrances interfere with our concentration, on the cushion or off.

Sensual desire. We see something and we want it, or we think of something and we want it. We want to be surrounded by good music. We want the room to be cooler or warmer. We want that new car. We want that great dinner. And we want them all right now. Once a thought like that enters the mind, it keeps coming back and back and back until we get what we want or despair of ever getting it. We obsess over it. We think about it night and day. We sacrifice the genuine good things in life for shiny baubles. The thoughts are incessant and obsessive. We cannot keep the mind on anything else for long.

Ill will (aversion). We hate being sick. We hate that nasty noise. We hate this food and we want something else. We wish that mean person who gives us such a rough time would go drop in a hole and vanish. Whenever life gives us something we really abhor, our mind gets stuck on it. It destroys our concentration power.

Restlessness and worry. We don't want to get cancer. It hasn't happened yet and it may never happen, but if it seems even remotely possible, we worry about it. We don't want to lose our job, or get a divorce, or be in a traffic accident. We worry and fret. We scheme how to get things and dwell on the possibility of not getting them. The thoughts keep us up at night and distract us from the good things right in front of us. Sometimes we just can't sit still, and we cannot even say why. Nervous anxiety fills us; the body trembles and the mind flits from one useless thing to another. We absolutely cannot concentrate in this state.

Sloth and torpor. Sometimes we are just too tired, mentally, physically, or both. Sleepiness feels sweet and we want it. We have just no drive or energy. Sometimes we just can't focus clearly. When we try to read, we read the same paragraph three times and it just does not make sense. When we try to meditate, the mind is like a swirling gray fog; everything is hazy and indistinct. So maybe we give up and go watch TV or something else that will pound its way in through the dullness. Concentration requires energy, vigor, clarity, and sharpness. In this state we just do not have it.

Doubt. Sometimes we start to meditate or do something else and we are full of indecision. We wonder, "Am I really getting anywhere with this? Is it really worth my time? How do I know if any of what I have been told is true? Am I doing it right? Am I doing it wrong?" There is just no certainty. The mind wavers and dithers and shies away from the task. We may put it off until we are totally sure of something or other. But total certainty in life seldom comes and the task never gets done. Sometimes life requires a bit of a gamble and a bit of trust. Without it we just can't keep the mind on one thing.

How the Hindrances Are Nourished

Hindrances appear as a result of three types of erroneous behavior: *wrong thoughts* (thoughts of greed, hatred, and cruelty); *wrong speech* (false speech, malicious speech, harsh speech, and gossip); and *wrong deeds* (killing, stealing, and misconduct in sensual pleasures).

In addition, there are some harmful habits that nourish hindrances:

Unmindful reflections. Whatever we dwell on embeds emotional responses in our minds. The repeated emotions turn into habits that trap us. We must pay attention to our habitual thoughts and the objects on which our perceptions habitually linger, or we contaminate the minds we are trying to cleanse.

Not listening to true Dhamma. It is not easy to escape from our trap. The route is subtle and easily misunderstood. We must examine the source of the ideas that we think are going to save us. Among other things, we must be sure that the source of the ideas has no hidden agenda. Many things can sound wonderful in words. To determine the worth of any particular system, we must carefully inspect what type of person that system actually produces. Systems that are spread through force, bigotry, or propaganda pressure are probably not going to move us in the direction of peace and wisdom.

Associating with unwholesome friends. We soak up ideas, attitudes, and actions from the people around us. We should seek to associate only with people who are equal to or better than we are.

CONCENTRATION AND MINDFULNESS BLOCK HINDRANCES

Concentration holds the hindrances at bay. Correspondingly, in order to achieve concentration, we must block these hindrances from our minds temporarily by using mindfulness. When we succeed in blocking the five hindrances, we experience a great relief. This relief slowly increases until it becomes joy.

Mindfulness and clear comprehension belong to the realm of the insight practice, but in order to practice jhana we must use mindfulness to overcome the obstacles to our concentration. The hindrances don't disappear automatically. Mindfulness and concentration must work together.

We must use mindfulness to know five things about the hindrances: when they are present; when they are absent; how they arise; how to let them go; how to prevent them from arising in the future.

TECHNIQUES FOR OVERCOMING HINDRANCES

When you are distracted by a hindrance during your meditation practice, take a moment to think about which hindrance is predominating in the mind. Then apply one or more of the methods in the list. We will look at all of these hindrances by looking at their symptoms, their nutriments (those factors that maintain the hindrances), and potential solutions to each one.

Sensual desire

Symptoms: Distracting thoughts about what you want to get, do, have, or attain. Most of our distracting thoughts have an element of wanting something to be different from the way it is. Planning is always like this. The thoughts are incessant and obsessive. You cannot keep the mind on anything else for long.

Nutriments: Giving frequent, unmindful attention to the thoughts in the desire category. The nourishment of sense desire is unmindful reflection, and the route to overcoming it is mindful reflection.

Solutions: You are dwelling on something. You cancel that by making the mind dwell on healthier things:

- *Pure mindfulness*—When a desire arises, notice that it is present. When it disappears, notice that it is absent.

- *Mindful reflection*—Generate a genuine, healthy desire to rise above this unmindful reflection and get rid of it. Generate its opposite, mindful reflection.

- *Self-encouragement*—You can actually talk silently to yourself, reminding yourself of wholesome intentions.

- *The Noble Eightfold Path*—The most direct way of getting rid of sense desire forever is the cultivation of the entire noble eightfold path. Recall the steps. Which one is lacking at this moment? Which one is most lacking in your life? Resolve to work on that.

Ill Will (Aversion)

Symptoms: When your thoughts reveal a motivation that is unkind or aggressive, even a little, you have ill will. In that condition you cannot appreciate the beauty of anything or anybody. When it reaches the level of grudge or hatred, you are like a pot of boiling water, very hot and confused. The thoughts are incessant and obsessive. You cannot keep your mind on anything else for long.

Nutriments: Dwelling on your angry thoughts. Ill will can start from a mild annoyance or some slight irritation. If you don't take care of it at that level, it gradually grows into aversion, resentment, anger, grudge, or hatred. This comes from unmindful reflection on the subject of your anger. You dwell on it. You contemplate it, think about it again and again. You feed it.

Solutions: Catch anger at the outset—Be mindful of it as soon as it arises. Don't let it build.

- *Isolate anger*—Isolate it in the mind as an event separate from the actions, persons, situations, or memories that trigger it. Let anger just mirror in your mind without being a person who is angry. Let it be just a pure energy.

- *Talk to yourself*—Give yourself a kind but thorough lecture.

- *Count breaths*—Count your breaths in the very special way described below.

- *"Homage to the Blissful One"*—Bring your respect for the Buddha and his teachings into play. Say, "Homage to the Blissful One, the Worthy One, the Fully Enlightened One." Say it three times. Remember the Buddha's infinite patience, compassion, and loving-friendliness.

- *Remember that your temper is dangerous*—and remember anger's miserable consequences.

- *Try to see the whole person*—Stop dwelling only on the negative aspects of the person or situation. Remember the good parts.

- *See impermanence and dependent origination*—Use anger to enhance your overall realization of the truth. See that anger and its causes are impermanent. Realize that anger and its causes are impermanent. See that anger arises dependent on causes and conditions.

- *Be kind to yourself*—Sometimes you are angry with yourself too. Forgive yourself. Recall your good qualities and what you are striving to become.

- *Remember that you will die*—Do you really want to pass away with this in your mind? Remember that, when you do or say something with anger to hurt somebody, you hurt yourself first. You hurt yourself even before you hurt the other.

- *Don't blame anybody*—Remember that it is just a situation. The other person has a viewpoint too and it looks as valid to him or her as yours looks to you.

- *Cultivate gratitude*—Use metta to cultivate gratitude toward everybody. It dissolves anger and ill will.

- *Talk to the pain*—Anger causes pain and pain causes anger. Talking to the pain, talking to your laziness, talking to aging, talking to fear—all these can be very useful and important.

Ill will is a very large topic. It's not just anger that sticks to us. It's things like sadness and fear and depression too. You can have ill will toward anything—the pain in your back or leg, the taste of your dinner, the house you live in or your salary. This section has presented remedies that apply to human relationships—your interactions with the people around you. But the general principles you have read on these pages apply to anything toward which you have aversion. I invite you to think about how you will apply what you have read to the real situations of your life—your illness, paying your taxes, and the death of your dearest friend.

Restlessness and Worry

Symptoms: You have "monkey mind," fear, tension, anxiety, and a nervous, jittery feeling manifest in a mind jumping continually from thought to thought. You just cannot settle down, mentally or physically. Sometimes it is all too subtle and you cannot pin it down. Sometimes it is so strong that you do not have enough focus to see any of it clearly.

Nutriment: Frequently giving careless attention to the thoughts of worry and the feelings of restlessness.

Solution: Count your breaths in the very special way described below.

Sloth and Torpor

Symptoms: Sloth and torpor is the traditional description given to all sleepy, lethargic, sluggish states of mind. *Sleepiness and drowsiness* is another common translation. Sometimes you are just too tired, mentally, physically, or both. Sleepiness feels sweet and you want it. You just have no drive or energy. Sometimes you just can't focus clearly. Concentration requires energy, vigor, clarity, and sharpness. In this state you just do not have it.

Nutriments: When you do mindfulness of breathing, body and mind become relaxed. You often feel sleepy and lethargic. Sleepiness is very sweet. You want to welcome it in, invite it to stay. But real joy does not arise from sleepiness or drowsiness. Don't deceive yourself by identifying the cloying sweetness of sleepiness with real joy. It makes you dull. You lose your energy. The Buddha said: "This Dhamma is for developing energy, not for developing laziness."

Solutions: Try one of the following techniques.

- *Mindful reflection*—In lethargy too, you must apply your cognitive form of mindful reflection. Conduct a silent monologue to rouse yourself, giving yourself encouragement and motivation.

- *Open your eyes*—Open your eyes and roll your eyeballs around for a few seconds. Close them and go back to your sitting mindfulness exercise.

- *Visualize a bright light*—Visualize a very bright light and focus your mind on it for a few seconds. As you are visualizing bright light, the sleepiness often fades away.

- *Hold your breath*—Take a deep breath and hold it as long as you can. Then slowly breathe out. Repeat this several times until your body warms up and perspires. Then return to your sitting practice.

- *Pinch your earlobes*—Pinch your earlobes hard with thumbs and index fingers. Really feel the pinch. Surprisingly, this can help.

- *Standing*—Stand up very slowly and very quietly. Try to do it so that even a person sitting next to you will not know. Do standing meditation for a few minutes until the sleepiness goes away. Once it is gone, return quietly to your sitting mindfulness practice.

- *Walking*—Do walking meditation for a few minutes until sleepiness disappears. Then return to your sitting practice.

- *Splash water*—Go and wash your face with cold water.

- *Rest*—Go take a nap for a few minutes. Sometimes sleepiness actually is a sign we may need sleep.

Doubt

Symptoms: You are uncertain about what you should be doing, in the moment or in your life. There is something you don't trust. You dwell on thoughts like "What?" "Why?" "Is it right?" "Is it wrong?"

Nutriment: Unmindful reflection on the thoughts of what you doubt. This is what sustains doubt. Having doubts is natural. Dwelling on the doubts so that they fill your mind and give you no peace—that is not natural. The solution to dwelling on doubt with unmindful reflection is to practice mindful reflection.

Solutions: Reflect mindfully on one of the following:

- *The Buddha*—The qualities of the Buddha, the Dhamma, and the Sangha.

- *The Dhamma*—Investigate the Dhamma and watch it work. Then think about what you have read and the changes you may have seen in yourself. You gain confidence from this and your doubt weakens. When you see and investigate the truth of Dhamma, your doubt gradually fades away.

- *Past success*—Any success you have had in overcoming greed, ill will, restlessness, and sleepiness.

BREATH COUNTING TO BLOCK HINDRANCES

In Buddhist cosmology, the demon Mara personifies unskillfulness, the "death" of the spiritual life. He is a tempter, distracting humans from practicing the spiritual life by making the mundane alluring or the negative seem positive. When the hindrances arise, you can use a skillful technique to defeat these armies of Mara by counting your breath in a very special way.

> Breathe in and out. Then count, *"One."*
> Breathe in and out. Then count, *"Two."*
> Breathe in and out. Then count, *"Three."*

Go on counting this way up to *ten*. Then count down from *ten* to *one*. Count up from *one* to *nine* and back down. Count up to *eight* and back to *one*. Then count up to *seven* and back to *one*. Continue decreasing the maximum number until you get to *one*. Then stay with one for a couple of seconds.

When you do this kind of counting, hindrances interfere. They take your mind away from your calculation. As soon as you realize that you are distracted, return to the counting.

When you have returned, maybe you have forgotten what number you last counted. Or maybe you don't remember whether you were counting in ascending order or descending order. Suppose you were distracted when you were at *six*. When you return, you don't remember whether you should go from *six* to *seven* or *six* to *five*.

Just start over. With kindness toward yourself, gently reprimand yourself. Make yourself repeat the entire counting all over again from the very beginning. When this happens to you a few times, you become determined not to let your mind go here and there. Then the mind stays on your breathing and you defeat Mara. Stop when you have full confidence in yourself and in your practice. Then go back to your normal meditation exercise.

How the Hindrances Are Eliminated

How do you "kill" a hindrance? You "watch it to death." You bathe it regularly in the fiery light of awareness and it melts away. You often don't notice hindrances dying. While you are doing the awareness process there is a sense of, "It's still there. It's still there. When will it ever go away?" But one day you say, "You know, I haven't seen such-and-such around lately. I wonder why? By George, it's gone at last!" We often see it when it is present and see it when it is gone, but fail to notice that "going away" stage in which it is becoming weaker and less frequent.

The hindrances are eliminated in three stages: *Stage one* is observing moral and ethical principles and restraining the senses. During this stage, gross expression of these tendencies is prevented from arising and the senses become relatively calm. This is the stage in which you employ mindful reflection by consciously thinking about the deep nature of what is meeting your senses.

Stage two is attaining jhana, during which the five hindrances are in abeyance. At this stage, conscious thought about the nature of your perceptions does not take place. Your senses are turned inward and recognition of the fundamental nature of your perceptions is wordless and automatic.

Stage three is final and complete. It is the attainment of full enlightenment. In this stage, all underlying tendencies are uprooted from the mind.

THE FETTERS

The fetters are underlying tendencies in the mind that act as the roots of the hindrances. The fetters are the roots and the hindrances are their offshoots. Desert plants must absorb every drop of precious moisture from the parched soil. To do this, the root system is often enormous, much larger than the portion of the plant we can see aboveground.

Fetters are also like cataracts in our eyes. When the mind is purified of hindrances by practicing jhana, it is like using eye drops to clear the eyes temporarily. But the ignorance is still there and confusion can arise again. Removal of these fetters is like surgically removing the cataracts from our eyes so that we can see perfectly again. When the fetters are removed from the mind's wisdom-eye, we can see the truth of the impermanence of all conditioned things. This leads to total freedom.

There are ten fetters, five lower fetters and five higher fetters. You will learn more about how the fetters are eliminated starting with chapter 12.

The Five Lower Fetters

Self—The view that you are a permanent self. The belief that some kind of "you-ness" lies at the center of your happiness. The idea that everything will be OK if you can get more things for "yourself" or get rid of certain situations or qualities or become different in some way.

Doubt—Fundamental doubts about the really important things, such as whether you can trust the Buddha, this Dhamma, and the Sangha. Doubts about the importance of morality. Doubts about key Buddhist doctrines such as the law of kamma and rebirth (not to be confused with reincarnation!).

Rites and rituals—The belief that you can free yourself by following set formulas and adhering to a particular belief system. Reliance on rites and rituals to do your spiritual work instead of finding the truth through your own efforts. Note that it is not just the *belief* in the rituals that does the harm, but the *attachment* to them.

Addiction to sensual pleasures—Believing that something or someone is going to come into your life and relieve the suffering that is inherent in all ordinary experience, that some pleasure will fundamentally change how you feel about yourself and the world.

Dependence upon hatred—Feeling that you can make everything all right by rejecting and attacking things.

The Five Higher Fetters

Desire for some fine material existence—Belief that continued existence in this world can relieve the inherent suffering that pervades all experience.

Desire for immaterial existence—Belief that everything will be OK if you continue to exist in some other state or place.

Conceit—Too much pride in yourself, a high and unjustified opinion of your own qualities and abilities. Self-involvement.

Restlessness—Always wanting things to change, never being satisfied with the moment.

Ignorance—Not seeing the world as it really is. Being blind to impermanence, suffering, selflessness, and the four noble truths.

DESTROYING IGNORANCE WITH JHANA

The fetters can be boiled down to three underlying tendencies—*greed*, *hatred*, and *delusion*. Of these, delusion or ignorance is the deepest. Ignorance cannot exist by itself. It needs to be fed. Its nourishment is the hindrances. When we hold the hindrances in abeyance, we can attain jhana. Concentration then weakens our greed, and greed is the principal cause of our suffering.

Then we use our jhanic concentration to gain wisdom, the knowledge of how things are at the deepest level. With the combined power of concentration and wisdom we fully eradicate the hindrances. Then we can rip the fetter of ignorance out by the roots.

The progression goes like this: you temporarily restrain the hindrances to attain jhana; then you use jhanic concentration to gain wisdom; with the combined power of your concentration and wisdom, you eradicate the fetters and begin to eliminate ignorance more easily from the roots; concentration weakens your greed, which is the cause of suffering; finally, wisdom and concentration weaken and destroy both the hindrances and the fetters altogether; when the hindrances and fetters are destroyed, destroying ignorance is easy.

The concentration gained by overcoming the hindrances is a very healthy state of mind that can be directed to comprehend reality. Here peace, happiness, and mental health are at their peak.

This clear understanding and very powerful concentration are united as a strong team to maintain perfect mental health. This is the reason the Buddha said, "Concentrated mind sees things as they really are."

SELF-TALK

I spoke before about "talking to the pain." We all have negativities arise that trouble us, on and off the cushion. Holding a conversation with yourself can be a very useful tool. What follows uses physical pain as an example of the kind of self-talk that can be useful for settling the mind in many situations.

When pain arises we must talk to the pain. We must say things like this:

> This pain is not something new. I have had this kind of pain before. It vanished after a while. This pain, too, is not permanent. It will vanish.
>
> I have suffered and suffered from pain—physical and psychological—that I have experienced throughout my entire life. All of it has passed eventually. My pain is not unique. All living beings are in one kind of pain or another.
>
> I must pay total undivided attention to this pain. The Buddha advised us to use pain as an object of meditation. It is one of the four establishments or foundations of mindfulness. He has advised us to know pleasant feeling as pleasant feeling, unpleasant feeling as unpleasant feeling, neither-pleasant-nor-unpleasant feeling as neither-pleasant-nor-unpleasant feeling.
>
> I must learn to be patient. The Buddha went through an enormous amount of pain when he was practicing meditation before his attainment of enlightenment. Even after the attainment of enlightenment he had pain. Once Devadatta threw a rock at

him and injured his foot. The Buddha tolerated it with patience.
    Pain is inevitable but suffering is avoidable. I should not suffer
from pain. I should use this pain in order to get rid of suffering.

In sports they say, "No pain, no gain." And really, there is no gain
without pain. It is even more so in spiritual practice. The Buddha
called it "upstream swimming."
    In "The Sword Simile" discourse the Buddha said,

> *Bhikkhus, even if bandits were to sever you savagely*
> *limb by limb with a two-handled saw,*
> *he who gave rise to a mind of hate toward them*
> *would not be carrying out my teaching.*
> *Herein, bhikkhus, you should train thus:*
> *"Our minds will remain unaffected,*
> *and we shall utter no evil words;*
> *we shall abide compassionate for their welfare,*
> *with a mind of loving-kindness, without inner hate.*
> *We shall abide pervading them*
> *with a mind imbued with loving-kindness;*
> *and starting with them,*
> *we shall abide pervading the all-encompassing world*
> *with a mind imbued with loving-kindness, abundant,*
>   *exalted,*
> *immeasurable, without hostility and without ill will."*

I highly recommend that you talk to the pain and the anger arising
from pain in this manner. Use your own words. With a bit of thought
you can modify this to other conditions that trouble you like the pain
of aging or divorce or the loss of a loved one.

You can talk to your laziness. You can talk to your fear and your anger and your greed. This kind of self-talk is very useful to get control of thought chains so you can function on the cushion and to direct your life.

7. The Purpose of Practice

*J*hanas can be an essential part of insight meditation. They can be used to develop the deepest possible insight into the essential features of our experiential world. The purpose of your meditation practice is to gain insight into the "three marks" of all existence: *anicca* (impermanence), *dukkha* (suffering), and *anatta* (selflessness).

Noticing changes without greed, hatred, and delusion is the essence of your mindfulness practice. Your breath and your feelings are tools. So too are your perceptions, attention, intention, and consciousness—they are all tools. They can help you understand impermanence. Once you are aware of change, you can find yourself longing for the power to stop the change. Every thought, every sensation—including the good ones, the ones you want to hang on to—they all slip away.

Unfortunately, you can't stop it. This is anicca, the impermanence of all existence.

And that makes you disappointed. You feel the unsatisfactoriness of this situation. This is dukkha, the inherently dissatisfying nature of all samsaric experience. You realize there is nothing that can stop the change, and then you also come to see there is no "myself" to do the stopping, and no essence of thing-out-there to do it to. This is anatta, the inherently selfless nature of all samsaric existence, the fact that everything you can identify as a discrete thing or activity is actually an accumulation of subcomponents and has no inherent existence of itself.

Thus, you come to experience the reality of impermanence, unsatisfactoriness, and selflessness. This is the knowledge and insight you gain from observing your own breathing, feelings, perceptions, intention, and consciousness. This is your mindfulness.

You practice it either on the cushion, or away from the cushion. You do it sitting, standing, walking, talking, and lying down. You do it while eating, drinking, wearing clothes, urinating, defecating, thinking, bending, stretching, running, writing, reading—performing any activity at all. It is all there for you to use for insight. You can notice the impermanence of anything you're engaged in, without using words or concepts to label those activities. Impermanence, unsatisfactoriness, and selflessness are not merely words or ideas. They are the intrinsic nature of all conditioned things.

This is the power of mindfulness. And jhana is where the pure truth of impermanence is seen deeply enough to carry over into all the other moments of your life.

Let's look at each of the three marks of existence in more detail.

IMPERMANENCE

Anicca is the Pali term for "impermanence" or "change." It's a word worth learning. It says more than its English translations. Anicca is not just a word or concept. *Anicca* is real. It is experience of what is actually going on in your body and mind.

Everything is changing constantly.

Yes, yes. You know this. You have heard all this before and you agree. The chair you are sitting in will one day fall apart and go to the junkyard. That is impermanence, right? Well, yes, it is. But only at the most superficial level. Knowledge of change at that level will not heal you; it will not free you; it lacks the power and clarity to carry you to liberation. Unless you gain strong concentration, you will never see it at the deep and subtle level that makes you free.

You need to sit in the place where the whole world of your experience is coming up and passing away so rapidly that there is just nothing to hang on to. Nothing lasts long enough for you to mentally glue it together into "something." As soon as you turn your attention to any occurrence, it goes "poof"! It vanishes as soon as pure awareness touches it. It all just comes up and goes away, leaving no trace. There is no time for such a trace to be left. As each thing comes up, it pushes the last thing out of the mind and there is no residue. You come out of this experience with no solid memory of anything that occurred. There is just the lingering impression of everything arising and passing away more rapidly than the mind can hold. This is termed "seeing things as they really are." You are not verbalizing or conceptualizing. You are just "seeing." This happens in the awareness of your deeply concentrated mind.

It all just comes up and goes away as a raging torrent without the slightest straw to grasp to keep you from drowning. Yet you do not drown. Because you are not really there. "Me" is just another "thing" that only exists when you glue your passing experience together in that artificial way. What does the seeing in this state is a calm, unruffled, pure *watchfulness* that does not get involved and does not exist as a thing. It just *watches*.

When you see things this way, you lose interest in trying to hold on to things. You see that it is futile and harmful and cannot lead to any truth or happiness. You lose interest in the attachment that you have to all those very, very crucially important things you worry about in your life—those things you just have to "get" in order to be happy; those worries you just have to sidestep to avoid unhappiness. It cannot be done. They are not really there to grasp or avoid. And you are not really there to do the grasping or avoiding. It is all just ceaseless change in action.

Grasping in this state is like trying to balance a tiny, tiny mustard seed on the tip of a moving needle. It is nearly impossible and why should you bother? Yet the desire is still present to grasp on to something pleasing and joyful and to run away from something disagreeable. You cannot do it and you see the futility. You realize, "This is the nature of my life. My body, my consciousness, all my ideas and memories and attitudes and wants and needs—they are all like this—fleeting, ephemeral and fruitless. Even 'I' am like this."

Why Is Seeing Impermanence So Important?

Impermanence is the slipperiest idea you have ever encountered and the most basic. It goes against everything you think you know about existence. The mind resists it both subtly and grossly. It slides into the mind easily and then slides right out again just as easily, without any impact. And it must have that impact. It is the basic idea you need to make you free.

You see things changing. You see it deeply down to the most incredibly fast, moment-by-moment level. Then you see it more broadly. You perceive it in everything you see and everything you ever could see. When you see anicca in all your experiences, your mind gets tired of this incessant change. This is the suffering, the dukkha, you experience in impermanence. This is the truth that the Buddha uncovered and expounded to us saying, "Whatever is impermanent, it is suffering."

Seeing suffering in all the aggregates of your experience, you become disenchanted. Being disenchanted you become dispassionate. Passion is the gluing nature of your mind. Passion is the glue that holds the self and the world together as apparent units of being.

When this gluing power is removed, there arises relinquishment, which leads to cessation of your suffering.

You apply mindfulness and attention without concepts. Ideas or thoughts are thorns, boils, wounds, and impediments. Without them you can focus the mind like a laser beam on the five aggregates. Then the mind can see that "I" exists only when the body, the feelings, the perceptions, the volitional formations, and the consciousness exist. They, in turn, exist within the parameters of impermanence. That burns everything. You don't find any "self" or "soul" or "I" in any of the aggregates.

Suppose you put many components together and make a flute. When you blow it, it produces a sweet sound. Suppose someone breaks this flute into little pieces. He burns each of them in search of the sound in the flute. He will never find the sound. You will never find the "I" in the aggregates. That is your discovery of anatta.

Not seeing impermanence, you tend to cling to impermanent things. You end up in suffering because impermanent things betray you when you try to hold on to them. They pull the rug out from under your feet. They deceive you. They make you believe that they are going to please you forever. They make you believe that they are going to give you permanent happiness, that your life is going to profoundly change forever when you have this solid, enduring thing or relationship or situation. They cheat you. They cannot stop changing, but they give you the impression that they will not change or pass. They tell you that you can enjoy their company forever.

When you see this undercurrent of unreality with the wisdom-eye, you are no longer confused. You no longer think they are going to make you happy forever. Seeing the impermanence of everything, you take precautions against their deceptive, constantly departing nature. At this stage, effort, mindfulness, and concentration work as a team to open your wisdom-eye so that you see everything related to the five aggregates as it really is. Supported by the luminous mind and shining with brilliant mindfulness, concentration and effort crack open the shell of ignorance. The wisdom-eye breaks in and dispels the darkness of ignorance. It sees the truths of selflessness, suffering, and impermanence as they really are.

Seeing Impermanence with Vipassana Awareness

There are two levels of seeing change. You can see it with vipassana awareness or with jhanic awareness. Let's look first at the vipassana experience of change.

You should begin every day with meditation, using your breath as the primary focus. As the breath becomes calm, subtle, and relaxed, the mind becomes calm and relaxed. The deeper you get into seeing this reality with unremitting energy, the more you will be filled with joy to see the truth unfolding within your experience in daily life.

Each moment is a new moment. Each moment is a fresh moment. Each moment brings you new insight and new understanding. You begin to see things that you have never seen before. You attain what you have never attained before. You see things from a totally new perspective. Each new experience brings you refreshing, calming, cooling joy and happiness.

Sometimes remarkable experiences accompany this new way of seeing the world. You may feel a calm and cool sensation spreading through your entire face, under your eyes, eyebrows, forehead, the middle of your head, and back of your head. You don't do anything artificial or deliberate to gain this happiness. It happens naturally when the conditions are ripe. Then you may experience a very subtle, very peaceful, but very sharp and clear vibration in your neck, shoulders, and chest area. As you go on breathing normally, simultaneous with this vibration, you may experience the expanding and contracting of the entire upper part of your body between the abdomen and the lower part of navel. You may experience every tiny little cell all over your body vibrating and changing, rising and falling with an inconceivable rapidity.

Not everybody feels this at the same points or in the same pattern. Some may experience this kind of phenomena elsewhere in the body or in another progression, or perhaps in a different way altogether. Do not go looking for this experience or think that something is wrong if you do not find it. The point is not the exact sequence of sensations. The point is what it means.

There is nothing static. Everything is dynamic. Everything is changing. Everything is appearing and disappearing. Feeling arises and passes away. Thought arises and passes away. Perception arises and passes away. Consciousness arises and passes away. You experience only changing. You cannot experience anything that is not changing.

Everything that you thought to be permanent is now seen to be impermanent and changing incessantly. You cannot make anything stay the same even for two consecutive moments. One moment seems to be pleasant and the mind wishes to keep it that way. Before the mind even makes this wish, it has changed. Mind moves with inconceivable rapidity. No matter how fast the mind moves to grab the pleasant experience, it changes before the mind reaches it. Its arising is like a dream. Millions of tiny little experiences arise and pass away before you blink your eyes. They are like lightening. No, much faster than that. You cannot keep up with their speed of change.

You may think, "Let me see the beginning, duration, and passing away of this experience."

Before this thought arises, the objects of your sense experience have arisen, reached their maturity, and passed away. Sometimes your mind can catch the beginning of an experience. But your mind cannot see the middle or the maturity of it. Or sometimes you may experience the middle of it but not the end of it. Sometimes you may experience the end of it but not the middle or the beginning. However, you are mindful of this change. That is good. At least you can notice the changes taking place. It is even better to notice how fast they change. You experience impermanence all day long, all night long, every waking moment. In samsara, everything is "permanently" impermanent.

At this point you may feel as if you are breathing with the rest of the world. You may feel every tiny little creature from little ants to great elephants, tiny fish to the giant whales, from small worms to huge pythons. All of them are breathing to your rhythm or you are breathing to theirs.

When you mindfully pay total attention to your body, feelings, perceptions, volitional formations, and consciousness, you experience every tiny little part of them constantly changing. When your mindfulness is established, your mind notices that every split second is new. Every molecule of your body, every feeling, perception, volitional formation, and consciousness itself—they are all changing incessantly, every split second. Your breath moves in and out with this change. Your feeling keeps changing. Your experience of this change—even that experience is changing too. Your attention and your intention to pay attention to notice the change are changing. Your awareness is changing.

When you hear a sound, you experience the change in the sound. You notice the change in any sound that hits your eardrum. If you keep paying attention to it, you notice that it is slowly changing. Similarly, any smell, any taste, any touch with the body—they all change constantly. Although they change all the time, you don't know that they change until you pay attention to them.

A feeling arises that depends on sight, sound, smell, taste, touch, and thought. This also changes. Any perception that arises and depends upon sight, sound, smell, taste, touch, and thought—this also changes. Any state of consciousness that arises and depends upon sight, sound, smell, taste, touch, and thought—this also changes. When you are paying attention to them, all of them change just like when you are paying attention to your breath. Your feeling of the breath, your perception of breath, your attention to breath, your intention to pay attention to breath, and your awareness of breath—they are all changing. They rise, change, and pass without ceasing.

SEEING IMPERMANENCE IN JHANA

You also need to see impermanence at a very deep level, the minute and inconspicuous changes taking place in every moment of consciousness. Before attaining jhana you know intellectually that everything is impermanent. When you experience jhana, you perceive impermanence at its most intense and subtlest level.

Before you gain right concentration, your awareness of the impermanence of all phenomena is shallow. Now it is very deep and powerful. You have left thought and sensation behind and your mind can penetrate impermanence more thoroughly than ever before. In jhana, the meditation subject as a *thing* has been left behind. The mind does not focus on any separate point beside its own collectedness. One-pointedness is the mind focusing on its own one-pointedness.

This is a preconceptual awareness, a state in which mindfulness, concentration, and equanimity work together in unison without being disturbed by any of your sensory stimuli. This is not thinking about impermanence. This is experiencing it directly. True insight wisdom comes from this experience, not from mere thinking.

What do you experience as impermanent? The jhana itself is all you see, and you see the impermanence of that. Your jhana comes and goes. The jhanic factors, like joy, happiness, equanimity, and one-pointedness, come and go and fluctuate. You clearly experience the impermanence of the jhanic factors themselves.

You see the impermanent nature of everything that fills your awareness, of all the jhanic factors. These realizations are not thoughts. They are dynamic actions or activities in the mind and body. The factors rise and fall and fluctuate and your awareness of that fluctuates along with them.

In jhana your mind is not being affected by greed, hate, delusion, or fear. At all other times words, ideas, concepts, or emotions interfere with your awareness of impermanence. Jhanic awareness is wordless. It is not thinking or speculation. It is not reflection or investigation. You have passed all that before you come to this level. This is the level where the mind sees things through the eye of wisdom. Words, thinking, investigation, or even reflection have no place. They would just get in the way. They are too slow and everything is moving too fast.

This is an experience of pure impermanence, the impermanence of the experiencing awareness itself.

SUFFERING

People ask, "Why don't we talk mainly about pleasure, joy, happiness, bliss, and peace instead of suffering?" Because suffering, *dukkha* in Pali, is important. It motivates us toward the practice that can make us truly free.

There *is*, of course, a certain degree of temporary pleasure in life. Life is certainly not without any pleasure. There is always some pleasure. But no pleasure comes without pain. What really dominates your life is not the pleasure, but the pain. Nearly everything you do in life is aimed at reducing and getting rid of this pain.

The Buddha gave a few examples of suffering. You must look at these examples impartially. If you get emotionally involved in the word "suffering," you simply suffer from your own misunderstanding and you dislike the subject without ever understanding what it is. Before we move into our discussion in detail of the jhanas, let's look directly at a few classes of suffering.

Birth is suffering. We enjoy our baby's birth. We celebrate it. Is that all we do with the baby's birth? We don't deny its pleasure and enjoyment. But is that all we have with the baby's birth? No, there are many more things.

Just imagine the amount of suffering the mother goes through during the pregnancy. Nine months she suffers emotionally and physically to take care of the fetus. Sometimes she enjoys thinking that she is going to have a baby. At the same time her anxiety is also growing. Her fear is growing. Her sense of insecurity is growing. Her discomfort is growing. The beauty she enjoys very much is changing.

At the delivery of the baby she suffers enormously. Some women die in childbirth. This is one fear many women have. They are also anxious about complications after birth. A woman never knows what kind of baby she is going to deliver—healthy, unhealthy, beautiful, ugly, intelligent, not so intelligent, one with criminal tendencies.

Once the baby is born, the mother and father must take care of the baby. They must sacrifice an enormous amount of their freedom, energy, and money to take care of the baby's education, well-being, happiness, peace, health, and general growth.

Meanwhile, is the baby totally free from suffering? Most of the time babies are born with a big cry. This cry continues throughout their lives—sometimes very loud, sometimes smoldering quietly inside them until it explodes with no notice.

Growth is suffering. Children have anxiety about growing. Adults have anxiety about growing. Children's growing is called growing and maturing. Adults' growing is called old age. At every step of growing, you have to make some adjustment, willingly or unwillingly. This adjustment is not always pleasurable. You have to accept changing situations and give up old habits. This is painful for anybody.

Sickness is suffering. You may think that sickness is suffering only when you are sick. When you are healthy you may treat a sick person in a most cruel way. You may hate the sickness. But it will come to you, too. Can you stop it with all kinds of insurance? No, you cannot stop sickness. It does not matter whether you are living in the most affluent country or the poorest country. You are subject to this. You can try to prevent some of the sickness but some comes to you whether you like it or not. This really is painful and it really is suffering.

Old age is suffering. When you are very young you may laugh at somebody when you see them trembling, walking unsteadily, talking with a tattered, wrinkled face and gray hair, not being able to cope with his own limbs. An old person cannot move as fast as he used to. He cannot talk as fast he used to. He cannot eat as much as he used to. His flesh and muscles are not as strong as they used to be. Eyesight is not good; hearing is not good. Teeth are not reliable. They fall out. They have to be replaced. He cannot do all the things he loved to do when he was young. Often there is pain. Is this not suffering?

Death is suffering. Although some people kill others, when it comes to their own death, everybody trembles. When the mind is totally distorted and in despair somebody may kill himself, but normally everybody is afraid of death. When somebody is living a long life he may say, "I am not afraid of death." This is true only when people are healthy and live long. When they come closer to death, they are afraid. We do everything to prevent death. This is the only truth we can never avoid. This is really painful and it really is suffering.

To be separated from loved ones is suffering. How many times have you experienced this reality in your own life? Have you felt this suffering when you separated from your friend? Your partner? Your parents? Your brothers? Sisters? Uncles? Aunts? Grandmother? Grandfather? Your sons? Your daughters? Your husband? Your wife? You could lose your job, or your ability to work at it. You could lose in a flood or a hurricane, for instance, all your property at once. And eventually, through trauma, disease, or, at the very least, aging, you can even lose control of your body and even your mind.

To be conjoined with an unloved one is suffering. You go to work. You have to work for somebody you hate. Is this pleasure? Your boss is very mean and giving you a very hard time. He treats you unfairly. Your landlord is very stingy. He does not fix your leaking roof. He increases your rent without giving you any additional service. Don't you think these situations are unpleasant?

Even to get what you want is suffering. Suppose you get a very expensive car. See how much you love it. But you must maintain it. You must insure it. While you are taking care of it, very much like you take care of your own life, somebody scratches it. You meet with an accident. This causes you lots of suffering.

All the five aggregates are suffering. Our aggregates—the constituents of our body and mind—are the home for all suffering. If the aggregates did not exist, no suffering would exist. The five aggregates are form, feeling, perception, volitional formations, and consciousness.

Form requires maintenance. Your body is a form. As everything is happening to the body you experience physical pain. You feel hunger so you eat. You feel the need to urinate so you urinate. You feel the need to defecate so you defecate. None of those things are very pleasant.

You experience heat, cold, and thirst. You must take care of them. You must wash the body. You must clothe it. You must take care of your physical health by eating right, exercising, and resting. You must do all these things every day.

In order to maintain this body you must have the means—money, a house, clothes, food, water, good air, and many more things. Without them you cannot maintain this body. You must work very hard to obtain all the means to support this body. This is suffering.

Feeling needs to be maintained in the same way. Every time your senses come in contact with their respective objects, this thing called feeling arises. You don't like unpleasant feeling. You always want the pleasant feeling. You always look for something that can give you happiness and avoid unhappiness. This is a real struggle. You eat, drink, sleep, rest, meditate, play games, sing, dance, and do many more things to make yourself happy. Nevertheless you still are not happy, are you? Come on, admit it. Your feelings are not easily satisfied. This is suffering.

Perception also needs to be maintained the same way. You always encounter conflicting perceptions. However you perceive something to be right now, it will change. And the change does not feel right. Somebody will come up with something that does not agree with your perception. You are in constant conflict with others with regard to your perceptions. This is suffering.

Volitional formation or thought creates more pain for you. Deciding is a problem. You think your decisions are perfect. Soon you find out somebody has made some other decision, which is approved by many and your own is looked down upon. They may think your mind is full of greed, hatred, and delusion, and with these emotional states, you have made the wrong decision. Their decisions have also been influenced by greed, hatred, fear, and confusion. Nobody seems to be able to make a clear and perfect decision. We keep changing our decisions, looking for new and better ones. This is suffering, too.

Consciousness is even trickier. You like to maintain a clear consciousness. Unfortunately, you cannot hold on to any consciousness for even two consecutive moments. As it is changing faster than the speed of light, you end up in frustration.

SELFLESSNESS

The Buddhist teaching of no-self says that the person I think I am is, in a certain way, not real, at least not in the way I conceive it and enact it in my daily life. But it's important to understand that this isn't a doctrine or a theory, it's just a description of what Buddhists generation after generation have verified as true. The "self" is an aggregation, a collection of subcomponents that can be broken down endlessly. Similarly, anything your mind can identify as a discrete item is actually an accumulation. There is no real self anywhere, not in you, not in anything you sense or can identify.

The term "no-self" points to a state beyond words. In our current condition, our attention catches or snags on most of the things we feel, perceive, and think. We want some things and hate other things and ignore everything else. Our lives are spent trying to get things, avoid things, achieve things, and run away from things. It all stems from a basic feeling of "I! Me! Mine!" We unconsciously think things like, "I am crucial. What I think and want and say is true and counts more than the opinions of others."

All religious traditions agree that selfishness lies somewhere near the root of our problems. No-self is a mode of perception in which "me" moves to the background and our attention flows smoothly through the world without snagging or catching on anything. Our attention is turned outward and we see things clearly. We are naturally attentive to the needs of others. We can learn this state of attention without changing our religious ideas at all.

The jhanas are particularly instructive in this respect. They are states of existence in which we move beyond our wants and needs and fears. We move into joy. We bring back peace and contentment to our lives and we find that we have not dissolved our personalities, gone crazy, or lost our souls. After that we may, if we wish, retain whatever concepts we wish about soul and afterlife and leave the philosophical hair-splitting to others.

Some historical background on selflessness may be helpful. The Buddha was born into Brahmanism, the religious context of ancient India. He saw clearly that the religion and philosophy of his society were simply not working. The doctrines were centered on the concepts of kamma and reincarnation and a hard-and-fast idea of the self, called *atman*. Religious activity was in the hands of a priestly caste called Brahmans. You needed to be born into this caste in order to interact with the gods, and the observances took the form of repetitive, empty rituals. Other castes essentially hired the Brahmans to perform the rituals. No one was getting even partially free except a few ascetics who lived in the forest and devoted themselves full time to yogic practices centered on austerities. The doctrine of atman was not setting people free. The Buddha saw this as a problem and taught the idea of *anatman* (literally, "no-self").

THE NO-SELF EXPERIENCE

So what is the experience of selflessness? It is simply the act of *not* seeing a collection of constantly shifting phenomena or perceptions as a single fixed entity. What is it really? It is actually a collection of phenomena or perceptions.

When we use the notion of self, we always use it in reference to forms, feelings, perceptions, volitional formations, and consciousness. Under very close examination, however, we don't find anything that can be identified as this "self." Although there is no such separate entity as "self," we use it as a conventional term to make our communication easy. Without using "I," "me," or "mine," our day-to-day communication becomes impossible. Just try it some time. Try to get your point across without ever referring to "me" or "I" or "mine." We need terms like "myself," "herself," "himself," or "itself" to say what we mean—and both the words and the concept of self are important for navigating the everyday world—but this does not mean that the collection of shifting things is a single fixed entity.

By seeing all forms, feelings, perceptions, volitional formations, and consciousness with the attitude, "This is not mine, this I am not, this is not my self," you can abandon the false notion of "I." It's not easy but it can be done. You can begin to escape from the delusion of self by viewing things like past, present, and future as mere conventions. Any comparative or evaluative thought is just a theory. That includes things like internal versus external, gross versus subtle, inferior versus superior, and far versus near. We have a widespread agreement to use these concepts, but that is all they are. They are concepts. You cannot find them. You cannot experience them. You can only think about them. Thinking in this way is very useful when applied to the exterior world. This is what has made humans the dominant species on the planet. But using such terms to apply to inner experience is fraught with hazards.

Have you ever *seen* Sunday or Monday? You say, "It is twelve o'clock." Have you ever seen "twelve o'clock," except on a dial in a clock? If you don't have a clock, how do you know it is twelve o'clock?

And how about the clock itself? When many parts are put together, you call it a clock. When those components are taken apart and separated, do you see a clock? No, all you see is a collection of pieces. The "clock" is a concept you use to refer to those pieces when they are put together in a particular way. You could take the same pieces and put them together some other way, to create an entirely different shape, and you would not perceive it as "a clock." The "self" is like that—a collection of components hanging together in a special way. Explore it, take it apart into its components, and it melts and disappears.

The scent of a lotus does not belong to the petals or to the stalk, or to the pistils. The scent belongs to the whole flower. Similarly, you speak of form, feelings, perceptions, volitional formations, and consciousness as "I am." You never speak of this "I am" apart from form, feelings, perception, volitional formations, or consciousness. "I am" is a concept that only applies to the entire collection of the aggregates. You only use "I" to refer to the whole assemblage when they are combined in a specific way. The notion "I am" exists in us only in relation to these five aggregates that are subject to clinging. Yet we do not regard any one thing among the aggregates as "This I am."

Suppose you send your clothes to a laundry to clean. They will clean them using various detergents. When the clothes are returned, you may find some lingering smell in the cloth. Then you put them in a sweet-scented drawer. The residual smell of cleaning vanishes. Similarly, when a person dwells contemplating the rise and fall of the five aggregates that are subject to clinging, a number of things are uprooted. The residual conceit "I am" is seen to be just that, a concept. The desire we call "mine" and the view we express as "myself" are both uprooted. They just fade, like the smell in the clothes.

At this point we have laid the groundwork in both theory and (hopefully) practice to be able to turn our full attentions to the jhanas in detail, and then later to how to cultivate and practice them.

8. The Jhana States

*A*s you practice jhana-oriented meditation, you move over time through a series of mental states that become more and more subtle as you proceed through them. You start where you are now and you go far, far beyond. You move beyond the range of concepts and sensory perceptions.

All human words and concepts are tied to perception. We depend heavily on vision and hearing as our primary perceptual mechanisms. We are tied to the realm of our senses and we have never known anything else. Even our abstract concepts are based on our perceptions. When we want to say we understand something, we usually say, "I see what you mean" or "I hear you." But what does "understand" mean when applied to a realm beyond vision, hearing, or any other material sense perception?

We really cannot talk about such things with any real precision. Our normal concepts just do not apply to the nonconceptual. Yet that is where the jhana states lead and we must use words to describe it. It is the only way we know how to communicate. As we proceed through the coming description of the jhana states, words become more and more metaphorical. It cannot be helped. All we have are the concepts of our perceptual realm, but we must keep in mind that we are not really telling the full truth. Only the experience itself will reveal the truth.

There are two categories of *mundane jhanas*. The states in the first category do not have names. They are simply numbered first, second, third, and fourth jhana. These are called the *material jhanas* or the *fine material jhanas*. Those who have attained these jhanas are called "those who live happily in this very life."

The second category is known as the *immaterial jhanas* because the meditation objects of these jhanas are pure concepts, not anything material. You center your mind upon a concept until it takes you into a direct, nonconceptual experience. Those who have attained these jhanas are called "those who are liberated and live in peace."

These two categories of mundane jhanas are followed by the *supramundane jhanas*, which we shall talk about in chapter 14.

THE MATERIAL JHANAS

The material jhanas are four states of experience that lie just beyond our ordinary cognitive, sensory world, but still have some relationship to it. Normal words can be used to describe some of the events and phenomena here, but we must remember that much is metaphorical. You "see" certain aspects of your experience, but it is not visual perception.

Some people can attain liberation without the material jhanas through the path of insight meditation alone.

The First Jhana

As you enter the first jhana, something remarkable happens. There is a total break with normal thought and perception. Your mind suddenly sinks into the breath and dwells. The breath is still there, but it is no longer a "thing," just a subtle thought, much like a memory or an afterimage. The world goes away. Physical pain goes away. You do not totally lose all sensation, but the physical senses are off in the background.

Wandering conscious thoughts stop. What remains are subtle thoughts of good will toward all beings.

Your mind is filled with rapture, bliss, and one-pointedness. "Rapture" or "joy" is like the leaping elation you feel when you finally get what you have been after. "Bliss" or "happiness" is like the rich, sustained satisfaction you feel when you have it. Joy may be physical, like hair rising all over your body. It may be momentary flashes or waves that shower you again and again. Happiness is more restrained, a gentle state of continuing ecstasy.

The Buddha offered a useful simile. A man has been wandering in the desert. He is on the verge of complete collapse due to dehydration. Bliss is like drinking all he wants and soaking in a bath of cool water. Happiness is like relaxing in the shade of a tree afterward.

The first taste of jhana is usually just a flash, but then you learn to sustain it for longer and longer periods. Eventually you can experience it whenever you meditate. It lasts as long as you have decided that it should last. In the first jhana, "joy" or "rapture" predominates.

You already put the hindrances on hold and let go of normal, conscious thought as you moved into the first jhana. Now it is time to let go of other things.

The Second Jhana
In the second jhana you drop even the subtle thought of the breath. The subtle thoughts of good will drop away. Your mind is now totally free of any verbal or conceptual thoughts, even that of the breath. All that remains is a subtle reflection of thought and sensation that is more like a memory or an afterimage. Joy predominates. There is happiness, mindfulness, and concentration.

The Third Jhana

It is hard to imagine that you could ever get bored with joy, but something like that takes place. Rapture is akin to excitement. It is coarse compared to the more subtle happiness and one-pointedness. Your mind turns toward bliss and one-pointedness in a way that is more delicate, refined, and stable.

Equanimity is growing. You gain a feeling of equanimity toward even the highest joy. It is just more material substance really. It is subtle, but it is still tying you to the hectic world of thought and the senses. You let it go and the joy fades away by itself.

In the third jhana, the more subtle "bliss" or "happiness" intensifies. It fills you and floods every cell of your body. Confidence rises. Mindfulness and concentration strengthen. The external world may be gone but body feeling is still present and it is wonderful. The body is very still. The breath is very gentle.

The Fourth Jhana

In the fourth jhana you go deeper still. You turn away from all mental states that would counter total stillness, even happiness. The turning away happens by itself, no effort required. Equanimity and one-pointedness get even stronger. Feelings of pain went away at the first jhana. In the fourth jhana, feelings of bodily pleasure go away, too. There is not a single thought. You feel sensation that is neither pleasant nor unpleasant. You rest in one-pointedness and equanimity. As your mind becomes progressively more still, your body and breath do the same. In the fourth jhana it feels like you have stopped breathing altogether. You cannot be roused. You emerge from the fourth jhana only at a predetermined time of your own choosing.

The fourth jhana is also the state in which mindfulness and concentration unite into an intense awareness that can penetrate deeply into the nature of existence. This is the ideal state in which to directly perceive the three primary qualities of all ordinary existence: anicca, dukkha, and anatta. You passed through jhanas one through three, simply allowing them to develop and pass. You pause at the fourth jhana. You *use* the state to see deeply into impermanence, suffering, and no-self.

THE IMMATERIAL JHANAS

The immaterial jhanas are four states that have very little relationship to our ordinary cognitive/sensory world. Normal words simply do not apply. These are called the "formless" jhanas. The first four jhanas are attained by concentration on a material form or the feeling generated by certain concepts such as loving-friendliness. You attain the formless states of the immaterial jhanas by passing beyond all perception of form.

To move into the first four jhanas, the mind turned away from one thing after another. To enter each successive formless jhana, you substitute one thing for another. You turn your attention toward ever more subtle objects of awareness. There is one-pointedness and equanimity in each of these states, but at each level they become more refined. Concentration gets stronger and steadier. No one can rouse you. You come out of jhana at a time you have predetermined for yourself.

The immaterial jhanas are not usually numbered. Each has an individual name that describes the sphere of awareness that the mind occupies or dwells upon. We give them numbers here just to show their order.

The Fifth Jhana: The Base of Infinite Space

Everything that happens in the mind can be thought of as existing "somewhere," as if in a mental space. You turn your attention away from the characteristics of whatever is in the mind and toward the "space" it occupies. This infinite space is your object of contemplation.

Anything you attend to could be likened to a signal being carried on some medium of communication. You turn your attention away from the signal and toward the carrier wave that conveys it. The mind as a space, medium, channel, or vehicle is your object of awareness.

Equanimity and one-pointedness now mature fully. You find yourself in a realm where all perception of form has ceased. You cannot be disturbed or disrupted from the outside, but the tiniest suggestion of the material senses remain. You ignore them totally, but if you turn your attention to any of them, the jhana is lost.

The Sixth Jhana: The Base of Infinite Awareness

Awareness of infinite space requires infinite awareness. You turn your attention toward that immeasurable alertness. The thought of infinite space drops away and what is left is infinite awareness without an object. You dwell in boundless consciousness, pure awareness of awareness.

The Seventh Jhana: The Base of Nothingness

The next jhana is often called the "base of nothingness." The infinite awareness of the previous jhana has no object. It is empty, vacant, and void. You turn your awareness toward this emptiness. The seventh jhana is pure focus upon no-thing-ness. Your awareness dwells on the absence of any object.

The Eighth Jhana:
The Base of Neither Perception nor Nonperception

Perception of no-thing-ness is still perception. Your mind gets bored even with that and swings away from any perception at all. Total absence of perception is sublime.

You turn your attention away from perception of the void and toward the peacefulness of total nonperception. If there is the slightest hint of desire to attain this serenity or to avoid the awareness of void, the transition will not occur.

There is no gross perception going on, yet there is still super-subtle awareness of the state itself. The eighth jhana is called "neither perception nor nonperception."

THE SUPRAMUNDANE JHANAS

The supramundane jhana states are an absolute prerequisite to liberation. They take place at the end of both the insight meditation path and the jhana path. The supramundane is where the two paths merge.

In this series of states, the fetters, deep-rooted tendencies of the mind that bind you, are burned away without a trace. This is where the meditator does the final work of escaping from samsara.

These states sound truly remarkable and appealing, do they not? But how do we get there? We'll start to answer that question with the next chapter.

9. Access Concentration

The transition point from nonjhana to jhana states is called *access concentration*. You don't find the term "access concentration" in the early Pali texts. But there *is* a state just before full concentration and we use the term "access concentration" to express that state. Access concentration is compared to the soft, weak muscles of a baby trying to learn to stand on his own feet. The baby's legs are not yet strong enough to stand, so he falls back on the ground.

You use the state of access concentration to battle and subdue the hindrances. Applying mindfulness in the state of access concentration allows you to step aside from each hindrance to deep concentration and put it temporarily on hold. Do that often enough over a long enough period and the hindrances "go to sleep." They are just mental habits and you have replaced them with the habit of mindfulness. In access concentration, the hindrances are restrained and generosity, loving-friendliness, compassion, joy, happiness, and concentration have arisen. Most meditators practice in access concentration for a good while before attaining jhana.

CHOOSING A MEDITATION SUBJECT

No single subject of meditation is suitable for every person. The Buddha recommended many different subjects of meditation to many different individuals, according to their needs. He knew that not every person makes progress at the same speed or at the same time. The Buddha has given you full freedom to determine how long you should do sitting meditation, walking meditation, lying down meditation, and standing meditation. In the entire teaching of the Buddha you can see that he always recognized individual differences and gave instructions according to these differences. He always showed how all these different methods lead to the same goal—attaining full liberation from suffering and entry into the perfect peace and bliss of emancipation. You may wish to seek the guidance of a teacher to arrive at a suitable meditation object for you.

Once that person has attained a jhana, no matter what object has been used for attaining it, the jhanic qualities are the same. The same object can also be used for both concentration meditation and insight meditation. For instance, the breath is often used for both. Pali literature mentions forty common meditation objects.

For the sake of convenience, in this book I usually describe the breath as our object of meditation. Most of what I say about the breath as a meditative phenomenon applies to other subjects, too.

A useful alternative to focusing on the breath is focusing on what is called a *kasina*. A kasina—the word means the "entirety"—is a physical object used as a meditation focus. Traditionally, these were circles used to represent certain concepts. Many were made of earth with coloring added. A traditional kasina was approximately nine inches in diameter. These objects are seldom used today, but they were a traditional method used at the time of the Buddha.

Today, *kasina* means "an object that represents a pure concept, the essence of all things with that quality." There are ten traditional kasinas, including colors and the four elements. Different people, depending on their particular inclination, use kasinas representing water, fire, air, blue, red, white, space, or consciousness. Each kasina represents a pure concept, the entire quality of something, the essence. The blue kasina represents blueness, the quality that is common to all blue objects—light blue, dark blue, royal, or aquamarine. All the shades of blue are included in this perception of blueness. Each of the kasinas represents a basic reaction in the mind, what your mind will do whenever you see anything that has the quality of blueness, yellowness, the liquidity of the water element, or any finite space.

You should select one meditation object and stay with it. Don't jump from object to object. Mixing up the object can confuse your mind. Suppose somebody asks you to dig a hundred-foot-deep hole in the ground to get water. You could dig ten holes each ten feet deep or twenty-five holes each four feet deep. You could then say logically that you have dug a hundred feet worth of holes. However, you would not get water. You should dig one hole, one hundred feet deep. Only then can you get water. Similarly, by trying all the meditation subjects, you could say logically that you have tried all of them but nothing worked for you.

When focusing on a meditation object, your objective is not to "become one with the object" and thus become deadened or stupid. Instead, you use these objects to gain a high degree of concentration by expanding each one everywhere—above, below, and across—making it undivided and immeasurable. The whole of your experiential world is filled with the quality that the kasina represents. Someone who contemplates deeply upon the earth kasina, for instance, fills his or her experiential universe with the quality of solidity. Such a person is said to be able to walk on water because the mind perceives everything everywhere as solid. Nevertheless, the person is not "one with" or "totally absorbed in" the kasina. He still perceives the external and internal universe.

Meditation objects are like launching pads. Once you have gained jhana, everything that follows after that is the same. The concentrated mind is on its own, alone, dependent upon nothing external. Whatever object has been used for abandoning hindrances and gaining concentration is left behind.

Imagine a swimming instructor encouraging a child to hold on to a kickboard in a shallow swimming pool. He wants to teach the child to float on the water. When the child is reasonably comfortable kicking in the water, the instructor slowly removes the board. Then the child gradually learns to float without the support of the kickboard. The subject of meditation is like the kickboard. It is used until the skill is built and then abandoned.

The Entry Point

If you have ever tried even a single period of meditation, you already know the initial stage. It is our normal mind.

Your focus wanders and wavers. The breath is there for you occasionally, but you keep losing it and you go off into daydreams and memories and imaginary conversations with who knows who. You notice the wandering and you pull yourself back to the focus. You fluctuate, vacillate, and swing back and forth between the breath and who knows what—distracting thoughts, feelings, and sensations.

Your first milestone comes when you detach from the world just a bit. The outer world with its sounds and sensations drifts into the background. They are still there, but they bother you less. Your thoughts are still there too, but they are quieter and they pull you away less often. You hear things, smell things, think things, but that does not disturb you so much. Some peace is present now and then. Your body becomes more and more still. You know you are headed in the right direction. Your mind begins to linger on the breath for short periods. You can feel yourself getting better at pulling it back.

This is the place where you usually start to have some real insights about your thought process. These thoughts and sensations really are annoying things! They really are disturbing. It is not a theory. The calm one-pointed focus is so much nicer. Eventually even nice thoughts are a bother compared to calm.

You start to see the hindrances too. Whether you call them that or not, you notice that certain thoughts and sensations are more jarring than others and you start learning to let them go, to let the hindrances pass without grabbing on to them.

CONCENTRATION STRENGTHENS

After a period of effort comes a noticeable strengthening of concentration. The mental attributes that will eventually mature into jhana—things like one-pointedness and bliss—become quite noticeable. This is your first major attainment. It is a state on the brink of genuine jhana. It is called "access" concentration because it is the doorway to the real thing.

Concentration is still unsteady but your mind keeps trying and it is getting easier. You fluctuate between your calm focus and your inner dialogue. You are still open to your senses. You hear and feel in the normal way, but it is off in the background. The breath is a dominant thought—an object, a thing—but it is not your sole focus. Strong feelings of zest or delight set in. There is happiness, satisfaction, and a special state of nonpreference called equanimity. They are very weak, but they begin to arise. They will mature.

Your attention touches the breath repeatedly, strikes at it, flicks away, and then begins to dwell upon it. You may feel lightness or floating. In the mind's eye you may see shimmering forms or flickers of light. These are not visual phenomena in the eyes. These phenomena are totally in the mind.

This is the realm of visions. If a deity or an entity is ever going to speak to you, this is where it will happen. Your normal thought patterns are being disrupted and deep imagery can come forth. Your visions may be beautiful or terrifying or just strange kaleidoscopic sequences without meaning. Whatever they are, you just let them be there and bring the mind back to the breath. They are nothing special, just more discursive thought in disguise.

ACCESS CONCENTRATION AND THE BREATH

As you continue to breathe, take note of the beginning, middle, and end of each inhalation, followed by a brief pause. Then note the beginning, middle, and end of each exhalation. This will assure that your mindfulness is strong as you approach jhana. If you do not pay careful, mindful attention, you will not be able to discern these separate stages in each breath. Each of these stages should be noticed at the place where you feel the touch of the breath. For that reason, it's very important to really find the place where the breath touches before jhana develops, and pay total mindful attention to that particular spot. By paying total attention, you also can notice the intrinsic nature of any phenomena as they arise.

As your breath becomes subtler and subtler, the details begin to be unnoticeable. Finally they disappear altogether, and the mind naturally stays only at the place where you noticed the touch of the breath. At that point, you begin to experience inhaling and exhaling as one single sensation.

Don't follow the breath all the way into the lungs or out of the nose. Just stay right with that one sensation.

The technique is like a person with a stiff neck pushing a baby on a swing. He cannot move his head, so he keeps it straight. When the swing comes right in front of him he taps it. The swing goes in the direction of his tap. When it comes back he taps it again in the other direction. It moves in the other direction. Keep your attention on the breath-spot. Do not follow the movement.

Here is another analogy. Imagine an electronic sensor mounted on a wall. Every time someone approaches this sensor, a light comes on. As soon as the person has passed by, the light goes off. Similarly, every time you inhale or exhale, your mind notices the sensation of your inhaling or exhaling at the place where the breath touches. It simply registers the sensation without following the movement.

Each time the mind wanders away from the breathing, you bring it back and keep it at the touch-point. Repeat that process, as often as necessary, until the mind stays easily with the breath, as it flows in and out, passing the place where you established your attention. Then you will be able to see every tiny part of the breath.

As you watch every part of your breath, it eventually becomes subtler and subtler until you cannot even notice its movement. All you notice is a strong but pleasant sensation at the place where you established your attention. First the mind lets go of noticing the beginning, middle, and end of the breath. Then the mind focuses only on the inhaling and exhaling. Finally, even the subtle breath is replaced by just that strong sensation at the touch-point.

Breathing in and out, you experience the feeling of your breath. And as the breath changes, so does the feeling. You perceive the changing breath and the changing feeling. The thought, "This is the breath—this feeling, this perception," is called *volitional formation*. You intentionally (or "volitionally") pay attention to the breath and its sensations. Your awareness or consciousness also changes as your breath, feeling, perception, and thought change. You realize that any state of consciousness also changes, whether it arises dependent upon sight, sound, smell, taste, touch, or thought.

While noticing the impermanence of breath, if the mind goes to a sound, notice the impermanence of the sound. Ignore your emotional or conceptual response to it. Just spot the impermanence. It comes and it goes. There is sound and then silence.

If the mind swings to a feeling, notice the impermanence of that feeling. If your mind fastens on a perception, notice the impermanence. If the mind goes to your own attention, notice the impermanence of attention itself. In other words, you pay attention to the impermanence of everything you experience, even your own paying attention. When the mind becomes stable and does not go to anything other than the breath, you stay with the breath and notice the impermanence of that alone.

When all the hindrances have subsided, joy arises. Develop that joy further and let go of your restlessness. Let the joy spread all through your mind and body. This is a right thought, too.

Pin your attention to the simple sensation of breath at the nostrils. Stay with it as the breath naturally slows down and becomes fine and light. Allow thoughts of the breath to drop away. Stay with the simple sensation. Just let the process happen. Don't try to rush it.

APPROACHING THE FIRST JHANA

In access concentration some interesting phenomena take place. People report dreamlike experiences and strange sensations of rising or floating or flowing. Some people report visions, but you should neither chase after these kinds of things nor worry if they do or don't come. Your attention is coming back to the object of meditation again and again, touching it and swinging away, then hovering around it closer and closer. As the first jhana approaches, there is a stage when your attention "sinks into" the meditation subject.

You attain the first jhana with the beautiful pleasant feeling arisen from having restrained hindrances and practicing metta. Your joy and happiness arise from being separated from all your physical worldly activities and from the hindrances that arise from those things. Now you can take a deep breath and relax. You can sit down quietly and enjoy the solitude and peace.

Even though your concentration in the first jhana is not very deep, you enjoy the freedom from all the hustles and bustles of worldly life. Concentration and equanimity are there too, though these two factors are not prominent in the first jhana. There is also one-pointedness or unification of mind. In the first jhana the joy and happiness you feel arise from seclusion and from the absence of the hindrances.

Some teachers lay a lot of emphasis on the importance of using the sensation of delight as a tool to enter jhana.

They recommend that, if you feel this delight only in one location, you should enlarge it. The whole body should be bathed and satu-rated with the feeling of bliss. This is a physical sensation, though not the kind that you are familiar with in ordinary life. It is similar to an extremely pleasurable sensory phenomenon, but not identical, far more subtle and gratifying.

You can take control of this feeling and, to some extent, direct it. Once you have learned to concentrate, you can get to the delightful sensation any time you wish and stay in it as long as you wish.

For instance, when doing the metta meditation described in chap-ter 4, feelings in the center of the chest may occur. This is usually a very enjoyable feeling of bodily warmth. As soon as it comes, you should let go of the metta practice, place your entire concentra-tion on the sensation, and expand it to suffuse the entire body. This physical feeling is similar to the more subtle feelings of joy and bliss in jhana. This feeling can be used as a bridge to allow you to slide naturally into jhana.

When you have taken care of all the hindrances, the breath becomes very subtle. You may not even feel it. You may think it has stopped. There is nothing to worry about. It is still going on. When all the disturbing factors are gone, the mind returns naturally to the breath. When breath becomes subtle enough that it is unnoticeable, your mind focuses on the memory of this subtle breath as your object for gaining concentration.

Watch for the sensation to change into a kind of vivid afterimage. Stay with that. Keep at it. Be persistent. This memory may then be replaced with a little spark of light. If so, that becomes your focus of attention. This is a very important moment, the moment just before true concentration. This spark is your signal. You are about to enter jhana.

At the beginning there may be just a fleeting experience that can be very hard to identify. The first time there may be just a strange, indefinable discontinuity that often evokes a startled, "What was that? What just happened?" Do not question such experiences. Any verbalized pondering will just lead you away from the goal. Just stay with your concentration practice. If some strange experience arises that you think might be jhana, pay no attention. When real jhana arises, you will know what it is.

If all goes well, in the next moment after experiencing the spark, you gain genuine jhanic concentration and hold it. There are thoughts of generosity, friendliness, and compassion that you have already cultivated by overcoming greed, hatred, and cruelty. They are not really "thoughts." You experience just the shadow of the generosity, friendliness, and compassion that are holding greed, hatred, and aversion at bay. The joy, happiness, and concentration in jhana have restrained drowsiness, restlessness, and doubt.

10. The First Jhana

*W*hen you enter the first jhana you are still in touch with your physical senses. Your eyes are closed but you can still hear, smell, feel, and taste. This is one definite indication of the first jhana, as opposed to others.

You don't fully lose thought either. Thoughts come now and again. Since you have been thinking all your life, your thoughts do not disappear all of a sudden at the attainment of the first jhana. They are like nervous habits—difficult to wipe out at once. They continue to haunt your mind periodically. Just ignore them. They are one of the things that will pull you out of jhana. You want to be able to maintain it as long as you wish.

This passage describes the moment you enter the first jhana with all the jhanic factors and qualities:

> *Quiet, secluded from sense pleasures, secluded from*
> *unwholesome states of mind,*
> *one enters and dwells in the first jhana,*
> *which is accompanied by applied thought and sustained*
> *thought,*
> *with rapture and happiness born of seclusion.*

A DIFFERENT KIND OF JOY

When you finally overcome the five hindrances, you experience a great relief. This relief slowly increases until it culminates in *piti*, joy. This joy is purely internal. It does not arise dependent on worldly or household pleasure. Nothing outside you causes it. It arises through renouncing outward pleasure.

This joy is called "nonsensual joy." It does not gush into the mind suddenly. You have been experiencing pain arising from the hindrances for a long time. You have been working very hard to overcome those that have caused you pain. Now, every time you overcome one of them, you experience a great relief that that particular pain has subsided. It is this relief, this freedom from that particular hindrance, that brings you joy. Now you no longer have the pain caused by that particular hindrance. It is gone. You rejoice.

This is the state that the Buddha explained to Ajatasattu in the *Samaññaphala Sutta*:

> But when he sees that these five hindrances
> have been abandoned within himself,
> he regards that as freedom from debt,
> as good health, as release from prison,
> as freedom from slavery, as a place of safety.

> When he sees that these five hindrances
> have been abandoned within himself, gladness arises.
> When he is gladdened, rapture arises.
> When his mind is filled with rapture,
> his body becomes tranquil.
> Tranquil in body, he experiences happiness.
> Being happy, his mind becomes concentrated.

Because the hindrances have been overcome, your joy continues to increase. It arises cumulatively, slowly filling up the entire mind and body. This is the stage where you feel that your entire body and mind are diffused with joy and happiness like sugar or milk or salt mixed with water.

The ordinary, material joy we are accustomed to arises from contacting things that are desired, agreeable, gratifying, and associated with worldliness. They are simple, basic things like seeing forms, hearing sounds, smelling smells, tasting tastes, touching tangibles, and thinking mind-objects. This is called *joy based on the household life.*

When you seek and know the impermanence, the change, the fading away, and the cessation of all these things, a different joy arises. You perceive the forms, sounds, smells, tastes, touches, and mind-objects as they actually are. You see with proper wisdom. You know they are all impermanent, suffering, and subject to change. You see that they are like this now and that they always were. Then a new joy arises. This is called *joy based on renunciation.*

So you overcome joy based on the household life by the joy based on renunciation that is attained in jhana. You can overcome grief based on the household life by the grief based on renunciation, too. You can grieve for the loss of your dog or your car or you can grieve over the unsatisfactoriness of all phenomena. One leads to further involvement with the source of grief and the other leads away from that involvement.

You overcome equanimity based on the household life by equanimity based on renunciation. Although equanimity is the ideally balanced state of mind, as long as it arises based on household life, it still is diversified. It is conditioned by individual things and circumstances. But the equanimity that arises in jhanic attainment is unified. It is based on the natural unity or one-pointedness of mind. It is based on concentration. This is the highest kind of equanimity.

To regard all your children as exactly equal and treat them all just the same is a wonderful worldly goal. To regard every experience—good or bad—as equal lies beyond that.

THE FIVE JHANIC FACTORS

Mindfulness is present in your jhana. You are awake. You notice (mindfulness) and recognize (clear comprehension) the components of your own experience. You do not notice the external world, but you are fully awake to the jhanic factors that comprise your internal experience. You are mindful of what is present, the five jhanic factors.

A "factor" is a feature or aspect of something. It is a dynamic thing, often a cause of something else, often something you must do or have to make that second thing come into existence. In this case, it is something that must be present for enlightenment to take place. It is also a quality that every enlightened being displays.

These five factors hold the first jhana together: *Vitakka*—Laying hold of a thought with applied attention. It is a directed thrust of the mind, a turning of attention toward a meditation subject, such as the right thoughts of renunciation, loving-friendliness, and compassion. Some English translators have called vitakka "initial thought," but not in the normal sense of those words. Vitakka lies beyond normal "monkey mind" cognitive thought. It is likened to the striking of a bell.

Vicara—Maintaining right thoughts with sustained application. Often rendered as "discursive thought," vicara is the mind roaming about or moving back and forth over thoughts. It is a sustained dwelling upon the meditation subject. It is likened to the reverberation or resounding of the bell after it is struck.

Piti—Sometimes translated as "joy," "rapture," "enthusiasm," "interest," or "zest." It is not a physical feeling. It may be described psychologically as "joyful interest." A high degree of piti is present in the first few jhanas. It is strongest in the second jhana.

Sukha—Sometimes translated as "happiness," "pleasure," or "bliss." It may be either a physical or a mental feeling. Sukha is an indispensable condition for attaining jhana. It is present in the first, second, and third jhanas and is strongest in the third.

Ekagatta—One-pointedness; unification of mind. It implies serenity and tranquility as well as single-pointed concentration.

Right Thoughts

Let's look more closely at the first two jhanic factors, vitakka and vicara.

In the first jhana, three *right thoughts* must be cultivated with applied thought (vitakka) and their opposites must be abandoned. When maintained with sustained application (vicara), these thoughts will become perfectly pure at the attainment of the supramundane jhanas and full enlightenment.

In jhana, these right thoughts buffer the mind, hold the hindrances at bay, and keep them from entering. They have the function of guarding the mind without clinging, keeping it steady and peaceful. This is not the kind of guarding where you hold something to your chest to keep anyone else from taking it. That is greed. This is a gentle, nongrasping function. What you are guarding is your own greedlessness. You hold it gently, like a baby.

The three right thoughts are renunciation, loving-friendliness (metta), and noncruelty (compassion). Let's look more deeply at each.

The First Vitakka: Renunciation

Renunciation begins with the thought of generosity. You are not attached to worldly wealth, position, and power. You renounce them.

You let them go. You give them away. You do not need them and you are happier without them.

The first step toward practicing generosity is giving up the desire to hold on to your trivial material possessions. This is what you do every time you let go of some petty thing and give it away for someone else to enjoy.

The second step is to cultivate the thought of abandoning your indulgence in sensual pleasure in both words and deeds. This is what you do temporarily when you go off to a meditation retreat. This is what you do in miniature every time you sit to meditate.

The third step is cultivating the thought of not getting involved with sensual pleasures, at least during your meditation. Abandoning the thought of desire for sensual pleasures by cultivating the resolve toward renunciation is called *factorial replacement*. It is replacing one thing with another, smothering one impulse by instilling its opposite.

Before he attained enlightenment, the Buddha divided his thoughts into two classes. He put the thoughts of sensual desires, thoughts of ill will, and thoughts of cruelty in one class and the thoughts of renunciation, friendliness, and compassion in the other class. When he noticed that one of the thoughts belonging to the negative category arose in him, he became fully aware of it and mindfully reflected that this particular thought was harmful to him, harmful to others, and harmful to both. Then that particular thought subsided. When another unwholesome thought arose in him, he used the same technique to overcome that thought. By this "mindful reflection" he abandoned negative thoughts one by one.

On the other hand, when thoughts of renunciation, friendliness, and compassion arose in him, the Buddha became mindful of their arising. Then he reflected that these thoughts aid wisdom. They do not cause difficulties. When he spent days and nights reflecting on these wholesome thoughts, the Buddha felt secure. There was no longer anything to fear from their opposites.

The Buddha's instruction is that you should do the same. As a result of the right thought of renunciation, the mind becomes very calm, relaxed, and peaceful. It has no concern for anything in the world. You just let things go. You pay no attention. Your clinging and craving for ordinary things subside.

The Second Vitakka: Loving-Friendliness

You have seen the danger of ill will. You have been cultivating the habit of not harboring ill will toward anybody. You have learned from experience how much you have suffered from your own ill will and that of others. After applying appropriate remedies you have succeeded in letting go of your anger and cultivating loving-friendliness. You take another deep breath of relief.

Generally, the last hindrance to leave the mind is hatred. When it is gone, metta arises naturally. The void is filled with feelings of friendliness toward everyone. When you no longer push things away, you naturally feel close to everything. You feel positive toward everybody. Everybody is your friend.

The Third Vitakka: Noncruelty

With the arising of this, you are now very glad that you are no longer cruel to people or animals. You have seen beings suffering from cruelty. You know quite well how animals and people suffer at the hands of cruel people. Having witnessed for yourself other people's cruelty, you may have felt the pain of the victims in your own heart. So you have decided not to be cruel and to cultivate compassion for all living beings.

Now you are totally at peace. You feel totally secure. You have no fear that anyone will hurt you. Thoughts of cruelty fade and you no longer have any desire to hurt or punish anyone. The natural result is compassion. You naturally feel and identify with the struggles others are going through and you have a natural desire to help them however you can. Your heart pours out to suffering beings everywhere.

The Importance of Vitakka and Vicara

Your vitakka in the first jhana is turning toward these three thoughts. They stay (vicara) in the mind, continuously supporting the first jhana.

Note the role of conscious thought in this progression. We use conscious thoughts, such as thoughts of loving-friendliness, to pervade the mind and push away hindrances. When the hindrances have been restrained, we carry the subtle residue of loving-friendliness into jhana. All the vitakkas work that way.

Note also that we must actually work at these vitakkas, applying considerable effort at the beginning to establish a firm ethical ground. You cultivate these conceptual thoughts day and night, on the cushion during formal meditation and off the cushion in your daily life. In your meditation work you make a conscious effort to replace unhealthy conscious thoughts with healthy ones. You replace unwholesome vitakkas with wholesome vitakkas. You root out greed, hatred, and cruelty and replace them with thoughts of letting go, loving-friendliness, and compassion for others. They become a wholesome habit that naturally permeates your jhana. The subtle remnants of these conscious thoughts prevent greed, hatred, and cruelty from invading your jhana.

Nevertheless, this is not some giant struggle. You cannot get these effects through straining. You simply cultivate the ground, and the seeds grow by themselves. After establishing a solid ethical foundation for your life and cultivating these wholesome thoughts, you reap the reward. Your mind is peaceful. You feel a great gladness in having given up your hectic, grasping ways. You feel secure. You feel that you have an infinite number of friends. This is the fertile ground that grows concentration.

When verbalized vitakkas turn into real, pure mental activities, they become jhanic factors. In jhana, most normal, conscious thoughts have been left behind. There are no more words.

"Thought" in Jhana

In English the word "thought" is always used to mean normal cognitive thinking, like "thinking" about what you will buy at the store. In Pali there is a whole range of words that can be translated into English as some kind of thought or component of the thinking process. We just don't have the terms to express these tiny but important differences unless we spend a lot of time learning a whole range of very subtle concepts.

It is probably easiest to understand the nature of "thought" in jhana if we speak first of using a kasina, a physical object, as our meditation subject. You start out by looking at the physical object. Then you shut your eyes and bring it to mind as a visual image. Eventually the object comes fully into focus when you attend to it with eyes shut. It is as clear as when you look at it with eyes open. This is your *learning sign*. You stop gazing at the physical object and focus solely upon the learning sign. You develop it by striking at it over and over with vitakka (applied thought) and maintaining it with vicara (sustained thought). It then turns into something more subtle, like an afterimage. This is called the *counterpart sign.*

As you practice this way, the *jhanic* factors grow in strength, each restraining its respective hindrance. Applied thought, for instance, counters sloth and torpor, eventually reducing it to a state of complete abeyance. When the hindrances are restrained and the defilements subside, your mind enters access concentration. This is when the learning sign is replaced by the counterpart sign.

The *Visuddhimagga*, an ancient commentary on the path of meditation, explains the difference between the learning sign and the counterpoint sign like this:

> *In the learning sign, any fault in the kasina is apparent. But the counterpart sign appears as if breaking out from the learning sign. It is a hundred times, a thousand times, more purified. It is like a looking-glass disk drawn from its case, like a mother-of-pearl dish well washed. It is like the moon's disk coming out from behind a cloud, like cranes against a thundercloud. But it has neither color nor shape, for if it had, it would be gross, cognizable by the eye, susceptible to comprehension by insight. But it is not like that. It is born only of perception in one who has obtained concentration, being a mere mode of appearance.*

The counterpart sign is the object of both access concentration and jhana. The difference between access concentration and the first jhana consists, not in their object, but in the strength of their respective jhanic factors. In access concentration the jhanic factors are still weak and not yet fully developed. In jhana they are strong enough to actually thrust the mind *into* the object with the full force, like a carpenter pounding a peg into wood or a stone sinking into water. In this process *applied thought* (vitakka) is the factor most responsible for bringing about the mind's sinking into the counterpart sign.

In metta meditation and elsewhere we speak of "thoughts" of loving-friendliness in jhana. Applied thought *in* jhana is associated with wholesome roots. It takes the form of wholesome "thoughts" of renunciation, benevolence, and harmlessness. What is the nature of these thoughts? You have to experience it to really understand. Words can only approximate. You use conceptual thoughts of metta to develop physical feelings. Then you turn your attention to the feelings and discover a subtle "color" or "flavor" in the mind that is the pure, nonconceptual feeling of metta. This is what you use to carry you into jhana and this vitakka is what you carry with you into jhana.

When using the breath as your object of focus, you use conscious thoughts to help you direct your attention onto the breath. You find the physical feeling. You drop conscious thought and dwell purely on the feeling. This is your learning sign. A spark of light sometimes appears. This signals the arising of your counterpart sign. The subtle afterimage of the physical feeling of the breath is what you carry with you into jhana.

The Seven Factors of Awakening

One of the most important aspects of the first jhana is that at this point, you begin your progress toward liberation through a succession of seven stages. Each stage leads to the next. They take place in the same order for each of us. No one ever skips any stage. Each stage is a natural outgrowth of the one before. These seven stages culminate in the attainment of *sotapanna*, "stream entry," the first stage of enlightenment. In each stage you develop a "factor of awakening."

The First Factor: Mindfulness

You need mindfulness to build jhana, but what is the proper domain for your mindfulness? What is your frame of reference in meditation? What do you concentrate on? You can't get jhana through concentrating on just anything. You must use certain specific subjects

510 BEYOND MINDFULNESS IN PLAIN ENGLISH

in your meditation. They must be things that promote dispassionate observation and reveal the truth of anicca, dukkha, and anatta.

Those proper objects of focus, the *four foundations of mindfulness*, are described in the *Satipatthana Sutta*. When using each object you must remain "ardent, alert, and mindful, putting aside greed and distress with reference to the world." That means you put some effort into the thing, do it with zest and vigor. Pay mindful attention to what you are doing and leave your day-to-day bothers behind while you are doing it. The four foundations of mindfulness constitute the basis and the guiding principles of concentration.

Mindfulness of the body focuses your attention on the body itself and its position and movement. You see that breathing is something that takes place within the body itself.

Mindfulness of feelings focuses on physical sensations. You watch them, looking constantly for their deeper nature, the way they are constantly changing and have no real substance other than what you give them with your mind. Tactile sensation is a feeling. Hearing is a feeling, too, if you ignore the other mental content that arises with it and just concentrate on the pure sensation of sound vibrations. The same is true for all the senses.

Mindfulness of consciousness focuses on watching thoughts and emotional reactions arise without getting involved in them. That includes things like discursive thoughts, internal conversation, pure concepts, and mental pictures. You see them as bubbles just coming up and going away without any particular meaning. You don't take them seriously.

Mindfulness of mental objects focuses on seeing the inherent nature of your whole experience: anicca, dukkha, and anatta. You face directly, in real time, the changing nature of everything you experience and everything material that you can experience. You see that none of it makes you really happy and that you are not really a somebody who is stuck in it all.

You can and must think about these things. That is valid practice. But remember that all such thoughts exist to guide you to the goal of the wordless experience of these things as the truth, exactly the way it is.

Mindfulness of impermanence in any of the four foundations is the entry point. Seeing anicca leads you to seeing dukkha and anatta. Seeing these three marks of existence leads you to liberation.

The Second Factor: Investigation

Out of mindfulness arises investigation.

While being mindful of the impermanence, unsatisfactoriness, and selflessness of one thing, the mind inevitably swings to some other thing. When that happens, you investigate that new object more closely, wordlessly looking for the impermanence, wordlessly asking, "Is this permanent or impermanent?" As you ponder that question and pay more mindful attention to this new object, you will see it as impermanent, unsatisfactory, and without self.

Can any object be permanent? The answer is "No." But don't take my word for it. Investigate for yourself.

Then you must investigate your mind and body with another question in mind: "Where can I find something permanent in this mind and body, with its perceptions, thoughts, feelings, and con- sciousness?" The answer will be, "Nowhere." But hearing this will not change you. You need to perform the investigation yourself, sin- cerely and exhaustively.

Concentration holds an object before mindfulness. Mindfulness then pays close attention to it. Then investigation finds that it is constantly changing, thus showing the signs of unsatisfactoriness and selflessness.

The Third Factor: Energy

Out of investigation arises energy.

This investigation arouses your energy to look for anything permanent and push away anything impermanent. Deeper mindfulness and investigation arouse stronger effort to see deeper, subtler aspects of anicca, dukkha, and anatta. Because this energy is aroused, you never tire in your mindfulness. You investigate the nature of impermanence, suffering, and the selflessness of your body. You delve into your feelings, perceptions, thoughts, and consciousness where you find the same thing. You do it with a vigor born out of spiritual urgency. You never tire of seeing tiny, perhaps even molecular, changes in the breath. Your effort helps you make progress.

This is the power of the energy factor of enlightenment. You have a natural energy in jhana. It carries over into your normal life, too.

The Fourth Factor: Joy

Out of energy arises joy.

Suppose you are traveling in a desert. You are hungry, thirsty, tired. You are full of worries, full of doubt as to where you should go. You need to get water, food, shade, and help. A man appears. His hair and clothes are dripping with water. Where did he come from? Where did he get this precious water you need so desperately?

You ask him. He points. He says, "Continue walking that way and you will find a forest. Right there, in a clearing in that forest, there is a natural lake."

You continue in the direction he pointed. Then, from a distance, you hear birds singing. You hear animal noises and people talking. As you get closer and closer, you hear people jumping into the water, swimming, and playing. As you get still closer you see all kinds of birds, animals, and human beings—boys, girls, teenagers, adults, old people. They are bathing, swimming, eating water lilies, lotus buds, lotus roots. They are drinking the water and relaxing on the bank of the lake. Seeing all this, your joy and gladness intensify.

Then you jump into the lake. You swim in it, play with the water. You drink all you want. You eat the delicious lotus roots and the water lilies. You frolic in the lake for hours. Then you come out of the water and stretch your arms and legs. You lie down on your back saying, "What happiness. I am happy! I am truly happy!"

In this image, the gladness that arises in your weary mind when you see that fresh lake is like the joy that arises in your mind in meditation. As you approach the lake and hear the sounds coming from it, your joy increases by degrees. When you jump into the water and drink, you are absolutely delirious with joy. As you eat the lotus roots and water lilies, you experience a deep tranquility. When you come out of the water and relax on the beach you are happy and deeply content. You might even fall asleep.

Similarly, in jhana, joy arises slowly and increases until it turns into tranquility and happiness. Normally you may use these two words— joy and happiness—to indicate states of excitement. Ordinarily, when you are excited you may jump up and down. You smile. You laugh. You hug someone. You talk a lot. You sing. You kiss someone you love. You dance and even cry out of such excitement. While expressing your excitement through all these activities, you may say, "I am happy." But this is not the happiness of jhana. Jhanic happiness is calm, peaceful, and smooth. It is not excitement. It is almost the opposite. Spiritual happiness makes you relaxed, calm, peaceful, and concentrated.

Sometimes, even in meditation, your eyes may be filled with tears when you are full of this deep joy. But, if you are mindful, you can become fully aware of your joy without shedding tears, without a murmur or a movement.

Once you have achieved the joy factor of enlightenment, you automatically feel so much loving-friendliness and compassion for all beings that a natural wish arises in your mind: "May all living beings live in peace and harmony!" When practicing this mindfulness of loving-friendliness, this compassion for all living beings, you appreciate whatever you have. You experience appreciation of whatever others enjoy, and you feel extremely grateful for everything you have received.

This is the power of joy. The joy of jhana carries over into a joy in your normal consciousness. It is a joy that fuels your life.

The Fifth Factor: Tranquility

Out of joy arises tranquility.

The calm, cool, and refreshing joy engendered by this practice makes your mind and body calm, relaxed, and peaceful. When the mind is calm and peaceful, you feel serene and tranquil. You are satisfied. The fever of anger is cooled. The fire of lust has subsided. Delusion is dispelled. Grief, pain, sorrow, lamentation, and despair have all disappeared. You no longer feel the burning of jealousy, fear, tension, anxiety, and worry. Instead, you feel safe and secure. Although you have not yet achieved your final goal, at this level you have temporary peace and happiness.

The power of the deep peace of jhana carries over. It begins to pervade your life. You live and practice your mindfulness with an ever-deepening tranquility.

The Sixth Factor: Concentration

Out of tranquility arises concentration.

The Buddha said, "One who is happy gains concentration. One whose mind is filled with loving-friendliness gains concentration very quickly." In the first jhana, your thoughts of friendliness, compassion, generosity, equanimity, joy, and happiness are very strong. They hold your attention effortlessly.

What creates this unification of mind, this one-pointedness? It is hard to say in words, but analogies may help. Imagine that in the distance there are mountains, traditionally, thirty-seven peaks and ridges, corresponding to the thirty-seven factors of enlightenment— things like the noble eightfold path, and the four foundations of mindfulness. These merge into seven major mountains, the seven factors of awakening. Their peaks are in the clouds. A fine drizzle is falling constantly. Tiny, tiny drops of water are showering down gently nearly all the time. Occasionally it rains harder. Drops are continually accumulating. Each of these drops is a tiny moment when one of the factors dominates your mind. We all have fleeting flashes of things like mindfulness, concentration, and certainty that what we are doing is right. This is a state of scattered mind. The factors you want to be unified are occurring in rare fits and starts.

These tiny mind-moment droplets seep into the ground, percolate through the soil and are purified. Harmful elements are filtered out and healthy minerals percolate in. The drops flow together, merge and surface as tiny springs. The springs create rivulets that flow together into streams. The streams flow together into creeks. This process continues and the water is rushing down the mountain, singing as it goes over rocks and crashing as it plunges in waterfalls. Every drop is laden with the potential factors of enlightenment accumulated within it. Eventually they form a mighty river, a huge river, like the Mississippi or the Nile or the Ganges.

But the power of this river is harnessed. Someone has been very clever and dammed the river where it flows through a gorge. It forms an enormous lake, a really big lake like Lake Superior or the Caspian Sea. The lake contains all the power of all the droplets that fell on the mountains, stored as potential energy in the weight of the water. Innumerable tons of water press against the dam, trying to release their power. Your mind is still scattered, but less so. The factors have gained great potential power through being unified, but the power has not yet sufficiently concentrated to create the effect you want.

Someone has been even more clever. They have put holes in the dam, small holes compared to the huge volume of water trying to pour through them. The water gushes with enormous force as it squeezes its way through those holes, turning its potential energy into the kinetic energy of movement. Now your mind is no longer scattered. The factors have been unified to release their power. Their power is now the power of concentration.

There are turbines mounted in the path of the raging flow. They spin huge generators, which convert the kinetic energy into electrical energy, enough power to light Canada or a whole section of Europe. This concentrated power flows through electric lines to light bulbs in cities and homes. It is the bright flame of mindfulness that reveals the luminous nature of the mind. With this much power behind it, mindfulness blazes through the accumulated dirt of lifetimes and produces liberation. Concentration has accumulated tiny mind-moments in which the various factors expressed themselves singly into a state in which they are all present together, constantly.

In this state of mind, with jhanic concentration, you continue to pay total attention to your experience of change. Your awareness of impermanence is much sharper and clearer than ever before because it is backed by right concentration. Previously, before you gained right concentration, your awareness of the impermanence of all phenomena was shallow. Now it is very deep and powerful. Your mind can penetrate impermanence more thoroughly than ever before.

This time you see not only impermanence, but also the fact that everything impermanent is unsatisfactory. Your mind gets tired of clinging to any pleasant experience, because the experience inevitably changes before the mind even reaches it. Even your mindfulness is changing. You may even begin to feel bored with it all.

Keep watching this boredom. You will notice that the boredom is also changing. The meditation subject, as a thing, has been left behind. The mind does not focus on any separate point beside its own collectedness. One-pointedness is the mind focusing on its own one-pointedness.

This power of jhanic concentration makes everything you do and think deeper. You apply the concentration in your daily life off the cushion and it takes your mindful investigation of everything to a higher level. You see more easily into the impermanence, suffering, and selflessness of everything you are doing.

Concentrated mind sees things as they really are. You become deeply disappointed with the mental rubbish you have been making and holding on to. You let it go at last. And then you are free.

The Seventh Factor: Equanimity
Out of concentration arises equanimity.

Once you can see that all of the components of the body and mind—in the past, present, and future—are impermanent, unsatisfactory, and selfless, something remarkable happens. Equanimity arises regarding all conditioned things. Your mind looks at everything with equanimity—wholesome, unwholesome, physical, verbal, and mental. Good, bad, or indifferent, it is all the same. It is being-ness. It is simply reality. Your viewpoint is imperturbable.

Then you feel a spiritual urgency. You accelerate your mindfulness practice and do it even more vigorously. When you are in this state of mind, you have deeper insights into the noble eightfold path. You use your mindfulness, your concentration, and your attention to recognize impermanence. You study and pierce unsatisfactoriness and selflessness in the body and mind. You realize that all those "wonderful" thoughts and feelings are constantly changing on a very subtle level—and the "terrible" ones are constantly changing, too.

11. The Second and Third Jhanas

*I*n your upward movement in any spiritual practice, you encounter obstacles. You must struggle with these to go to the next higher attainment. You must let go of your lower desires to secure what you have attained. It has to be done without greed in order to proceed with greater perseverance. It is like climbing a ladder. You must let go of the lower rung that you are standing on and securely hold on to the one you have grabbed. You must lift one foot to step on the higher rung. It takes a willingness to let go. If you feel comfortable with the rung you are standing on and cling to it, you can't climb another step. You are stuck on the first rung of the ladder.

> *Knowing this body to be like a clay pot,*
> *Establishing this mind like a fortress,*
> *One should battle Mara with the sword of insight,*
> *Protecting what has been won,*
> *Clinging to nothing.*

This is the situation you are in when you have attained the first jhana. Joy and happiness have arisen from abandoning hindrances. Being away from all worldly affairs is wonderful. This is a very enticing and attractive situation. Sensual desire is left behind, so becoming attached to that is not possible. Nevertheless, genuine peace, joy, and happiness are unimaginable while you are involved in worldly affairs. Now you have something you never had before. This is an ideal state in which to get stuck.

The *Dhammapada* stanza quoted above says the body is like a clay pot. It is very fragile. It can break any time. In order to protect it, the Buddha advises us to build a fortress around it with the mind. The mind is even more fragile, delicate, fast changing, fickle, and unsteady. But, building this wall with such a mind, you are asked to fight Mara and gain some ground. Once you have gained ground, then you must protect it without attachment to it. That is hard.

When you are attached to something, you protect it. If you don't attach to something you let it go. The Buddha advised us to protect what you gained without attachment. This is the nature of spiritual achievement. If you are attached to the jhana you have attained, you cannot make progress. Nor can you make use of it. In order to protect your fragile body, you must use the even more fragile mind and build a fortress around it to fight Mara. These two fragile objects should be made strong with mindfulness. You have gained joy, happiness, and peace in jhana. These must be protected with mindfulness, without attachment to them. Only when you don't attach to joy, happiness, and peace can you fight Mara. Attachment is Mara's bait. If you swallow this bait, you lose the battle.

ATTAINING THE SECOND JHANA

The attainment of the second jhana does not take place by wishing or willing or striving. When the mind is ready to attain the second jhana, it automatically lets go of the first jhana. You don't even have to wish to go to the second jhana. When the mind is ready, it glides into the second jhana by itself. But only if you let it.

When you attained the first jhana, you let go of your many activities and all the hindrances that were such firm habits of mind. The second jhana is called "jhana without thought." To attain the second jhana you must let go of vitakka (applied thoughts of generosity, loving-friendliness, and compassion) and vicara (maintaining those thoughts with sustained application). Part of their function is to form words, to turn subtle thought into speech.

In meditation, especially in a retreat situation, we observe silence. We say that we observe "noble silence." In reality, as there are thoughts in the mind, our ordinary silence is not *real* noble silence. Word formation must totally stop to qualify our silence as "noble." The second jhana does not have discursive thought or sustained thought. Here your internal silence is truly noble. It is a genuine noble one's jhana. In this state, the mind really becomes calm.

The moment your thinking or subtle thoughts vanish from your mind, you are aware that you have entered the second jhana. But as soon as the thought, "This is the second jhana," appears in your mind, you lose it. Try again and again until that thought does not appear. You can stay with the awareness of second jhanic experience without the concept "this is the second jhana." This is a very delicate balance. Only with full awareness can you maintain it.

Before attaining the first jhana you practiced mindfulness to attain it. In the first jhana you use mindfulness to maintain an unfluctuating level of the jhana. Mindfulness plays a very important role in the first jhana to prevent hindrances from entering. Whenever you lose mindfulness, you lose the first jhana. Your jhanic concentration is not very strong and you can lose it very quickly.

The second jhana is more stable. Altogether, the second jhana has numerous factors, including internal confidence. This was absent in the first jhana. By overcoming the hindrance of doubt, you developed a certain degree of confidence in the Buddha, Dhamma, and Sangha and in ethical principles. When you attain the second jhana, that confidence becomes stronger. Due to the fact that you have already experienced the first jhana, you experience even deeper confidence in your attainment and in the Buddha, Dhamma, and Sangha. You are making progress. You see that for yourself and it is beyond all possibility of doubt. Your upward path is very clear.

The second jhana also has a deeper level of concentration. You do not have to watch out for hindrances. The first jhana is still close to the hindrances and to all material experiences. The second jhana is still close to vitakka and vicara, but remote from hindrances. You should always be mindful of the possibility of losing the jhana. This is why you have cultivated mindfulness from the beginning.

With the subsiding of applied thought and sustained thought
one enters and dwells in the second jhana,
which has internal confidence and unification of mind,
is without applied thought and sustained thought,
and is filled with rapture and bliss born of concentration.

As vitakka and vicara drop out of the picture, rapture, happiness, and one-pointedness remain. When thought drops away, you experience your entire body and mind filled with joy and happiness. This joy continuously replenishes itself with more and more joy. It is like a lake that has a spring underneath, continuously flowing with fresh water. From time to time it is cleansed by a very light rain shower that washes away whatever little dirt may fall upon the surface. Your mind is continuously refreshed and cleansed with new joy. It is constant and springing ever anew.

ATTAINING THE THIRD JHANA

Now you are approaching the third jhana. Without wishing, the mind loses interest in the lower jhana and moves into the higher one. Joy is fading away. You don't do anything to make it fade. It does that naturally, by itself. This happens for two reasons. The first is that the mind loses interest in the second jhana. The second reason is that joy is affected by time and becomes impermanent.

You clearly experience the impermanence of the jhanic factors. That experience takes place while in jhana, as you are coming out of jhana, and when you reflect on the factors afterward. You don't have to spend any great deal of time to see the impermanence of the jhanic factors. The mindfulness you have cultivated does it.

In the preliminary stage, before attaining jhana, you had to make a strenuous effort to stay with the practice of moral principles. You disciplined yourself using the fourfold effort you learned in chapter 3; you learned to pick up good habits and drop bad ones. The mind was like a wild animal. It experienced the mundane enjoyment of sensual pleasures. Greed, hatred, delusion, and all the minor defilements were very strong. You needed a great deal of effort to overcome them, cultivate wholesome mental states, and maintain them. You have passed that stage. Holding off the defilements during meditation is much easier now.

Mindfulness and concentration united in the first jhana and were struggling to appear clearly. In the second jhana they became stronger, but still did not have enough strength to come out fully. In the third jhana they emerge completely and join hands. You can see them very clearly in the third jhana formula.

> *With the fading away of rapture,*
> *one dwells in equanimity, mindful and discerning;*

and one experiences in one's own person
that bliss of which the noble ones say:
"Happily lives one who is equanimous and mindful";
thus one enters and dwells in the third jhana.

The third jhana and fourth jhana are called "concentration with-out joy." Happiness (sukha) predominates, replacing the joy (piti) that has faded. When you are mastering the second jhana your mind keeps losing interest because of the coarseness of joy. It becomes more and more interested in the happiness, concentration, mindful-ness, clear comprehension, and equanimity that begin to show up. When the mind completely loses interest in joy, it glides into the third jhana without your wishing or thinking. When the conditions for attaining the third jhana are present, mind itself chooses to move into it.

The third jhana has thirty-one factors. The joy drops away. It is seen to be coarse in comparison with the more refined happiness of the third jhana. The joy of the second jhana is like getting some-thing. The happiness of the third jhana is like taking pleasure in it afterward. It is smoother, more unperturbed than joy.

When you attained the second jhana you experienced a very strong confidence from your success. As you are going through the practice of mastering the second jhana, your mind notices that the joy is getting weaker. Its opposite hindrance, restlessness and worry, is still haunting the mind from time to time. Each time you attain the second jhana your mind loses a bit of interest in joy. The mind-fulness that you have practiced, even at the preliminary stage, before attaining the first jhana, is emerging, getting stronger.

You developed mindfulness and clear comprehension in the preliminary stage. They were present in the first jhana and second jhanas, too. Since the other factors in those jhanas were grossly dominating the mind, they did not come to prominence. Equanimity and clear comprehension also emerge in the third jhana. Now that the other jhanic factors have become weak, equanimity, mindfulness, and clear comprehension emerge to polish the third jhana.

MASTERY OF JHANA

You should not rush on to attain any higher jhana without thoroughly mastering the lower ones. You put your attention on fully mastering the first jhana before you attempt to attain the second. When you attain the first jhana many times, the mind loses interest in it because the shadow of thought is still lurking in the background.

It is a bit like the boredom you know in normal consciousness. Suppose you were struggling to obtain something you like very much. One day you get it. When you enjoy it for the first time, it is really wonderful. It is very tempting. You just love it. But as you go on enjoying it repeatedly for a long time, you lose interest in it. The pleasure you derive from that object or relationship gradually begins to diminish. Eventually the mind does not pay any attention to the object. It becomes just another thing you have, part of the backdrop of your life. The mind turns toward something else.

Similarly, you have been delighted with the subtle thoughts of renunciation, loving-friendliness, and noncruelty that pervade the first jhana. After attaining the first jhana several times, you lose interest in these thoughts. Suppose you have attained the first jhana ten times. Each time, interest in these thoughts wears out a little. On the eleventh occasion, the mind may drop them completely. (Pay no attention to the numbers. It is just an example. You will work through the jhanas at your own pace.)

This means that, when the mind loses interest in the first jhana and is ready to drop it completely, you don't have to make any volitional effort to move on to the second jhana. It just happens. It happens in the same sequential order for everyone. When the preparatory state is well established, what comes next will simply happen—naturally. That is the nature of Dhamma.

Then your mind naturally goes to the second jhana. Confidence is strong in the second jhana because you have seen the result of the first jhana. After attaining the second jhana many times, you find it not giving you that same joy and happiness born of concentration that you experienced at the beginning of the second jhana. After attaining it many times, the same thing that happened in the first jhana happens in the second jhana. Joy becomes stale. Can you really turn away from a state of joy? Yes. The joy of jhana is not excitement as we know it in ordinary consciousness, but it is still a bit keyed up when compared with other, more refined states of mind. Restlessness can haunt you so long as joy is there. The mind loses interest in joy, which is dominant in the second jhana. Then the mind glides into the third jhana, where a more refined state of happiness is dominant.

THE STEPS OF MASTERY

How do you accomplish this "mastery" we speak of? Does it come all at once? No. Like many other things, there are natural steps in the process:

Step 1: Adverting. "Advert" means to turn the attention to something. Adverting, in this case, is the ability to bring your attention mindfully to the jhanic factors one by one after emerging from jhana.

That period right after your meditation session is very fruitful. Do not let this important opportunity pass you by. You should reflect on your jhana, especially when it has become stable, when you can attain it wherever you want, whenever you want, and for as long as you want. Then you can see it clearly.

Remember, the hindrances are not dead, just restrained. As any of these restrained hindrances becomes strong, you lose the jhana. You should find out which impediment has disturbed your jhana. Repeat the steps you followed to overcome that particular impediment. After it is once again subdued, you re-attain the jhana.

Step 2: Attaining. "Attaining" is your ability to enter jhana quickly. It improves with practice. Since you have already attained it, even though you lost it, you can attain it again quickly. Do so as promptly as you can, in this sitting, or the next, or as soon as you can set up the proper conditions. Do not let your mind forget how to do it. Strike while the iron is hot.

Step 3: Resolving. "Resolving" is the ability to make a decision to remain in the jhana for exactly a predetermined length of time. You resolve or decide to spend a certain amount of time in jhana. This ability is weak in the lower jhanas and grows in the higher ones.

You cannot determine to stay too long in any jhana lower than the fourth. The hindrances are only weakly restrained and still haunt the mind. Then you lose jhana. You should resolve to re-attain the jhana and to remain there for a certain period of time. Your ability will not be perfect. You will lose it again.

You must then resolve to see what has gone wrong. You find the reason. It is always one of the mental impurities that has snuck into your mind. Once you have found the particular hindrance that is causing the trouble, resolve to prevent it from arising again. Decide to overcome that particular impurity and to cultivate the wholesome state that supports the jhana. Be determined to maintain that wholesome state again.

This is the function of mindfulness in jhana. You apply mindfulness outside the jhana to find out the problem. You apply mindfulness within the jhana to maintain the state that preserves the jhana. So, with mindfulness you can overcome these impurities and with mindfulness you can re-attain and preserve the jhana.

Step 4: Emerging. "Emerging" means that you come out of the jhana without difficulty exactly at the predetermined time. You don't wait in jhana until you lose it. Here you attain jhana at will and come out of jhana at will. This is part of mastery.

Step 5: Reviewing. "Reviewing" means the ability to review the jhana and its factors with retrospective knowledge immediately after adverting to them. You have noticed the factor. Now you consciously review it. What you want to review is your progress on the path, how this jhanic experience has helped you. You review how you obtained jhana and what its benefits are. You consider how it has helped you overcome your own defilements and what defilements remain to be handled.

BEING IN JHANA

Why do you have to do all this after attaining a jhana? Jhana is like a juggling act. You keep things suspended in the air or balanced. Then you drop them. Then you start over. It takes a lot of practice and you need to figure out why you dropped the balls.

Being in jhana is like juggling five balls at once. They are the five jhanic factors. You are holding them all in the air without letting any of them fall to the ground. If one falls, they all fall. You must pick them up and start juggling all over again. What would make a ball fall? You are distracted—by fatigue, onlookers, vehicles, sounds, or even by the joy of jhana.

While you are in jhana, a hindrance will appear in your mind. Maybe your body is hurting so much that your attention goes there. Maybe you hear a loud noise. Maybe you want lunch. Then you lose your jhana. You must start it all over again. Fortunately, you don't have to start from scratch because you have already learned to restrain hindrances. Simply go through these five steps of mastery and attain jhana again.

Have you ever seen a seal suspending a big ball in the air on its nose? He can hold it for a while. Then it falls to the ground. Then his trainer must pick it up and give it to him to do the same thing. Similarly, you can hold your concentration for a while. As soon as something disturbs your mind, you lose it. Then you pick it up again. Do not fret. You are learning, just like the seal.

Have you ever seen a balloon being suspended in the air for hours or days by a tube blowing air? That is a juggling act too. Once you manage to restrain the hindrances by balancing all the jhanic factors, your concentration stays with you for a long time. You are learning this juggling act called jhana.

12. The Fourth Jhana

*I*f you continue refining your mindfulness, you can end up in the highest material jhana—the fourth. Here, mindfulness and equanimity are purified and come to a new level. Mindfulness acts as a shepherd for equanimity and keeps it in superb balance. The mind is pure, white, without stain, free from idiosyncrasies. It is soft, pliable, steady, and imperturbable.

All unsteady minds are upset by the thought of selflessness and suffering. Those minds are subject to an unpleasant emotional reaction when they investigate suffering. A foundation of well-developed equanimity corrects that. Unsteady minds want to experience only happiness, even though happiness never comes without suffering. It's like a buy-one-get-one-free deal. You get the second one, whether you want it or not. But when you are in the fourth jhana, steeped in extremely powerful and pure mindfulness and equanimity, your mind will not react emotionally to the words "suffering," "selflessness," and "impermanence" or to seeing the real things directly.

In the fourth jhana, nonverbal, nonconceptual realization begins to take place on a regular basis. The broad base of the eight steps of the noble eightfold path gradually narrows down to the last step, concentration. The factors of enlightenment come together. Endowed with this powerful concentration, the fourth jhana penetrates the five aggregates and sees their impermanence, unsatisfactoriness, and selflessness at a nearly subatomic level. This is not inferential or theoretical knowledge. It is nonverbal, nonconceptual, and experiential, a direct seeing of the intrinsic nature of the aggregates.

Similarly, when you direct such an extremely powerful, clear mind toward the four noble truths, your understanding becomes completely clear. The four noble truths that you realize at this level are not gross in nature. They are the finest level of the four noble truths. Jhana gradually gathers the force, power, and strength of concentration, to crack open the long-established shell of ignorance and get the full vision of liberation.

In this state verbal communication has totally ceased. The pure concentrated mind with pure mindfulness and equanimity clearly comprehends things without the sound of words or the vibration of thoughts. This is not the verbalizing or thinking stage. You already passed that long ago during your rational thinking phase. There you practiced the investigation factor of enlightenment in a verbal way, a way that took place before your mind became concentrated.

In the fourth jhana, you don't think conceptually about suffering, the cause of suffering, the end of suffering, or any of the rest. You just know, directly. This is the level where the mind sees things through the eye of wisdom. Words, thinking, investigation, or even reflection have no place. They would just get in the way. They are too slow and everything is moving too fast. Every cell in the body undergoes change every moment. When the body changes at this inconceivable rapidity, no mind without powerful concentration can keep up. You need steadiness, pliability, softness, and purity to notice that flashing, incessant change. This sharpness of the mind is present only in the concentrated mind.

You must use this sharpness. You must focus your mindful attention on form, feeling, perception, thoughts, and consciousness so deeply that they disappear as discrete units. There is a single field, a range of form, feeling, perception, volitional formations, and consciousness. All that activity is happening within that range. Whatever notions you have had of "I" or "mine" or "I am" vanish. There is no "I" doing any of it.

JOINING BOTH

In the fourth jhana, concentrated mind penetrates the veil of pleasantness, pleasure, permanence, and self more clearly than ever before. It sees displeasure, suffering, impermanence, and nonself, craving, conceit, and wrong view more clearly. Tranquility and insight shake hands. This state is called "joining both."

In Brazil there is a thrilling sight. The river Solimões and river Negro are two tributaries of the Amazon. These two giant rivers join at Manaus to make the Amazon River. The water in the two is different in color and they flow side by side for nearly six kilometers before they mix. I have seen this for myself on one of my teaching trips to Brazil. Mindfulness and concentration work that way in the fourth jhana. They blend together to form one mighty river.

You do not abandon this jhana. You don't let it subside. You don't overcome it as you did with the previous jhanas. You use it. You have been working very hard to attain this. It is not to be let go of like other jhanas, always passing on to something higher. You use it for developing insight.

The defilements you eradicate at this level are deeply settled in the mind. Only this kind of nonverbal, nonconceptual mindfulness with clear comprehension and equanimity can reach the very root of those deeply embedded defects. You simply direct attention onto your own underlying tendencies. Jhana opens the door. Working together, mindfulness and concentration weaken the fetters, so that later, in the supramundane jhanas, you can destroy them altogether.

Attaining the fourth jhana is called "Purification of Mind." From this purification wisdom arises.

> *With the abandoning of pleasure and pain,*
> *and with the previous disappearance of joy and grief,*
> *one enters and dwells in the fourth jhana,*
> *which has neither pain nor pleasure*
> *and has purity of mindfulness and equanimity.*

Once you have attained the fourth jhana, you will not feel any need to come out of it. Equanimity predominates and you have strong "neither pleasant nor unpleasant" feelings. You stay as long as you have planned to stay. The world cannot disturb you. Pleasure and pain are abandoned. This "neutral feeling" is something that will persist throughout all the jhanas above the fourth.

In addition to the qualities that we have already mentioned, there are many mental factors in the fourth jhana (though six of them are repetitions from earlier jhanas). Once you have attained and mastered the fourth jhana, you can re-attain it any time without any problem.

COMING OUT OF JHANA TO PRACTICE VIPASSANA

Many people teach that we must come out of jhana to practice vipassana. Is that true?

The real question is, "Can your jhanic concentration penetrate things as they really are?" If the answer is "No," then your concentration is the absorption variety we spoke of earlier. It may well be wrong jhana. If the answer is "Yes," then your concentration is not absorption. It is right jhana.

According to the Buddha's teaching, when the mind is concentrated, you can see things as they really are. If your concentration is absorption without mindfulness, then you *should* come out of it because you are in wrong jhana. However, you *can* see things while you are in right jhana, and those things bear the stamp of the triple marks of all experience. They show anicca, dukkha, and anatta, which is what you are looking for and the reason you're doing all of this. So why should you come out of it to see things as they really are?

When we read about the way that the Buddha used his own fourth jhanic concentration, as given in many suttas, we have no reason to believe that he came out of jhana to develop the three kinds of knowledge that he used for seeing past lives, seeing beings dying and taking rebirth, and knowing that his own defilements had been destroyed.

If you can see things as they truly are when you are in access concentration, there is no reason to come out of it to practice vipassana. You are already achieving the goal of the practice. But, if you can see things as they actually are in access concentration, then you should be able to see things even better when you are in full right jhana, which is clearer and stronger than access concentration.

Should you come out of jhana and reflect upon the jhanic factors in order to understand the impermanence, suffering, and selflessness of jhanic factors themselves? It is virtually impossible to find evidence in the suttas that one should come out of jhana to practice vipassana. If you come out of jhana to practice vipassana, you lose the jhanic qualities because your hindrances return. The jhanic state is a perfect state of mind to focus on the four noble truths, impermanence, unsatisfactoriness, and selflessness and to attain liberation by eliminating the fetters.

EQUANIMITY BASED ON DIVERSITY

Equanimity is the hallmark of the fourth jhana. Equanimity is a most altruistically balanced state of mind. A meditator in this state of mind is called "One who is living happily here and now." Happiness here is synonymous with peace and bliss.

A mind that grabs on to things constantly is constantly swept away, distracted. It cannot stay steady and uninvolved. It cannot simply see what is there. Equanimity releases you from this distraction. It is the dominant factor in the fourth jhana and it is the reason that the jhana can yield deep wisdom.

The equanimity that is sometimes present in normal consciousness depends on diversity, dividing conscious attention into apparently enduring "things." In vipassana meditation, you stay in the realm of diversity. You are still in touch with your senses. When you practice well, as each thing arises in the mind, you spot it and you pull yourself back to equanimity. Your equanimity is very rapid but not quite instantaneous. Each sensory experience arises and passes away in a flash. The mind does not hold on to it. Yet there is a measurable moment of its arising.

When we get immersed in the pleasantness or unpleasantness of a sensory object, we fail to notice its impermanence. The function of equanimity is to break this attachment reaction and reveal the impermanence of everything we experience in samsara.

Equanimity based on diversity can be explained with regard to six senses (including consciousness) and the objects of the six senses.

The eye and forms. When you see a form with your eyes, you begin to grasp on to it. Then you rapidly pull back into equanimity. If it was pleasant, you forget the pleasantness and register it as just a visual phenomenon. You use your equanimity to see the impermanence of what you saw.

The ear and sounds. When you hear a sound with the ear, you pull back to equanimity very quickly. If it was an unpleasant sound, you just drop the unpleasantness. It is simply a sound. You use your equanimity to see the impermanence of what you heard.

The nose and odors. When you smell an odor with the nose, you rapidly establish equanimity. You register it as simply an odor, neither pleasant nor unpleasant. You use your equanimity to see its impermanence.

The tongue and flavors. When you taste a flavor with the tongue, it is regarded as simply a flavor. You drop the wonderfulness or the horribleness or the neutrality. You see its impermanence.

The body and tangibles. When you touch a tangible with the body, you just register it as a touch. You establish your state of non-preference swiftly. You see the impermanence.

The mind and mind-objects. When you recognize a mind-object with the mind, you let it be just something held in the mind, neither good nor bad. You let it be just a mental phenomenon, inherently impermanent.

When you have "equanimity based on diversity," you spot and pull back from every sensory thing that arises in your perceptual world. When you do this well and consistently you are doing a good job at what is called "guarding your senses."

All this starts with mindfulness, of course. All the seven factors of enlightenment begin with mindfulness. Your mindfulness must be sharp enough that you quickly notice yourself becoming involved in these perceptions. Only then can you establish the equanimity you need to drop the near-instantaneous reaction that follows.

EQUANIMITY BASED ON UNITY

A different sort of equanimity develops in the fourth jhana, where consciousness is unified by concentration. In the fourth jhana and beyond, sensory impressions do not arise at all. Your equanimity is not based on any of the six senses. It arises based purely on concentration or one-pointedness of mind, along with mindfulness. There is no room for sensory experience and thus equanimity is smooth and continuous. It takes no time because it is uninterrupted. When mindfulness is present, awareness of impermanence is smooth and steady.

The perfection of equanimity allows all the other factors to unite. This is where the factors of enlightenment you have been cultivating all come together. All the wholesome things you have been doing in your daily life—little by little, here and there—consolidate and produce results in the fourth jhana. When the fourth jhana is attained, its equanimity is based on this unity of mind. The mind is well unified in the second jhana. It becomes perfectly unified in the fourth jhana because your senses are not responding to sensory stimuli.

When you see impermanence in ordinary consciousness, it can be quite distressing. Everything is slipping away, all the time. You are attached to it and you want it to last. All the things you love are being lost or will be lost. You have strong emotional reactions to this. That is natural. However, in the fourth jhana, there are no emotional reactions. Equanimity and mindfulness are strong and clear. They become equal partners. You see impermanence, suffering, and selflessness, smoothly, without response. It just is as it is.

Light and Vision

At the very beginning of this book we said that the mind is luminous. Jhana is where you see that clearly. The mind is filled with a beautiful light. You see everything clearly.

When you attain the fourth jhana, this luminosity becomes prominent. Speaking of this luminous mind, the Buddha says:

It has become malleable, wieldy, purified,
bright, unblemished, and rid of defilement.
It is steady and attained to imperturbability.

Luminosity is not explicitly stated in this formula but it is implied by purity, brightness, an unblemished state, and a state free from defilement. This luminosity is very powerful. The Buddha used it to develop supernormal powers. Seeing previous lives and beings dying and taking rebirth are mundane supernormal powers. More significant is the kind of knowledge that can see the four noble truths and destroy the defilements.

In jhana there is also an experience similar to visual light but not a product of the ordinary material senses. So long as a meditator is in right jhana, there is both light and vision. That is the state where the mind is perfectly clear to see the truth as it really is. Effort, mindfulness, and concentration work as a team to open the wisdom-eye that allows you to understand all things as they really are. Luminous mind shines most brilliantly, making the brightest vision.

We humans put a lot of emphasis on vision. Mindfulness and clear comprehension are often expressed as "seeing." After attaining enlightenment the Buddha met people said to have very little dust in their eyes. One who has attained the stream-entry fruition state (eliminating the belief in the self) is known as "One who has entered the vision." *Seeing* the truth is heavily emphasized in the texts. When the Buddha attained enlightenment he said, *"Eye* arose in me."

You can see the truth only when the wisdom-eye is clear. The wisdom-eye temporarily removes confusion or dust. Ignorance, expressed as fetters, has confused your mind for a long time. When the fetters are removed from the mind, your wisdom-eye can see the truth of impermanence in all conditioned things.

Explaining his own attainment of jhana, the Buddha said that he gained light and vision and soon both of them disappeared. Having considered the reason for this disappearance, he found that one of the imperfections had arisen in his mind and his concentration had fallen away. When concentration was there, light and vision were there. When concentration fell away, he lost both light and vision. Then he restarted the practice with mindfulness until he once again gained concentration, vision, and light.

Even a very tiny speck of dust can distort the clarity of a great, powerful telescope. Then it cannot bring to human eyes its pristine clarity of images. Your heart, brain, and nervous system do not operate to their maximum capacity if there is a single iota of dirt in them. It is far more important for the mind that is dealing with spiritual matters to remain totally free. Otherwise it cannot even temporarily recall previous lives or see beings dying and taking rebirth according to their kammas, as the Buddha did. Above all, and most importantly, it cannot destroy all the defilements. This is not intellectual speculation. This is seeing with a pure, clean, well-concentrated mind.

Only in the state of the fourth jhana are equanimity, mindfulness, and one-pointed concentration powerful enough to perform these feats. Once you come out of the fourth jhana, or any jhana for that matter, the mind begins to weaken in its strength and power. The longer you are out of jhana, the weaker the power and strength of jhana become until the hindrances return in their full strength. Then your mind is nearly as it was before attaining jhana. You have the residue of jhana, but not the full strength and power.

It is very much like when you climb a mountain. At the top you have a huge, wide vision of the surrounding countryside. The world looks vast from up there. So long as you are there you can see all the surrounding area as far as your eyesight and visibility goes. If you come down even one step, you lose that vision. It is not the same. The farther down you go, the narrower your vision.

Similarly, so long as you are in the fourth jhana, the clarity, purity, steadiness, stainlessness, whiteness, equanimity, and imperturbability of the mind remain. When you come out they become weak. Eventually they are lost.

SIGNLESSNESS, NONSTICKINESS, AND VOIDNESS

In spite your mastery of jhana, you lose jhana. This is because your jhanic attainments are impermanent. Everything, even your long-sought jhana, is impermanent! You realize that everything operates within the boundary of this all-pervading impermanence. What is lost is lost forever. It is totally gone. There is no sign left behind. This is an experience of *signlessness*. You can see this directly in jhana and conceptually in your review afterward.

The concentrated mind can penetrate impermanence at three levels—rising, peaking, and passing away. These are the three minor moments of each instant of impermanence in body, feelings, perceptions, volitional formations, and consciousness. They occur in your concentrated mind like mustard seeds dropping into a hot frying pan. Your experience breaks into tiny pieces with a popping sound. It is like a drop of water dropping into a hot pan. It shatters into tiny particles, and evaporates quickly, without leaving any sign behind. Although you have known that everything is impermanent, this is the first time you experience impermanence at this intensity, at its subtlest level.

Repeated loss of what you have gained is very frustrating. This is unsatisfactoriness or dukkha. Desire is the glue that sticks thoughts, ideas, feelings, and perceptions to the mind. You see with the eye of wisdom that this glue, affected by all-pervading impermanence, is drying, weakening. Its grip is slipping away. At this point, nothing sticks to the mind. This is called *nonstickiness*.

You realize that there is no way to keep your jhanic attainment. You will always lose it when you come out of jhana. This sense of loss deepens your frustration. What is this "you" that keeps gaining and losing a whole world of experience? It is not really there. There is just experience, rising and falling, coming and going. This is your insight into the reality of selflessness, anatta. You see void or vacuum in what has been lost. This is called *voidness*.

These insights, however, are not very deep. These experiences of signlessness, nonstickiness, and voidness are superficial. But they are very useful.

USING THE FOURTH JHANA

You pause at the fourth jhana rather than passing on to some higher state. You *use* the fourth jhana. There is no transition from the fourth jhana to any intermediary state. The qualities of the fourth jhana provide the mind its best opportunity for seeing the finest level of change in the five aggregates. The mind is pure, clear, and refined.

The Buddha was always mindful. His mind was always pure, clean, equanimous, imperturbable, bright, shining, and steady. Yet, still he attained the fourth jhana to get the sharpest and most powerful one-pointed concentration. Only when you are in the deepest level of meditation do you experience the minute level of the changes taking place in your mind and body. Words, thoughts, and concepts stop, but the feeling of impermanence goes on. This is where you perceive that the Dhamma is unaffected by time. This means that the element of Dhamma that the Buddha taught us is always present. You experience it only when you are mindful and concentrated in deep meditation.

You cannot put this experience into words. This is the state where the law of Dhamma is distinctly present in your mind. It is here that you see suffering, but you do not suffer from suffering. You can see the truth of all dhammas, all feelings, all consciousness, all thoughts, and all perceptions. The truth that you see in all of them is that they all are flowing through the awareness. They are just flowing through. Nothing is sticking. The attention does not snag on anything. It just flows.

You must go through rigorous training. It takes all the elements we have discussed to gain concentration of this quality—virtue, restraint, mindfulness, clear comprehension, contentment, making effort, choosing a secluded place, and metta practice. As you are not attached to these wholesome thoughts, in spite of the fact that they are very pleasing, you can stay mindfully in this state without coming out of it and without being attached to it. This is the state you protect without being attached to it.

> Protecting what has been won,
> clinging to nothing.

Your attention, mindfulness, and concentration work together to see the impermanence, unsatisfactoriness, and selflessness of these jhanic factors themselves, which are not thoughts but dynamic actions or activities in the mind and body. Mind can easily notice them as they occur. In fact, in jhana they are clearer and more prominent than at any other time.

Even after coming out of jhana, you remember the factors that were present in jhana. But then what you have experienced is all gone. Reflecting on the impermanence, unsatisfactoriness, and selflessness of these factors is most effective while you are participating in them, not before or after.

You experience the impermanence of anything best while you are actually experiencing it. What you do after or before your experience is intellectualizing or philosophizing, using logic and reason.

Probably the most important of the ancient teachers of the past is Venerable Buddhaghosa. He created the great Theravada compendium called the *Visuddhimagga*, or *Path to Purification*. One thing he pointed out is that one meaning of jhana is to burn up the factors opposing jhana. You cannot burn them by thinking about them. You burn anything when the objects are there, actually present.

Defilements have "influxes" and "outfluxes." They flow into the mind and brew there, becoming ever more potent. Then they flow out with even more force. They manifest as harsh words and evil deeds and emotional uproar. In jhana, you burn these influxes and outfluxes directly. They are deep down in your subconscious mind, but they are coming up to the conscious level in small, subtle doses during jhana.

The jhanic state is very calm, peaceful, and quiet. Your concentration, with mindfulness and equanimity purified, can reach these influxes and outfluxes and uproot them. It is not impeded by emotional reaction. If you try to do this outside jhana, you will be simply trying to use your logical, rational thinking to eliminate them. It will not be successful. You can burn or eliminate them in a deep, concentrated state of mind. That is the time the mind is fully qualified to eradicate them. For defilements to burn, they must arise in the mind. They must be burnt as they are arising, neither before nor after.

Jhana can help you burn the ill influences out of the mind in other ways too. Sometimes, while listening to the Dhamma, your mind can go into deep concentration. You can see the meaning of the Dhamma, see the meaning of life, and remove the roots of greed, hatred, and delusion while sitting right there on that very same spot. That is why, when the Buddha gave Dhamma talks, many people—monks, nuns, men, and women—attained stages of enlightenment. These mental states become crystal clear when the mind is free from hindrances and other psychic irritants.

You might even remember something like this. It happens to everyone. While listening to a talk, you lose the thread. For a while, your mind is not on the talk. It is somewhere else, deeply engaged in something else. After some time your mind returns. During the time your mind was thinking of something else you did not even hear the speaker.

The same mental process can take place while listening to a Dhamma talk. While the speaker is giving the Dhamma talk, your mind goes into the deep meaning of the words he utters. Then you see the intrinsic nature of the things the speaker says. The Dhamma becomes perfectly clear. You realize the perfection of the Buddha's teaching through a little window of vision into the clarity and purity of Dhamma. As this realization arises, your mind experiences the pristine purity of Dhamma and your doubt vanishes.

At this moment you enter the path of "stream entry."

13. The Immaterial Jhanas

You do not need the immaterial jhanas to achieve liberation. What is essential is the practice of the noble eightfold path. However, the practice of the immaterial jhanas can contribute to the growth of calm and insight. They can embellish the spiritual perfection of a meditator, so the Buddha included them in his discipline. They are options for you if you are inclined to develop them.

THE FOUR ARUPPAS

The four immaterial jhanas are called the *aruppas* or "peaceful immaterial liberations transcending material form." They are not designated by numerical names like their predecessors, but by the names of their objective spheres: the base of boundless space; the base of boundless consciousness; the base of voidness; the base of neither perception nor nonperception.

They are called "formless" or "immaterial" for two reasons: First, they are achieved by overcoming all perceptions of material form (*rupa*), even of the subtle material form of the counterpart sign of your meditation object. And second, they are the subjective counterparts of the immaterial planes of existence.

The movement from any lower jhana to its successor involves the elimination of the coarser jhanic factors. The refinement of

547

consciousness that occurs hinges upon actual changes in the composition of the states. However, when you ascend from the fourth jhana to the first immaterial jhana, and from one immaterial jhana to another, there are no changes in these compositional factors. The fourth jhana and all four formless jhana attainments have precisely the same factors of consciousness. The factors in each higher attainment are subtler than those in its predecessors, more peaceful and more sublime, but they do not differ in number or in their essential nature.

You achieve the climb from one formless attainment to another by changing the object of concentration, not by eliminating or replacing component factors. All five states contain the same two jhanic factors: one-pointedness and "neither painful nor pleasant" feeling.

THE FIRST ARUPPA: THE BASE OF BOUNDLESS SPACE

The four formless attainments must be achieved in sequence, beginning with the base of boundless space and culminating in the base of neither perception nor nonperception. The motivation that leads you to seek the immaterial states is a clear recognition of the dangers posed by gross physical matter. You might also be repelled by matter as a result of considering the numerous afflictions to which your physical body is vulnerable. You can have eye diseases, ear diseases, and all the other things that bodies are plagued with.

If you want to escape these dangers, you must first attain the four material jhanas. You enter the fourth jhana, taking as your object any of the kasinas except the limited space kasina. At that point you have risen above gross matter, but you still have not completely transcended all material form. The self-luminous counterpart sign, the object of your jhana, is still a material form. To reach the formless attainments you must genuinely yearn to rise completely above the materiality of the kasina. The countersign's materiality is the counterpart of gross matter. It shares the defects of matter.

Why should you be afraid of ordinary, physical matter? Buddhaghosa gives us a simile. Suppose a timid man is pursued by a snake in the forest. He flees. Later he sees something resembling the snake. It might be a palm leaf with a streak painted on it, a creeper, a rope, or a crack in the ground. He becomes fearful and anxious. He does not want to look at it.

You can be frightened by seeing the danger in gross matter, as the man was afraid of the snake. You can flee from gross matter and escape by reaching the fourth jhana. You can observe that the subtle matter of the kasina is the counterpart of gross matter and not want to look at it.

Once you have generated a strong desire to reach the immaterial jhanas, you must achieve the five steps of mastery of the second and third jhanas you learned in chapter 11. Then, after emerging from the jhana, you perceive its defects and the benefits of the next higher attainment. The defects are:

The fourth jhana has an object of material form. It is still connected with gross matter.

It is close to happiness, a factor of the third jhana.

It is coarser than the immaterial attainments.

You then see the *base of boundless space* as more peaceful and sublime than the fourth jhana and as more safely removed from materiality. The method for attaining this first formless jhana is to extend the kasina mentally "to the limit of the world-sphere, or as far as you like." You then remove the kasina by attending exclusively to the space it covered.

The original physical kasina provides the preliminary sign for concentration. You keep focusing your mind on it until the mental image or learning sign appears. This memorized mental image is apprehended as clearly as the physical object. Concentration on the learning sign gives rise to the counterpart sign. This conceptualized image is used as the object for access concentration and the material jhanas.

After entering each jhana, you learn to extend the sign outward by degrees, making the visualized kasina cover increasingly larger areas—up to a world system or more. Now, to reach the base of boundless space, you must remove the kasina and attend exclusively to the space it has been made to cover.

> *When he is removing it,*
> *he neither folds it up like a mat*
> *nor withdraws it like a cake from a tin.*
> *It is simply that he does not advert to it*
> *or give attention to it or review it;*
> *it is when he neither adverts to it*
> *nor gives attention to it nor reviews it*
> *but gives his attention exclusively*
> *to the space touched by it*
> *[regarding that] as "space, space,"*
> *that he is said to "remove the kasina."*

Taking as your object the space left after the removal of the kasina, you advert to it as "boundless space, boundless space," or simply as "space, space." You strike at it with applied and sustained thought. You cultivate this practice again and again, repeatedly developing it until the concept reaches maturity. When your development is fully matured, a new moment of consciousness arises with boundless space as its object.

> *With the complete surmounting of perceptions of matter,*
> *with the disappearance of perceptions of resistance,*

with nonattention to perceptions of variety,
aware of "unbounded space,"
he enters into and dwells in
the base consisting of boundless space.

Several phrases in this formula may benefit from some clarification: "With the complete surmounting of perceptions of matter" means that you transcend all material perceptions, both the ordinary perception of the physical kasina and its subtle counterpart sign. You have left behind the mental objects you used to achieve and sustain the material jhanas.

"With the disappearance of perceptions of resistance" means that every physical perception contains a striking of the sense organs upon some sensory object. There is always a slight resistance, a moment of felt impact. You also leave this behind.

"With nonattention to perceptions of variety" means that every time you experience any one thing, you are distinguishing that object from all other perceptions. You are chopping your experiential world into pieces. You leave this sense of diversity behind as well.

"Unbounded space" means that since there are no separate perceptions, no boundary for the space can be perceived. There can be no "beginning" or "middle" or "end." It is boundless.

What results are discrete moments of consciousness, with discrete names in the Pali language. There are three or four moments of access concentration, still in touch with the physical senses and characterized by equanimity. Then follows the moment of complete engagement in the subtle feeling of boundless space.

A note relative to the limited space kasina—there's a small tricky point here. You can use any of the kasinas except the limited space kasina, which is meant to stand for any restricted space. Meditators usually concentrate on a hole in a wall, the space inside a keyhole, a window—something like that. The objective of this exercise is to expand your meditation object until it fills and represents boundless space. You cannot expand limited space to boundless space. Limited means limited. This meditation object simply will not work for this exercise.

THE SECOND ARUPPA: THE BASE OF BOUNDLESS CONSCIOUSNESS

To attain the second aruppa, you must achieve full mastery over the first and then see its defects. It is still close to the material jhanas and it is less peaceful than the attainments above it. You reflect on these defects until they are real to you. Then the mind naturally develops indifference toward the first aruppa and you turn your attention toward the second.

> By completely surmounting the base
> consisting of boundless space,
> aware of "unbounded consciousness,"
> he enters and dwells in
> the base consisting of boundless consciousness.

You focus upon the consciousness that is aware of that boundless space. This consciousness is also boundless and even more refined. You advert to it as "boundless consciousness" or simply as "awareness, awareness." Your object is awareness but you always keep that boundless, infinite nature in mind.

These are normal conscious thoughts and you turn to them again and again. You repeat to yourself over and over "awareness, awareness." The hindrances are restrained and the mind enters access concentration. You continue to cultivate the counterpart sign that results. There follows a moment of complete engagement in the "base of boundless consciousness."

THE THIRD ARUPPA:
THE BASE OF NOTHINGNESS (VOIDNESS)

To attain the next aruppa, the base of nothingness, you fully master the base of boundless consciousness. Then, after reviewing it, you become convinced that this attainment is imperfect due to its proximity to the base of boundless space. It is gross compared to the next higher jhana. By recognizing these defects, you remove your attachment. You perceive that the base of nothingness is more peaceful. The formula is:

> *By completely surmounting*
> *the base consisting of boundless consciousness,*
> *aware that "there is nothing,"*
> *he enters upon and dwells in*
> *the base consisting of nothingness.*

To concentrate on the base of nothingness, you give attention to the nonexistence, the voidness, and the secluded aspect of the base of boundless space. The consciousness of boundless space was an experience. It is gone. It is no longer present in your mind. You attend to that absence. The boundless space contained nothing. That too is absence. You attend to that absence.

The *Visuddhimagga* explains it this way: A monk sees a group of monks assembled in a hall. Then he goes away. When he returns they are gone. He does not think about the monks or where they have gone. He just concentrates on their current absence, the total vacancy of the hall.

You advert to this absence over and over. You think to yourself, "there is not, there is not" or "void, void," or "nothing, nothing." The hindrances are restrained. Access concentration ensues. You continue to attend to the subtle counterpart sign that replaces the conscious thoughts. When this practice matures, there arises a moment of full engagement, a consciousness "belonging to the base of nothingness."

The base of boundless consciousness and base of nothingness are both concerned with the consciousness of the base of boundless space. However, they relate to it in opposite ways. The second aruppa objectifies it positively, focusing upon its content, the consciousness or awareness that fills the infinite space. The third aruppa focuses on its lack of content.

The "base of boundless consciousness" that must be surmounted is both the second immaterial jhana and its object.

THE FOURTH ARUPPA: THE BASE OF NEITHER PERCEPTION NOR NONPERCEPTION

If you choose to go further and reach the fourth and final aruppa, you must first achieve the five steps of mastery over the base of nothingness. Then you contemplate the defectiveness of that attainment and the superiority of the base of neither perception nor nonperception. You can also reflect upon the inherent unsatisfactoriness of perception. You can think, "Perception is a disease. Perception is a boil. Perception is a dart. The state of neither perception nor nonperception is more peaceful. It is sublime." This ends your attachment to the third aruppa and arouses a desire to attain the next.

The fourth aruppa has as its object the four mental aggregates that constitute the attainment of the base of nothingness: feeling, perception, mental formations, and consciousness. The second aruppa took as its object the consciousness belonging to the first aruppa. Similarly, the fourth aruppa takes as its object the consciousness of the third aruppa and its associated states.

Focusing on these four mental aggregates of the base of nothingness, you advert to that state as "peaceful, peaceful." You review it, strike at it with vitakka, and sustain the thought with vicara. The hindrances are restrained. The mind enters access concentration. You then pass into total engagement in the base of neither perception nor nonperception.

By completely surmounting
the base consisting of nothingness,
he enters and dwells
in the base
consisting of neither perception nor nonperception.

You attain the fourth aruppa by passing beyond the base of nothingness. Yet this fourth attainment has the third as its object. You reach the fourth aruppa by focusing upon the base of nothingness as "peaceful, peaceful."

How can you overcome the base of nothingness if you attend to it? The *Visuddhimagga* provides an answer. Although you attend to the third aruppa as peaceful, you have no desire to attain it. This is because you have already decided that the fourth aruppa is more peaceful and sublime.

Buddhaghosa gives the example of a king who sees craftsmen at work while proceeding along a city street. He admires their skill but does not want to become a craftsman himself. He is aware of the superior benefits of kingship.

The name "base consisting of neither perception nor nonperception" suggests the abstruse nature of this jhana. On one hand, it lacks gross perception. On the other, it retains a certain subtle perception. Lacking gross perception, it cannot perform the decisive function of perception—the clear discernment of objects. Thus it cannot be said to have perception. Yet it retains an extremely subtle perception. Thus it cannot be said to be without perception. Perception, feeling, consciousness, contact, and the rest of the mental factors continue here, but are reduced to the finest subtlety. This jhana is also named the "attainment with residual formations."

The commentaries illustrate the meaning with the following anecdote. A novice smears a bowl with oil. An elder monk asks him to bring the bowl to serve gruel. The novice replies, "Venerable sir, there is oil in the bowl." The monk tells him, "Bring the oil, novice. I shall fill the oil tube." The novice says, "There is no oil, venerable sir."

What the novice said is true in both cases. There is "no oil" since there is not enough to fill the tube. Yet there is no utter absence of oil since some remains in the bowl.

With this fourth formless jhana, the mind has reached the highest possible level of development in the direction of serenity. Consciousness has attained the most intense degree of concentration. It has become so subtle and refined that it can no longer be described in terms of existence or nonexistence. Yet even this attainment, as we will see, is still a mundane state. From the Buddhist perspective, it must finally give way to insight. Insight alone leads to true liberation. We cover these points in the final chapter.

14. The Supramundane Jhanas

There are said to be four stages in the supramundane enlightenment process. They are: stream-enterer; once-returner; never-returner; arahant.

The stages occur in this order and we will look at each of them in this chapter. You attain the supramundane jhanas at the moment of stream entry.

Those who attain mundane jhanas restrain hindrances but don't destroy them. Mundane jhana attainers live happily so long as they do not lose their jhanic attainment. Those who attain the supramundane jhanas, on the other hand, destroy the hindrances as well as fetters.

Attainers of mundane jhana alone may still have the desire to "be reborn in the Brahma realms," which is to say, to gain some better circumstance than they have now. They may still have hopes for some future self, different from and better than their present situation. But supramundane jhana attainers destroy any desire whatsoever to be born in any form or shape. It is written that, if the meditator attains the supramundane jhanas without attaining full enlightenment, he will be reborn a limited number of times, and only in higher planes of existence.

The final step of the path is the wisdom of full liberation. Everybody who attains any stage of enlightenment attains that state in supramundane jhanic concentration. Attaining full enlightenment brings rebirth to an end completely.

The Supramundane Noble Path

The supramundane jhanas are also called the Supramundane Noble Path. You began your practice with the mundane noble eightfold path. There was still some doubt in your mind. When you overcome doubt, you see the truth for yourself and enter the Supramundane Noble Eightfold Path. From that moment onward, until you attain full enlightenment, you are following the supramundane level of the noble eightfold path.

Each of the factors of the noble eightfold path has two aspects. The *mundane* aspect is "subject to the cankers, pertaining to the side of merit, and maturing in the foundation of existence." The *supramundane* aspect is, "noble, free from cankers, supramundane, and a factor of the path."

Even at the mundane level of the path, you have to develop right view, right resolve, right speech, right action, right livelihood, right effort, and right mindfulness to attain right concentration. Now each must be developed fully, all the way to the supramundane level. Supramundane unification of mind is a noble, stainless state that abolishes any unwholesome mental condition.

Progress on the noble eightfold path can be roughly divided into four phases. Each corresponds to a person's level of jhanic attainment: *Uninstructed worldlings* are blocked by hindrances and fetters. They generally have no personal acquaintance with jhana.

Instructed worldlings have entered the mundane path. If they employ jhana at all, it is the mundane jhanas, in which hindrances are held at bay but not removed from the mind.

Noble disciples have crossed over into the Supramundane Noble Path. They employ the supramundane jhanas to eradicate the fetters that hold hindrances in place and bind them into samsara.

Arahants have no further work to do. The fetters are gone and they use the jhanas for "pleasant abiding."

All the steps of the noble eightfold path are mental states. That is true of both the mundane and the supramundane expressions of the path. When you see deeply, as a real experience, with your own wisdom-eye, that all conditioned things are impermanent, your mind-state changes. Your superficial understanding of impermanence becomes a deep understanding and you attain the stream-entry path. From that point onward, the noble eightfold path becomes the Supramundane Noble Path and you start demolishing the bridges that connect this life with the next.

DESTROYING DOUBT

To attain stream entry, you must overcome doubt, which is classified as both a hindrance and a fetter. When you attain the mundane jhanas, you restrain doubt, but when you attain stream entry, you destroy it. It is easier to destroy doubt if you have weakened it. You learned to sidestep doubt in order to enter jhana. That made it weak enough that you can subject it to the intense scrutiny of mindfulness and burn it up forever.

There are two personality types who have less trouble with doubt: The first type, the *faith-follower*, is a person whose primary vehicle for the attainment of enlightenment is faith. He follows a devotional path based on deep faith in the Buddha, Dhamma, and Sangha. Due to this strong faith, he can attain the stream-entry path without attaining any mundane jhana. His faith allows him to destroy doubt.

The second type, the *Dhamma-follower* or *wisdom-follower*, is a person whose primary vehicle on the path is a deep understanding of the Dhamma. He uses the intellect extensively. His reason leads him to the deep, wordless understanding that is true wisdom. He can attain the stream-entry path through penetrative insight alone, without attaining jhana. His insight allows him to destroy doubt.

Only these personality types can go directly to the supramundane jhanas to destroy the fetters. Others need the mundane jhanas to weaken them first.

So are you either of these types? Be honest. What happens to the rest of us? Do we still have a chance for liberation? The answer is a resounding "Yes!" And this is precisely what jhanas are for.

STAGES OF THE SUPRAMUNDANE NOBLE PATH

Each of the four stages of the Supramundane Noble Path is divided into a path phase and a fruition phase. Both phases have definite characteristics. For each stage, there is a specific realization that marks the beginning of the path phase and another that signals "graduation" to the fruition phase. Each stage is marked by the elimination of one or more of the fetters. The order in which these are destroyed depends on your personality type. Faith-followers destroy the fetters in one order. Dhamma-followers proceed by another sequence.

The Abhidhamma Pitaka is an ancient work that provides a detailed analysis of the principles that govern mental and physical processes. It is a detailed scholastic reworking of doctrinal material appearing in the suttas, according to schematic classifications and numerous lists.

In the Abhidhamma texts, there is some suggestion that the path and the fruition periods can arise very rapidly, almost simultaneously.

I feel that each phase may take a moment, a lifetime, or anywhere in between. The texts say that reflection on what is being accomplished at each stage of the process is very important, and there must be time for this reflection to take place. In addition, some texts talk about the comparative amount of merit obtained from offering gifts to someone who is in one or another of these stages. To me this means that people remain in each stage long enough to be distinguished from one another.

Other suttas imply that the path phase arises first. Then the meditator associates with the path phase, develops it, and cultivates it before attaining the fruition state. This means that the person has time to associate, cultivate, and develop the path before attaining the fruition state. Even if somebody's attainment seems instant, he still must attain the path first and afterward attain fruition. Attaining path and fruition at once is impossible. It is never mentioned in any sutta.

When you practice the Supramundane Noble Path, you become one of the "eight noble disciples of the Buddha." A "noble disciple" is one who enters the noble eightfold path at the supramundane level. This is the stage at which "his fetters fade away." Such a person has already attained at least stream entry with concentration at the supramundane jhanic level.

In each phase of each stage, it is important to reflect on the process. The ancient texts lay out four things to reflect on: what defilements have been destroyed, which ones remain to be handled, the path that led to that destruction, the fruition that resulted.

Stream Entry

The first supramundane jhana destroys the first three fetters: belief in a permanent self, doubt, and attachment to rites and rituals. The precise order in which these three fetters are eliminated depends on your personality. If your path is faith, then at the attainment of the stream-entry path you will first destroy doubt. If your path is wisdom, then at the attainment of the stream-entry path you will first destroy the notion of self. The description below follows the first of these options.

Path. At the path phase of stream entry, you "attain the Dhamma, understand the Dhamma, and fathom the Dhamma." You cross beyond doubt, do away with perplexity, gain intrepidity, and establish yourself in the Buddha's teaching without depending on others. Up until now your doubt has been held at bay by the joy of the second jhana. This is the level at which you experience the complete disappearance of doubt. No sign remains of your previous confusion concerning the Buddha, Dhamma, Sangha, and morality.

You go on practicing the noble eightfold path at the supramundane level. Your belief in attaining liberation by following rites and rituals disappears without a trace. You realize that no ritual that you have been following in the past could bring you the knowledge you have gained. Only the practice of Dhamma and the gaining of right concentration have done that.

Fruition. You attain stream-entry fruition when you overcome the belief in a separate self. There is still a lingering sense of "I" in the mind, but you don't take it seriously.

This awareness arouses your firm confidence in the Buddha, Dhamma, and Sangha, the noble disciples who became noble by following the Buddha and his teaching. You now have full confidence that there is life before this life, and that there are beings who have followed the Buddha's path and attained full liberation from suffering.

With confidence, the strength of your faith, and the clear understanding that there is no self, you proceed. You pay attention to the impermanent nature of your bodily and mental experiences. You remember that all your past physical and mental experiences have changed. Similarly, all physical and mental experiences of the future will change, too. All past, present, and future experiences arise and pass away. You understand that the five aggregates, form, feeling, perceptions, thoughts, and consciousness, are all of the same nature, arising and passing away. They are all due to causes and conditions. When those conditions change, they pass away.

Knowing that there is birth before and after death, fear arises. You realize that if you don't liberate yourself from suffering immediately, you will be reborn. You will suffer through the same pain, sorrow, grief, and despair. You may fear that you will die without liberating yourself from all this suffering. Knowing this, you wish to liberate yourself from samsara altogether. You want never to be born again.

Once-Returner

The second supramundane jhana weakens your addiction to sensual pleasure and hatred.

Path. Now you see the five aggregates constantly, every single tiny event, in every single breath. You notice that every intentional occurrence in your body and mind involves all five aggregates. As they involve themselves in each and every thing you intentionally do, you see their tiny little parts in a constant state of flux. They change without remaining the same for even a fraction of a second. When the gross part of your lust vanishes you enter the once-returner's path.

Fruition. When the gross part of your hatred vanishes, you enter the once-returner's fruition stage.

If you have been a person prone to hate, the first fetter to be overcome is the gross part of lust. If you have been more prone to lust, you overcome the gross part of hatred first. Whichever fetter has been predominant will be the last to be overcome. Notice that we said "the gross part" of anger and desire. The subtle part of each remains.

Never-Returner

The third supramundane jhana destroys for good addiction to sensual pleasure and hatred. One meditator may first destroy greed for sensual pleasure. Another might destroy hatred first. This difference depends, as before, on the person's temperament and character.

Path. With more vigor, courage, confidence, and clarity than ever, you practice the noble eightfold path at the supramundane level. When the loving-friendliness, compassion, appreciative joy, and equanimity that were initiated at the attainment of the first jhana come to fruition, the subtle level of hatred totally vanishes from your mind. At that moment, you enter the never-returner's path.

Fruition. Then, when the last remnant of craving for sensual pleasures vanishes forever, you enter the state of never-returner's fruition.

Arahant

The fourth supramundane jhana destroys the final five fetters: desire for material existence, desire for immaterial existence, conceit, restlessness, and ignorance. When you make the jump from mundane right concentration to supramundane right concentration, your luminous mind can be permanently purified from external defilements. The result is arahantship.

Path. Here all desire for material existence evaporates. As you progress on that path, desire for material and immaterial existence, conceit, and restlessness each vanish from your mind.

Fruition. Finally, the last residue of the I-maker and the last iota of ignorance of the four noble truths are erased from your mind. At that point, you attain the fruition of full enlightenment.

Then this thought arises: "Birth is exhausted, lived is the holy life, done is what was to be done, there is nothing more to be done."

At this point, you have attained liberation, the ultimate goal of Buddhist practice, through a long, arduous process of awakening.

And it all began with the simple observation of a breath going in and out.

Glossary

ABANDONING: Giving up unwholesome habits.

ABHIDHAMMA: The Abhidhamma is Theravada Buddhism's gigantic compendium of everything known about meditation and related subjects.

ACCESS CONCENTRATION: The improved ability to focus exclusively on the breath or other object for longer and longer periods. It marks the boundary between ordinary meditation and the jhana states of deep concentration.

ADVERTING: To turn the mind or attention toward something. The ability to bring your attention mindfully to the jhanic factors one by one after emerging from jhana. This is part of jhana mastery.

AGGREGATES: The five traditional constituents of body and mind: form, feeling, perception, thought, and consciousness.

ANATTA: No "self"—The realization that neither "I" nor any other conditioned "thing" is actually self-existing in its essence. All apparent things are temporary collections of impermanent elements undergoing continuous and sometimes subtle change.

ANICCA: *Impermanence*—The realization that all things arise and pass away and that their very nature is incessant change. Anicca is the actual experience of what is going on in one's body and mind. The body, mind, and everything in our sensory world is changing constantly.

ARAHANT: Advanced meditators who have reached the goal of complete liberation from suffering. It is the fourth stage of the supramundane path to enlightenment, during which all desire for material existence evaporates. The last residue of the I-maker and the last iota of ignorance of the four noble truths are also erased from one's mind. *See also* Stages of the Supramundane Path.

ATTAINING: The ability to enter jhana quickly. It improves with practice and is part of jhana mastery.

AWARENESS: Having knowledge of (e.g., "He had no awareness of his mistakes"). A state of elementary or undifferentiated consciousness (e.g., "The crash intruded on his awareness").

BHIKKHU: A fully ordained monk. A member of the Buddha's Sangha or community of followers.

BOJJHANGAS: In Pali, the seven factors of enlightenment: mindfulness, investigation, energy, joy, tranquility, concentration, and equanimity. The word comes from *bodhi*, which means "enlightenment," and *anga*, which means limb.

CESSATION: Ending—the Buddha's third noble truth, the promise that suffering has an end. Cessation with no further rebirth is nibbana, liberation, freedom from suffering.

CLEAR COMPREHENSION: *See* Sampajanna.

CONCENTRATION: Concentration is a gathering together of all the positive forces of the mind, tying them into a bundle, and welding them into a single intense beam that will stay where one points it.

COUNTERPART SIGN: The object of focus is called a "preliminary sign" or "learning sign" and is used for learning. The meditator gazes at it until he or she memorizes it. The memorized picture is called the "counterpart sign," which the meditator holds in mind and uses as the meditation object to enter jhana.

CRAVING: Desire to have more or less of something. The existence of objects in the world does not cause craving to arise in one's mind automatically. But when one encounters them and reflects on them in an unwise manner, craving is the result. Craving is one of the most powerful of the unwholesome roots, the deepest forces of the mind, the ones that feed the fetters. It is the cause of suffering. Once craving is eliminated, suffering will be eliminated.

DELUSION: The confused belief in a permanently existing self or soul. We believe that there must be something real and permanent called *I* or *me* that is identical with the body and mind or is within the body and mind.

DEPENDENT ARISING: Anything that depends for its existence on impermanent and ever-changing causes and conditions. All such things arise, remain for a time, and then disappear.

DHAMMA (CAPITALIZED): The teachings of the Buddha. When lower-cased, *dhamma* is phenomena; also the true nature of phenomena, as taught by the Buddha—his profound insight that all conditioned phenomena are impermanent (*anicca*), suffering (*dukkha*), and selfless (*anatta*).

DISCURSIVE THOUGHT: Discursive means "proceeding to a conclusion by reason or argument rather than intuition." In this book we divide "thought" into two categories. *Discursive thought* is the one-concept-leading-to-the-next variety of thought you hear most of the time, like a voice speaking in your head. *Subtle thought* is nonverbal and intuitive.

DISPASSION: The opposite of attachment. One of ten special percep-tions that arise as a result of mindfulness meditation. Mindful that everything that arises as a result of causes and conditions is imper-manent, unsatisfactory, and selfless, one experiences dispassion and abandons the belief that attachment to anything in this world can make one permanently happy.

DOUBT: One of the five hindrances. Does one have to accept every-thing one's teacher says on faith, without proof and without any analysis of your own? No. But certain doubts are deadly: Emotional doubt is doubt about the Buddha, the Sangha, and morality. Intellec-tual doubt is doubting essential aspects of the Dhamma.

DUKKHA: *Suffering, unsatisfactoriness*—The realization that some amount of suffering exists in every experience within samsara.

EMERGING: This means that one attains jhana at will and comes out of jhana at will and without difficulty at a predetermined time. One doesn't wait in jhana until one loses it. This is part of jhana mastery.

ENLIGHTENMENT: Full and complete liberation from suffering. By attaining enlightenment, the Buddha and arahants have attained cessation. Having eliminated the fetters that bind someone to the cycle of births and deaths, they will not take rebirth in any form anywhere.

FACTORS OF ENLIGHTENMENT OR FACTORS OF AWAKENING: *See* Thirty-Seven Factors of Enlightenment.

FAITH FOLLOWER: Someone whose primary vehicle for the attainment of enlightenment is faith. He or she follows a devotional path based on deep faith in the Triple Gem and, based on that faith, can attain the stream-entry path without first attaining any of the mundane jhanas.

FETTERS: The ten deep-rooted habits and underlying tendencies of the unenlightened mind that bind us to one unsatisfactory life after another. The fetters arise directly from the contact of our senses with sensory objects and consciousness and are fed by the three poisons: greed, hatred, and delusion. The ten fetters are: belief in a permanent self, skeptical doubt, dependence on rituals, craving for sensual pleasure, ill will, craving for a fine material existence, craving for an immaterial existence, conceit, restlessness, ignorance. The first five fetters are called lower, the last five higher. Hindrances are the offshoots of fetters. *See also* Hindrances.

FOUR ELEMENTS: An analytical system to help one focus on the four foundations of mindfulness. The elements are *earth* (solidity—the earth element represents solidity, heaviness, solidness, compactness, and is characterized by hardness or softness); *water* (liquidity—the water element has a moist or flowing quality); *air* (oscillation—the air element is experienced primarily as motion or stillness); *fire* (heat—the fire element manifests as heat or cold or any sense of temperature in between, or as the dry sensation that goes with heat).

FOUR FOUNDATIONS OF MINDFULNESS: *See* Satipatthana.

THE FOUR NOBLE TRUTHS: The Buddha's first essential teaching, delivered at the Deer Park near Varanasi after he achieved enlightenment: (1) the truth of suffering, (2) the truth of the cause of suffering—craving, (3) the truth of cessation—the end of suffering, and (4) the noble eightfold path—the step-by-step method to ending suffering.

HINDRANCES: Negative tendencies or distractions that hamper concentration and obstruct or impede our spiritual progress along the path. They include sense desire, ill will and sloth, torpor, restlessness and worry, and skeptical doubt. Concentration meditation suppresses the hindrances temporarily, but only the jhana states of concentrated meditation can eliminate them. In samadhi meditation we focus our minds on a certain object in order to suppress these hindrances and thus attain the mundane jhanas. *See also* Fetters, Restlessness and Worry.

IDDHIPADDA: Spiritual powers that develop as a result of deep concentration meditation. They help us to destroy the fetters and to progress to higher and higher states of accomplishment.

IGNORANCE: Not knowing the basic insights of the Buddha, especially the four noble truths.

ILL WILL: When one's motivation is unkind or aggressive, even a little, one will have ill will. In that condition one cannot appreciate the beauty of anything or anybody. It is like a man who is sick and cannot enjoy delicious food because his taste buds are affected.

INSIGHT MEDITATION: Also called *vipassana* or *mindfulness meditation*. Focused awareness that helps us gain insight into the nature of the body, feelings, thoughts, and phenomena.

JHANA: The stages of deep concentration meditation that take meditators beyond ordinary mindfulness into a series of deeply tranquil, harmonious, and powerful states. The sequence of mental states become more and more insubstantial as we proceed through them. The word *jhana* derives from *jha* (Sanskrit *dyai*). It means to "burn," "suppress," or "absorb." Jhana is a deep, tranquil state of meditation, a balanced state of mind where numerous wholesome mental factors work together in harmony to make the mind calm, relaxed, serene, peaceful, smooth, soft, pliable, bright, and equanimous. In that state of mind, mindfulness, effort, concentration, and understanding are consolidated.

The first four jhanas are states of experience that lie just beyond our ordinary cognitive, sensory world but still have some relationship to it. Qualities of the first jhana include very little normal thought or sensation, subtle thoughts of good will and compassion, joy, happiness, equanimity, mindfulness, and concentration. In the second jhana subtle thought drops away, joy predominates, and happiness, equanimity, mindfulness, and concentration are noticeably present. In the third jhana joy drops away, happiness predominates, and equanimity, mindfulness, and concentration grow. Qualities of the fourth jhana include purified mindfulness and equanimity, mindfulness and concentration fused into a unit, and direct perception of anicca, dukkha, and anatta.

The fifth, sixth, seventh, and eighth jhanas are four states that have very little relationship to our ordinary cognitive and sensory world. They are the immaterial or formless jhanas and are usually referred to individually as the *base of infinite space*, the *base of infinite consciousness or awareness*, the *base of nothingness*, and the *base of neither perception nor nonperception*. In the fifth jhana one dwells on the mental "space" within which experience takes place and expands that to infinity. In the sixth jhana one dwells on the infinite awareness or consciousness that has that experience. In the seventh jhana one turns one's attention to the nothingness, the total voidness, within that awareness. The eighth jhana is a state of awareness that is so subtle that it cannot be called perception or nonperception.

JOY: The ordinary, material joy we are accustomed to arises from contacting things that are wished for. When you seek and know the impermanence, the change, the fading away, and the cessation of all these things, a different joy arises called *joy based on renunciation*.

KAMMA: The universal principle of cause and effect. Our countless actions of body, speech, and mind are causes. Our present life and everything that happens to us are the effects that arise from the causes we created in this life or previous lives. In general good actions lead to good results and bad actions to bad results.

KASINA: A physical object used as a meditation focus. Traditionally kasinas were circles used to represent certain concepts. Kasina means an object that represents a pure concept, the essence of all things with that quality.

LEARNING SIGN: *See* Counterpart Sign.

LIBERATION: Termination of bondage and complete freedom from suffering. The state of being free from the cycle of repeated births and deaths in samsara propelled by kamma and craving. *See also* Nibbana.

LIGHT: *See* Luminous.

LUMINOUS: Referring to the bright and radiant nature of the basic mind. Jhana is where one sees that clearly. The arising of the counterpart sign is often experienced as light. The mind is filled with a beautiful light, and one sees everything clearly.

METTA: A state of mind characterized by loving-friendliness. A meditation procedure in which you generate loving-friendliness toward yourself and all beings.

MINDFUL REFLECTION: A thought process that takes in what is happening at the moment in the mind and body. It includes the deep nature of what one is experiencing, the effects that perception is having on one, and the effects that it will have on the mind in the future. It sometimes includes "talking to yourself."

MINDFULNESS: The quality of mind that notices and recognizes.

NEVER-RETURNER (NONRETURNER): The third level of achievement on the path to complete liberation, during which one eliminates the subtle remnants of hatred and greed for sensual pleasure. A meditator who reaches this level will never be born in the human realm again. Rebirth will be in a pure abode where practice continues toward complete liberation. *See also* Stages of the Supramundane Path.

NIBBANA: Literally "extinction" (Sanskrit *nirvana*). The highest and ultimate goal of Buddhist aspiration—liberation, the absolute extinction of greed, hatred, delusion, and clinging to existence; freedom from the life-after-life cycle of births and deaths. *See also* Liberation.

NOBLE EIGHTFOLD PATH (THE PATH): The eight steps to freedom from suffering: skillful understanding, skillful thinking, skillful speech, skillful action, skillful livelihood, skillful effort, skillful mindfulness, and skillful concentration. The entire noble eightfold path is divided into two parts—mundane and supramundane—depending on whether the eight factors are partially or fully developed. The eight steps of the path must all be in place in one's life in order to create the peaceful, settled atmosphere one needs to cultivate jhanas.

NONSTICKINESS: A state in which nothing sticks to the mind. It all just flows through.

ONCE-RETURNER: The second level of achievement on the path to complete liberation, during which one eliminates the gross parts of lust and hatred. A meditator who reaches this level will take rebirth in the human realm at most one more time before achieving enlightenment. *See also* Stages of the Supramundane Path.

PALI: The ancient scriptural language of Theravada Buddhism.

PRELIMINARY SIGN: *See* Counterpart Sign.

RESOLVING: The ability to resolve or decide to remain in jhana for exactly a predetermined length of time. This ability is weak in the lower jhanas and grows in the higher ones. This is part of jhana mastery.

RESTLESSNESS AND WORRY: One of the five hindrances. The "monkey mind" jumps about constantly and refuses to settle down. *See also* Hindrances.

REVIEWING: The ability to review the jhana and its factors with retrospective knowledge immediately after adverting to them. One has noticed the factor, now one consciously reviews it. This is part of jhana mastery.

RIGHT CONCENTRATION: Right concentration (*samma samadhi*) is defined and explained in terms of the first five jhanas—mindfulness gradually increases as jhana practice is developed. Mindfulness is the prerequisite and the basis of concentration; it necessarily supports right concentration. Mindfulness and concentration become pure in the fourth jhana owing to the presence of equanimity. In the noble eightfold path concentration is qualified as *right concentration* in order to differentiate it from wrong concentration. Concentration without mindfulness is *wrong concentration*. *See also* Right Jhana, Wrong Concentration.

RIGHT JHANA: Mindfulness is present in every state of right jhana, along with the other seven factors of awakening. *See also* Right Concentration.

SAMADHI: *Jhana* and *samadhi* are closely connected ideas but are not the same thing. *Jhana* is limited in meaning: there must be five jhanic factors present. *Samadhi* means concentration in general. It derives from a prefixed verbal root that means "to collect" or "to bring together." This suggests concentration or unification of mind. Samadhi can be either wholesome or unwholesome.

SAMAPATTI: The deepest stages of samadhi. In some Buddhist texts the terms *samadhi* and *samapatti* are used synonymously.

SAMATHA: *Samatha*, meaning "serenity," is almost interchangeable with the term *samadhi*. Samatha, however, comes from a different root that means "to become calm" and is sometimes translated as "calm abiding." Both terms are defined as "one-pointedness of mind." This peaceful, one-pointed mind suppresses the hindrances and settles the emotional commotion of the mind, making the mind calm, peaceful, and luminous. It can only be wholesome.

SAMPAJANNA: Clear comprehension, clarity of consciousness. *Sampajanna* means remaining fully awake and conscious of everything your body is doing and everything you are perceiving in the midst of any activity. It is a turned-within monitoring of everything going on in the mind and body.

SAMSARA: The life-after-life cycle of birth, illness, aging, and death characterized by suffering.

SATI: "To remember" in Pali. It is also what is translated as "mindfulness": paying direct, nonverbal attention from one moment to the next to what is happening.

SATIPATTHANA: Four foundations of mindfulness—one can't get jhana through concentrating on just anything. One must use certain specific subjects in one's meditation that promote dispassionate observation and reveal the truth of *anicca* (impermanence), *dukkha* (suffering), and *anatta* (no "self"): Mindfulness of body (including breath), mindfulness of feeling (physical sensation), mindfulness of consciousness (thoughts), and mindfulness of dhammas (phenomena as mental activities, especially the primary ones, anicca, dukkha, and anatta).

SECLUSION: The jhana practitioner must leave behind all work, people, and family concerns, that is to say, all normal worries and unease. Physical separation is essential but not enough; mental separation is also needed. In this "liberation from attachment," one lets go of attachment to things, people, situations, and experiences.

STAGES OF THE SUPRAMUNDANE PATH: The enlightenment process is said to have stages. They are stream-enterer, once-returner, never-returner, and arahant, in that order. Each stage is marked by the lessening or elimination of one or more of the fetters. The order in which these fetters are destroyed depends on one's personality type. Faith-followers destroy the fetters in one order. Dhamma-followers proceed by another sequence. Each stage consists of a "path" and a "fruition" phase. *See also* Arahant, Never-Returner, Once-Returner, Stream-Enterer.

STREAM-ENTERER: The first milestone on the path to complete liberation, characterized by clarity and confidence in the Buddha's noble eightfold path. This is the moment one really sees the Dhamma and eliminates doubt, dependence on rituals, and the notion of "self." *See also* Stages of the Supramundane Path.

SUFFERING: *See* Dukkha.

SUNNATA: Emptiness of self. The wisdom that sees that there is no permanent self or soul and that everything that exists in samsara, including every human being, is impermanent, unsatisfactory, and selfless.

SUPRAMUNDANE JHANA: The states of jhanic consciousness that the noble ones have in the phases of enlightenment called stream entry, once-returner, never-returner, and arahant. Complete burning of the fetters leading to escape from samsara. Supramundane unification of mind is a noble, stainless state that abolishes any unwholesome mental condition. It is written that if the meditator attains supramundane jhana without attaining full enlightenment, he or she will be reborn a limited number of times and only in higher planes of existence. Attaining full enlightenment brings rebirth to an end completely.

SUTTA: Buddhist scripture, especially a narrative or discourse delivered by the Buddha or one of his well-known disciples.

THERAVADA: The Buddhist "tradition of the elders" that practices meditation as a path to nibbana, permanent liberation from suffering. It adheres to the Pali scriptures and is the primary tradition of Buddhist practice in Sri Lanka, Myanmar, Thailand, Laos, and Cambodia. It is also practiced in numerous Dhamma centers in the West.

THIRTY-SEVEN FACTORS OF ENLIGHTENMENT: Liberation is said to have components. A "factor" is a component or aspect of something. It is a dynamic thing, often a cause of something else, often something one must do or have in order to make that second thing come into existence. In this case, a factor is something that must be present in order for enlightenment to take place. The thirty-seven factors are the four foundations of mindfulness, the four bases for spiritual power, the four efforts, the five spiritual faculties, the five spiritual powers, the noble eightfold path, and the seven factors of enlightenment, or awakening.

UNMINDFUL REFLECTION: Total immersion in a thought process without noticing what is happening at the moment in the mind and body. It neglects to observe the deep nature of what one is experiencing, the effects that thought is having on one, and the effects that it will have on the mind in the future.

VIPASSANA: *Insight*—especially into the true nature of the self and phenomena. The intuitive understanding and perception that everything that is conditioned is impermanent (*anicca*), suffering (*dukkha*), and selfless (*anatta*).

VITAKKA/VICARA: *Vitakka* is called "thought" or "thought conception." It is the laying hold of a thought and is likened to the striking of a bell. *Vicara* is called "discursive thought." It is the mind roaming about or moving back and forth over thoughts. It is likened to the reverberation or resounding of the bell. Vitakka and vicara are present in normal consciousness and in the first jhana but absent in every jhana above the first.

VOIDNESS: Things flow through the mind. They leave no trace. One sees a void or vacuum in what has been lost. The word may also refer to the immaterial seventh jhana, perception of nothingness.

WISDOM-FOLLOWER: Someone whose primary vehicle on the path is wisdom, a deep understanding of the Dhamma. He or she uses the intellect extensively. Reason leads the follower to the deep, wordless understanding that is true wisdom. A wisdom-follower can attain stream entry through penetrative insight alone, without attaining jhana.

WRONG CONCENTRATION: Wrong concentration is absorption concentration without the other seven factors of the noble eightfold path. Without them, vipassana is not successful. There is no mindfulness in wrong concentration. Because you have not developed jhana with mindfulness, you become attached to the jhanic state. When you come out of wrong jhana, jhana that doesn't have mindfulness, you may think the experience you had was enlightenment. How do you know your concentration is wrong concentration? One clue is the absence of all feeling. You will not have any feeling only after attaining the highest jhana, the attainment of the "cessation of perception and feelings." Until then, you should still have feelings and perceptions. *See also* Right Concentration, Right Jhana.

Index

A

abandoning, 384, 492, 504, 519
  perception of, 347
  See also renunciation
Abharaja Kumara, 186
Abhidhamma, 198, 560–61
absorption, 389, 534–35
acceptance in vipassana practice, 36–37, 109, 135, 149–50, 182
access concentration, 360, 489–98, 535
  choosing a meditation subject, 489–92
  counterpart signs and, 508
  entry points for, 492–93
  immaterial jhanas and, 554, 555
  strengthening, 493–94
  See also concentration
accomplishment, the four bases of, 369
action(s)
  purpose of, 234–38
  right, 409, 558
  skillful, 368
  suitability, 238–39
addiction, 564
  to sensual pleasures, 458
adverting (step of mastery), 526–27
aggregates
  breath meditation and, 437–38
  fourth jhana and, 531–32
impermanence and, 466–68
selflessness and, 478–80
as suffering, 475–76
supramundane jhanas and, 563
understanding, 255–56
  See also consciousness; feeling(s); five aggregates; form; perception; volitional formations
aging. *See under* Buddha
agitation, 105, 124, 147, 217. *See also* restlessness
air element, 212, 213, 258–59, 437, 438–41
Akkosana, the story of, 190, 287, 288
Alarakalama, 391, 392
algae, ponds covered with
  metaphor of, 421
alters, 406
Amazon River, 533
Ananda (disciple of Buddha), 188, 207, 219, 232, 261
anatman. *See* no-self
anatta, 140, 141, 394, 485, 535. *See also* selflessness
anger, 44, 151, 185, 411–12, 425
  becoming aware of, 288–91, 329
  dealing with, 187–91; key points for, 291–92, 307–8
  mindfulness of, 290–93
  overcoming, 450–52
  supramundane jhanas and, 563

"talking" to, 461
  See also feeling(s)
Angulimala, 178–79, 188
anicca, 140. See also impermanence
Anuruddha (disciple of Buddha),
  325, 326, 331
anxiety, 32, 99, 162, 387–88, 437, 452
  about growing, 474
  concentration and, 446–47
  See also fear; feeling(s)
appamada, 142. See also mindfulness
appreciative joy, 176–77
arahants, xvi, 371–72, 557, 559, 564
architecture, 383
aruppas, four, 547–56
asceticism
  avoiding, 80, 98
  See also Five Ascetics
atman, 478
attachment, 411, 412
  Buddha on, 520
  clear comprehension and, 243–44
  death and, 268
  dispassion and, 347
  equanimity and, 536
  fetters and, 458
  impermanence and, 236, 465
  liberation from, 405
  meditation on the body and, 249
  to positive mental states, 125–26, 132
  to rituals, 458
  See also clinging
attaining (step of mastery), 527
attainment
  immaterial jhanas and, 548, 553
  impermanence of, 541
  supramundane jhanas and, 557–58
  voidness and, 542
  See also awakening; enlightenment
attention
  access concentration and, 496, 498

Buddha on, 214
  building awareness with, 232
  to feelings, 278, 279–85, 290
  fourth jhana and, 532, 543
  intention and, 229
  "joining both" state and, 533–34
  mindfulness and, 219
  right concentration and, 390, 394
  selflessness and, 477–78
  to thoughts, 308, 314–16
  See also bare attention; mindful-
    ness
attitudes conducive to meditation,
  35–39, 73–74
aversion, 6, 32, 108, 123, 147, 290,
  329. See also ill will; rejecting,
  hindrance of
awakening, 509–14. See also attainment; enlightenment
awareness
  the aggregate of consciousness as,
    303
  as alertness, 72
  application to mental states, 127
  balancing concentration with, 26,
    150–52, 197
  goal of, 14, 15, 138, 155, 163
  importance of, xiv, xv
  infinite, 486
  meditation as, 155
  mindfulness meditation and, xx,
    xxi, 354
  See also bare attention; conscious-
    ness; mindfulness; specific topics

B

bare attention, 136, 138, 139, 141,
  393–94
  mindfulness as, 136, 138, 139, 141
beginner pitfalls
  burnout, 79

discursive thought, 71
excitement over extraordinary sen-
    sations, 100
forcing breath, 69
trying too hard, 18, 80, 105–6
See also *specific pitfalls*
bells, use of, 406
Beyond Mindfulness in Plain English,
    xxii–xxiii, 358
bhavana, 28
bhikkhus, xvii, 381, 461
    defined, xvii
birth, 473, 499
    end of, for arahants, 371–72
    kamma and, 305
    See also *under* Buddha; rebirth
blame, 451
blaming, avoiding, 291
bliss, 388, 393, 503
    access concentration and, 493, 497
    equanimity and, 536
    jhana mental states and, 483, 484
    See also rapture
body
    access concentration and, 492–93,
        497
    clear comprehension and, 393–95
    developing energy and, 453
    equanimity and, 536–37
    five spiritual faculties and, 414
    fourth jhana and, 532
    identification with, 170
    impermanence and, 541
    jhana mental states and, 484
    metta meditation and, 422, 423, 426
    mindfulness of, xvii, 203, 394, 510
        (*see also* body elements; body
        parts)
    observing change in physical expe-
        rience, 54–55, 198
    vipassana awareness and, 468–71

See also breath; breath-body; eyes;
    pain; posture; sensations
body elements
    meditation on, 248–49
    mindfulness of, 255–60
body hair, mindful meditation on, 251
body-mind complex, 41–43, 57, 304.
    See also mind-body system
body movement
    mindfulness of, 219–20
    observing, 163
    slow movement as aid to mindful-
        ness, 152
    See also stillness during meditation
body parts
    first five, 249–52
    internal and external, 212–13
    meditation on, 248–49
    seeing the many, xvii
    thirty-two, 252–55, 258, 259
bojjhangas (seven factors of enlight-
    enment), 352. *See also* enlighten-
    ment: factors of
boredom, 39, 102–3, 162, 164
    vs. mindfulness, 102–3
    mindfulness of, 162, 164
Brahma realms, 557
Brahmanism, 478
Brazil, 533
breath
    access concentration and, 493–96
    and the aggregates, 214–15
    bringing attention back to, 67, 71,
        74, 119
    concentration aids using, 49–52,
        112–13
    controlling, 68–70, 101, 112
    finding, 69
    following passage of, 69
    forcing, 69
    holding, 453–54

impermanence and, 468–71
jhana mental states and, 482–84
length of, 48–49
losing the sensations of, 391
resolve to follow, 74
subtle, 49, 52, 53
vipassana awareness of, 437–38
See also *specific topics*
breath-body
four elements of, 438–41
mindfulness of, 211–12
breath coordination, 161–62
breath meditation, 435–43, 490–92
Buddha's instructions on, 208–10
developing a daily practice, 441–43
four elements and, 437, 438–41
internal and external elements and,
212–13
key points for, 217–18
mindfulness and, 443
mindfulness training and, 207–8,
372
overcoming restlessness and worry,
332–33
patience and joy and, 215–16
walking meditation and, 229
See also breath
breath practice
avoiding discursive thought during,
71, 72
avoiding sinking mind during, 72
breathing normally during, 48, 70
calmness experienced during, 49,
55, 72–73
developed through mindfulness, 41,
55, 161
discovering the present moment
through, 48, 69, 74, 167
farmer simile, 53
focusing at abdomen, 54, 56
focusing at chest area, 54, 56

focusing at nostril tip, 48, 51, 68, 69
gatekeeper analogy, 52
as home base, 48, 57, 67–68
investigative attitude toward, 70–71
lightness experienced during, 52
observing changing consciousness
through, 39, 54–55, 197–198
observing changing physical experience through, 54–55, 198
observing heat, 55
observing rhythm of expansion and
contraction, 56
perceiving elements through, 55
perceiving impermanence through,
55–57
perceiving interconnectedness
through, 38–39, 68
perceiving selflessness through,
55–57
perceiving unsatisfactoriness
through, 55, 57
realizing universality through,
38–39, 68
Satipatthana Sutta on, 65
shifting to other objects of attention, 57, 118
signs experienced during, 52, 53–54
breathing
deep, 112
as fascinating procedure, 70–71
in and out, 113; perception of, 348
breaths
counting, 49–51, 112–13, 451, 452,
454–55
focusing on connection point between, 51
pause between: eliminating the, 51;
observing the, 46
Buddha (Siddhartha Gautama), 460
on abandoning unwholesome
thoughts, 301–2

Alarakalam and, 391–92
on attachment, 520
on birth, aging, and death, 261–62, 267, 270, 305–6
Brahmanism and, 478
on breath meditation, 207–11
clear comprehension of, 243
on concentration, 514
on contentment, 402
decision to teach Dhamma, 365
on developing energy, 453
discourses, 198
on domain, 233–34, 240
doubt and, 521–22
on the elements, 258, 259
enlightenment of, 380–81, 504–5, 538, 539
and enlightenment of others, 544–45
exchange with Akkosana, 287
faith in, 383
fetters and, 458
Fire Sermon, 404
on the five hindrances, 500–501
following the example of, 380–84
fourth jhana and, 535, 538–40, 542
on harmful and beneficial feelings, 289
homage to, 451
on impermanence, xv, 466
instruction on pain, 279
instruction to Anuruddha, 325, 331
instruction to Mahakassapa, 351
instructions for meditation, 489–90
on internal and external, 213
life experiences, xviii–xix
and looking within, xix, xx
loving-friendliness of, 178, 186, 188–90
on luminous mind, 538–39
on mindfulness practice, xvi–xx, 352–53
on the nature of the mind, 379
noble eightfold path and, 408
on overcoming hindrances, 334–35
pain and, 460–61
on parts and elements, 247
on purification of mind, 235–36
reflecting on qualities of, 454
on self-hatred, 248–49
on the senses, 414–15
stepmother of, 402
on stream entry, 370
on suffering, xiv, xv, xix, 276, 289, 466, 473
supramundane jhanas and, 559, 561, 562
"The Sword Simile" discourse, 460–61
unorthodoxy of, 30, 83
See also *Satipatthana Sutta*
buddha nature, 166
Buddha statues on alters, 406
Buddhaghosa, 198, 544, 555
Buddhism
    antiauthoritarian attitude, 30
    empiricism, 30, 140
    faith and, 12, 30, 140
    Tantra, 27
    theological religions compared with, 196
    Theravada, 196, 198
    Zen, 26, 198
    See also *specific topics*
Burmese posture, 222

C
Cakkhupala (disciple of Buddha), 220
calmness, 242

during breath practice, 49, 55, 72–73
carpenter analogy, 51, 69
cemetery contemplation, 268–70
chairs, sitting in, 63, 222
change
  the constant experience of, 321
  incessant nature of, 5–6, 168
  inherent in present moment, 47, 54, 168
  mindfulness as awareness of, 137
  momentary concentration, 54
  observed in consciousness, 54–55, 198
  observed in mental phenomena, 54–55, 126, 168, 198
  observed in physical experience, 54–55, 198
  observed through breath practice, 39, 54–55, 198
  See also impermanence
choices, mindfulness meditation and, xxi
Cinca, 189
citta (mind and heart), 303
clarity, mindfulness meditation and, xxi
cleansing the mind, 305–7
clear comprehension, 393–95, 402, 448, 524–25, 539
  aspects of, 233, 234, 372
  in daily life, 243–44
  domain and, 233–34, 239–40
  of eating, 245–46
  nondelusion, 240–41
  purpose, 234–38
  suitability, 238–39
clinging, 391, 405, 467, 480
  avoiding, in meditation, 36
  five aggregates of, 204
  five spiritual faculties and, 414

mindfulness of, 293–94
right thoughts and, 503
as suffering, 277, 366–67
See also attachment
clock, concept of, 479–80
clothing worn during meditation, 60–61, 96
colors, perception of, 490–91
common ground, recognizing, 418
compassion
  access concentration and, 498
  arising from meditation, 11
  arising from wisdom, 19
  cultivating loving-friendliness through, 89–90
  as a form of virtuous conduct, 401
  metta meditation and, 420–23, 425
  morality and, 19
  vs. pity, 176
  renunciation and, 504
  supramundane jhanas and, 564
compassionate thought, 114
comprehension, clear. See clear comprehension
conceit, 344
concentration, x, 522–24
  on all activities, 162–64
  balancing awareness and, 26, 150–52, 197
  blocking hindrances with, 448–49
  breath meditation and, 435
  in Buddhist tradition, 26
  classification of, as one of the five spiritual faculties, 412, 413
  in contemplation, 25
  deep relaxation and, 14–15.
  defined, 72, 146
  developing, 445–62, 493–94
  eliminating the pause between breaths as aid to, 51
  farmer simile, 53

fear arising from, 104
fetters and, 457–59
forced nature of, 145
fourth jhana and, 534–35
hindrances and, 394
hindrances to, 147, 388, 446–57, 492, 493, 496–98
importance of, 378–80
inability to concentrate, 101–2
vs. insight, 15
jhana mental states and, 14–15, 483–85
jhanas and, 387–97
"joining both" state and, 533–34
in Judeo-Christian tradition, 25
meditation factor, 19
mental dullness as byproduct of, 109
vs. mindfulness, 145–52
mindfulness and, 41, 392–93; balancing, 150–52
momentary, 54
needed to observe mental phenomena, 66–67
noble eightfold path and, 410
as one of the seven factors of awakening, 514–17
and overcoming distraction, 111–16
prayer as, 25
preconceptual awareness and, 471
right, 408, 410
signs of, 52, 53, 112–13
slowing mental processes through, 66, 127
stages of deep (see jhana(s))
as tool, 146
unwholesome, 146
vipassana meditation and, 15, 150, 197
wrong, 390–92

See also access concentration; jhana; jhanas; mind wandering; samatha
concentration meditation (samatha), xxi, 197, 198, 306, 369
as factor of enlightenment, 359–63
mental state of, 14–15, 316
skillful, 368
concentration path, 377–85
conceptions, overcoming, 259
conceptualization, 128–30, 134, 167
moment of, 134
suspended during meditation, 127–30
confusion, 295
consciousness, xviii
aggregate of, 214–15, 303–5, 438
boundless, 486, 552–54
vs. mind, 303–5
mindfulness of, 394, 510 (see also mind: mindfulness of)
observed during meditation, 39, 54–55, 57, 198
observing changes in, 39
See also awareness; specific topics
contemplation, 23, 25
contentment, 401–2, 443, 478
corpses, contemplation of, 262, 269
cosmology, 455
counterpart signs, 507, 508, 547–50
counting, to deepen mindfulness, 217
craving, 293–95, 306, 402, 404–7
becoming aware of, 289, 293–95
for immaterial existence, 344
sensory, 343
See also desire
cruelty, 447, 498, 505–6, 526

D
daily life, bringing awareness to

through breath coordination, 161–62

carryover from seated meditation, 154–56

through concentration on activities, 162–64

as goal of practice, 138, 155, 163

through mindfulness of motion, 160–61, 163

through mindfulness of posture, 159

seated meditation as practice for, 153–54

spontaneous, 154

taking advantage of spare moments, 162

walking meditation as practice for, 155–56

danger, perception of, 346–47

death, 451, 474
anger and confusion at time of, 292
Buddha on, 261–62, 305–6
cemetery contemplation, 268–70
key points for mindfulness of, 270–71
near-death experiences, 264–66
preparing for, 266–67
three kinds of, 262–64

defilements, 379, 380, 384, 404, 523, 539, 540
"burning up," 544
supramundane jhanas and, 564
See also hindrances

delusion, 394, 401, 406–7, 414, 459
becoming aware of, 289, 295–96
freedom from, 309
mental state of, 315

dependent origination, 451

depression, 99, 135, 164

desire, 123, 125–26, 147, 393, 404
becoming aware of, 289, 293–95
fetters and, 458
for fine material existence, 458

as hindrance, 327–28
jhana mental states and, 487
sensual, 446, 449–50
supramundane jhanas and, 557, 563, 564
See also craving

despair and grief, ending, 237

detachment, 32, 104, 345

Devadatta, 188, 279, 460–61

developed mental state, 316

Dhamma (teachings of Buddha), 85, 383, 413, 453, 458, 544–45
Buddha's decision to teach, 258, 365
fourth jhana and, 542, 543
investigation of, 355, 356
as island or refuge, 240
listening to Dhamma to deal with anger, 292
metta meditation and, 423
not listening to, 448
overcoming hindrances, 326
preliminaries for meditation and, 402, 413
qualities of, 455
reciting intentions and, 442
second jhana and, 522
supramundane jhanas and, 559, 562
the truth as within, xix

Dhamma-follower (wisdom-follower), 560

Dhammapada, 10, 188, 277, 520

dhammas (phenomena)
definitions and meanings of, xviii, xx, 343
mindfulness of, xvi, xviii, 203–4; cultivating, 373

dirty rag, metaphor of, 420

disciples, noble, 559, 561

discouragement, 107–8

dispassion, perception of, 347

dissatisfaction. See unsatisfactoriness

distraction(s), 242, 315–16, 399, 435–
    36, 446–47
  bliss of meditation as, 125–26
  categorization into hindrances,
    122–25
  dispelled through mindfulness, 119,
    121, 149
  frame of reference, 67
  grasping and, 119
  observing, 117–22, 126
  structuring environment for mini-
    mal, 75, 77–78
  techniques for dealing with, 111–16,
    119–22, 125
  See also hindrances
divorce, 420
domain, 233–34, 239–40
doubt, 125, 147, 217, 333–34, 447,
    454–55, 521
  access concentration and, 498
  fetters and, 458
  skeptical, 342–43
  supramundane jhanas and, 558–60
dreams, 496
drinking liquids, clear comprehen-
    sion of, 245
drowsiness during meditation, 100–
    101, 123–24
dukkha, 140, 169. See also suffering;
    unsatisfactoriness
dullness, 330–32
  dispelled through mindfulness, 109
  of mind, 109

E
earlobes, pinching your, 454
earth element, 212, 213, 252, 256–57,
    437–41
easy style posture, 222
eating, 395, 401–3, 409
  clear comprehension of, 245–46

key points for mindful, 246
ecstasy
  getting trapped in jhanic, 396 (see
    also bliss)
  See also rapture
effort, 36, 76, 105–6, 148
  required for mindfulness, 148
  right, 392–93, 410, 558
  skillful, 357, 361, 368
ego, 396, 397
  extinguished through mindfulness,
    85, 114, 166
  hindrances arising from, 23, 86, 165
  as sense of separation, 165
  tantric practices aimed at under-
    standing, 26–27
  thought and, 26
  See also self
egoless awareness, mindfulness as,
    85, 136, 148
Eight Mindful Steps to Happiness:
    Walking the Buddha's Path, 368
eightfold path. See noble eightfold
    path
ekagatta, 503. See also one-
    pointedness
elements
  of the body, 255–60
  of the breath, 212–13
  perceived through breath practice,
    55
  See also four elements; specific el-
    ements
elephant analogy, 67
emerging (step of mastery), 528
emotions
  canceling negative emotion with
    skillful thought, 114–15
  mindfulness of, 280
  as nonsensory feelings, 277

observed during meditation, 42, 57, 108, 115, 135
ending grief and despair, 237
overcoming sorrow and lamentation, 236–37
during walking meditation, 228–29
See also feeling(s); mental phenomena, observing; specific emotions
emptiness
base of, 486 (see also voidness)
of self (sunnata), 241
energy, 391, 401, 405, 412, 413, 512
concentration and, 447, 515–16
as factor of enlightenment, 357–58
needed for meditation, 85
overcoming sloth by developing, 453–54
enlightenment, 383, 397, 457, 487, 512–14
of Buddha, 365, 380–81, 504–5, 538, 539
defined, xxiii
factors of, 204, 351–63, 509–14, 537
fourth jhana and, 531–32, 539
mindfulness and, 352–54, 537
mindfulness leading to, 120, 143–44, 164
through mindfulness of physical movements, 219, 220
as promise of Buddha, xxiii, 351
supramundane jhanas and, 557–65
See also attainment; awakening; liberation; nibbana
equanimity, 176, 177, 296–97, 360–61, 401, 501–2, 564
access concentration and, 493, 497
based on diversity, 536–37
based on unity, 537–38
fourth jhana and, 531–32, 534, 536–37, 540, 541
highest form of, 501–2

immaterial jhanas and, 551
impermanence and, 472
jhana mental states and, 484–86
metta meditation and, 420
mindfulness and, 538
as one of the seven factors of awakening, 517–18
preconceptual awareness and, 471
right concentration and, 390
third jhana and, 523–25
eternal death, 264
ethics, 20. See also morality
expectations, 36
eyes, 453, 457, 490–91, 493, 536
closed during meditation, 47
opening, 453

F
faith, 12, 30, 140, 377–78, 383, 391, 412, 413, 559–62
faith-follower, 559, 560
family, 402, 425, 427–29, 473–75
fear, 387–88, 425, 452, 474
of death, overcoming, 264–66
dispelled through mindfulness, 104
during meditation, 39, 42, 73, 93, 103–4, 135
See also anxiety
feeling(s)
aggregate of, 214, 437
attention to, 278, 279–85, 290
beneficial, 296–97, 302
building concentration and, 387–89
fourth jhana and, 533, 534
how they arise, 281–82
impermanence and, 541
metta meditation and, 426–27
mindfulness of, xvii–xviii, 210, 214, 242, 276–77, 372–73, 394, 406–8, 510; investigation of, 355; key

points for, 284–85; meditating on, 282–83; overview, 203
selflessness and, 478–79
as suffering, 475–76
types of, xvii–xviii, 277–78, 280–81, 287–90; harmful, 290–96; unpleasant, 277–78, 290–93
See also emotions; pain; suffering; *specific feelings*
fetter(s), 337–38, 340–45
defined, 385
fourth jhana and, 535
higher, 457–59
ignorance, wisdom-eye, and, 539
jhana mental states and, 487
lower, 457–58
supramundane jhanas and, 559–63
See also hindrances
field analogy, 11
fire, three kinds of, 414
Fire Sermon (Buddha), 404
five aggregates
breath and, 214–15
breath meditation and, 437–38
of clinging, 204, 339–40
equanimity and, 360, 361
fourth jhana and, 531–32
impermanence and, 466–68
Sariputta on, 275
selflessness and, 478–80
and sitting meditation, 223–24
as suffering, 475–76
supramundane jhanas and, 563
wandering mind and, 239
See also aggregates; consciousness; feeling(s); form; perception; volitional formations
Five Ascetics, 380–81
five mental hindrances, 203
Buddha on, 500–501
See also hindrances

five precepts, 400–401
flutes, 467
focus, mindfulness meditation and, xxi, 218, 353, 359–61
form
aggregate of, 214, 437
equanimity and, 536
jhana mental states and, 485
selflessness and, 478–79
as suffering, 475–76
Foundations of Mindfulness Sutta. See *Satipatthana Sutta*
four elements
breath meditation and, 437–41
overview and nature of, 438–41
See also elements; *specific elements*
four foundations of mindfulness. See mindfulness: four foundations of
four noble truths, 381–84, 535, 539, 565
fetters and, 459
fourth jhana and, 532
in their three phases and twelve aspects, 381
key points for practicing the path of, 372–73
mindfulness of, 366–67
mindfulness of the eightfold path, 367–69
suffering and, xix
summary of, 204, 365–66
See also truth
fourfold effort, 400
friends
associating with unwholesome, 448
help from, 291
friendship, 402, 420, 421, 425
fruition phase of Supramundane Noble Path, 560–65
full lotus posture, 220–21

G

generosity, 114, 115, 401, 498, 503–4
  practicing, 291
gentleness in meditation, 27, 37, 73,
  79, 148, 182
good, bad, neutral categories of experience, 6, 31, 39, 170
grasping, 6, 32, 36, 86, 119, 169
gratitude, cultivation of, 291, 452
greed, 312, 313–14, 387–88, 394, 425,
  498
  concentration and, 447, 459
  dispelling: through the experience
    of impermanence, 42; through
    mindfulness, 44, 45, 55, 114, 120,
    142, 143; through skillful thought,
    114
  five spiritual faculties and, 414
  for noble feelings, 125–26
  origin of, 38, 86, 165
  preliminaries for meditation and,
    401, 402, 404, 406–7, 411, 414
  right thoughts and, 503
  supramundane jhanas and, 564
greedy thought, 66, 114, 115, 120
grief and despair, ending, 237
growth as suffering, 474
guilt, 115

H

habits. See mental habits
hair, mindful meditation on, 250–51
half lotus posture, 221–22
hand position during meditation, 62,
  63, 96
happiness, 8, 10
  mindfulness meditation and, xxi
hateful thought, 114, 115
hatred, 290–91, 308, 314–15, 343–44,
  394, 414, 447, 459, 498

dispelling: through benevolence,
  86; through loving-friendliness,
  86, 91, 185, 188; through mindfulness, 44, 45, 143; through skillful
  thought, 114
fetters and, 458
loving-friendliness and, 505
metta meditation and, 420, 423, 429
mindfulness and, 406–7, 411
origin of, 38, 86
preliminaries for meditation and,
  401, 402, 406–7, 411, 414
self-hatred, 86, 179, 248–49
supramundane jhanas and, 563, 564
See also ill will
head hair, mindful meditation on,
  250
healing the body, 253–54
heat, observing in breath practice, 55
heat element, 212, 213, 258, 437–41
"high quality" pleasant feelings, 297
hindrances, 446–47, 500–501, 508,
  527
  arising from ego, 23, 86, 165
  breath counting to block, 455–56
  breath meditation and, 436
  categories of, 122–25
  to concentration, 147
  concentration and, 388, 394, 446–
    57, 492, 493, 496–98
  concentration and mindfulness
    block, 448–49
  concentration meditation and,
    306–7, 326–35, 361–63
  defined, 385
  dispelling: through loving-friend-
    liness, 86, 184–85, 188; through
    mindfulness, 142–43, 165–66
  elimination of, 456–57
  fetters and, 457–59
  five spiritual faculties and, 413

fourth jhana and, 540
as habits, 388
how they are nourished, 447–48
metta meditation and, 425
noble eightfold path and, 410
overcome through experience of
  impermanence, 42
preliminaries for meditation and,
  400, 410, 413
second jhana and, 522
supramundane jhanas and, 557, 559
techniques for overcoming, 449–55
third jhana and, 524
See also fetters; five mental hindrances
Hinduism, 26
"Homage to the Blissful One," 451
honesty, 384, 410
  in mindfulness, 44
human condition, 399

I

"I, me, mine." *See* self
ignorance, 42, 44, 45, 170–71, 345,
  404, 457, 459, 532
  dispelled through mindfulness, 44,
  45
  luminosity and, 539
  mindfulness and, 411
ignoring
  habit of, 6, 31
  negative mental states, 318
ill will, 329–30, 446, 450–52, 505
  renunciation and, 504
  See also anger; hatred
immaterial existence, craving for, 344
immaterial (formless) jhanas, 385,
  482, 485–87, 547–56
impartial watchfulness, mindfulness
  as, 135–36
impermanence, 451, 495–96

of attainment, 541
of body, 30–31, 43, 44
breath meditation and, 435, 443
clear comprehension and, 394
concentration and, 394, 515–16
consciousness and, 541
described, 464–66
equanimity and, 536, 538
feelings and, 278, 296
fetters and, 459
fourth jhana and, 531–32, 535,
  543–44
importance of recognizing, 466–68
inherent to all existence, 30–31
investigation of, 355
jhana mental states and, 485
longevity and, 262
mindfulness and, 407, 412, 511
mindfulness meditation and, xxi,
  215, 242, 320
of negative mental states, 318–19
overcoming hindrances through the
  experience of, 42
perception of, 345–46; in all
  thoughts and conceptions, 348;
  through breath practice, 55–57;
  as goal of practice, 27, 55, 171;
  through mindfulness, 140–41
seeing, in jhana, 471–72
suffering in reaction to, 31
third jhana and, 523
vipassana awareness and, 468–71
See also change
impure states, 235
impurities, perception of, 346
India, 478
insight meditation, 141–44, 196, 197,
  306–7. *See also* vipassana
intentions, recitation of, 442–43
intuition, 12, 21, 161, 414
investigation, 511

as factor of enlightenment, 354–56
investigative attitude in meditation,
    28, 30, 37, 70–71, 94

J

jealousy, 38, 39
jhana, 14–15, 17. See also concentra-
    tion
jhana mental states, mindfulness
    and, 483–85
jhana road map, 385–86
jhana(s), x, xxii, 358–61
    being in, 528–29
    benefits of, 395–96
    concentration and, x, xxii
    defined, 358, 385, 388–89
    destroying ignorance with, 459
    eighth, 486–87
    factors in, 524–25, 534, 543, 544
    fifth, 485–87
    first, 482–83, 496–518, 520–21
    fourth, 484–85, 531–45, 549
    highest, 390, 392
    hindrances and, 457
    immaterial (formless), 385, 482,
        485–87, 547–56
    importance of metta meditation
        for, 425
    mastery of, 525–26
    material, 385, 482–85
    mundane, 482
    nature of, 388–90
    potential pitfalls of, 396–97
    preliminaries for meditation, 399–
        415
    right, 389, 390
    second, 483, 519–29
    seeing impermanence in, 471–72
    seventh, 486
    sixth, 486
    states, 481–87

supramundane, 385, 487, 557–65
    third, 484, 519–29
    "thought" in, 507–9
    See also concentration
"joining both" state, 533–34
joy, 215–16, 295, 358–59, 388, 496–97,
    500–502, 519–20
    appreciative, 176–77
    concentration and, 448
    in daily life, 395
    as a form of virtuous conduct, 401
    impermanence and, 472
    jhana mental states and, 483, 484
    material jhana states and, 385
    as one of the seven factors of awak-
        ening, 512–14
    second jhana and, 522
    supramundane jhanas and, 564
    third jhana and, 523, 524
    turning away from the state of, 527
    uplifting, 358
Judeo-Christian meditation, 25
juggling, metaphor of, 528–29

K

kamma (karma/principle of cause
    and effect), 305, 458, 478, 540
kasina, 490–91, 507, 548–52
killing, avoidance of, 447
kindness
    meditation and, 421, 427
    mindfulness and, 411
    to oneself, 451, 456
    See also loving-friendliness
knowing, 303

L

labeling, 407
lamentation and sorrow, overcoming,
    236–37
laziness, 330–32

key points for overcoming, 331–32
learning signs, 507–9, 549
lens analogy, 146
lethargy, 123–24, 147
    dispelled through mindfulness, 124
    See also drowsiness during meditation; dullness: of mind
liberation, 197
    attaining, 238
    four noble truths and, 381–84
    fruits of the path, 369–72
    meditators who have reached, xvi
    mental state of, 317
    progress on the path toward, 237–38
    See also attainment; enlightenment; nibbana
light
    appearance of sparks of, 509
    deep mind and, 379
    visualizing bright, 453
    See also luminosity
listening and speaking with mindfulness, 45
livelihood
    right, 409, 558
    skillful, 368
loving-friendliness (metta), 85–91, 330, 505, 508–9, 526, 564
    acting from, 176, 186
    beginning meditation session with, 87, 89, 91
    cultivating, toward different types of people, 419–24
    cultivating compassion through, 89–90
    cultivating morality through, 90
    dirty cloth analogy, 180
    dispelling hindrances through, 86, 184–85, 188
    expanded to all beings, 86–87, 185, 191–94

five spiritual faculties and, 413
    innate capacity for, 177–82
    jhana mental states and, 485
    joy and, 513–14
    meditations on, 426–33
    mindfulness and, 173, 186–87, 412
    motherhood analogy, 176–77
    peaceful mind necessary for, 173–74
    the power of, 173–94
    practicing, 182–87
    purification through, 89
    recitations, 87–88, 179, 191–93
    resistance to, 185
    responding to anger with, 187–91
    strengthened through practice, 183
    in thought and action, 418–19
    toward enemies, 89–91, 182–84, 193
    toward neutral people, 182
    toward self, 86, 182
    universal, 191–94
    See also metta meditation
"low quality" pleasant feelings, 297
luminosity
    Buddha on, 539
    fourth jhana and, 538–41
    supramundane jhanas and, 564
    See also light
lust, 39, 42, 113, 143, 146, 165, 247, 289
    dispelled through mindfulness, 143
lying down posture, 231–32

M

Maha Rahulovada Sutta, 213
Mahacunda (follower of Buddha), 352
Mahakassapa (follower of Buddha), 351
Mahakotthita (follower of Buddha), 337–38

Mahapajapati Gotami, 402
Mahayana Buddhism, 197
Mara, 455, 456, 520
material existence, fine
  craving for, 344
meditation
  attitudes conducive to, 35–39,
    73–74
  bond created by, 175
  in Buddha's life, 178, 186, 188–90
  Buddhist, 26–27
  choosing subjects of, 489–92
  contemplation compared with, 25
  energy needed for, 85
  gumption needed for, 3
  mindfulness and, 29, 76–77, 141–
    44, 150, 155 (see also mindfulness
    meditation)
  misconceptions about, 14–24
  overcoming resistance to, 107–8
  personal transformation arising
    from, 12, 34
  preliminaries for, 399–415
  purpose of, 12, 122
  stages of deep (see jhana(s))
  time needed to see results of, 24, 34
  two types of, 306–7
  See also breath meditation; metta
    meditation; vipassana; specific
    topics
meditation benches, 222
meditation practice
  choosing the environment for,
    77–78
  group practice, 78
  length of sitting session, 47, 80–82,
    156
  scheduling, 75–76, 78–80, 101
memory, xv, 57, 103, 104, 129, 142,
  482, 492, 498
mental dullness. See dullness

mental factors, universal, 42
mental habits
  cleansing the mind of, 305–7
  cultivation of thoughts as, 120, 302
  developing negative, 5, 75,
  instilling new, 154
  overcoming, 208, 236, 239, 441, 489
  perceptual, 32
mental notes during meditation, 46,
  113, 119, 158, 159
mental objects, 281–82
  equanimity and, 537
  mindfulness of, 394, 510–11
  nonperception and, 556
mental phenomena, observing, 101
  concentration needed for, 66–67
  without conceptualization, 128–30
  See also specific mental phenomena
mental states
  attachment to positive, 125–26, 132
  awareness of, 320
  birth, growth, and decay stages of,
    126, 128–29
  eight pairs of, 312–17
  key points for meditation on, 320–21
  overcoming negative, 318–19
  working with, 318–19
  See also specific mental states
metta (loving-friendliness), 173. See
  also loving-friendliness
metta meditation, 441–43, 496–97,
  543
  general instructions, 426–27
  importance for jhana, 425
  overview, 417–33
  six formal types of, 426–33
  thought and, 508–9
Middle Way, 381
mind
  cleansing the, 305–7
  clear comprehension and, 393–95

vs. consciousness, 303–5
craziness of, 19, 71
discipline of, 8–9, 19
as gatekeeper, 52
luminous character of, 379
mindfulness of, xviii, 203, 303–7
    (*see also* consciousness); key
    points for practicing, 307–9
muddy water analogy, 47, 75–76,
    436
purification of, 10, 41, 46, 89, 235–
    36, 534
as set of events, 35
sinking, 72
tranquility of, 197
unity of, 538
See also conceptualization; mental
    phenomena, observing; thought;
    specific topics
mind-body system, 214. *See also*
    body-mind complex
mind wandering, 218, 239
  bringing mind back to object of at-
    tention, 67, 71, 74, 119
  observing, 117–18
  what to do when it happens, 49–52
  See also "monkey mind"
mindfulness, 410–12, 502–3, 509–11
  basic premise and benefits of, xiv–xv
  beyond, xxii–xxiii
  described, 29, 133–38, 143 (*see also*
    egoless awareness)
  experience of, 133, 139
  forcing, 148
  four foundations of, xvi–xx, 372,
    373, 394, 510–11 (see also *Satipat-
    thana Sutta*)
  fundamental activities of, 138–41
  goal of, 41
  inclusive nature of, 149
  lost and found, 242–43

nature of, xiv–xvi
not limited by conditions, 147–48, 152
process of, 141
reestablishing true, 102–3
reminder function of, 138–39, 141–43
right, 392–93, 410, 558
skillful, 368 (*see also* skillful effort)
strengthened through practice, 131,
    150
translations of the word, xv
See also *specific topics*
Mindfulness in Plain English, xiii
mindfulness meditation
  getting started with, xx–xxi, 202
  purposes of, 234–38
  See also breath meditation; medi-
    tation: mindfulness and; *specific
    topics*
mirror-thought, mindfulness as, 135
mitra, 177. *See also* loving-friendli-
    ness
momentary death, 263
moments, stolen, 162
monastery, controlled environment
    of, 147
"monkey mind," 71, 72, 151, 452, 502.
    See also mind wandering
morality, 20, 456, 506–7, 522–23, 562
  arising from meditation, 10, 20–21
  arising from mindfulness, 191
  bath in ocean analogy, 19
  compassion and, 19
  cultivated through loving-friendli-
    ness, 90
  as habit pattern, 12
  intuitive, 20–21
  levels of, 19–20
  mental control prerequisite to, 19, 20
  noble eightfold path and, 408, 410
  precepts as guide to, 186

as preliminary for meditation, 400–401

as prerequisite to meditation, 18–19

motion. *See* body movement

movement. *See* body movement

muddy water, cup of

  analogy of, 47, 75–76, 436

mustard seeds, metaphor of, 541

N

nails, mindful meditation on, 251

Nakulapita (householder follower of Buddha), 275, 276

near-death experiences, 264–66

negative mental states, overcoming, 318–19

neutral feelings, 277, 295

never-returner (nonreturner), 371, 557, 564

nibbana, 86, 171, 204

  beneficial actions and, xiv

  defined, xiv

  as eternal death, 264

  freedom from delusion, 315

  as the highest quality pleasure, 297

  mindfulness and, xiv, 373

  mindfulness practice and, 247

  See also enlightenment; liberation

no-self, 485, 533, 535. *See also* self

no-self experience, 478–80

noble disciples, 559, 561

noble eightfold path, xix, 204, 367–73, 515, 517, 531–32

  hindrances and, 450

  immaterial jhanas and, 547

  mindfulness of the, 367–69

  practicing, 408–10

  supramundane jhanas and, 558, 559, 562, 564

nondelusion, 234, 240–41

nonconceptual awareness, mindfulness as, 136

nonreturner (never-returner), 371, 557, 564

nonstickiness, 542

nothingness. *See* voidness

O

objects of attention, 98, 147–48

  identified in Pali canon, 198

  importance to mental focus, 47, 65–67

  shifting, 57, 118, 130, 148

observation

  mindfulness as nonjudgmental, 135

  mindfulness as participatory, 137

  obsession/obsessive thoughts, 33, 66, 114–15

old age, as suffering, 474

once-returner, 371, 557, 563

one-pointedness, 472, 493, 501–3, 540

  jhana mental states and, 483–86

  second jhana and, 522

overpowering negative mental states, 319

P

pain, 80, 96–99, 218

  dealing with, 279–80

  jhana mental states and, 482–83

  metta meditation and, 424

  mindfulness of, 98–99

  observing, in meditation, 97–99, 127–28

  resistance reaction, 97, 98

  selflessness of, 98, 128

  vs. suffering, 95

  "talking" to, 452, 460

  See also suffering

pain-pleasure connection, 93

pain reduction, 96

through proper clothing, 96
through proper posture, 60, 61,
   96–97
through relaxation, 97–98
Pali literature, 198. See also *specific
   works*
passana
   as root of vipassana, 28
path
   fruits of the, 369–72
   as one of the four noble truths, 366
   See also noble eightfold path
Path of Freedom, The (Upatissa). See
   Vimuttimagga
Path of Purification, The (Buddhaghosa). See *Visuddhimagga*
path phase of Supramundane Noble
   Path, 560–64
patience, 24, 36, 73, 82, 94, 99, 149–
   50, 215–16, 329
   mindfulness as essence of, 149–50
peace, 173–74, 242, 283
perception, xxi
   aggregate of, 437
   fourth jhana and, 533
   immaterial jhanas and, 547, 554–56
   impermanence and, 541
   jhana mental states and, 481,
      485–87
   of nondelight in the whole world,
      348
   and nonperception, 486–87, 554–56
   selflessness and, 478–79
   as suffering, 475–76
   See also seeing things as they really
      are
perceptions, ten, 345–49
phenomena. *See* dhammas
physical sensation. *See* sensations
piti, 502–3. *See also* joy
pity, 176

pleasant states, attachment to, 125–
   26, 132
pleasant vs. unpleasant vs. neutral
   division of experience, 6, 31, 39,
   170
pleasurable feelings, suffering and,
   277, 293–94
pleasure-pain connection, 93
poisons, three, 414
ponds covered with algae, metaphor
   of, 421
posture, 96–97, 159
   rules regarding, 59–60
postures
   in breath meditation, 209, 217
   learning from, 229–30
   lying down, 231–32
   mindfulness of, 219–20, 222–24
   purpose of various, 59–60
   sitting, 220–24
   standing, 224–26
   traditional, 61–63
   walking, 226–28
   in walking meditation, 230–31
practice, goals of, xx–xxi, 27, 46, 55,
   170–71
   awareness, 14, 15, 138, 155, 163
   fivefold nature of, 46
   insight, 15
   jhana as goal in itself, 14–15
   liberation, 197
   of mindfulness, 41
   rapture as goal in itself, 22
   setting too high, 73
   transformation of life experience,
      153
prayer, 25
precepts as guide to morality, 186
preconceptual awareness, 127–30,
   134, 167–68, 471

preconceptual nature of mindful-
    ness, 134
pregnancy, 473
present moment
    breath practice as path to discover-
        ing, 46, 69, 74, 167
    change inherent in, 47, 54–55, 168
    focusing on, xx, 209, 362
    mindfulness as awareness of, 136
    observing in meditation, 46, 47,
        54–55, 69, 74, 129
presymbolic, mindfulness as, 138
pride, 38, 44, 344
prison inmates, 423
problems, 37
    dealing with, 93–109
    See also *specific problems*
psychic irritants. *See* hindrances
psychic powers, 16–18
puddles, metaphor of, 421–22
purification
    and happiness, 10
    through loving-friendliness, 89
    meditation as means of, 10–11
    of mind, 10, 41, 46, 89, 235–36, 357
    of psychic irritants, 10, 89–90
purpose
    of actions, 234–38
    recalling your, 115–16

R

rapture, 14, 22, 125, 197. *See also* bliss
reaction, observing, 32–33
reality, construction of, 31
rebirth, 305, 371, 478, 539
    fetters and, 458
    supramundane jhanas and, 557, 558
    See also samsara
recitations, 83–85, 87–88, 179, 191–93
reflection(s)
    mindful, 406–8, 449, 453

unmindful, 448, 454
rejecting, hindrance of, 6, 36, 123
relaxation, 22, 60, 62, 97–98, 108
    meditation as a technique of, 14–16
remembering, xv. *See also* memory
*Removal of Distracting Thought
    Sutta, 318*
renunciation, 409, 503–5
    joy based on, 501
    mastery of jhana and, 526–28
    thought and, 508–9
replacing negative mental states, 318
resentment, 42, 45, 89, 178, 185
resistance to meditation, 107–8
resolve, right, 409, 558
resolving (step of mastery), 527
restlessness, 12, 39, 81, 105, 124, 156,
    217, 332–33, 344–45
    access concentration and, 496, 498
    concentration and, 446–47, 452,
        459
    fetters and, 459
    overcoming, 452
restraint, practicing, 291
reviewing (step of mastery), 528
rituals, 83–84, 458, 561
    clinging to, 343
rules of conduct, 408–10

S

samadhi, 72. *See also* concentration
Samaññaphala Sutta, 500–501
samatha, xxi, 197, 198. *See also* con-
    centration meditation
samsara, xiv, 470, 487, 536, 559
Sangha, 85, 454, 458, 522
    five spiritual faculties and, 413
    supramundane jhanas and, 559, 562
sanity, role of mindfulness in achiev-
    ing ultimate, 142

Sariputta, 45, 247, 275, 276, 337–38, 370

sati, xv, 72, 133, 136, 142. *See also* mindfulness

Satipatthana Sutta (Foundations of Mindfulness Sutta), xvi–xvii, 27, 65, 202–4, 510

scheduling practice, 75–76, 78–80, 101

seclusion, 404–6, 543
  five spiritual faculties and, 414

seeing things as they really are, 33, 41, 139–40. *See also* perception

self
  attachment to, 244, 247
  belief in a permanent, 342
  building concentration and, 391, 396
  comparison with others, 38
  confusion about, 295
  consciousness of, 478–80
  construction of, 33–34, 128, 170–71
  emptiness of, 241
  evil arising from false sense of, 33
  false notion of, 479
  fetters and, 458
  five spiritual faculties and, 414
  ignorance arising through notion of, 42
  impermanence and, 467
  mindful reflection and, 407
  and other, barrier between, 396
  perception of the absence of, 346
  supramundane jhanas and, 562
  See also ego; no-self

self-discipline, 82
self-hatred, 86, 179, 248–49
self-talk, 460–62
selfishness, 22–23, 45, 148, 149
selfless awareness, 85, 128, 136, 148, 168

selfless nature of mindfulness, 85, 136, 148

selflessness
  of the body, xvii
  consciousness and, 478–80
  ignorance dispelled through realization of, 42, 170–71
  of mindfulness, 85, 136, 148
  of pain, 98, 128
  perceived through breath practice, 55–57
  perceived through mindfulness, 28, 140–41, 166
  perception of, as goal of practice, 27, 55, 170–71

sensations
  of the body, losing the, 391
  of the breath, 210
  as confusing, 295–96
  feelings as, 276–77
  observing, 42, 100
  odd, 100
  See also pain

sense bases, six internal and six external, 204

sense consciousness, five kinds of, 240

senses, 438–41, 495, 497–98
  breath meditation and the, 435–36
  Buddha on the, 414–15
  building concentration and the, 389
  eliminating hindrances and the, 456, 457
  equanimity and the, 536, 538
  fetters and the, 458
  guarding your, 537
  jhana mental states and the, 481, 482
  metta meditation and the, 426
  mindful reflection and the, 406–8
  as "oceans," 414–15

renunciation and the, 504
restraining the, 402–4
vipassana awareness and the,
470–71
sensory pleasure
binding nature of, 294
craving for (*see also* craving); as a
fetter, 343
desire as willingness to have, 327
separation from loved ones, 475
seven factors of enlightenment,
351–63
sexual feelings, experiencing during
meditation, 39, 42, 113. *See also*
lust
sexuality, 446
sickness, as suffering, 474, 475
signlessness, 541
silence, noble, 521
sitting posture, 220–24
six internal and six external sense
bases, 204
skeptical doubt. *See* doubt: skeptical
skillful effort, 357, 361, 368
skillful thinking, 368
skin, mindful meditation on, 252
sleep difficulties, 231
sleepiness, 100–101, 123, 218, 330,
391, 453–54, 498
sloth, 447, 453–54, 507–8
and torpor, 330–32
slow movement as aid to mindfulness, 152, 160–61
smiling with the heart, 216
sorrow and lamentation, overcoming,
236–37
sound(s), 297
as distraction, 77
observed in meditation, 57, 130–31
space, boundless/infinite, 485–86,
548–53

speaking and listening with mindfulness, 45
speech
avoiding unwholesome, 403
false, 401, 447
harsh, 447
malicious, 447
metta meditation and, 421, 423, 424
noble eightfold path and, 409
right, 409, 558
skillful, 368
wrong, 447
spiritual accomplishments resulting
from meditation practice, xx–xxi
spiritual feelings, 288
spiritual powers (*iddhipada*), 369
spiritual urgency, 266, 283
spontaneous nature of mindfulness,
166
stagnation, 16
standing meditation, 224–26, 332
steps of mastery, 526–28. *See* adverting, attaining, resolving, emerging, reviewing.
stillness during meditation, 46–47, 60
stolen moments, 162
"stone buddha" syndrome, 150
stream-enterer, 370–71
stream entry, 509, 539, 545
supramundane jhanas and, 557,
559–63
stupor, 109
sublime states, 176–77
suffering, 463–64, 472–77
as within, xix–xx
birth as, 473
body parts and, 251, 252
Buddha on, xiv, xv, xix, 276, 289,
466, 473
building concentration and, 391,
397

causes of, 6–8, 29, 31–32, 91, 128, 169, 276, 277, 318, 365–67
cessation of, 8–10, 34, 42, 43, 149, 154, 347, 365–67
clear comprehension and, 394
consciousness as, 475, 477
craving and, 403–4
defilements and, 380
disillusionment with, 393
equanimity and, 538
fetters and, 459
five aggregates as, 475–76
four noble truths and, 381–84
fourth jhana and, 531, 535
growth as, 474
impermanence and, 466–68
inherent to human experience, 3–5, 7, 169
jhana mental states and, 485
as liberated from arahants, 371–72
liberation from, xvi, xxiii, 238
metta meditation and, 418, 420, 422, 424, 426–33
mindfulness and, 411
as one of the four noble truths, 365–67
our responsibility for, 234
vs. pain, 95
right concentration and, 393, 394
separation from loved ones as, 475
See also pain
sunnata (emptiness of self), 241
superstitions, 268
Supramundane Noble Path, 558–65
supreme mental state, 316–17
suspension of disbelief, 377–78
suttas/sutras, 198. See also specific suttas
"Sword Simile" discourse, 461
sympathetic (appreciative) joy, 176–77

T
tantra, 26–27
tantric approach to awareness, 26–27
teacher, role of, 198
teachers, 384, 397, 427–29, 497, 544
teeth, mindful meditation on, 251–52
tension vs. mindfulness, 106
theory phase of four noble truths, 381
Theravada Buddhism, 196, 198, 377, 544
thinking, skillful, 368
thought
  the aggregate of: and the breath, 214; domain and, 240; investigation of, 355; wholesome and unwholesome, 244
  avoiding discursive thought during meditation, 37–38, 71, 72
  ego and, 26
  experience of, 139
  freedom from, 167
  nature of, 507–9
  observed during meditation, 32, 54–55, 57, 66–67, 127
  See also mind
thoughts
  canceling one thought with another, 113–15
  cultivating beneficial, 305–8, 318–19
  relinquishing harmful, 305–7, 318–20
  right, 503
  skillful vs. unskillful, 114
  wrong, 447
time
  length of sitting session, 47, 80–82, 156
  needed to see results of meditation, 24, 34
  scheduling practice, 75–76, 78–80, 101

seen as a concept, 167
time gauging and timing distractions, 111–12
Tipitaka, 198
torpor, 447, 453–54, 507–8
and sloth, 330–32
trance, 15
tranquility, as factor of enlightenment, 359
transformation arising from meditation, 12, 34, 153
trust in yourself, 73
truth, 396–97, 543, 558
as within, xix
about reality, 241
Dhamma as, 356
enlightenment and, 539
See also four noble truths
Two Kinds of Thought Sutta, 301–2, 306

U
Uddakaramaputta, 392
unconscious becoming conscious, 5, 76, 104, 105, 115, 119, 127
understanding, skillful, 368
unification of mind. See one-pointedness
universal characteristics of all conditioned things, 360
universal nature of all beings, 208
universality, realizing through breath practice, 38–39, 68
unsatisfactoriness
inherent to human experience, 3–5, 7
perceived through breath practice, 55, 57
perceived through mindfulness, 140–41
perception of, as goal of practice, 27, 55, 171

unwholesome thoughts, 301–2, 318–19
Upali (householder follower of Buddha), 236
Upatissa, 198

V
verbalizing mentally during meditation, 46, 113, 119, 158, 159
vicara, 502, 503, 506–7, 521, 522
view, right, 408–9, 558
Vimuttimagga (The Path of Freedom, by Upatissa), 198
Vinaya, 198
vipassana (insight meditation), 141–44, 396, 405, 437–38, 534–37
acceptance in, 36–37, 109, 135, 149–50, 182
approach to awareness, 23–24, 27, 74, 85
context of the tradition of, 195–98
empirical nature of, 28, 30, 34, 37, 167–69
as means of perceiving reality, 29, 33, 39, 41, 196
practice of, ix, x, xxii
See also insight meditation
vipassana, etymology of the term, 28–29
vipassana awareness, seeing impermanence with, 468–71
vipassana bhavana, 28–29
virtuous conduct, seven forms of, 401
vision, 494, 496, 538–41
Visuddhimagga (The Path of Purification, by Buddhaghosa), 198, 508, 544, 553–55
vitakka, 502–9, 521, 522, 555
voidness (nothingness), 542, 547, 553–55
base of, 486

volitional formations, 437–38, 470,
    475–79, 495, 533, 541
  impermanence in, 541
  overview and nature of, 437–38, 495
  paying attention to, 413, 470
  self/"I" and, 467, 478–80

W
walking, mindfulness of, 228–29
walking meditation, 155–58, 226–31,
    454, 490
  key points for, 230–31
wandering mind. See mind wander-
    ing
watchfulness, impartial
  mindfulness as, 135–36
water element, 212, 213, 252, 257–58,
    437, 438–41
weapons, three, 414
willing suspension of disbelief,
    377–78

wisdom, 11, 19, 41, 44, 114, 142, 148–
    49, 390, 391, 408, 411–14, 459
  arising from mindfulness, 148–49
  concentration and, 378–79
  enlightenment and, 539
  fetters and, 457, 459
  fourth jhana and, 534, 539
  impermanence and, 467, 472
  preconceptual awareness and, 471
  renunciation and, 504–5
  supramundane jhanas and, 557–58
wisdom-follower, 560
worldlings, uninstructed/instructed,
    558
worldly feelings, 288
worry, 32, 39, 113, 125, 332–33. See
    also anxiety

Z
Zen approach to awareness, 26
Zen Buddhism, 26, 198

About the Author

VENERABLE HENEPOLA GUNARATANA was ordained as a Buddhist monk at the age of twelve in Malandeniya, Sri Lanka. He is the bestselling author of *Mindfulness in Plain English* and several other books—including his autobiography, *Journey to Mindfulness*. He travels and teaches throughout the world, and currently lives at Bhavana Society Forest Monastery in West Virginia.

More Books by Bhante Gunaratana from Wisdom Publications

MINDFULNESS IN PLAIN ENGLISH

EIGHT MINDFUL STEPS TO HAPPINESS
Walking the Buddha's Path

BEYOND MINDFULNESS IN PLAIN ENGLISH
An Introductory Guide to Deeper States of Meditation

MEDITATION ON PERCEPTION
Ten Healing Practices to Cultivate Mindfulness

THE FOUR FOUNDATIONS OF MINDFULNESS IN PLAIN ENGLISH

JOURNEY TO MINDFULNESS

THE MINDFULNESS IN PLAIN ENGLISH JOURNAL

LOVING-KINDNESS IN PLAIN ENGLISH
The Practice of Metta

About Wisdom Publications

Wisdom Publications is the leading publisher of classic and contemporary Buddhist books and practical works on mindfulness. To learn more about us or to explore our other books, please visit our website at wisdompubs.org or contact us at the address below.

Wisdom Publications
199 Elm Street
Somerville, MA 02144 USA

We are a 501(c)(3) organization, and donations in support of our mission are tax deductible.

Wisdom Publications is affiliated with the Foundation for the Preservation of the Mahayana Tradition (FPMT).